Economic Analysis of Law in European Legal Scholarship

Volume 2

The purpose of this book series is to publish high quality volumes in the growing field of law and economics research in Europe, from a comprehensive theoretical and practical vantage point. In particular, the series will place great emphasis on foundational and theoretical aspects of economic analysis of law and on interdisciplinary approaches in European legal scholarship. Following Nobel laureate Ronald Coase's famous essay "The Problem of Social Cost" (1960) fifty years ago, law and economics has become the lingua franca of American jurisprudence. In recent decades, law and economics has also gained widespread popularity in Europe and its influence on legal scholarship is growing significantly. Therefore, the Economic Analysis of Law in European Legal Scholarship academic book series illustrates how law and economics is developing in Europe and what opportunities and problems – both in general and in specific legal fields – are associated with this approach within the legal traditions of European countries. Rather than further exploring economic analysis as such, the main focus of this series lies on the implementation of economic methods in legislation and legal adjudication from a European perspective. It takes into account the particular challenges the European legal systems face. Volumes will address law and economics research in Europe from a critical and comparative viewpoint. The studies in this series are strong and bold narratives of the development of economic analysis of law in European legal scholarship. Some are suitable for a very broad readership. Contributions in this series primarily come from scholars in Europe. The purpose is to provide the next generation of European lawyers with the models and skills needed to understand and improve the economic analysis of law in their own legal field. The series includes monographs focusing on specific topics as well as collections of essays covering specific themes.

More information about this series at http://www.springer.com/series/11927

Klaus Mathis
Editor

European Perspectives on Behavioural Law and Economics

Springer

Editor
Klaus Mathis
Faculty of Law
University of Lucerne
Lucerne
Switzerland

ISBN 978-3-319-11634-1 ISBN 978-3-319-11635-8 (eBook)
DOI 10.1007/978-3-319-11635-8
Springer Cham Heidelberg New York Dordrecht London

Library of Congress Control Number: 2014954244

Printed on acid-free paper

Springer is part of Springer Science+Business Media (www.springer.com)

Foreword

On 10 and 11 April 2014, the law faculty of the University of Lucerne, Switzerland, had the honour to host the 3rd Law and Economics Conference on Behavioural Law and Economics. During two days, the participants explored the delicate relationship between law and economics, between jurisprudence and economic science. The dichotomy between law and economics is well-known, but has—at least in Europe—not managed to establish itself as the leading analytical concept in either legal or economic studies. On the contrary, it has been faced with severe criticism, especially from the legal community.

The conflict might well be illustrated from the viewpoint of legal theory and by—for once—relying on systems theory. Systems theory denies that a given social system may be influenced by another social system according to the concept and strategy of the latter. In this theory, different systems—like law and economics—use different codes, in our example profit and loss instead of legality and illegality. The two systems are not interpenetrative, that is to say, they use a different "language". Any mutual influence is dependent on a decision to allow so by the affected system. If other systems seek more influence, this is labelled "colonization". The polemics triggered by this reference to evil imperialist empires are accepted, if not intended. The situation is thus regarded as illegitimate. Analysing law in terms of economics seems to be evil, and—for academics even worse—utterly useless.

It might be argued, however, that this would be a misinterpretation of the relationship between law and economics. Regrettably, if there ever was an era which can be called the era of law—with jurisprudence as the leading human science—this era is in decline. In the past five decades, economics has taken over. However, the decline of jurisprudence is not due to the rise of economic science, but due to inherent boundaries of normative concepts.

Additionally, economic analysis has posed unpleasant questions to the law, questions about the legitimation of certain legal rules. This was not the first attack on the law, but it was a unique one. The political theory of Marxism had already claimed to unmask the law as instrument of power of the bourgeoisie. Later, deconstructivism challenged my beloved doctrinal analysis for being a (rather political) instrument of dominant groups in society. These theories maintain that the way the law is used in conflict resolution is not based on any source of legitimacy other than power.

Economic analysis, however, argues that people need not rely on legal rules to solve conflicts, but can turn to cheaper economic negotiations instead.

Both the law and jurisprudence have been affected by these critics. The law was stripped stark naked, so to speak. It lost its impressive clothes, but it survived. What is left might be called the "naked truth". Let me elaborate on this thought: jurisprudence has often been criticized for being unscientific—how can it successfully produce lasting academic insights, if its own basis is subject to changes by the legislator at any time? It is not easy to defend the "legal science" against this attack. But one can build on the pieces of the law surviving the academic fire ignited by other sciences. Some insights of jurisprudence proved to be immune to these challenges. They may be characterized as an understanding of the law common to all human beings and thus reaching the realm of "everlasting legal insights".

Nonetheless, economic science has taken over. It seems that there is a new era of a specific human science. However, it was not until 2004 that lawyers could buoyantly say: "The Empire Strikes Back". There was a young Jedi Knight then, Klaus Mathis, pointing his laser sword of legal reasoning against the "dark side of the (economic) force", asking for the legal and normative assumptions of the economic analysis of law in his book "Efficiency Instead of Justice?". In contrast to *Star Wars*, the battle did not end up in economics identifying the law as its natural father. However, it tremendously helped to sharpen the arguments on both sides and gather further insights. In particular, it led to the claim that economics may be biased in itself and that anyone dealing with economics should be well aware of its normative assumptions. Likewise, in the behavioural approach to economics—turning to psychology and the social sciences—the profile of the academic discipline was further sharpened.

The members of the law faculty of the University of Lucerne are highly honoured that leading scholars accepted their invitation to come to Lucerne in order to spark a different kind of academic fire, one that will corroborate and confirm the ideas and thoughts of our Jedi Master. This publication is meant to spread a heated debate in and around Lucerne as well as throughout the vast world of law and economics.

Lucerne
August 2014

Prof. Dr. Sebastian Heselhaus
Vice Dean of the Faculty of Law
University of Lucerne

Preface

This anthology, “European Perspectives on Behavioural Law and Economics”, arises from the 3rd Law and Economics Conference from 11 to 12 April 2014 held at the University of Lucerne. The conference was organized in partnership with Notre Dame Law School and their Program on Law and Market Behavior. The main focus of the conference lay on the talks on European legal questions by European legal scholars. They were complimented by insights from distinguished scholars from the United States in order to foster the dialogue between the two different legal cultures. The thematic scope of this volume spans both the theoretical and practical developments of behavioural law and economics.

I take this opportunity to thank all those who have contributed to the organization of the conference and to the successful completion of this volume. First of all, I thank Avishalom Tor from the Program on Law and Market Behavior, Notre Dame University, for co-organizing the conference. I also thank Julia Wetzel, MLaw, and lic. phil. Ariel David Steffen for their diligent proofreading and flawless coordination and organization of the conference. A special thank goes to the Swiss National Science Foundation (SNSF), the Research Commission (FoKo) of the University of Lucerne, the Charitable Foundation Gambit, Hergiswil, as well as the Bank Julius Baer, Geneva, for supporting the conference. Finally, I am grateful to Neil Olivier, Diana Nijenhuijzen and Corina van der Giessen at Springer Publishers for overseeing the publishing process, as well as to Prachi Mehta and her team from Crest Premedia Solutions Private Limited for the careful typesetting.

Lucerne — Prof. Dr. Klaus Mathis
August 2014 — Editor

Introduction

The traditional neo-classical microeconomic theory explains human behaviour by using rational choice. According to this model, people tend to maximize the difference between expected utility and cost ("expected utility theory"). This theory includes three assumptions: (1) unbounded rationality, (2) unbounded self-interest, and (3) unbounded willpower. Behavioural economics questions these assumptions and endeavours to render economic analysis more realistic by underpinning it with psychological insights.

In recent years, the influence of behavioural economics on the economic analysis of law has gained momentum. Behavioural law and economics (BLE) generates a better theoretical understanding of legal phenomena and offers a multitude of applications in legislation and legal adjudication. This anthology highlights the theoretical foundations as well as the various applications of BLE in European legal culture. By the same token, it fosters the dialogue between European and American law and economics scholars.

In part I, the authors discuss the foundations of BLE from different perspectives:

Thomas S. Ulen describes why BLE is so important and how it has altered significant areas of substantive law. The author moves on to discuss criticisms of BLE, finding that some of those criticisms have merit and raise serious issues that legal scholars should investigate further. Finally, Ulen debates some differences between the structure of legal faculties and prevailing scholarly practices in Europe and North America and how these may have an impact on how quickly legal scholars address the open questions in BLE.

Avishalom Tor's contribution explores the next generation of BLE and the awaiting substantial challenges. In terms of both impact and potential, together with the empirical legal studies movement, the behavioural approach to law and economics is perhaps the most significant development in legal scholarship in recent decades. Furthermore, the author finds that the impact of the behavioural approach has not abated. Tor concludes that although BLE has come a long way, additional jurisdictions and legal fields are in need of exploration and much further analysis is required even in more familiar legal territories.

Klaus Mathis and Ariel David Steffen investigate individual and social decision-making from the perspective of rational choice, on the one hand, and behavioural economics, on the other hand. Highlighting how the law may help individual and social decision-makers to avoid cognitive biases in order to maximize individual and social utility, they argue that insights from rational choice and behavioural economics are both equally indispensable to do so. They conclude that the two approaches are not mutually exclusive, but complement each other: future research should thus be directed at a combined application of rational choice and behavioural economics.

In part II, the contributions explore the modern applications of law and economics from various angles:

Kai Purnhagen investigates the intrinsic need of the EU to establish an internal market even against the nation states' will through the reliance on the responsiveness of the peoples of Europe. Purnhagen argues that data gained from behavioural research is the right tool to cure such a market failure in EU internal market law. He concludes that by combining responsive regulation and behavioural economics, the EU is able to listen to its people and motivate Member States to act in everyone's best interest.

In her contribution, Anne-Lise Sibony explores in what ways behavioural insights could be used to shape the interpretation of European law on unfair practices. She argues that insights from social psychology are relevant to the interpretation of the EU directive on unfair practices. In order for such insights to be put to actual legal use, Sibony finds that it is important to address the question of how they should be used and incorporated.

The model consumer is well educated, well informed and capable of making informed decisions. With the rise of digitalisation, however, it has become increasingly difficult to remain informed and up to date. Martin Engel and Johanna Stark explore the phenomenon of consumer choice in B2C contracts by analysing how much of contemporary consumer choice matches considerate and responsible decisions. In their conclusion, the authors outline how current strategies may be updated to increase their effectiveness towards creating consumer empowerment and consumer confidence.

Mark Schweizer demonstrates how insights from cognitive psychology explain the appeal of a higher standard of proof in civil law than the "preponderance of the evidence" or "balance of probabilities" standard utilized in common law. These insights, according to Schweizer, may explain the rigid rejection of any attempts to lower the standard of proof in civil matters in Germany. The intuitive rejection of the "balance of probabilities" standard, the author believes, may be the result of loss aversion, omission bias and status quo bias, which all act together to make a higher standard of proof seem appealing in civil law jurisdictions.

The essay by Edgar Klinger and Günter Bierbrauer investigates the new interdisciplinary research between psychology and civil law and discusses why parties in a civil trial prefer litigation over informal settlement. The analysis by Klinger and Bierbrauer shows that disputants who file claims in a civil court need to understand their case not only from a legal perspective, but also from the dynamics of the trial in order to advise disputants on how to best satisfy their needs and to avoid potential risks.

Rainer Baisch and Rolf H. Weber elaborate on how the findings of behavioural finance research have influenced the traditional understanding of the processes which allow for the functioning of the financial markets. Perceptions, which used to be based on the assumptions of rational behaviour, gradually allow for human flaws. Ultimately, the authors note that the tendency of the reputable market participant to behave accurately and in line with the requirements should bolster the confidence that costumers will be advised on a new level.

In her contribution, Geneviève Helleringer analyses the protection of retail investors from poor investment decisions. The purpose of disclosure regulation is to correct the information asymmetry provided to the potential retail investor, relating to the characteristics of the financial products and the motivations of the intermediary advisor. Helleringer finds that there is a need for the introduction of a research agenda design, focused on the limits deriving from motivation in the use of financial information and in good decision-making, disentangling finance and emotion.

Andreas Heinemann explores the potential benefits of behavioural economics for competition law. After a summarizing the most important behavioural findings from a competition law perspective, the author presents and explores the practical aspects. Behavioural economics not only influences basic concepts of competition law but also affects the analysis of the specific conduct relating to it. According to Heinemann, it seems more appropriate to describe this development of behavioural economics in competition law as a "behavioural turn" than a "behavioural revolution" since traditional analysis is not replaced but merely complemented. Finally, the author notes that behavioural antitrust has the potential to overcome the ideological confrontations between the classical antitrust schools and may help to solve specific problems.

The contribution by Mariusz J. Golecki compares and contrasts the approach taken by the United States and the United Kingdom with regard to defamation and libel laws from an economic perspective. Applying the standard rational choice theory various law and economics scholars proposed different alternatives based on the balance between public good and actual damage to the individual. Golecki ultimately suggests that a more modern approach to judicial process requires the reference to cognitive limitations of adjudicators and systemic errors committed by judges, as the divergence between prediction and post-diction may lead to a lower level of risk-aversion and a higher level of publication.

This volume is testament to the growing and thriving law and economics movement in Europe. The European law and economics community has steadily grown and the yearly law and economics conference at the law faculty of the University of Lucerne has successfully become a guiding star in the vast sky of law and economics.

Lucerne
August 2014

Prof. Dr. Klaus Mathis
Editor

Contents

Contributors

Rainer Baisch Rechtswissenschaftliche Fakultät, University of Zurich, Zurich, Switzerland

Günter Bierbrauer University of Lucerne, Lucerne, Switzerland

Martin Engel Center for International Law, University of Munich, Munich, Germany

Mariusz J. Golecki Department of Legal Theory and Philosophy of Law, Faculty of Law and Administration, University of Łódź, Łódź, Poland

Andreas Heinemann Commercial, Economic and European Law, University of Zurich, Zurich, Switzerland

Geneviève Helleringer Law Department, Essec Business School, Cergy-Pontoise, France

Institute of European and Comparative Law, Oxford University, Oxford, United Kingdom

Edgar Klinger Berufsakademie Ost-Friesland, Lienen, Germany

Klaus Mathis Faculty of Law, University of Lucerne, Lucerne, Switzerland

Kai Purnhagen Law and Governance Group, University of Wageningen, Wageningen, The Netherlands and Law School, Erasmus University, Rotterdam, The Netherlands

Mark Schweizer University of St. Gallen, Zurich, Switzerland

Anne-Lise Sibony University of Liège, Liège, Belgium

Johanna Stark Center for International Law, University of Munich, Munich, Germany

Ariel David Steffen Faculty of Law, University of Lucerne, Lucerne, Switzerland

Avishalom Tor The School of Law, University of Notre Dame, Notre Dame, IN, USA

Thomas S. Ulen College of Law, University of Illinois, Champaign, IL, USA

Rolf H. Weber Rechtswissenschaftliche Fakultät, University of Zurich, Zurich, Switzerland

Part I
Foundations

Chapter 1
European and American Perspectives on Behavioural Law and Economics

Thomas S. Ulen

Abstract Behavioural law and economics is one of the two most significant developments currently going on in legal scholarship. In this essay, I seek to describe, first, why behavioural law and economics is so important and to give a brief example of how it has altered the law-and-economic analysis of one significant area of substantive law—criminal law and punishment. Second, I discuss some criticisms of behavioural law and economics, finding that some of those criticisms have merit and raise serious issues that legal scholars should investigate further. I describe two recent articles that find a common behavioural policy prescription of using "nudges" to be not just ineffectual but damaging. Finally, I speculate on some differences between the structure of legal faculties and prevailing scholarly practices in Europe and North America that may have an impact on how quickly legal scholars in those two areas address the open questions in behavioural law and economics.

1.1 Introduction

I want to divide my remarks into three parts. I begin with a very brief overview of the general impact of behavioural economics on the field of law and economics and on the reasons for its relatively rapid acceptance and development within law and economics. Second, I discuss some criticisms of behavioural studies and two interesting recent articles on some policy implications of behavioural economics. Finally, I speculate on some possible differences between behavioural law and economics in Europe and North America.

T. S. Ulen (✉)
College of Law, University of Illinois, East Pennsylvania Avenue, 504,
Champaign, IL 61820, USA
e-mail: t-ulen@illinois.edu

K. Mathis (ed.), *European Perspectives on Behavioural Law and Economics*,
Economic Analysis of Law in European Legal Scholarship 2,
DOI 10.1007/978-3-319-11635-8_1

1.2 Behavioural Law and Economics, Generally

Behavioural law and economics is, I believe, one of the two most important innovations that is going on in legal scholarship today.[1] As is well known, behavioural considerations began in the 1970s with experiments by Kahneman and Tversky in cognitive and social psychology that were designed to test the predictions of rational choice theory. For various reasons, the results of those experiments—broadly speaking, those results were that rational choice theory does not accurately predict much human choice behavior—remained unknown to many economists and to lawyers familiar with economics and law and economics until the 1990s. However, once the experimental criticisms of rational choice theory became widely known, they had very different impacts on the fields of economics, law, and law and economics.

I think that it is fair to describe the reaction of the field of economics to behavioural findings as being lukewarm.[2] Economists had for decades been perfectly content to assume that individuals are, in all their choices, rational maximizers. Not only was that assumption a congenial one with which to begin economic analysis, it also produced some cogent and empirically supported predictions of core economic decisions. One small piece of this tepid reaction may be found in the fact that the undergraduate economics curriculum does not have a widely used microeconomics textbook that stresses the importance of behavioural findings.[3]

In contrast, legal scholars are widely and enthusiastically aware of behavioural findings. Why this significant difference? I can think of three important reasons why behavioural findings have had a deeper impact on law than on economics. First, law is, by comparison to economics, more concerned with practical matters than is economics and less concerned about theoretical purity. Put somewhat differently, the field of law pays more attention to its applicability to real-world matters and less attention to the theoretical niceties of discussions among scholars than does the field of economics. Legal scholars spend almost as much time talking to practitioners, including lawyers, judges, and policymakers, as to one another—at least by comparison to the relative time that economists talk to private and public-sector economists and among themselves.

This greater orientation of the legal academy toward the practical comes with a scepticism about theorizing. As a result, when there is an academic innovation in law (which, as I shall argue later, is more likely than in economics and some other academic disciplines), the less realistic the innovation seems, the greater the burden

[1] The other important trend in legal scholarship, one closely related to behavioural law and economics, is empirical legal studies.

[2] Pessendorf 2006. There are, of course, significant exceptions to this characterization. John List at the University of Chicago, Matthew Rabin at the University of California, Berkeley, Sendhil Mullainathan at Harvard, and others have been prominent in their use of behavioural economics. I also believe that it is true that European economists have been more congenially disposed toward behavioural economics than have North American economists.

[3] The only exception to this statement of which I am aware is Frank 2014.

on the innovator to demonstrate the innovation's utility. When law and economics came to the legal academy, those legal scholars who were already familiar with economics found nothing objectionable in the microeconomic assumption that decision makers are rationally self-interested. But those lawyers and legal scholars who had not yet grown comfortable with that assumption found it difficult to accept.[4] And I can testify from personal experience that trying to persuade legal audiences that the assumption of rationally self-interested decision makers was a reasonable one to make was not likely to be successful. As a result, when behavioural accounts began to find their way into legal scholarly discourse, the findings that human beings are predictably and systematically prone to decision-making and judgmental errors were congenial to many, if not most, of those in the legal academy.

The second reason that I think behavioural findings have had a greater impact on law than on economics has to do with another fundamental difference between the two fields: There is no core methodology in the doctrinal study of law that must be displaced by innovation while rational choice theory has been the core methodology of microeconomics for almost 60 years. The field of law is defined not by a common methodology that lawyers all over the world (or even regionally or nationally) use to study their subject. What unites the legal academy is not a methodology but rather a subject matter—namely, the formal obligations that we call "law" and its close substitutes, such as social norms. Economics, on the other hand, is a field that has a core methodology—rational choice theory—and no strong commitment to a core subject matter. Indeed, rational choice theory has long been applied to matters of supply and demand far beyond the boundaries of markets.

One of the important implications of this difference between the disciplines of law and economics is that scholarly innovation may be more difficult in economics than in law (and, more generally, in those academic disciplines that are defined by a core methodology or by a related phenomenon, a central "paradigm," as Thomas Kuhn called it).[5] For example, an innovative way of doing economics that seeks to displace the core, prevailing methodology of rational choice has got a nearly impossible task. Indeed, without the core methods of rational choice theory, what is left of microeconomics? There are generations of scholars who have been trained in the application of rational choice theory, and their willingness to abandon that fundamental assumption is limited. This reluctance in other disciplines is the source of a famous quip by Max Planck: "Science advances funeral by funeral."

In law there is no core methodology of investigation that has to be displaced. The field is united by subject matter, not method. So, an innovation—such as law and economics—does not need to undertake the difficult task of displacing a prevailing

[4] I recall that when I first began presenting papers to law faculties in the early 1980s and would begin my presentation by saying that I would be assuming rational choice by decisionmakers, someone would ask some version of the question, "Who *are* these rational decisionmakers you're talking about?"

[5] Thomas Kuhn 1996.

methodology. Rather, almost any innovation that helps us better understand law has a willing audience within the legal academy.[6]

There are other conditions that must be present for the legal academy to be open to innovation. For example, there must be competition within the discipline for resources, including prestige, money, students, and the like, in order for there to be a return to innovating. A legal professoriate that does not have to compete is one that is likely not to innovate.[7]

Third and finally, it is very important to remember that before the relatively quick adoption of behavioural findings within legal scholarship there had been a prior important innovation—law and economics—that paved the way for behavioural law and economics. There is a really important point to be made here about this: Legal scholarship, like most academic fields, is not static. It is changing; it is dynamic; it follows a path of development that I believe is not only discernible but is a development toward better and better scholarship. To be blunt, I think that the legal scholarship that is being produced worldwide today is much, much better than that with which I became familiar in the late 1970s and early 1980s. And typically there are no sudden changes in an academic discipline (or in art, for that matter). Rather, the changes are foreshadowed by prior developments so that an adept historian of a discipline can usually demonstrate that today's innovation is a natural outgrowth of prior innovations. Sir Isaac Newton memorably made this point about the cumulative and collective aspects of academic innovation: "If I have seen further, it is by standing on the shoulders of giants."[8]

So, I suggest that law is generally more open to scholarly innovation than is economics. But there is an unseemly side to this observation. Some of our colleagues who champion behavioural law and economics have done so for what I think are inappropriate reasons. There are those in the legal academy who have been opposed to law and economics because they are suspicious of what seem to them to be politically undesirable implications of some law-and-economic analysis. To speak plainly, some opponents of law and economics do not like the fact that, as they see it, law and economics frequently favours market-oriented, non-regulated solutions to problems.[9] (For what it is worth, I think that this view is factually wrong and speaks ill of those who hold it.) For those people, the principal value of behavioural findings is to demonstrate that because rational choice theory is an unwarranted

[6] There is, of course, a downside to this willingness. The field must develop a sense for what innovations have promise and make sense and which do not. The experience of law with one innovation of the late 1980s and early 1990s—critical legal studies—illustrates that law is able to make this distinction between promising and unpromising innovations.

[7] Garoupa and Ulen 2008.

[8] Another Newton quote that is apt: "Men build too many walls and not enough bridges." Law seems to have been building bridges to other disciplines more than almost any other social science, with the predictable result that there is a very high level of intellectual fervor in legal scholarship, at least in North America.

[9] In European terms, law and economics seems to be associated with neo-liberal political views. In U.S. terms, the association would be said to be with conservative or neo-conservative politics.

assumption and because law and economics relies on that assumption, law and economics is wrong.

This view of the role of behavioural law and economics is wrong in a number of ways. The most important way in which it is wrong seems to me to be that it profoundly misunderstands the means by which any academic discipline evolves and how law and economics has been evolving. Behavioural law and economics is a natural outgrowth of "rational choice theory"-based law and economics. And, indeed, I think that the criticisms that traditional legal scholars have leveled against the RCT-based law and economics of the 1980s were precisely the goad that got law-and-economics scholars to take behavioural findings more seriously than they have been taken by most economists.

The body of work that had become the received wisdom of law and economics has been amended but not scrapped entirely by the development of behavioural law. Take, as an example, some emerging scholarship in the economic analysis of crime and punishment. Under the late Gary Becker's hypothesis (1968), potential criminals compare the expected benefits of crime with the expected costs and rationally decide to refrain from committing crime if those expected costs exceed the expected benefits and to commit crime if the benefits exceed the costs. An important implication of this hypothesis is that society can deter crime by increasing the expected costs of crime[10] (including by increasing the opportunity cost of crime by making legitimate work more likely, more constant, and more rewarding).

State and federal governments in the U.S. sought to implement this analysis (and thereby to deter crime) by such policies as reducing the variance in criminal sentencing[11] and increasing the certainty of harsh criminal sanctions. For example, the United States, between 1980 and 2007, increased the number of prisoners incarcerated in jails and prisons from roughly 500,000 to roughly 2.5 million.[12] The U.S. has only 5 % of the world's population but 25 % of its total prisoners and has by far the highest rate of imprisonment of any nation.

Beginning in the early 1990s and continuing through today, violent crime in the U.S. has declined to levels not seen since the 1950s. And non-violent crime has also declined significantly, although by not quite as much. On one reading of the evidence, the policies inspired by the Becker hypothesis were successful at reducing

---

[10] The expected costs of crime are the product of the probabilities of detection, arrest, and conviction and the value of the sanctions imposed on the guilty criminal. Becker implied that, all other things being equal, it was more efficient to raise those expected costs by raising the value of the sanction rather than by raising the probabilities of detection, arrest, and conviction.

[11] Through the 1980s state and federal sentencing guidelines moved from a system of indeterminate sentencing (under which judges had a range within which to sentence a convicted criminal for a given crime, with the judge having discretion as to where within that range to place any given criminal; additionally, parole boards had discretion to release convicted criminals who had not completed their sentence but had exhibited some desirable behavior during imprisonment) to one of determinate sentencing (under which judges had relatively little discretion in sentencing, and parole boards virtually went out of business).

[12] The very large numbers of prisoners in U.S. jails and prisons peaked in 2007 and has declined slightly since then.

crime—presumably on the ground that they deterred the general population and the specific population that was incarcerated.

Despite the surface plausibility of the contention that deterrence policies, as implemented from 1980 on, explain the decline in crime, there is an emerging scepticism about some aspects of the Becker hypothesis. Let me give three brief examples. First, there is controversy about what really caused the significant declines in violent and non-violent crimes since 1991.[13] It is not obvious, for example, that the increase in the numbers of incarcerated and the increased length of average incarceration have been a significant factor. For example, Donohue and Levitt very famously—and controversially—found that up to half of the decline in crime since the early 1990s should be attributed to the legalization of abortion in 1973.[14]

Second, there is recent evidence that the U.S. has gone too far in its propensity to use imprisonment as a deterrent.[15] Raphael and Stoll contend that a significant number of prisoners could be released from federal and state prisons with almost no increase in violent crime and a very small increase in property crimes.[16]

Third, Robinson and Darley argue, using behavioural and empirical insights, that criminals are not much deterred by imprisonment.[17] There is additional empirical evidence suggesting that if prisoners are deterred from crime by imprisonment, that effect comes mostly from the incapacitating effects of incarceration.[18]

The central point that I want to stress with this brief example is that this story of the relationship between a scholarly hypothesis, empirical evidence, and policy implementation based on that hypothesis and evidence illustrates a perfectly natural and conventional process of knowledge-acquisition. It is not a story of academic failure or of political hubris. Rather, it is a story of a familiar set of steps leading from the academy to the real world and back to the academy and then back to the real world. In the first step, a scholar proposes a plausible explanation of a real phenomenon, such as Becker's 1968 article. Then, other scholars gather data and subject that hypothesis to searching statistical scrutiny.[19] Then, policymakers are persuaded to implement policies (such as determinate sentencing and increasing the number of police) on the basis of the hypothesis and evidence. But then there is new evidence that is not entirely consistent with the older hypothesis. For instance, the moratoria on the implementation of the death penalty (in all states between 1972 and 1976 and in Illinois after 1999 and elsewhere at other dates) were not (as might have been predicted from the Becker hypothesis) accompanied by an increase in

---

[13] Donohue and Levitt 2001; Levitt 2004; Zimring 2008.

[14] Donohue and Levitt attributed half of that 50% explanation to the fact that there were fewer 18-year-old men in the population as of 1991 and another half to the fact that the young men born in the years after 1973 were less likely to commit crime than the young men who were not born. Cooter and Ulen 2012, Ch. 12.

[15] Raphael and Stoll 2014.

[16] Raphael and Stoll 2014, p. 17.

[17] Robinson and Darley 2004.

[18] Barbarino and Mastrobuoni 2014.

[19] For example, Ehrlich 1975; Cooter and Ulen 2012, Ch. 13.

crimes punishable by death.[20] Nor was there an increase in crime with the onset of the Great Recession in 2008, as might have been expected from the Becker hypothesis. Rather, these and other similar anomalies excited a new round of scholarship, which has led to questioning of the continued applicability of the Becker hypothesis and its implications.

In the same way, the story of the increasing influence of behavioural findings on law (and on law and economics) is not a story of the failure of law and economics. It is, rather, the story of one of the very best aspects of the freedom of intellectual pursuit. Moreover, this story is a thrilling testament to the wonderful power of academic openness and progress. Law and economics is becoming a "normal science".[21]

1.3 Some Criticisms of Behavioural Law and Economics

I turn now to a consideration of some powerful criticisms of behavioural law and economics. Let me be clear. While I think that some of the critics raise some good points, I do not believe that their criticisms, taken together, should cause a moment's hesitation in pursuing more behavioural research. Nor are those criticisms principally directed at behavioural findings like those presented in the Luzern conference. That is, the findings that all of us are prone to use shortcuts and misleading heuristics to draw inferences about the world are solid. Remember that these are empirical findings, not mere hypotheses about human behavior.

So, why bring up these criticisms? Because they raise some valid issues that those who see some promise in behavioural research should be aware of. Many of the criticisms have to do with the policy implications of behavioural law and economics or are reminders of how much more there is to learn about human decision-making. Typically, these critics point out that behavioural investigation is relatively new, that some of its findings are internally contradictory (some people are unaware of their judgmental shortcomings; others are achingly aware of them), differ over the life cycle, may be amenable to "nudges", or may require significant limitations of choice.[22]

One example comes from John List of the University of Chicago Department of Economics. He has published several articles that show that greater market experience undoes some biases, such as the endowment effect.[23] Another argument against behaviouralism as being an important point comes from the early work of Gary Becker, who showed, theoretically, that a few rational traders can, through devices like arbitrage, correct the adverse effects of a large number of what he

[20] See Donohue and Wolfers 2005.

[21] Cooter 2011.

[22] Thaler and Sunstein 2008.

[23] List 2003, 2006, 2008.

called irrational traders.[24] That contention is open to question, but it is one to take seriously.

Greg Mitchell[25] and Mitchell and Jon Klick[26] have made some important criticisms of behavioural law. Mitchell notes that "individuals [and societies may] differ greatly in their propensities to act rationally and that situations differ greatly in their propensities to elicit rational behavior from individuals".[27] Moreover, our first-order thoughts—our initial reactions—may well lead to biased outputs, but Mitchell notes that those first-order thoughts are frequently corrected by our second-order thoughts.[28] That is, we sometimes—perhaps often—stop and think before proceeding on the basis of our initial (often mistaken) intuition. If so, then an important policy consideration is this: How can we prime or trigger these second-order thoughts?[29] Finally, Mitchell and Klick warn that to the extent that governmental policymakers devise laws to prevent individuals and organizations from making cognitive errors and misjudgements, they are removing incentives to take care and to learn.[30] If people believe that the government will protect them from making a mistake (or that firms will be adequately deterred from making unsafe products because of fear of liability), then why should they investigate the qualities or safety of the products they buy? If we learn importantly from our own and others' mistakes, then this cognitive and moral hazard that might flow from laws (or inappropriate beliefs) that protect us from our cognitive errors may diminish our learning.

Additionally, some philosophers have recently argued that personal autonomy is a strong fundamental value and that the extent to which we use behavioural findings to interfere with individual autonomy, we may be unnecessarily limiting our abilities to order our lives in ways that we choose. We all know or should know that cigarette-smoking is dangerous to our own and others' health. Assuming that a smoker takes steps to prevent her smoking from harming others, why shouldn't she be allowed to smoke?[31] Clearly, going forward we need to be sensitive to the tradeoffs between protecting personal autonomy and protecting individuals and groups from the adverse consequences of their own cognitive and judgmental errors.

Finally, there are two important recent articles in the law literature that are critical of behavioural law and economics and that are worthy of your attention. These articles question the ability of libertarian paternalism or soft paternalism—the use

---

[24] Becker 1962.

[25] Mitchell 2002a, b, 2005, 2009.

[26] Mitchell and Klick 2006.

[27] Mitchell 2002a, p. 73.

[28] Mitchell 2009.

[29] This topic is one of the central concerns in Kahneman 2011. Kahneman distinguishes between System I thinking, which is quick, intuitive, and capable of generating a rapid response, and System II thinking, which is slow, deliberative, balanced, and interested in getting the right response. There is a popular literature, Gladwell 2005, and a scholarly literature, Gigerenzer 2007, that is far more well-disposed toward intuition, as being a form of crystallized experience.

[30] Mitchell and Klick 2006.

[31] Spector 2012; Rebonato 2013; Conly 2013.

of "nudges"—as a policy to debias judgmental errors and decision biases. Prior to these critical articles, there has been great excitement about the ability of simple nudges to achieve individually and socially desirable results. For example, telling electricity customers how much electric power they are using by comparison to their neighbors has a greater impact on power usage than does increases in the price of that power.[32]

Ryan Bubb and Richard Pildes argue that behavioural economics has not taken its findings seriously enough in its policy recommendations: Behavioural findings argue strongly for mandatory regulations, not for libertarian paternalism.[33] Consider the case of retirement savings. There the "behavioural market failure" is that consumers, left to their own devices and because of their myopia regarding the future and their present bias, do not save enough for their retirement. Thus, the average American, who will retire at 62 and live to be 80, has accumulated only about $ 45,000 in savings for her retirement by the time she stops working.[34]

The central recommendation of behavioural analysis is to change the default rule for employer-provided defined contribution plans from opt-in to opt-out of automatic enrolment on the ground that defaults are sticky and that very few will opt-out. Bubb and Pildes assert that the "result is that the adoption of automatic enrolment has in practice *lowered* retirement savings for many workers and on net likely lowered average retirement savings".[35] The reason for this finding is apparently that while the number of people saving is greater under automatic enrolment, the percentage of income saved in most automatic enrolment schemes (3 %) is lower than

[32] Vandenbergh et al. 2011; Robinson and Hammit 2011; Sunstein 2013. The central behavioural finding that argued in favor of changing the default as a "nudge" was the discovery that people do not typically move away from a default position; those defaults, in the parlance of the literature, are said to be "sticky." The results of changing the default can be large, without much apparent change in the well-being of those subject to the default. So, for example, the choice between an opt-out regime for donating one's organs for transplantation (the organs are presumed to be available for transplantation unless the donor takes steps to opt out of donation) and an opt-in system (in which the donor's organs are presumed *not* to be available unless the donor takes steps to opt in to the transplantation system) may seem to be inconsequential. But the differences are profound: The U.S. has an opt-in system and only about 28 % of people take steps to do so. By contrast, in the six European countries that have an opt-out system, the donation rates vary between 85 and 99+ percent.

[33] Bubb and Pildes 2014.

[34] Schwartz Center for Economic Policy Analysis, Department of Economics, The New School 2012. Retirement account balances by income: Even the highest earners don't have enough. http://www.economicpolicyresearch.org/guaranteeing-retirement-income/528-retirement-account-balances-by-income-even-the-highest-earners-dont-have-enough.html. The more detailed figures are even more startling. For the two lowest personal income quartiles (those with annual incomes of less than $ 27,500), the mean total savings for those who are 50–64 years of age in the lowest quartile are $ 16,034, with a median of $ 0; for those who are 50–64 in the next highest quartile, the median total savings are $ 21,606, with a median of $ 0. For those in the highest quartile (annual personal income of greater than $ 52,201) the mean total savings are $ 105,012, with a median of $ 52,000. For the purposes of rough accounting, most financial planners suggest total savings equal to 20 times one's annual income on the eve of retirement as a prudent amount.

[35] Bubb and Pildes 2014, p. 7.

the percentage that was saved, on average, under the older opt-in rule. Additionally, precisely the wrong people opt-out of automatic-enrolment plans.

Bubb and Pildes recommend a mandatory retirement saving account, like that in effect in Australia and other nations, in which the minimum that each person saves is 9% of his or her income.[36]

Another important recent article, by Lauren Willis, urges us to see that the case for nudges is more complex than previous literature might have led us to believe.[37] In 2010 legislation changed the default option for checking-account overdraft fees in order to protect consumers. Prior to 2010, the prevailing regime was an opt-out regime in which banks automatically provided overdraft protection (at huge fees) unless customers affirmatively chose not to participate. Because of the stickiness of defaults and because most consumers do not expect to overdraw their accounts and, therefore, do not pay attention to the announced fees, almost all consumers stayed with the default of paying for overdraft protection. After 2010, by law the regime became an opt-in regime in the hope that bank customers would stick with the default of no overdraft protection.

But that is not what happened. Within two years of the introduction of the opt-in alternative regime, more than half of the customers at several large banks sampled by the Consumer Financial Protection Bureau had opted into the new overdraft charges system. Why did the new default prove to be slippery, rather than sticky? Professor Willis finds that there is one principal reason for the failure of this nudge: The system of overdraft charges is so lucrative to banks (accounting for more than 30% of profits at many banks before 2010) that after 2010 they were willing to spend a great deal of effort and money to get people to opt in to the system of overdraft protection. For instance, banks made it very easy to opt in at an ATM or by phone or in person. They also sold the overdraft charges as a form of insurance that was attractive to many people; in fact, it was most attractive to those who would have most benefited from sticking with the default of not opting in.

So, the lesson to be learned from these examples is that nudges work, except when they don't. And that's not terribly helpful. There needs to be much more research to distinguish the circumstances in which defaults are sticky and when they are slippery, when they improve individual and social well-being and when they do not.

The criticisms surveyed briefly in this section raise some very big issues that the field of behavioural law and economics needs to address. Moreover, as these last two criticisms suggest, we need to be cautious in rushing to implement policies based on behavioural analyses until we have better, more complete information.

---

[36] Bubb and Pildes consider two additional instances in which individuals make decisions that are either sub-optimal for themselves or for society or both and in which nudges have been recommended as corrective but do not work.

[37] Willis 2013.

1.4 American and European Behavioural Law and Economics

Finally, are there any significant differences between North America and Europe in their capacities to add to the literature on behavioural law and economics? I think that there are.

First, there are some important structural differences between Europe and North America that may influence behavioural work going forward. Of these differences, the most important is the degree of competition among law schools. Competition among law schools in North America is ferocious. As a result, the returns to scholarly innovation are very high. I know that things are changing in Europe in this regard so that there is an increasing amount of competition across national boundaries for both undergraduate and graduate students and for faculty. As competition among European law schools increases may come greater incentives to innovate. But even so, the mood within most of the European law schools with which I am familiar is the cozy, practice-oriented, quiet life that used to characterize U.S. law schools 35 years ago. I am not sure what will cause European law schools to recognize the ferment that is going on in legal scholarship and to embrace that ferment, but until they do so, I fear the North American law schools will stay ahead of their European brothers and sisters in the law.

Second, I think that a vital part of our scholarly work going forward is to design and perform experiments and other empirical work that apply the insights of behavioural science to specific legal topics or fill in the many gaps in our understanding of real human decision-making. At the moment, we may have exhausted the insights of taking the work of Kahneman and Tversky and showing that it may impact our particular areas of law. We need to move to the next phase: Doing experiments and other empirical investigation ourselves that demonstrate these behavioural effects and their implications for substantive law. There are, of course, numerous distinguished legal scholars, both in Europe and North America already doing these experiments, but we need more of them.

My intuition (it is nothing more than that) is that North America is ahead of Europe in this regard, too. Most of the top law schools in the U.S. (less so in Canada) have many legal scholars with law degrees and Ph.D.'s in a behavioural or social science. For example, at the University of Illinois College of Law we currently have 14 of 39 faculty members with either joint degrees in law and a Ph.D. or a Ph.D.[38] They understand and have already done empirical work and know how important it is to produce one's own results rather than simply to rely on the work of others. Moreover, the fact that there are so many on our faculty (which I do not think is unusual for a top-40 law school) with graduate-school training means that there is a great deal of interaction (and respect) between those faculty who are traditionally trained lawyers and those who also have Ph.D.'s so that even those of my colleagues

[38] When I joined the law school faculty in 1982, I was the first person to have a Ph.D. (and only a Ph.D.) to join that faculty since the founding of the law school in 1897.

who have never done empirical work are aware of its being done, of its importance, and of the professional value of more scholars' getting involved in this work.

Relatedly, my suspicion is that in North America the ease of doing cross-disciplinary work with those in other behavioural and social sciences—even those in other departments, not just those who are colleagues within law faculties—is easier than it is in Europe. There is no particular impediment in Europe to your doing more work with psychologists, economists, anthropologists, statisticians, and others in your great universities. So, I think that may be an avenue for you to explore if you are eager to do your own experiments and other empirical work in behavioural law and economics.

1.5 Conclusion

What we have learned from the remarkable behavioural literature of the past thirty years has fundamentally changed how we do and ought to think about legal and economic decisions. But it is worthwhile remembering that we are only at the beginning of what can be and should be known about human decision-making and how law can help to channel that decision-making into what is best for each individual and for society collectively. Dramatic and important as the behavioural findings have been thus far, I am confident—but not overly optimistic—that future scholarship on these matters from both European, American, and other legal academies will be even more exciting.

Acknowledgment I want to thank Avishalom Tor and Klaus Mathis for organizing the Lucerne conference and inviting me to attend. I also want to thank Julia Wetzel, Ariel Steffen, and the IT people at Lucerne and Tyler Hunter at Illinois for arranging for me to speak to the conference by video.

Bibliography

Barbarino, Alessandro, and Giovanni Mastrobuoni. 2014. The incapacitation effect of incarceration: Evidence from several Italian collective pardons. *American Economic Journal of Economic Policy* 6:1–37.

Becker, Gary S. 1962. Irrational behavior and economic theory. *Journal of Political Economy* 70:1–13.

Becker, Gary S. 1968. Crime and punishment: An economic analysis. *Journal of Political Economy* 76:169–217.

Bubb, Ryan, and Richard H. Pildes. 2014. How behavioral economics trims its sails and why. *Harvard Law Review* 127:1593–1678.

Conly, Sarah. 2013. *Against autonomy: Justifying coercive paternalism*. Cambridge: Cambridge University Press.

Cooter, Robert D. 2011. Maturing into normal science: The effect of empirical legal studies on law and economics. *University of Illinois Law Review* 2011:1475–83.

Cooter, Robert D., and Thomas S. Ulen. 2012. *Law and economics*. 6th ed. Upper Saddle River: Prentice Hall.

Donohue III, John J., and Steven D. Levitt. 2001. The impact of legalized abortion on crime. *Quarterly Journal of Economics* 116:379–420.
Donohue III, John J., and Justin Wolfers. 2005. Uses and abuses of emprical evidence in the death penalty debate. *Stanford Law Review* 58:791–845.
Ehrlich, Isaac. 1975. The deterrent effect of capital punishment: A question of life and death. *American Economic Review* 65:397–417.
Frank, Robert H. 2014. *Microeconomics and behavior*. 9th ed. New York: McGraw-Hill/Irwin.
Garoupa, Nuno, and Thomas S. Ulen. 2008. The market for legal innovation: Law and economics in Europe and the United States. *Alabama Law Review* 59:1555–1633.
Gigerenzer, Gerd. 2007. *Gut feelings: The intelligence of the unconscious*. New York: Viking.
Gladwell, Malcolm. 2005. *Blink: The power of thinking without thinking*. Boston: Little Brown.
Kahneman, Daniel. 2011. *Thinking, Fast and Slow*. New York: Farrar, Straus, and Giroux.
Kuhn, Thomas. 1996. *The structure of scientific revolutions*. 3rd ed. Chicago: The University of Chicago Press.
Levitt, Steven D. 2004. Understanding why crime fell in the 1990s: Four factors that explain the decline and six that do not. *Journal of Economic Perspectives* 18:163–190.
List, John A. 2003. Does market experience eliminate market anomalies? *Quarterly Journal of Economics* 118:41–71.
List, John A. 2006. The behavioralist meets the market: Measuring social preferences and reputation effects in actual transactions. *Journal of Political Economy* 114:1–37.
List, John A., and Daniel L. Millimet. 2008. The market: Catalyst for rationality and filter of irrationality. *Berkeley Electronic Journal of Economic Analysis and Policy* 8:1–51.
Mitchell, Gregory. 2002a. Why law and economics' perfect rationality should not be traded for behavioral law and economics' equal incompetence. *Georgetown Law Journal* 91:67–167.
Mitchell, Gregory. 2002b. Taking behavioralism too seriously? The unwarranted pessimism of the new behavioral analysis of law. *William & Mary Law Review* 43:1907–2021.
Mitchell, Gregory. 2005. Libertarian paternalism is an oxymoron. *Northwestern Law Review* 99:1245–1278.
Mitchell, Gregory. 2009. Second thoughts. *McGeorge Law Review* 40:687–722.
Mitchell, Gregory, and Jonathan Klick. 2006. Government regulation of irrationality: Moral and cognitive hazards. *Minnesota Law Review* 90:1621–1663.
Pessendorf, Wolfgang. 2006. Behavioral economics comes of age: A review essay of advances in behavioral economics. *Journal of Economic Literature* 44:712–721.
Raphael, Steven, and Michael A. Stoll. 2014. A new approach to reducing incarceration while maintaining low rates of crime. The Hamilton Project, Discussion Paper 14-03. Washington: The Brookings Institution 1–25.
Rebonato, Riccardo. 2013. A critical assessment of libertarian paternalism. Working Paper 1-68, University of Oxford and University of Edinburgh. www.ssrn.com. Accessed 8 June 2014.
Robinson, Paul H., and John M. Darley. 2004. Does criminal law deter? A behavioral science investigation. *Oxford Journal of Legal Studies* 24:173–205.
Robinson, Lisa A., and James K. Hammitt. 2011. Behavioral economics and regulatory analysis. *Risk Analysis* 31:1408–1422.
Spector, Horacio. 2012. Autonomy. In *The routledge companion to social and political philosophy*, ed. Gerald F. Gauss and Fred D'Agostino, 573–584. New York: Routledge.
Sunstein, Cass R. 2013. *Simpler: The future of government*. New York: Simon & Schuster.
Thaler, Richard H., and Cass R. Sunstein. 2008. *Nudge: Improving decisions about health, wealth, and happiness* (Revised ed.) New York: The Penguin Group.
Vandenbergh, Michael P., Lisa S. Bressman, and Amanda Carrico. 2011. Regulation in the behavioral era. *Minnesota Law Review* 95:715–781.
Willis, Lauren E. 2013. When nudges fail: Slippery defaults. *University of Chicago Law Review* 80:1155–1229.
Zimring, Franklin E. 2008. *The great American crime decline*. Oxford: Oxford University Press.

Thomas S. Ulen Champaign, United States. Swanlund Chair Emeritus, University of Illinois at Urbana-Champaign, Professor Emeritus of Law, University of Illinois, College of Law Champaign, IL 61820, t-ulen@illinois.edu. Fields of Interest: Economics and Law, Economic Analysis of Law, Quantitative Methods of Legal Decision-Making.

Chapter 2
The Next Generation of Behavioural Law and Economics

Avishalom Tor

Abstract The paper examines some of the important tasks awaiting the next generation of scholarship in behavioural law and economics. Some of these tasks reflect the need for expanding the *breadth* of the behavioural approach to law while others involve the mission of increasing its *depth*. The following sections examine each category in turn.

2.1 Introduction

Behavioural law and economics (BLE) seeks to inform legal analysis by drawing on both the methods and the extensive findings of behavioural decision research, the psychology of judgment and decision-making, and related fields.[1] In terms of both impact and potential, together with the empirical legal studies movement, the behavioural approach to law and economics is perhaps the most significant development in legal scholarship in recent decades.[2] Legal scholars by now have examined at least some of the behavioural lessons for the law in most legal fields, though the systematic application of this methodology is still in its early stages.[3] Indeed, two early programmatic articles that outlined some key features of BLE are heavily cited: Jolls, Sunstein, and Thaler's "*A Behavioural Approach to Law and Economics*," published in 1998, had over 2000 citations in Google Scholar by the end of 2013;[4] Similarly, Korobkin and Ulen's "*Law and Behavioural Science: Removing the Rationality Assumption from Law and Economics*," published 2 years later, had over 1000 Google Scholar citations by the same time.[5] More significantly,

[1] Jolls et al. 1998; Korobkin and Ulen 2000; Tor 2008.

[2] Ulen 2011.

[3] Langevoort 1998; Zamir and Teichman 2014.

[4] Google Scholar 2013a.

[5] Google Scholar 2013b.

A. Tor (✉)
The Law School, University of Notre Dame, Eck Hall of Law 3163,
Notre Dame, IN 46556-0780, USA
e-mail: ator@nd.edu

K. Mathis (ed.), *European Perspectives on Behavioural Law and Economics*,
Economic Analysis of Law in European Legal Scholarship 2,
DOI 10.1007/978-3-319-11635-8_2

however, a formal citation study from late 2011 counted the former article among the 100 most-cited law reviews of all time, with 783 citations in the law review literature alone.[6] The same study also ranked the latter article 25th among all law review articles since 1990, with 424 citations. Thus, regardless of the precision of different citation measures, beginning in the late 1990s, the scholarly impact of these articles and, by extension, of behavioural law and economics in general, has been substantial.

Furthermore, the impact of the behavioural approach has not abated. Scholars continue to engage in behavioural analyses of legal questions, increasing both the sophistication of their analyses and the range of legal fields they study. Perhaps even more telling, signs of the growing awareness of behavioural law and economics can be found outside the domain of pure scholarship: In the United States, Cass Sunstein, a prominent behavioural scholar, served as the administrator of the Office of Information and Regulatory Affairs throughout most of the first term of the Obama administration. As one magazine colourfully described, this position "[is] an obscure but exceedingly powerful perch that enabled Sunstein to put his imprint on everything from fuel efficiency standards and the redesign of the food pyramid to the rules for the landmark health care and Wall Street overhauls."[7]

Given the nature of the present volume, moreover, it is important to note that regulatory interest in behavioural law and economics is not limited to the United States. In the United Kingdom, the "Behavioural Insights Team" in the Cabinet Office "applies insights from academic research in behavioural economics and psychology to public policy and services."[8] In the same vein, behavioural studies—both empirical and theoretical—were undertaken by the Office of Fair Trading in the areas of consumer protection and competition law.[9] The European Commission and the OECD exhibit a similar interest in the behavioural approach: The former organized a series of conferences and issued reports on the policy implications of behavioural findings with an emphasis on consumer markets and suggested environmental initiatives on the same basis.[10] The latter also focused on the consumer policy implications of behavioural economics.[11]

Notwithstanding these accomplishments, however, my remarks here will focus on some of the important tasks awaiting the next generation of scholarship at the "frontiers" of behavioural law and economics. Some of these tasks reflect the need for expanding the *breadth* of the behavioural approach to law while others involve the mission of increasing its *depth*. The following sections examine each category in turn.

---

[6] Shapiro and Pearce 2012, 1491.

[7] Newmyer 2013.

[8] Government of the United Kingdom Cabinet Office 2014. The unit's website also states that "[i] n addition to working with almost every government department, we work with local authorities, charities, NGOs, private sector partners and foreign government, developing proposals and testing them empirically *across the full spectrum of government policy*." (emphasis added).

[9] Armstrong and Huck 2010; Bennett et al. 2010; Huck et al. 2011.

[10] European Commission 2010; 2012; Organisation for Economic Co-Operation and Development 2010. *See also* Van Bavel et al. 2013, 8.

[11] Van Bavel et al. 2013.

2.2 Breadth

2.2.1 Legal Systems

This volume embodies one area of necessary and important development in the breadth of BLE—namely, the application of behavioural insights and methods to jurisdictions beyond that of the United States, in Europe and elsewhere. The study of behavioural applications in a broader range of legal systems is important since both the specific legal rules and institutions of different countries and their respective cultures can vary dramatically. Thus, different legal systems both differently shape human behaviour and are differently shaped by it, therefore meriting closer scholarly scrutiny at the level of specific jurisdictions.

One familiar example of cultural-legal differences is the different role assigned to common law courts compared to civil law courts. The adversarial nature of common law systems defines the role of judges as adjudicators who decide between the different presentations of the law and the evidence offered by the litigating parties' advocates. Within this framework, therefore, the judge is not responsible for finding the truth in any absolute sense. In civil law countries, on the other hand, judges determine both the facts of the case and the applicable law and, indeed, are charged with deciding the truth of the legal matter at hand. And though such formal distinctions are subject in practice to many caveats, they still generate substantial differences in the ultimate legal rules of evidence and procedure and the resulting conduct of the relevant legal actors—judges, advocates, and the parties—in common law versus civil law jurisdictions.[12]

Most importantly for present purposes, however, these differences in legal culture may have further behavioural consequences beyond those directly commanded or incentivized by the law. To illustrate, it would be of interest to test whether common law judges, who view their role as adjudicators, are influenced more strongly than civil law judges by the sentencing or damages anchors offered by prosecutors and plaintiffs, respectively.[13] Similar behavioural differences between the two legal families may be found for other legal actors as well. For instance, litigating parties who hold different perceptions of the role of the courts and the judicial process are also likely to hold different views of what constitutes a fair trial.[14]

Yet it is not only the law that can differently shape the behaviour of legal actors, but also the broader social and cultural institutions it is embedded in. Specifically, a significant and growing literature documents systematic cross-cultural differences in different areas of judgment and decision-making, from probability judgments, through risk perceptions, to risk preferences and beyond.[15] Researchers also find substantial variation across cultures in individuals' economic behaviour in common

[12] *See, e.g.*, Hazard 1998.

[13] Guthrie et al. 2001; 2007; Wistrich et al. 2005. This is not to say, however, that civil law judges are expected to exhibit no anchoring effects, since behavioural studies show that even completely irrelevant anchors can still impact legal decisions.

[14] Leung and Morris 2001; Lind et al. 1997; Tyler 2006.

[15] Weber and Hsee 2000.

economic games that reveal people's social preferences for cooperation, reciprocity, and more, such as the ultimatum game, public goods games, and the dictator game.[16] Naturally, we should expect such systematic cross-cultural differences to impact both the nature of a given culture's legal institutions and the ways in which these institutions, in turn, affect individuals' behaviour.

2.2.2 Legal Fields

Besides increasing the geographic and cultural breadth of BLE research, scholars are beginning to tackle important legal fields that, until recently, received little behavioural study. For example, the first behavioural study of intellectual property law—examining the question of copyright duration—was published in 2002,[17] but almost none followed until the last few years.[18] Similarly, besides one early precursor, the first law review article that started developing a behaviourally-informed approach to competition law was also published in 2002.[19] Despite a few early follow-ups, however, the legal community—both scholars and enforcement officials—had only started addressing behavioural antitrust in earnest in the late 2000s, as I discuss in detail elsewhere.[20] At any rate, BLE research in intellectual property and competition law—much like in many other fields that received more intense study already earlier on—requires much further development.

2.3 Depth

As important as is its increasing breadth, the mission of increasing the *depth* of BLE scholarship—in terms of both methodology and substance—is even more significant to the long-term success and impact of the behavioural approach to law and economics.

2.3.1 Methodology

The most common methodology in behavioural law and economics involves drawing on the large extant body of empirical behavioural research and applying its findings to legal questions.[21] This strategy is both economical and effective, using

---

[16] Henrich et al. 2005.

[17] Tor and Oliar 2002.

[18] Buccafusco and Sprigman 2010, 2011; Feldman 2006; Garcia 2014; Johnson 2012; Newman 2013; Sprigman et al. 2013.

[19] Gerla 1985; Tor 2002.

[20] Tor 2014a.

[21] Tor 2008.

well-established findings that often have broad legal ramifications. However, many of those questions that are particularly important to lawyers find no straightforward answers in the existing empirical literature, as extensive as it is. Behavioural decision researchers in the basic disciplines of psychology, economics, and related fields are primarily concerned with identifying general patterns of human judgment and decision behaviour and understanding their genesis. From the perspective of these researchers, questions of how behavioural phenomena apply in a particular legal context, how they interact with one another, how they are shaped by legal and market institutions, and so on, generally are of limited interest, involving merely applied science of secondary significance.[22]

To advance their research agenda, therefore, behavioural-legal scholars must also engage in empirical studies, using both observational tests with real-world data of legal significance and experiments structured to examine specifically-legal questions. These two empirical methodologies complement both one another and the theoretical applications of existing behavioural findings that are more commonly found in the BLE literature. Observational tests of legal questions, the cornerstone of the empirical legal studies movement, are becoming increasingly popular among legal scholars. Yet these studies, which possess the important advantage of bringing new data from the field to bear on legal debates, rarely address behavioural questions. Observational scholars typically study empirical regularities in data on legal institutions or decision makers. These studies are valuable, though subject to familiar limitations, such as dependence on the availability of relevant observational data and on the nature of that data when available. More pertinently, however, only occasionally do observational studies examine the impact of psychological variables on legally-relevant judgment and decision behaviour.[23] Indeed, most empirical scholars have limited psychological training or behavioural interests, and they are generally unconcerned about the behavioural foundations of the empirical patterns they observe. The effects of empirical scholars' limited interest are compounded, moreover, by the objective difficulty of discerning the psychological antecedents of behaviour through observational methods.[24]

For these reasons, experimental methods often are a necessary complement to observational studies. The basic logic of a controlled randomized experiment is straightforward, and not unique to behavioural decision research.[25] Researchers randomly assign participants to groups, administering treatment to the experimental group but not to the control group and then statistically analysing the data to determine whether the treatment had any effect.[26] The controlled randomized experiment

[22] Tor 2008.

[23] Marotta-Wurgler 2011; Marotta-Wurgler 2013.

[24] Gazal-Ayal and Tor 2012.

[25] Note there are other kinds of experiments that are not discussed here. See: Rosenthal and Rosnow 1991. Field experiments that study decision-making in the specific context of interest, for instance, seek to retain experimental control, while increasing the external validity of the subject pool. *See*, *e.g.*, Feldman 2006.

[26] Rosenthal and Rosnow 1991.

possesses some advantages over observational studies in which randomization and control usually are not possible. Yet experiments are inevitably removed from the natural legal environment—participants often differ from the legal actors of interest, and the laboratory design cannot (and should not) replicate the full richness of the real-world—and so are subject to concerns regarding their external validity.[27] Over time, however, experimental researchers have developed various means for addressing external validity problems, using different types of participants, infusing experimental designs with greater realism, and more. There is also significant evidence that even simulation or survey studies using no monetary incentives for performance largely correspond with the findings of field studies, where available, or of experiments using monetary incentives.[28] Indeed, a growing number of scholars now conduct experimental legal studies, though such research still is not widespread.

Nonetheless, given the relative novelty of experimental research in law, a distinct experimental-legal methodology is yet to develop. Most studies of this type employ the traditional methods of experimental psychology, which are also those typically used by judgment and decision researchers and behavioural economists.[29] Nearly all of the remaining studies, comprising a non-negligible minority of experimental research in law, adopt instead those somewhat different methods developed by experimental economists in recent decades. In the longer term, however, the behavioural approach to law would benefit greatly from developing its own variant (or variants) of experimental methods, adopting the conventions of psychologists or economists to its own needs and preferences.

For instance, some experimental economics conventions may be useful for behavioural-legal scholarship, at least occasionally, though the practices of experimental psychology and behavioural economics often will be better suited for the task. Motivating participants with monetary incentives for performance—as experimental economists do—may be beneficial, for instance, when studying legally-relevant phenomena in economic settings. Many other legal questions, however, involve situations where non-monetary factors—such as social norms, fairness, or other social preferences—play a pivotal role, so that extensive reliance on monetary incentives may distort rather than improve experimental results.[30] Similarly, the more abstract designs, which aim to avoid specific context, that experimental economists favour may be less productive for the study of behaviour within concrete legal and social institutions. BLE scholars, on the other hand, are interested primarily in questions in which the law and related institutions play a pivotal role shaping social behaviour, so their research will benefit often from the employment of somewhat richer, legally-embedded experimental designs.[31]

---

[27] McAdams 1999.

[28] Anderson et al. 1999; Camerer and Hogarth 1999; Tor 2008.

[29] Camerer et al. 2004.

[30] Tor 2007.

[31] Rachlinski 2000; Tor 2007.

2.3.2 *Substance*

To advance its mission, behavioural law and economics also needs to address some foundational questions that concern the behavioural study of legal questions across the board. A number of distinct questions comprise this category, and some of these—like the degree to which behavioural insights justify different forms of paternalism—already have received substantial scholarly attention, if not always a thorough analysis.[32] Other issues—such as the role of legal and market institutions in facilitating and inhibiting more rational behaviour—have not been subjected to any systematic study until recently.[33] Besides the important task of further exploring the above and similar issues, however, the next generation of behavioural law and economics scholarship will also need to tackle additional foundational questions that so far have received little or no legal analysis. The remainder of my remarks here will therefore focus on one challenge in the latter category—namely, the impact of individual differences in rationality on the analysis and design of legal rules and institutions—explaining its significance and offering some initial guidance on how to account for it in future BLE scholarship.

To date, the legal literature largely has neglected to examine the implications of individual differences in rationality for the law.[34] Yet those robust deviations from rationality that behavioural studies document at the *population* level are the product of substantial individual-level heterogeneity in judgment and decision behaviour, rather than the individual-level uniformity that most legal scholarship implicitly assumes.[35] Thus, different legal actors deviate from rationality to different degrees with respect to different behavioural phenomena. Some are more overoptimistic, for instance, while others are less so; some exhibit more biased judgments in hindsight, others show a greater degree of loss aversion, still others are more susceptible to framing effects than their peers are, and so on.[36]

The behavioural evidence reveals some systematic individual differences variables that explain a portion of variance in deviations from rationality. Factors such as cognitive ability,[37] thinking style,[38] risk-taking propensity,[39] personality traits[40] and more explain some of the individual differences with respect to some behavioural phenomena, but ultimately account only for a small fraction of the overall observed heterogeneity in rationality. The correlation *within* individuals among many of the

[32] Camerer et al. 2003; Klick and Mitchell 2006; Rachlinski 2006; Sunstein and Thaler 2003; Thaler and Sunstein 2008; Zamir 1998.

[33] Tor 2014a, b. Some aspects of this important issue have captured the attention of scholars in the narrower debate regarding the merits and demerits of a behavioural approach to competition law.

[34] Mitchell 2002; Prentice 2003; Rachlinski 2006.

[35] Mitchell 2002.

[36] Tor 2014c.

[37] Cokely and Kelley 2009; Stanovich and West 1998.

[38] West et al. 2008.

[39] Mahoney et al. 2011.

[40] Lauriola and Levin 2001; Levin et al. 2002.

familiar deviations from rationality is small as well.[41] Altogether, therefore, the current state of the art does not offer us an effective means for identifying ex-ante individuals' degree of rationality on the basis of their personal characteristics. It is also apparent that the behaviour of most legal actors, most of the time, cannot be classified into stable categories of the "rational" and "boundedly rational" across the board.

What then do these individual differences in rationality mean for legal analysis? Intuitively, such heterogeneity would appear generally to weaken or "dilute" behavioural-legal arguments, which often take the form of "people exhibit behaviour X that deviates from the assumptions of rationality and, therefore, the legal rule should be (or is) Y instead of the Z that would have been appropriate if the world were populated by rational actors." After all, insofar as the "if" portion of BLE arguments is recast as a more diluted "some people exhibit behaviour X some of the time," perhaps the legal "then" conclusion that follows should be more modest as well.

However, a closer evaluation of the dilution claim reveals that even while some behavioural-legal arguments indeed lose force once substantial individual differences in rationality are acknowledged, many other analyses remain compelling. Behavioural analyses of law may or may not be robust to heterogeneity in rationality depending on a number of behavioural and legal processes. On the basic behavioural level, processes of both dilution and selection may take place. Then, once the law comes into play, legal trade-offs and legal selection may impact the ultimate robustness of the specific BLE argument at hand further.

On the behavioural level, heterogeneity in rationality and thus the degree of dilution can vary greatly. In some cases, a dramatic majority of decision makers exhibits the relevant behavioural phenomenon (e.g. the hindsight bias) to a substantial degree. Yet, in other cases only a smaller fraction of the population substantially deviates from rationality (e.g. preferences reversals due to framing effects). Behavioural dilution is therefore more of a concern for the legal analyst in the latter than in the former case.

Moreover, legally-relevant behaviour takes place in specific contexts, which may select for or against rationality and thereby inhibit or facilitate behavioural dilution. This is often the case, for example, with overoptimism and related phenomena: Decision makers exhibit different degrees of optimistic bias in judging their ability, performance, or prospects, but those who are more biased naturally tend to select for different behaviours from those chosen by their less-biased counterparts. One consequence of this dynamic is that the optimistically biased tend to be overrepresented among those who engage in activities that require a greater degree of risk-taking.[42] However, while processes of behavioural selection can diminish the significance of behavioural dilution, (i.e. diminishing the proportion of the boundedly rational in a particular context) they can also have the opposite effect of facilitating dilution, such as where a limited number of more and less biased actors repeatedly compete with one another in an environment where better judgment is associated with better outcomes (e.g. a skill-based tournament).[43]

---

[41] Appelt et al. 2011.

[42] Tor 2002.

[43] For a more systematic discussion of how market environments, for instance, can facilitate rationality or inhibit it, see Tor 2014a.

Beyond the basic processes of behavioural dilution and behavioural selection, some legal policies that benefit less rational actors impose costs on their more rational counterparts—thereby generating potentially significant tradeoffs—while other policies do not exert such effects. Indeed, concerns about the potential trade-off costs of behaviourally-motivated policies have been voiced by commentators in the ongoing debate over "soft" paternalistic interventions, in areas such as consumer protection, public health and safety, personal finances, and more.[44] Yet the design of legal rules outside the domain of the familiar paternalism debate—that is, rules that do not seek to impact the rationality of individuals' behavior or exploit their bounded rationality—nevertheless may entail similar trade-off costs for which BLE analyses should account. To illustrate, a legal rule that is hostile to liquidated damages clauses due, say, to concerns about contracting parties' biased judgments has the effect of penalizing some less-biased parties by distorting their agreed-upon allocation of contractual risks.[45] Notably, however, policy makers sometimes can eliminate or at least reduce legal trade-off costs by designing appropriate rules. The trade-off costs of a rule that applies greater scrutiny to liquidated damages clauses may be reduced somewhat, for example, by permitting courts to override such clauses only in the limited circumstances in which clear indicia of biased judgments at the time of contract are available.[46]

Besides generating possible trade-offs, legal rules themselves may further select for or against rationality, thereby additionally diminishing the importance of behavioural phenomena for the law or instead making them more legally-relevant. Notably, selection effects are distinct from instances in which the law aims to "debias" individuals—improving the rationality of their judgments or decisions—or to "nudge" them towards behaviours that better approximate rationality.[47] Some selection effects may occur in the latter instances as well, but such effects are not limited to those cases in which the law seeks specifically to align behaviour with rationality.[48] Indeed, selection effects are more broadly relevant for legal design because they may occur any time a legal rule differentially affects decision makers depending on their degree of rationality. To illustrate, some jurisdictions allow attorneys to offer plaintiffs contingent fee (CF) arrangements, so that plaintiffs bear no fees if they lose but pay a substantial fraction of their winnings if they win the case. Many plaintiffs find contingent fee arrangements attractive, in part due to loss aversion; they are willing to forego a significant portion of the claim's expected value to avoid the risk of a smaller, painful loss, because the pain of a potential loss is greater than the pleasure of a comparable gain.[49] Even if CFs serve an important function for loss averse plaintiffs, however, they also tend to generate significant social costs and harm some plaintiffs who end up overpaying for legal services.[50]

[44] Camerer et al. 2003; Rachlinski 2006.

[45] Hillman 2000

[46] This is not to say, of course, that such a rule would be more efficient overall, only to illustrate the relative malleability of tradeoffs.

[47] Jolls and Sunstein 2006; Thaler and Sunstein 2008.

[48] Bubb and Pildes 2014.

[49] Zamir and Ritov 2010.

[50] Brickman 2003.

Hence, the smaller the proportion of plaintiffs that is substantially loss averse, the more limited the benefits of CF arrangements overall. Yet even if not all plaintiffs are loss averse, contingent fee arrangements create some legal selection effects: Among plaintiffs who resemble one another in all respects except their degree of loss aversion, the more loss averse find CFs more attractive than their less loss-averse counterparts. Consequently, the ultimate pool of plaintiffs who end up with contingent fees rather than alternative fee structures includes more of the loss averse compared to the ex-ante pool of plaintiffs overall. In this way, the tendency of CF arrangements to select for loss aversion renders the initial heterogeneity in rationality of the plaintiff population less relevant when evaluating the respective benefits and costs of this particular fee structure.

2.4 Conclusion

Despite its young age, behavioural law and economics already has accomplished much. Its impact on the legal and policy discourse is significant in the United States and, more recently, in Europe as well. Nevertheless, substantial challenges still await the next generation of BLE scholarship in its mission of increasing both the breadth and depth of its legal methodology. Additional jurisdictions and legal fields are in need of exploration and much further analysis is required even in more familiar legal territories.

Empirical and experimental tools will also benefit from their gradual adaptation to the interests and queries peculiar to legal scholars, as distinct from those favored by their psychological or economic predecessors. And overarching questions that affect many disparate behavioural-legal inquires demand additional systematic study. Indeed, this is an exciting time for those involved in behavioural law and economics, with abundant opportunities for meaningful scholarly contributions to the field in particular and to the law more generally.

Acknowledgements This essay is based on my opening remarks at the third Law and Economics Conference in Lucerne on "Behavioural Law and Economics: American and European Perspectives" and benefited from the comments of conference participants. Christina Brunty and Dean Nickles provided excellent research assistance.

Bibliography

Anderson, C. A., James J. Lindsay, and Brad J. Bushman. 1999. Research in the psychological laboratory: Truth or triviality? *Current Directions in Psychological Science* 8 (1): 3–9.
Appelt, Kirstin C., F. Milch Kerry, Michel J. J. Handgraaf, and Elke U. Weber. 2011. The decision making individual differences inventory and guidelines for the study of individual differences in judgment and decision-making research. *Judgment and Decision Making* 6 (3): 252–262.
Armstrong, Mark, and Steffen Huck. 2010. Behavioral economics as applied to firms: A primer. *Competition Policy International* 6:3–45.
Bennett, M., J. Fingleton, A. Fletcher, L. Hurley, and D. Ruck. 2010. What does behavioral economics mean for competition policy? *Competition Policy International* 6:111–137.

Brickman, Lester. 2003. The market for contingent fee-financed tort litigation: Is it price competitive? *Cardozo Law Review* 25:65–128.
Bubb, Ryan, and Richard H. Pildes. 2014. How behavioral economics trims its sails and why. *Harvard Law Review* 127:1593–1678.
Buccafusco, Christopher, and Christopher Sprigman. 2010. Valuing intellectual property: An experiment. *Cornell Law Review* 96:1–46.
Buccafusco, Christopher, and Christopher Sprigman. 2011. The creativity effect. *The University of Chicago Law Review* 78:31–52.
Camerer, Colin F., and Robin M. Hogarth. 1999. The effects of financial incentives in experiments: a review and capital–labor–production framework. *Journal of Risk and Uncertainty* 19:7–42.
Camerer, Colin, Samuel Issacharoff, George Loewenstein, Ted O'Donoghue, and Matthew Rabin. 2003. Regulation for conservatives: behavioral economics and the case for "Asymmetric Paternalism". *University of Pennsylvania Law Review* 151:1211–1254.
Camerer, Colin F., George Loewenstein, and Matthew Rabin, eds. 2004. *Advances in behavioral economics*. vol. 2. New York: Russell Sage Foundation. (Princeton, N.J. and Oxford: Princeton University Press.)
Cokely, Edward T., and Colleen M. Kelley. 2009. Cognitive abilities and superior decision making under risk: A protocol analysis and process model evaluation. *Judgment and Decision Making* 4 (1): 20–33.
European Commission. 2010. Behavioural economics. http://ec.europa.eu/consumers/behavioural_economics/index_en.htm.
European Commission. 2012. Future brief: Green behaviour. http://ec.europa.eu/environment/integration/research/newsalert/pdf/FB4.pdf.
Feldman, Yuval 2006. The behavioral foundations of trade secrets: Tangibility, authorship, and legality. *Journal of Empirical and Legal Studies* 3 (2): 197–236.
Garcia, Kristelia. 2014. Penalty default licenses: A case for uncertainty. *New York University Law Review* 89:(forthcoming).
Gazal-Ayal, Oren, and Avishalom Tor. 2012. The innocence effect. *Duke Law Journal* 62:339–401.
Gerla, Harry S. 1985. The psychology of predatory pricing: Why predatory pricing pays. *Southwestern Law Review* 39:755–780.
Google Scholar. 2013a. Scholar search. http://scholar.google.com/scholar?hl=en&as_sdt=5%2C31&sciodt=0%2C31&cites=12390685775047939328&scipsc=&as_ylo=&as_yhi=2013.
Google Scholar. 2013b. Scholar search. http://scholar.google.com/scholar?hl=en&as_sdt=5%2C31&sciodt=0%2C31&cites=9021820348227555800&scipsc=&as_ylo=&as_yhi=2013.
Government of the United Kingdom Cabinet Office. 2014. Behavioural insights team. https://www.gov.uk/government/organisations/behavioural-insights-team.
Guthrie, Chris, Jeffrey J. Rachlinski, and Andrew J. Wistrich. 2001. Inside the judicial mind. *Cornell Law Review* 86:777–830.
Guthrie, Chris, Jeffrey J. Rachlinski, and Andrew J. Wistrich. 2007. Blinking on the bench. *Cornell Law Review* 93:1–44.
Hazard Geoffrey C. Jr. 1998. Discovery and the role of the judge in civil law jurisdictions. *Notre Dame Law Review* 73:1017–1028.
Henrich, Joseph, et al. 2005. "Economic man" in cross-cultural perspective: Behavioral experiments in 15 small-scale societies. *Behavioral and Brain Sciences* 28:795–855.
Hillman, Robert A. 2000. Limits of behavioral decision theory in legal analysis: The case of liquidated damages. *Cornell Law Review* 85:717–738.
Huck, Steffen, Jidong Zhou, and Charlotte Duke. 2011. Consumer behavioural biases in competition a survey. Office of Fair Trading.
Johnson, Eric E. 2012. Intellectual property and the incentive fallacy. *Florida State University Law Review* 39:623–680.
Jolls, Christine, and Cass R. Sunstein. 2006. Debiasing through law. *Journal of Legal Studies* 35:199–241.
Jolls, Christine, Cass R. Sunstein, and Richard H. Thaler. 1998. A behavioral approach to law and economics. *Stanford Law Review* 50:1471–1550.
Klick, Jonathan, and Gregory Mitchell. 2006. Government regulation of irrationality: Moral and cognitive hazards. *Minnesota Law Review* 90:1620–1663.

Korobkin, Russell B., and Thomas S. Ulen. 2000. Law and behavioral science: Removing the rationality assumption from law and economics. *California Law Review* 88:1051–1144.

Langevoort, Donald C. 1998. Behavioral theories of judgment and decision making in legal scholarship: A literature review. *Vanderbilt Law Review* 51:1499–1540.

Lauriola, Marco, and Irwin P. Levin. 2001. Personality traits and risky decision-making in a controlled experimental task: An exploratory study. *Personality and Individual Differences* 31:215–226.

Leung, Kwok, and Michael W. Morris. 2001. Justice through the lens of culture and ethnicity. In *Handbook of justice research in law*, eds. J. Sanders and V. Lee Hamilton, 343–378. New York: Springer.

Levin, Irwin P., Gary J. Gaeth, Judy Schreiber, and Marco Lauriola. 2002. A new look at framing effects: Distribution of effect sizes, individual differences, and independence of types of effects. *Organizational Behavior and Human Decision Processes* 88 (1): 411–429.

Lind, E. Allan, Tom R. Tyler, and Y. J. Huo. 1997. Procedural context and culture: Variation in the antecedents of procedural justice judgments. *Journal of Personality and Social Psychology* 73:767–780.

Mahoney, Kevin T., Walter Buboltz, Irwin P. Levin, Dennis Doverspike, and Daniel J. Svyantek. 2011. Individual differences in a within-subjects risky-choice framing study. *Personality and Individual Differences* 51:248–257.

Marotta-Wurgler, Florencia. 2011. Will increased disclosure help? Evaluating the recommendations of the Ali's "Principles of the Law of Software Contracts." *University of Chicago Law Review* 78:165–186.

Marotta-Wurgler, Florencia. 2013. Set in stone? Change and innovation in consumer standard-form contracts. *New York University Law Review* 88:240–285.

McAdams, Richard H. 1999. Experimental law and economics. In *Encyclopedia of law and economics*, eds. B. Bouckaert and G. De Geest, 539–561. Cheltenham: Edward Elgar.

Mitchell, Gregory 2002. Taking behavioralism too seriously? The unwarranted pessimism of the new behavioral analysis of law. *William and Mary Law Review* 43:1907–2021.

Newman, John M. 2013. Copyright freeconomics. *Vanderbilt Law Review* 66:1409–1469.

Newmyer, Tory. 22 February 2013. Meet Cass Sunstein–Obama's superego. *Fortune Magazine*.

Organisation for Economic Co-Operation and Development. 2010. *Consumer policy toolkit*. Paris: OECD Publishing.

Prentice, Robert A. 2003. Chicago man, k-t man, and the future of behavioral law and economics. *Vanderbilt Law Review* 56:1663–1777.

Rachlinski, Jeffrey J. 2000. The "New" law and psychology: A reply to critics, skeptics, and cautious supporters. *Cornell Law Review* 85:739–766.

Rachlinski, Jeffrey J. 2006. Cognitive errors, individual differences, and paternalism. *University of Chicago Law Review* 73:207–229.

Rosenthal, Robert, and Ralph Rosnow. 1991. *Essentials of behavioral research: Methods and data analysis*. 2nd ed. New York: McGraw-Hill.

Shapiro, Fred R., and Michelle Pearce. 2012. The most-cited law review articles of all time. *Michigan Law Review* 110:1483–1520.

Sprigman, Christopher Jon, Christopher Buccafusco, and Zachary Burns. 2013. What's a name worth?: Experimental tests of the value of attribution in intellectual property. *Boston University Law Review* 93:1389–1435.

Stanovich, Keith E., and Richard F. West. 1998. Individual differences in framing and conjunction effects. *Thinking and Reasoning* 4 (4): 289–317.

Sunstein, Cass R., and Richard H. Thaler. 2003. Libertarian paternalism is not an oxymoron. *University of Chicago Law Review* 70:1159–1202.

Thaler, Richard H., and Cass R. Sunstein. 2008. *Nudge: Improving decisions about health, wealth, and happiness*. New Haven: Yale University Press.

Tor, Avishalom. 2002. The fable of entry: Bounded rationality, market discipline, and legal policy. *Michigan Law Review* 101:482–568.

Tor, Avishalom. 2007. On contractual defaults and experimental law and economics. *Journal of Institutional and Theoretical Economics* 163:26–29.

Tor, Avishalom. 2008. The methodology of the behavioral analysis of law. *Haifa Law Review* 4:237–327.
Tor, Avishalom. 2014a. Understanding behavioral antitrust. *Texas Law Review* 92:573–667.
Tor, Avishalom. 2014b. The market, the firm, and behavioral antitrust. In *Oxford handbook on behavioral economics and the law*. Oxford University Press. (forthcoming)
Tor, Avishalom. 2014c. (unpublished manuscript). Law in a behaviorally-complex world.
Tor, Avishalom, and Dotan Oliar. 2002. Incentives to create under a "lifetime-plus-years" copyright duration: Lessons from a behavioral economic analysis for Eldred v. Ashcroft. *Loyola of Los Angeles Law Review* 36:437–492.
Tyler, Tom. 2006. *Why people obey the law*. Princeton: Princeton University Press.
Ulen, Thomas S. 2011. *European and American perspectives on behavioral law and economics*.
Van Bavel, René, Benedikt Herrmann, Gabriele Esposito, and Antonios Proestakis. 2013. Applying behavioural sciences to EU policy-making. *Joint Research Centre Scientific and Policy Reports* 1–21.
Weber, Elke U., and Christopher K. Hsee. 2000. Culture and individual judgment and decision making. *Journal of Applied Psychology* 49:32–61.
West, Richard F., Maggie E. Toplak, and Keith E. Stanovich. 2008. Heuristics and biases as measures of critical thinking: Associations with cognitive ability and thinking dispositions. *Journal of Educational Psychology* 100 (4): 930–941.
Wistrich, Andrew J., Chris Guthrie, and Jeffrey J. Rachlinski. 2005. Can judges ignore inadmissible information? The difficulty of deliberately disregarding. *University of Pennsylvania Law Review* 153:1251–1345.
Zamir, Eyal. 1998. The efficiency of paternalism. *Virginia Law Review* 84:229–286.
Zamir, Eyal, and Ilana Ritov. 2010. Revisiting the debate over attorney's contingent fees: A behavioral analysis. *Journal of Legal Studies* 39:245–288.
Zamir, Eyal, and Doron Teichman. 2014. *The Oxford handbook of behavioral law and economics*. Oxford: Oxford University Press.

Avishalom Tor University of Notre Dame, United States. Professor of Law and Director of the Notre Dame Research Program on Law and Market Behavior (ND LAMB), Notre Dame Law School, IN 46614. ator@nd.edu. Fields of Interest: Behavioural and Experimental Law and Economics, Competition Law, Corporate Governance, Judgment and Decision Making.

Chapter 3
From Rational Choice to Behavioural Economics

Theoretical Foundations, Empirical Findings and Legal Implications

Klaus Mathis and Ariel David Steffen

Abstract This article considers how individual decision making is explained in rational choice, on the one hand, and in behavioural economics, on the other hand, and analyses the corresponding implications for the maximization of individual and social utility. Special emphasis is placed on whether and how the law can and shall positively influence non-utility-maximizing behaviour resulting from cognitive heuristics and biases.

3.1 Introduction

The value maximization premise of neo-classical rational choice theory assumes that, when confronted with various alternative courses of action, the rational and self-interested *homo oeconomicus* will choose the alternative that *maximises his or her individual utility*. Within welfare economics, welfare is used as a measure for evaluating social conditions.

Empirical knowledge obtained by social psychologists over the past thirty years from experiments and field studies partly refute rational choice theory. This knowledge has also been profitably used within economic theory under the heading of *behavioural economics*. In particular, the image of the rational, utility-maximising *homo oeconomicus* must be revised, since people often use *cognitive heuristics*, which may result in systematic *cognitive biases*. Accordingly, they make decisions that neither serve their own interests nor maximise social welfare. These findings

K. Mathis (✉) · A. D. Steffen
Faculty of Law, University of Lucerne, Frohburgstrasse 3, 6002 Lucerne, Switzerland
e-mail: klaus.mathis@unilu.ch

A. D. Steffen
e-mail: ariel.steffen@unilu.ch

K. Mathis (ed.), *European Perspectives on Behavioural Law and Economics*,
Economic Analysis of Law in European Legal Scholarship 2,
DOI 10.1007/978-3-319-11635-8_3

have undermined the traditional explanatory model for economics. As Richard A. Posner concisely puts it:

> What is called "behavioral economics" [...] has undermined the economic model of man as a rational maximizer of his self-interest and helped to expose the rampant exploitation by business of consumer psychology. Businesses know, and economists are learning, that consumers are easily manipulated by sellers into making bad choices—choices they would never make if they knew better [...].[1]

In this regard, the question arises as to the extent to which the law can and shall react to these new insights from behavioural research.

This paper discusses, in a first step, how individuals make decisions according to rational choice theory and the criteria by which welfare economics evaluates social conditions (3.2). It will then critique rational choice theory from the perspective of behavioural economics, commenting on various deviations from the assumptions underlying rational choice theory (3.3). Finally, the results will be summarised in a concluding paragraph (3.4).

3.2 Rational Choice Theory

According to the paradigm of neo-classical micro-economic theory, human conduct is understood as the *rational choice* between various alternatives under conditions of *scarcity*. The micro-economic approach is based on the economic paradigm. The core element of this paradigm is *homo oeconomicus*, who acts rationally under conditions of scarcity. The unit of analysis is the *individual* (*methodological individualism*). This individual disposes of limited resources and is unable to satisfy all of his or her needs, but must make an optimum choice amongst various alternatives. In principle, all human conduct—including interpersonal relations—is governed by the law of scarcity and thus represents a potential field for the application of economic theory. Thus, *economics* as a science refers to a *method* rather than to a specific subject. Applying the economic approach to a "non-economic" field—such as, for example, by Gary S. Becker to the family, crime and the law—is at times dismissed as "economic imperialism".[2]

3.2.1 Individual Decisions

Under the rational choice model, the individual's decision-making position can essentially be accounted for with reference to two factors: preferences and restrictions. Preferences refer to people's internal motives, and restrictions to their external incentives. The behavioural economic model attempts *to account for changes in*

---

[1] Posner 2013, p. 212.

[2] Mathis 2009, p. 21 et seqq.

behaviour as a reaction to external incentives, and hence to changes in restrictions. Whilst preferences are an important factor in accounting for human conduct, they are assumed to be unalterable in the short term and are thus both incapable of explaining changes in short-term behaviour and impracticable as an instrument for regulatory policy.

An individual's values, which have developed through the process of socialisation, manifest themselves as *preferences* in the utility function. According to this approach, the individual assesses the available options (i.e. weighs up advantages and disadvantages in the form of benefits and costs) of each alternative and chooses the alternative with the highest gain, assuming identical restrictions. *Restrictions* limit the individual's room for manoeuvre and thus all possible courses of action available to him or her. In the textbook case of consumer decisions by a private household, relevant restrictions are the disposable income, on the one hand, and the relative prices of consumer goods, on the other hand. Further restrictions include time or legal norms.

The restrictions that apply to the conduct of individuals are normally relatively easy to identify. By contrast, it is difficult to determine individuals' preferences. Leaving aside direct questioning (with all associated difficulties), preferences can, as a rule, only be determined indirectly by making inferences regarding individuals' order of preference via observing both behaviour and restrictions. Moreover, preferences are generally more stable than restrictions and change relatively slowly, if at all.[3] *It is therefore assumed that the conduct of individuals can be systematically influenced by changing incentives.* By the same token, it is presumed that a similar systematic influencing of preferences will be difficult, at least in the short term. For example, traffic volumes may be reduced more effectively and more quickly by increasing fuel prices than by calls to refrain from using a car.

The rational choice theory intentionally reduces people to a few individual characteristics, since a key feature of economic modelling is the focus on important aspects whilst disregarding less important matters. Human decision-making processes are an extremely complicated phenomenon and are influenced by an unwieldy large number of factors. In order to be able to engage with this phenomenon scientifically, it is necessary to *reduce complexity*.[4] Indeed, the aim of the economic approach is not to explain the actual behaviour of any given person; such matters must be left to psychologists. Economists are rather interested in the behaviour of large groups of individuals, so called "aggregates", such as, for example, the behaviour of consumers or businesses. They look for *patterns* within the behaviour of the group as a whole, or at least the majority of the relevant group.

In his renowned paper on "The Methodology of Positive Economics" (1953), Milton Friedman defends the neo-classical theory against the criticism that it is reductionist and based on false assumptions.[5] According to Friedman, the underlying assumptions do not constitute actual assertions relating to reality, but are rather *"as*

[3] Kirchgässner 1988, p. 111 et seqq.

[4] Homann and Suchanek 2000, p. 392.

[5] See also below, sect. 3.3.

if" assertions. Thus, maximising utility does not mean that any given individual actually seeks to do so, but rather that the result of his or her behaviour is the same as it would have been had he or she acted in this way.[6] A theory is a *forecasting tool*, and not a mirror of reality. Thus, the effectiveness of a theory is not to be judged on the basis of how realistic its premises are; on the contrary, its effectiveness is to be ascertained by testing how practical a given hypothesis—devised with the assistance of the theory—in reality is. Indeed, as a general rule, the more significant a theory is, the more unrealistic its assumptions will be:

> Truly important and significant hypotheses will be found to have "assumptions" that are wildly inaccurate descriptive representations of reality, and, in general, the more significant the theory, the more unrealistic the assumptions [...].[7]

Friedman is interested, first and foremost, in creating a usable tool for economists: hypotheses should provide useful forecasts on the basis of as little information as possible.[8] Richard A. Posner adopts a similar stance to Friedman in stressing the explanatory and predictive power of economic theory. However, the premises as such need not be accurate:

> An important test of a theory is its ability to explain reality. If it does a lousy job, the reason may be that its assumptions are insufficiently realistic; but we need not try to evaluate the assumptions directly in order to evaluate it. Judged by the test of explanatory power, economic theory is a significant (although only partial) success. [...] Another test of scientific theory is its predictive power, and here too economics has had its share of success, most dramatically in recent years.[9]

Drawing on a comparison with natural sciences—which acts as a model for economic theory—Posner shows that theories may still be very useful, even if they are based on partially false assumptions:

> Newton's law of falling bodies is unrealistic in its basic assumption that bodies fall in a vacuum, but it is still a useful theory because it predicts with reasonable accuracy the behavior of a wide variety of falling bodies in the real world.[10]

In objection to this *instrumentalism*, it may be countered that "explaining" means more than simply "forecasting". Friedman's methodology does not explain reality or expand knowledge. Such theories do not result in any new knowledge regarding the structural interrelations between situations.[11] As Michael Scriven aptly puts it:

> [T]here certainly seem to be occasions when we can predict some phenomenon with the greatest success, but cannot provide any explanation of it. For example, we may discover that whenever cows lie down in the open fields by day, it always rains within a few hours. We are in an excellent position for prediction, but we could scarcely offer the earlier event as an explanation of the latter. It appears that explanation requires something "more than" prediction; and my suggestion would be that, whereas an understanding of a phenomenon

[6] Frank 1976, p. 19.

[7] Friedman 1953, p. 14.

[8] Hotz 1982, p. 304.

[9] Posner 1998, p. 18.

[10] Posner 1998, p. 18.

[11] See Pheby 1988, p. 83.

> often enables us to forecast it, the ability to forecast it does not constitute an understanding of a phenomenon.[12]

It may also be argued that businesses competing with one another have no alternative than to maximise profit, as they would otherwise go bankrupt and be excluded from the market.[13] When viewed in this sense, the logic of the market has already been instilled into *homo oeconomicus* and any other behaviour will be eliminated through the naturally selective process of competition:

> [It] must be noted that Friedman shares Smith's optimistic view of the market. However, this assumes that businesses and families can make decisions about the future—even in a world full of uncertainty—which are appropriate for the situation often enough. It also implies that, owing to competition, there is only a small likelihood that the indolent, the foolish, the inept—but also the unlucky and the weak—will perform a decision making function over the long term.[14]

This view may be countered by objecting that entrepreneurs and their advisers have absorbed economic theory during their studies, with the result that businesses operate according to the rules of economic theory, which in turn prove to be true as a self-fulfilling prophecy.

3.2.2 Social Decisions

On a social level, welfare economics deals with the maximisation of welfare through the efficient allocation of resources. Efficiency is generally defined as *Pareto efficiency* or *Kaldor-Hicks efficiency*.[15]

A particular state will be regarded as *Pareto-optimal* where it is impossible to improve the situation of an individual without worsening the situation of another individual. The Pareto principle is drawn from the model of the free market. Assuming that individual economic operators have freedom of choice and are free to act, each market participant is free to conclude market transactions, or to decide not to do so. This freedom guarantees that every market transaction will represent an improvement in Pareto efficiency. The law, by contrast, is *mandatory in nature.* This means that the concept of Pareto efficiency needs to be adjusted in order for it to be of use for the law.[16] Nicholas Kaldor and John R. Hicks transformed the Pareto criterion into an instrument that can be applied to the law. The Kaldor-Hicks test stipulates that a change will involve an improvement whenever the winners consider their gains to be greater than the losers consider their losses to be.[17]

---

[12] Scriven 1962, p. 176 et seqq.

[13] Homann and Suchanek 2000, p. 422.

[14] Meyer 1978, p. 41. On Adam Smith's market optimism see Mathis 2009, p. 108 et seqq.

[15] On the efficiency criteria and their philosophical foundations, see Mathis 2009; see also Eidenmüller 2005.

[16] Fletcher 1996, p. 158.

[17] Baumol 1972, p. 402.

The *Kaldor-Hicks criterion* differs from the Pareto principle in that it not only envisages alternative decisions which leave nobody worse off, but also decisions that are beneficial for some but detrimental for others. Whilst the winners must *hypothetically* be able to compensate the losers, an actual compensation payment is not mandatory. The Kaldor-Hicks test thus denotes a *potential* rather than an actual increase in Pareto efficiency.[18]

The concept of Kaldor-Hicks efficiency is widespread within welfare economics. It is this concept that underlies the *cost-benefit analysis* used to measure the net social benefit of investments. For example, a new railway line will be assessed by comparing economic costs discounted to the present day (e.g. construction and environmental costs) with economic benefits discounted to the present day (e.g. additional profits for the railway company and improved passenger comfort). Cost-benefit analyses may be used in the legal domain in order to assess regulations. However, there are limits to this method of evaluation: alongside the technical difficulties in measuring costs and benefits, the cost-benefit analysis is criticised because it disregards the *problem of distributing* gains and losses associated with projects and regulations.[19]

3.3 Behavioural Economics

The traditional rational choice approach and its basic assumptions are being challenged by more recent approaches to research, which may be classified together under the term behavioural economics.[20] The goal of this line of research is to critically analyse the psychological foundations of economics and to provide a more realistic account of them.[21] The aim is to increase the explanatory power of the economic model by providing a better psychological foundation.[22]

The first fundamental criticism is directed against the *assumption of rational behaviour*. As early as the 1970s, Herbert A. Simon objected to this concept of *perfect rationality*:

> There can no longer be any doubt that the micro assumptions of the theory—the assumptions of perfect rationality—are contrary to fact. It is not a question of approximation; they do not even remotely describe the processes that human beings use for making decisions in complex situations.[23]

A further milestone was achieved by Daniel Kahneman and Amos Tversky's *Prospect Theory* (1979) which, building on Simon's work, further relativised the

[18] See contra Mathis 2009, p. 47 et seqq.

[19] Mathis 2007b, p. 1545.

[20] For an overview see Mathis 2007a, p. 118–120.

[21] This also makes it possible to refute more effectively the objection that economists frequently dedicate their efforts to constructing abstract models in their ivory towers.

[22] See e.g. the volume by Camerer, Loewenstein and Rabin 2003; a good overview is also provided by Kahneman 2011.

[23] Simon 1979, p. 510.

assumption of rationality. Their theory is based on empirical observation and describes how individuals perceive their wins and losses. Kahneman and Tversky found out that most people are *loss averse*. Thus, their negative perception of, for example, a fine of CHF 1000.00 will be more intense than their positive assessment of an equivalent gain. They also found out that people make probability assessments on the basis of particular indicators (known as *anchors*), which are often arbitrary.[24]

In his book "Thinking, Fast and Slow" (2011), Kahneman differentiates between two systems of human thinking:[25]

> System 1 operates automatically and quickly, with little or no effort and no sense of voluntary control.[26]

System 1 is an intuitive system of thought, in which judgments are made quickly and unwittingly.

> System 2 allocates attention to the effortful mental activities that demand it, including complex computations. The operations of System 2 are often associated with the subjective experience of agency, choice, and concentration.[27]

System 2 is a rational system of thought, in which judgments are made on the basis of thorough consideration, which requires a certain amount of time.

Each way of thinking has its own benefits and drawbacks: the rational approach of *System 2* enables human beings to analyse a problem thoroughly and to make well-considered decisions. However, this requires time and effort. *System 1* has the advantage of requiring hardly any time and being practically effortless. This system relies on a form of cognitive rules of thumb, known as *heuristics*, which are fundamentally useful, if not even necessary, in order to resolve complex everyday situations without dedicating a significant amount of time to the matter. However, in some cases its application leads to significant *systematic biases*.[28] In the same way as optical illusions may result in reality being misread, so can mental heuristics result in incorrect evaluations.[29]

Behavioural economics also calls into question the *theory of self-interest*. In reality, most people do not always act according to their best self-interest. There are indications that a consideration of fairness and mutual benefit are important within bilateral negotiations and market operation. More recent behavioural economics research has attempted to explain how social, economic and legal conditions influence the tendency to engage in reciprocal conduct (i.e. providing mutual satisfaction).[30]

---

[24] See overall Kahneman and Tversky 1979, p. 263–292.

[25] In their paper published in 1974 entitled "Judgement under Uncertainty: Heuristics and Biases", Amon Tversky and Daniel Kahneman demonstrated that people rely on mental heuristics in complex decision-making scenarios (this paper is also reproduced in the annex to the book "Thinking, Fast and Slow").

[26] Kahneman 2011, p. 20.

[27] Kahneman 2011, p. 21.

[28] Tversky and Kahneman 1974, p. 1124.

[29] Guthrie, Rachlinski and Wistrich 2001, p. 780.

[30] See e.g. Fehr and Fischbacher 2002, C1-C33; Gintis, Bowles, Boyd and Fehr 2005.

Finally, the neo-classical model of human behaviour implicitly presupposes the highly unrealistic assumption of unbounded *willpower*. Most economists see behaviour as a simple decision-making process in which a choice is made between different alternatives. Implementing the decision is either completely disregarded, or it is assumed to run smoothly. In actual fact, however, people normally have to motivate themselves in order to achieve a desired form of behaviour. There might be conflicts between two or more opposing motives and people may be tempted to seek short-term gains at the cost of long-term goals. For example, we may be unable to give up smoking contrary to our better judgment.[31]

3.3.1 Individual Decisions

On an individual level, behavioural economics studies human conduct through empirically investigating its implications for economic processes. In order to do this, data is usually generated artificially in laboratory experiments, though real-life data is also increasingly being used. Particular focus is placed on the cognitive heuristics and biases that contrast with *homo oeconomicus*. The following paragraphs will explain briefly the most important heuristics and their related biases.

Availability Bias The *subjectively perceived likelihood* of an event will be higher, the easier and quicker a person is able to imagine or remember such an event:[32]

> [P]eople might resolve a question of probability not by investigating statistics, but by asking whether a relevant incident comes easily to mind.[33]

Thus, it is possible that a judgment regarding the likelihood of a traffic accident is dependent upon how vividly one can imagine such an event. A person who has recently witnessed a traffic accident will generally assess the likelihood of traffic accidents to be significantly higher than a person who has not witnessed a traffic accident in a long time.[34] In addition to the *individual cognitive availability*, the *general cognitive availability* has to be considered as well. The media play a central role in this respect. The fact that deaths from car accidents are more widely reported than, say, deaths from cancer, promotes the idea that more people die from the consequences of traffic accidents than from cancer. In actual fact, however, the opposite is true.[35]

Furthermore, it is also necessary to consider *illusory correlations*. Since people look out for *positive contingencies*, they overestimate the frequency of the general occurrence of events. For example, there is a widespread belief that there is a correlation between consuming drugs and committing crimes. By the same token, *negative contingencies* are often hardly taken into account. A person may take drugs

[31] See Loewenstein 2000, p. 51–76.

[32] Tversky and Kahneman 1974, p. 1127.

[33] Jolls 2009, p. 77.

[34] Jungermann, Pfister and Fischer 2010, p. 173.

[35] Jungermann, Pfister and Fischer 2010, p. 174.

without ever committing a crime, or may commit a crime without ever having taken drugs.[36]

Hindsight Bias According to popular folk wisdom, "hindsight is always 20/20". Indeed, many events—especially those with a tragic outcome—appear to be foreseeable *after* the fact. Baruch Fischhoff was one of the first to study this phenomenon, which subsequently came to be known as *hindsight bias*. He asked how knowledge of the outcome of a course of events affects its *ex post* assessment. His starting hypothesis of a retrospective overestimation of the likelihood of an event has been substantiated in various experiments.[37] Knowledge of the outcome of a course of events influences those making *ex post* judgments by leading them to believe that people should have been able to anticipate future events more accurately than was actually possible. This bias is also known as the *knew-it-all-along effect* or as *creeping determinism*.[38]

Numerous subsequent studies have since independently confirmed that judgments made in retrospect tend to overestimate the foreseeability of events.[39] Following Fischhoff, Jeffrey J. Rachlinski elaborated on the hindsight bias: Rachlinski argues that people feel the urge to reconcile a particular outcome of a course of events with its respective causes—both of which are *ex ante* unknown—in a *coherent whole*. This has the effect that information that appears to be particularly relevant *ex post* is regarded as particularly relevant *ex ante*. By the same token, information pointing to an alternative course of events is disregarded.[40]

According to Rachlinski, this cognitive error is enhanced by *motivational factors*: many people seek *stability* and *foreseeability*. Moreover, since the foreseeability of an unfortunate event implies its avoidability, hindsight bias may have an extraordinary reassuring effect, as it makes uncontrollable events appear to be controllable.[41] Even if an event is regarded as singular and thus utterly unforeseeable, it is more agreeable to ascribe the event to the normal order of things, thereby rendering the future—allegedly—controllable.

Anchoring Effect The *anchoring* or *reference point* effect postulates that people frequently make probability judgments intuitively or with reference to *anchored points of view* that are often entirely arbitrary.[42] The anchoring effect may result both in inaccurate numerical estimates as well as biased memories. In a study by Kahneman and Tversky, students were asked to estimate the proportion of African UN member states. Before the students gave their estimates, the two groups of test participants span a wheel of fortune, which stopped—"by chance"—on 65 for group one and on 10 for group two. In group one, the students on average estimated that African states made up 45% of UN members, whilst in group two, the estimated

[36] Jungermann, Pfister and Fischer 2010, p. 174.

[37] Fischhoff 1975, p. 292.

[38] Fischhoff 1975, p. 288.

[39] See Christensen-Szalanski and Fobian-Willham 1991.

[40] Rachlinski 2000, p. 97.

[41] Rachlinski 2000, p. 97 et seqq.

[42] Tversky and Kahneman 1974, p. 1128; Jungermann, Pfister and Fischer 2010, p. 174 et seqq.

figure averaged 25 %. The entirely arbitrary figure provided by the wheel of chance had an influence on the participants' estimates—in other words, it served as an *anchor*.[43] Even if people acknowledge the invalidity of an arbitrary anchor, it nonetheless operates as a starting point for subsequent estimates. People simply adjust either upwards or downwards from it.[44]

The anchor effect can also lead to biased memories, as the following example illustrates: a test participant is asked to estimate the length of the river Rhine. Since the person does not know the precise length, she guesses it to be 1050 km. A few weeks later, the test participant is informed of the actual length of the Rhine (1230 km) and asked to remember what length she estimated. If the test participant is no longer able to recall her original estimate, she thinks about what she might most probably have estimated, arriving at a length of 1150 km.[45] The inaccurate memory is adjusted to the information provided immediately before the second estimate. The information serves as an anchor.

Confirmation Bias *Confirmation bias* refers to people's tendency to attempt to confirm a hypothesis they have already made. This means that information confirming a given hypothesis is perceived more accurately and given greater weight. By the same token, data confirming the hypothesis is actively sought after whilst data falsifying the hypothesis is disregarded.[46]

Egocentric Bias *Overoptimism* and *overconfidence* are two closely related phenomena, which are usually summarised under the term *egocentric bias*:

> People routinely estimate [...] that they are above average on a variety of desirable characteristics, including health, driving, professional skills, and the likelihood of having a successful marriage.[47]

Overoptimistic people overestimate the likelihood of positive events whilst at the same time underestimating the risk of a negative occurrence. For instance, it is unrealistic if most drivers expect themselves to be less likely than other drivers to be involved in an accident—because, if true, the average statistical likelihood would have to be lower than it is.[48] Overoptimistic assertions are often based on *overconfidence*. Thus, most drivers consider themselves to be more skilled than the average driver, which gives them the impression to be able to avoid an accident by skilful driving.

Loss Aversion In 1979, Daniel Kahneman and Amos Tversky empirically observed *loss aversion*. The theory postulates that individuals ascribe greater weight to losses than to equivalent gains.[49] Consequently, potential gains are often not realised, as they are associated with potential losses on the same or a slightly lower level. As

[43] Tversky and Kahneman 1974, p. 1128.

[44] Guthrie, Rachlinski and Wistrich 2001, p. 788.

[45] Cf. Jungermann, Pfister and Fischer 2010, p. 175.

[46] Schweizer 2005, p. 178.

[47] Guthrie, Rachlinski and Wistrich 2001, p. 811 et seqq.

[48] Englerth 2007, p. 95.

[49] Kahneman and Tversky 1979.

a result, a neutral or positive expected value is distorted and turned into a negative expected value. As a result, the potential gains will not be realised.

Status Quo Preference The *status quo preference* is closely related to loss aversion: since change is associated with uncertainty or risk[50]—and hence with potential losses—people tend to privilege the status quo over change.[51]

Endowment Effect The *endowment effect* may be interpreted as a sub-form of the status quo preference.[52] Rationally speaking, a person should ascribe the same value to a good, irrespective of whether she possesses it or not. However, empirical studies have shown that people demand more money for goods in their possession than they are willing to pay for them.[53] In other words: the amount that a person is willing to pay in order to *buy* an object (*willingness to pay*) is always lower than the amount for which the person is willing to *sell* the object (*willingness to accept*).

Framing Effect Rationally speaking, it is immaterial whether, given a specific likelihood, a particular alternative for action is formulated positively in the form of potential gains or negatively as potential losses. In actual fact, however, people tend to favour an alternative when it is *framed* positively and to reject it when it is framed negatively (*framing effect*).[54] For example, people generally favour a rate of employment of 95 % compared to an unemployment rate of 5 %, even though both states are identical. The more concrete, personal and emotional the formulation, the greater the effect appears to be.[55]

3.3.2 Social Decisions

Whilst systematic cognitive biases lead people to take decisions which maximize neither their own nor social utility, recent behavioural economics research into the way in which individuals take decisions has revealed new ways of influencing behaviour. It is thought that these insights may successfully be used to entice individuals to behave in manners that is optimal for them as well as society as a whole. The law—as an instrument for regulatory policy—is ascribed a prominent role in

[50] A fundamental definition of risk goes back to Frank H. Knight's paper "Risk, Uncertainty and Profit". Knight differentiates between the term "risk" as quantitatively measurable uncertainty and the term "uncertainty" for all non-quantifiable uncertainties. Accordingly, a decision will always involve risk if the probability of occurrence is known. By the same token, if the probability of occurrence is unknown, the decision will involve uncertainty (see Knight 1964, p. 19 et seqq.). People react more sensitively to risk than to uncertainty and to events that turn the impossible into the possible or the possible into the certain than to mere increases in likelihood (see Tversky and Fox 1995, p. 269 and 281).

[51] Cf. Kahneman und Tversky 1979.

[52] Both the endowment effect and the *status quo* preference are based on loss aversion (cf. Kahneman, Knetsch and Thaler 1991, p. 199).

[53] Kahneman, Knetsch and Thaler 1990.

[54] Kahneman and Tversky 1981.

[55] See e.g. Jolls and Sunstein 2006.

this respect.[56] There are essentially two ways in which the law can contribute to eliminate biases:

On the one hand, it may attempt to prevent the occurrence of boundedly rational behaviour by excluding all non-value maximizing options *ex ante*, for instance by means of prohibitions.[57] A hazardous product, for example, might not be approved by public authorities in order to protect consumers who underestimate the hazard risk (due to overoptimism). However, it is questionable whether this method is proportional, since it considerably impinges on individual autonomy.

On the other hand, it is also possible to help people overcome their cognitive biases via *debiasing*.[58] Debiasing may be achieved through *nudging*, that is to say by changing the individual's *choice architecture*[59] (i.e. the framework conditions under which a specific decision is made) order to nudge[60] the individual in a particular direction.[61] Nudging occurs, for example, where *default rules* apply. A classic example of a default rule is the opt-out solution for organ donation. According to an opt-out default, all people are assumed to be organ donors after their death—unless they expressly opt-out during their lifetime. In comparison to the opt-in solution, where organs are only removed if express consent had been provided by the donor, such a rule can result in significantly higher figures for donations.

The following example relating to consumer protection explains how the law may contribute to mitigate cognitive biases. By deploying opposing heuristics (the availability heuristic and the framing effect), consumers' overoptimism may successfully be debiased.[62]

Although rational choice theory assumes that consumers can make mistakes, these are based exclusively on *information asymmetry* between producers and consumers. Producers know their product, including its hazards, better than consumers, and can exploit this fact to their benefit. According to rational choice theory, minimising the information deficit can lead to an efficient result.[63] However, behavioural scientists assume that the information deficit is unable to account for all deviations from an efficient result. Even without information asymmetry, *overoptimism* might lead to inefficient results.[64] The law can take such a socially undesirable situation as a reason for expanding *product liability* or prohibiting a particularly hazardous product.[65] However, this leads to high economic costs: in the former case in particular for producers and courts, in the latter case mainly for consumers who

[56] On the law and economics analysis in conjunction with bounded rationality overall, see *inter alia* Jolls, Sunstein and Thaler 1998, Korobkin and Ulen 2000, Parisi and Smith 2004 and Sunstein 2000.

[57] See Rachlinski 2003, p. 1168.

[58] Cf. Thaler and Sunstein 2008.

[59] Thaler and Sunstein 2008, p. 81 et seqq.

[60] However, such an instrument may also be used in order to steer individuals in a politically desirable direction, which may involve more than mere debiasing.

[61] Cf. Thaler and Sunstein 2008.

[62] See Jolls and Sunstein 2006.

[63] See e.g. Stiglitz 1986, p. 90–91.

[64] *Inter alia*, Latin 1994, p. 1243–1244.

[65] See e.g. Prentice and Roszkowski 1991–1992.

would still be able to benefit from the use of a hazardous product.[66] A measure that only addresses boundedly rational (biased) behaviour and leaves rational behaviour intact is preferable. In this case, overoptimism may be debiased by both availability bias and framing effect:

Since the brain considers readily accessible data to be more likely to occur than data that is less readily available, overoptimism may be mitigated by the *availability bias*.[67] This may involve legislation obliging businesses to stress not only the positive but also—and in particular—the negative characteristics of their products in advertising.[68] The negative characteristics will spring more readily to mind, with the result that negative characteristics will not be crowded out by positive characteristics, enabling consumers to make a more balanced judgment. In Switzerland and Germany, for example, both health warnings and deterrent images must be applied to tobacco products (e.g. "Smoking causes fatal lung cancer" along with a picture of a healthy white lung and a black lung damaged by smoking). In order to ensure that consumers do not become accustomed to warnings and pictures (*wear-out effect*), these have to be changed from time to time.[69]

The *framing effect* is one of the most important factors influencing human decision-making.[70] Based on loss aversion, the framing effect may also be used as availability heuristic in order to counter overoptimism by ensuring that the formulation of a particular scenario focuses on potential losses rather than potential gains.[71] The more a given loss is presented in a tangible and personal manner, the greater its effect will be.[72] The private anti-smoking campaign conducted by the American Legacy subtly uses the framing effect by using authentic farewell notes written by terminally ill smokers: "To my children, I don't want you to be sad! Remember me, and forgive me for leaving you so soon. When it's over, mom will just be sleeping."[73] By exploiting the personal, emotional genre of the farewell note, which unequivocally draws out negative aspects, the loss is made *emotionally tangible*, reducing overoptimism. A narrative campaign that uses the framing effect has the additional benefit that the brain will regard it (subjectively) as being more likely to occur, since *real factual reports* are both more memorable and more readily retrievable than statistics.[74]

However, this tactic is not unproblematic: on the one hand, consumers might be unable to cope with the *flow of information*. Hence it is expedient to limit the approach to products for which overoptimism is a known evil. On the other hand,

---

[66] Cf. e.g. Schwartz 1988.

[67] Jolls and Sunstein 2006, p. 209–210.

[68] Jolls and Sunstein 2006, 216.

[69] See e.g. Craig, Sternthal and Leavitt 1976.

[70] See e.g. Thomas and Millar 2011, p. 139–149.

[71] In actual fact, a study on breast cancer prophylaxis by self-examination showed that stressing the negative effects of failing to carry out self-prophylaxis had a significantly greater impact on behaviour than stressing the positive effects (see Meyerowitz and Chaiken 1987, p. 505).

[72] Cf. Jolls and Sunstein 2006.

[73] See http://women.americanlegacy.org/about/ads.cfm (visited on 20 April 2014).

[74] See e.g. Jolls and Sunstein 2006.

such an approach might *shoot over the mark*, which would occur, for example, if arguments referred exclusively to worst-case scenarios.[75] Thus, it is of the utmost importance to strike the right balance at all times when selecting scenarios.

By helping individuals to overcome their cognitive biases, the law can contribute to increasing utility not only on an individual but also on a social level. The major advantage of debiasing through the law lies in the fact that it is a *relatively mild instrument*, as the individual can continue to decide autonomously. Changing the decision-making architecture on the individual level is generally preferential to eliminating choices (prohibition), as long as it involves pure debiasing and not politically motivated nudging.[76] The presented method for debiasing does not open the floodgates to manipulation: first, it is limited to overcoming boundedly rational (biased) behaviour and second, in a state governed by the rule of law any encroachment, including debiasing mechanisms, must be *transparent* end *democratically legitimated.*

That said, there are indeed serious problems with the approach. Generally speaking, it has to be borne in mind that boundedly rational behaviour induced by cognitive biases may in many situations be the lesser evil: the cost of avoiding biased behaviour may quickly surpass the incurred welfare penalty resulting from it.[77] This is not unlikely, especially if it is considered that the debiasing attempt may overshoot the mark. Thus, any debiasing by the law should only be considered if the potential gain on both the individual and the social level is high.[78] Also, it is unnecessary to intervene through legislation where people are able to overcome their biases by themselves, for example by means of *introspection.*[79] By the same token, if there is an information deficit, the authorities should limit their action to providing information in a way that is as neutral as possible.[80]

Finally, public officials are not omnipotent and are often ill-informed about the actual preferences of the general public. Moreover, they themselves are not free from self-interest or biases:

> The real problem lies [...] in identifying what people do or would want, and in deciding whether choice architects can be trusted. Perhaps choice architects do not know what people would want, if properly informed, and perhaps their own motivations are not pure. Perhaps the very idea of what people would want, if properly informed, raises difficult conceptual puzzles, at least in some cases, and creates unacceptable risks of overreaching by choice architects.[81]

---

[75] Sunstein 2002.

[76] Rachlinski 2003, p. 1224.

[77] Jolls and Sunstein 2006, p. 225 and 234.

[78] Jolls and Sunstein 2006, p. 230.

[79] Cf. Jolls and Sunstein 2006, p. 226, see also Rachlinski 2003, p. 1206–1219 and Rasmussen 1998, p. 1697–1698.

[80] However, Jolls and Sunstein 2006, p. 232 correctly point out that information can never be entirely neutral since it is inevitable to make linguistic choices when putting thoughts into words. This means that it is virtually impossible to draw a clear line between "neutral information" and "steering manipulation".

[81] Sunstein 2014, p. 158.

Indeed, steering behaviour using the tools of behavioural economics may represent a step back to a time before public choice, when the state was regarded as a *benevolent dictator*. The rational choice approach can provide valuable insights in this respect. Furthermore, rational choice fundamentally questions the need for debiasing through the law in general and in particular in cases involving politically motivated nudging. However, government action always has an impact on the decision-making architecture of individuals, irrespective of whether such an outcome was intended or not.

3.4 Conclusion

The insights gathered by behavioural researchers over the past thirty years can no longer be disregarded by economists. This accounts for the corresponding shift within law and economics from the traditional economic analysis towards the behavioural economic analysis of law. On the one hand, the law faces new challenges due to this *behavioural turn*. On the other hand, the same development opens up new possibilities for mastering them, amongst others *libertarian paternalism*.[82]

Despite the sustained interest in the results of behavioural research in both academia and in practice, it should be noted that, in contrast to rational choice theory, behavioural economics does not offer an all-embracing model based on a limited number of parameters. Its insights are not derived from a general theory, but rather stem from disparate empirical observations. In spite of all the criticism, in most cases the rational choice approach provides robust explanations and forecasts, whilst behavioural economics deals with—albeit important—marginal phenomena.

The two approaches are not mutually exclusive, but complement each other: whilst the rational choice theory is based on system 2, modern behavioural economics often aims at overcoming system 1. However, the usefulness—economic or otherwise—of cognitive rules of thumb is too often overlooked. Future research should thus strive to reconcile rational choice theory with behavioural economics.

Acknowledgements We would like to sincerely thank Thomas Roberts for his translation as well as Julia Wetzel, MLaw, Luca Langensand, MLaw, and Philipp Anton Burri for their careful proofreading.

Bibliography

Baumol, William. 1972. *Economic theory and operations analysis*. 3rd ed., 400–402. London: Prentice Hall.

Camerer, Colin F., George Loewenstein, and Matthew Rabin, eds. 2003. *Advances in behavioral economics*. Princeton: Princeton University Press.

Christensen-Szalanski, Jay J., and Cynthia Fobian-Willham. 1991. The hindsight bias: A meta-analysis. *Organizational Behavior and Human Decision Processes* 48:147–168.

[82] Cf. Sunstein and Thaler 2003; also see Mitchell 2005.

Craig, Samuel, Brian Sternthal, and Clark Leavitt. 1976. Advertising wearout: An experimental analysis. *Journal of Market Research* 13:365–372.

Eidenmüller, Horst. 2005. *Effizienz als Rechtsprinzip. Möglichkeiten und Grenzen der ökonomischen Analyse des Rechts*. 3rd ed. Tübingen: Mohr Siebeck.

Englerth, Markus. 2007. Behavioral law and economics—eine kritische Einführung. In *Recht und Verhalten,* eds. Christoph Engel, Markus Englerth, Jörn Lüdemannand, and Indra Spiecker genannt Döhmann, 60–130. Tübingen: Mohr Siebeck.

Fehr, Ernst, and Urs Fischbacher. 2002. Why social preferences matter—The impact of non-selfish motives on competition, cooperation and incentives. *The Economic Journal* 112:C1–C33.

Fischhoff, Baruch. 1975. Hindsight ≠ Foresight: The effect of outcome knowledge on judgement under uncertainty. *Journal of Experimental Psychology: Human Perception and Performance* 1:288–299.

Fletcher, George P. 1996. *The basic concepts of legal thoughts,* 158. New York: Oxford University Press.

Frank, Jürgen. 1976. *Kritische Ökonomie, Einführung in Grundsätze und Kontroversen wirtschaftlicher Theoriebildung*. Reinbek: Rowohlt.

Friedman, Milton. 1953. *Essays in positive economics*. Chicago: University of Chicago Press.

Gintis, Herbert, Samuel Bowles, Robert Boyd, and Ernst Fehr, eds. 2005. *Moral sentiments and material interests. The foundation of cooperation in economic life*. Cambridge: MIT Press.

Guthrie, Chris, Jeffrey J. Rachlinski, and Andrew J. Wistrich. 2001. Inside the judicial mind. *Cornell Law Review* 86:777–830.

Homann, Karl, and Andreas Suchanek. 2000. *Ökonomik: Eine Einführung*. Tübingen: Mohr Siebeck.

Hotz, Beat. 1982. Ökonomische Analyse des Rechts—eine skeptische Betrachtung. *Wirtschaft und Recht* 34 (4): 293–314.

Jolls, Christine. 2009. Behavioral law and economics. In *Law and economics—A reader,* ed. Alain Marciano. New York: Routledge.

Jolls, Christine, and Cass R. Sunstein. 2006. Debiasing through law. *Journal of Legal Studies* 35:199–241.

Jolls, Christine, Cass R. Sunstein, and Richard Thaler. 1998. A behavioral approach to law and economics. *Stanford Law Review* 50:1471–1550.

Jungermann, Helmut, Hans-Rüdiger Pfister, and Katrin Fischer. 2010. *Die Psychologie der Entscheidung. Eine Einführung*. 3rd ed. Heidelberg: Springer.

Kahneman, Daniel. 2011. *Thinking, fast and slow*. New York: Farrar, Straus and Giroux.

Kahneman, Daniel, and Amos Tversky. 1979. Prospect theory: An analysis of decision under risk. *Econometrica* XVLII:263–292.

Kahneman, Daniel, and Amos Tversky. 1981. The framing of decisions and the psychology of choices. *Science* 211 (4481): 453–458.

Kahneman, Daniel, Jack Knetsch, and Richard Thaler. 1990. Experimental tests of the endowment effect and the coase theorem. *Journal of Political Economy* 98:1325–1348.

Kahneman, Daniel, Jack Knetsch, and Richard Thaler. 1991. Anomalies: The endowment effect, loss aversion, and status quo bias. *The Journal of Economic Perspectives* 5 (1): 193–206.

Kirchgässner, Gebhard. 1988. Die neue Welt der Ökonomie. *Analyse und Kritik* 10:107–137.

Knight, Frank H. 1964 (1921). *Risk, uncertainty and profit*. (Reprint). Boston: Houghton Mifflin Company.

Korobkin, Russell, and Thomas Ulen. 2000. Law and behavioral science: Removing the rationality assumption from law and economics. *California Law Review* 88:1051–1144.

Latin, Howard. 1994. "Good" warnings, bad products, and cognitive limitations. *UCLA Law Review* 41:1193–1295.

Loewenstein, George. 2000. Willpower: A decision theorist's perspective. *Law and Philosophy* 19:51–76.

Mathis, Klaus. 2007a. Behavioral economics. In *Encyclopedia of law and society—American and global perspectives,* ed. David S. Clark, vol. 1, 118–120. Thousand Oaks: SAGE Publications.

Mathis, Klaus. 2007b. Utility maximization. In *Encyclopedia of law and society—American and global perspectives*, ed. David S. Clark, vol. 3, 1542–1545. Thousand Oaks: SAGE Publications.
Mathis, Klaus. 2009. *Effizienz statt Gerechtigkeit? Auf der Suche nach den philosophischen Grundlagen der Ökonomischen Analyse des Rechts*. 3rd ed. Berlin: Duncker & Humblot. (Mathis, Klaus. 2009. *Efficiency instead of justice? Searching for the philosophical foundations of the economic analysis of law*. Dordrecht: Springer.)
Meyer, Willi. 1978. Die Methodologie der positiven Ökonomie und ihre Folgen. In *Neuere Entwicklungen in den Wirtschaftswissenschaften: Verhandlungen auf der Arbeitstagung des Vereins für Socialpolitik, Gesellschaft für Wirtschafts- und Sozialwissenschaften in Münster 1977*, ed. Ernst Helmstädter, 19–46. Berlin: Duncker & Humblot.
Meyerowitz, Beth E., and Shelly Chaiken. 1987. The effect of message framing on breast self-examination: Attitudes, intentions, and behavior. *Journal of Personality and Social Psychology* 52:500–510.
Mitchell, Gregory. 2005. Libertarian paternalism is an oxymoron. *Northwestern University Law Review* 99 (3): 1–42.
Parisi, Francesco, and Vernon Smith. 2004. *The law and economics of irrational behavior*. Stanford: Stanford University Press.
Pheby, John. 1988. *Methodology and economics: A critical introduction*. Houndmills: Macmillan.
Posner, Richard A. 1998. *Economic analysis of law*. 5th ed. New York: Aspen Publishers.
Posner, Richard A. 2013. Why is there no Milton Friedman today? *Econ Journal Watch* 10 (2): 210–213.
Prentice, Robert A., and Mark E. Roszkowski. 1991–1992. "Tort reform" and the liability "revolution": Defending strict liability in tort for defective products. *Gonzaga Law Review* 27:251–302.
Rachlinski, Jeffrey J. 2000. A positive psychological theory of judging in hindsight. In *Behavioral law and economics*, ed. Cass R. Sunstein, 95–115. Cambridge: Cambridge University Press.
Rachlinski, Jeffrey J. 2003. The uncertain psychological case for paternalism. *Northwestern University Law Review* 97 (3): 1165–1225.
Rasmussen, Robert K. 1998. Behavioral economics, the economic analysis of bankruptcy law, and the pricing of credit. *Vanderbilt Law Review* 51:1679–1703.
Schwartz, Alan. 1988. Proposal for products liability reform: A theoretical synthesis. *Yale Law Journal* 97:353–419.
Schweizer, Mark. 2005. *Kognitive Täuschungen vor Gericht. Eine empirische Studie*. Zürich.
Scriven, Michael. 1962. Explanations, predictions and law. *Minnesota Studies in the Philosophy of Science* 2:170–230.
Simon, Herbert A. 1979. Rational decision making in business organizations. *American Economic Review* 69:493–513.
Stiglitz, Joseph E. 1986. *Economics of the Public Sector*. New York: W. W. Norton.
Sunstein, Cass R., ed. 2000. *Behavioral law and economics*. Cambridge: Cambridge University Press.
Sunstein, Cass R. 2002. Probability neglect: Emotions, worst cases, and law. *Yale Law Journal* 112:61–107.
Sunstein, Cass R. 2003. *Why societies need dissent*. Cambridge: Harvard University Press.
Sunstein, Cass R. 2014. *Why nudge?* New Haven: Yale University Press.
Sunstein, Cass R., and Richard H. Thaler. 2003. Libertarian paternalism is not an oxymoron. *The University of Chicago Law Review* 70 (4): 1159–1202.
Thaler, Richard H., and Cass R. Sunstein. 2008. *Nudge: Improving decisions about health, wealth and happiness*. New Haven: Yale University Press.
Thomas, Ayanna K., and Peter R. Millar. 2011. Reducing the framing effect in older and younger adults by encouraging analytic processing. *The Journals of Gerontology Series B: Psychological Sciences and Social Sciences* 67B (2): 139–149.
Tversky, Amos, and Craig R. Fox. 1995. Weighing risk and uncertainty. *Psychological Review* 102 (2): 269–283.
Tversky, Amos, and Daniel Kahneman. 1974. Judgment under uncertainty: Heuristics and biases. *Science (New Series)* 185 (4157): 1124–1131.

Klaus Mathis Lucerne. Prof. Dr. iur., MA in Economics. Professor of Public Law and Law of the Sustainable Economy at the University of Lucerne. CH-6002 Lucerne, Frohburgstrasse 3, P.O. Box 4466, klaus.mathis@unilu.ch. Fields of Interest: Public Law (Law of Sustainable Development, Economic Constitutional Law), Economic Analysis of Law, Legal Philosophy and Legal Theory.

Ariel David Steffen Lucerne. Lic. phil., University of Basel. PhD Candidate (SNSF) in Behavioural Law and Economics at the University of Lucerne. CH-6002 Lucerne, Frohburgstrasse 3, P.O. Box 4466, ariel.steffen@unilu.ch. Fields of interest: Behavioural Law and Economics, Humanistic Psychology, Positive Psychology, Political Philosophy, Philosophy of Law, Philosophy of Mind, Ethics, Empathy, Public Policy as well as Classical and English Philology.

Part II
Applications

Chapter 4
Why Do We Need Responsive Regulation and Behavioural Research in EU Internal Market Law?

Kai Purnhagen

Abstract Due to its intrinsic need to establish an internal market even against the nation states' will, EU law has always had to rely on the responsiveness of its peoples in order to make the establishment of the internal market a success. As to this need, top-down macro-economic regulation without a social bottom-up backup by the peoples of Europe has mostly failed. This creates a "legitimacy market failure" of the EU internal market, which needs to be cured by responsive regulation. Data gained from behavioural research are the right tools to cure such a market failure in EU internal market law. The provision of hard data from behavioural research is the most promising way to do so as it leaves room for Member States to behave opportunistically only if they present more convincing data. By combining responsive regulation and behavioural economics, the EU is able to first listen to its people and second incentivize Member States to act in the best interest for its peoples and the internal market.

4.1 Introduction

Quality of regulation in the internal market has become a fashionable topic for policy makers and scholars alike.[1] This contribution is yet another recommendation how to design "better" and "smart" regulation in the EU internal market. I will start from the background of economic regulation, which in my view is the classical point of departure of internal market law. In this logic, intervention into the European internal market is only possible if regulators identify (and cure!) a market failure within a given legal framework. After some necessary clarifications (4.2) I will illustrate that internal market witnesses a "legitimacy market failure", which is the outcome

[1] See e.g. European Governance—A white paper, COM(2001) 428 final; Mandelkern Group on Better Regulation, Final Report, 13 November 2001 and the articles in S. Weatherill (ed.) Better Regulation (Oxford 2007); as well as Allio 2011; McColm 2011; Radaelli 2007; Wiener 2006.

K. Purnhagen (✉)
Law and Governance Group, University of Wageningen, Wageningen, The Netherlands
and Law School, Erasmus University, Rotterdam, The Netherlands
e-mail: Kai.Purnhagen@wur.nl

K. Mathis (ed.), *European Perspectives on Behavioural Law and Economics*,
Economic Analysis of Law in European Legal Scholarship 2,
DOI 10.1007/978-3-319-11635-8_4

of the specific multi-level character of EU law (4.3). This legitimacy market failure, I argue, needs to be addressed by a combination of responsive regulation and behavioural research. It is this behavioural approach that provides the EU with the means it needs to secure legitimacy in its regulation and even expand its regulative capacity against the Member States' to the extent that it could even regulate in areas where it was not explicitly provided with any competence norm (4.4).

4.2 Terminological and Political Clarifications

Disclosing the preconceptions behind a scholarly piece is a necessary requirement of scientific honesty.[2] The writing of this piece has been strongly influenced by the "New Legal Realism" movement.[3] Within this movement, this piece shall be understood as a specific EU internal market reading of what Victoria Nourse and Greg Shaffer have dubbed "new governance theory"[4] and the "behavioural wing"[5] of new legal realism. For the purposes of this paper I hereby understand classical law and economic analysis as a model which describes the extent to which law is well suited for an intended task or purpose, based on deductive analysis and the assumption of rational individual behaviour.[6] New governance theory and behavioural economics then add to this assumption by setting classical law and economics models on a more realistic footing: Building on the insights of institutional analysis, "new governance theory" places the individual in its institutional context of internal market integration in order to achieve regulatory goals more effectively.

"New governance theories" aim at enabling regulators to constantly gain new insights about markets so they can continuously revise these norms "in light of shared experience."[7] Julia Black and Rob Baldwin provided a specific regulatory reading of "new governance theory", which they dubbed "really responsive regulation."[8] It sets economic regulation on a more realistic footing, as regulation manages societal interdependencies in order to achieve the respective regulative goal.[9]

Behavioural economics widens the *homo oeconomicus* concept in a different direction: Rather than building on a functional analysis of rationally acting market participants, it seeks to identify systematic departures from rational acting by

---

[2] Ackermann 2007, p. 9.

[3] See Nourse and Shaffer 2009, pp. 61–138; Miles and Sunstein 2013, p. 81; critical Leiter 2013.

[4] Nourse and Shaffer 2009, pp. 88–90.

[5] Nourse and Shaffer 2009, pp. 76–77.

[6] See Macneil 2000, p. 697.

[7] Simon 2006.

[8] Black and Baldwin 2010. The link between new governance theories and responsive regulation was also illustrated by Walker and de Búrca: "New Governance is seen as a highly pragmatic and flexible approach to and modality of regulation, a method for ensuring maximum responsiveness and adaptability, with an emphasis on open-ended and provisional goals, and ensuring revisability and corrigibility," see Walker and de Búrca 2007.

[9] Bizer and Führ 2002, p. 5.

empirical research and make policy recommendations based on these insights.[10] In this sense, while (neo-) classical law and economics provide some normative and simplifying assumptions as a basis for analysis, behavioural law and economics "represents a frontal assault within economics"[11] as it attacks the heart of the analysis of rational acting agents.

For the purposes of this paper I will combine both theories in the concept of "responsive behavioural regulation". My analysis is based on the conviction that classical law and economics provide a top-down theory to shape law and society, while responsive regulation has a much stronger basis for analysis as it starts in the realities of social life with a view to regulate bottom-up. Seen through the lens of EU internal market regulation, one may hence bluntly relate (neo-) classical top-down law and economics to what is known as 'the economy' of internal market regulation, while responsive regulation represents more 'the social', bottom-up perspective.[12] Behavioural economics is then a way to back up society's responsiveness to regulation by hard data. In this sense, I limit the value of behavioural economics not only to the task of harvesting biases in order to justify regulatory intervention.[13] It is in fact also a tool to assess market behaviour in order to ensure really responsive regulation[14] backed up by hard data in order to warrant a sound establishment of the EU internal market.

I use the term "legitimacy" as an umbrella term, which I borrowed from political science, and translate it into the world of law and economics. In political science, the term legitimacy embraces input-, output-, and throughput legitimacy.[15] "Input legitimacy" describes that "political choices are legitimate if and because they reflect the 'will of the people'—that is if they can be derived from the authentic preferences of the members of a community".[16] Output legitimacy finds that "political choices are legitimate if and because they effectively promote the common welfare of the constituency in question."[17] Throughput legitimacy is geared towards the process between output- and input-legitimacy.[18] In the world of law and economics, political decisions are thus "output"-legitimate if they create efficiency. They are "input"-legitimate, if they meet the "real" demands of the people, hence if they meet the expectations and shortfalls as expressed by institutional and behavioural economics. "Throughput" legitimacy then looks at the process of how these decisions

[10] Nourse and Shaffer 2009, p. 77.

[11] Nourse and Shaffer 2009, p. 77.

[12] This distinction is, of course, a simplification. (Neo-) classical law and economics likewise knows a number of market failures which enable "social" regulation, which also translate into internal market law, see Franck and Purnhagen 2014, p. 332.

[13] Jolls and Sunstein 2007.

[14] See on the term and the parameters affiliated with it Black and Baldwin 2010.

[15] The difference between input and output legitimacy date back to the work of Easton 1965 and have been advanced mainly by Scharpf 1970; Scharpf 1997; Scharpf 1999.

[16] Scharpf 1999, p. 7.

[17] Scharpf 1999, p. 7.

[18] Bekkers and Edwards 2007, p. 35.

come into being, which is mainly described by game theory. Within this context I will mainly use the term "legitimacy" to describe "input"-oriented legitimacy in the way behavioural law and economics may detect it.

Finally a disclaimer. In this piece I make a highly abstract theoretical argument. In order to back it up, I will draw on research in several regulatory domains.[19] As this piece would like to stay cognitively accessible to its reader, this approach cannot accommodate the wishes of people who expect in-depth analysis of these respective domains. I will only present these domains insofar as they are needed to accommodate the argument. The research into these domains as presented here will hence remain largely superficial.

4.3 The Legitimacy Market Failure of EU Internal Market Law

I will show that EU internal market regulation needs to counterbalance a legitimacy market failure by responsive regulation. Resorting to examples from various areas of EU internal market regulation, I will illustrate that wherever the EU did not regulate responsively, it was forced to remedy this lack of taking into account 'the social' reactively. For illustration purposes, I will choose three examples of economic regulation where the EU was forced to correct a decision in favour of efficiency due to behavioural concerns. I will illustrate this with the example of the cheese manufactured from non-pasteurised milk (4.3.1), standardisation of consumer products (4.3.2) and authorisation of GMO's (4.3.3).

4.3.1 Cheese from Raw Milk, or: Frenzy French Fromagers?

Consuming cheese made from raw milk can cause health issues. This has been the outcome of studies[20] and is an accepted fact in EU internal market regulation.[21] Relying on this evidence that products produced with raw milk can cause several diseases such as *Listeria*, *Salmonella* and *E. coli*, EU officials voted largely in favour of a ban on products manufactured with untreated milk.[22] There is, however, an exception to the ban when untreated milk products meet certain safety

[19] See on the term "domain" Dyson 2014, pp. 115–137.

[20] See especially Danielsson-Tham et al. 2004, p. 153. There are also studies which have proven that these threats may also come from consuming pasteurized milk, see Koch et al. 2010, p. 1581.

[21] See especially Art. 3 of Council Directive 92/46/EEC of 16 June 1992 laying down the health rules for the production and placing on the market of raw milk, heat-treated milk and milk-based products. See for the USA FDA, The Dangers of Raw Milk: Unpasteurized Milk Can Pose a Serious Health Risk, available at http://www.fda.gov/downloads/Food/FoodborneIllnessContaminants/UCM239493.pdf.

[22] See Art. 3 of Council Directive 92/46/EEC of 16 June 1992 laying down the health rules for the production and placing on the market of raw milk, heat-treated milk and milk-based products.

requirements. Attaining these standards requires expensive testing machinery that is usually beyond the budget of a traditional small French *fromager*. Indeed, cheeses in most southern European countries such as in France, Italy, Spain, Greece, and Portugal are manufactured with unpasteurised milk. Relying on experiences resulting from the work of several generations of dairy farmers and cheese producers alike testify to the safety of these cheeses. As these cheeses are regularly marketed locally in small numbers, in terms of safety reputational mechanisms might work as well as top-down safety regulation from Brussels. Additionally, there are a fair amount of cheese lovers around the world who simply prefer cheese made with unpasteurised milk over those manufactured with pasteurised milk, and do not care about the risks involved.[23] If one takes into account that representatives from northern European countries with only a little raw-milk cheese production were mainly involved with food regulation at EU level at this time, this regulation gets a peculiar twist. Southern cheese manufacturers hence feared that the hidden political agenda was to gain some comparative advantage for northern cheese producers over the southern ones, using scientific data as a shield and the EU as a primary tool to achieve that goal.

They were thus concerned that not only their livelihood, but also their way of life and cultural identity would be sacrificed for the unifying forces of Brussels' (and increasingly Parma's) administration. Indeed, the broader fear was that the variety of European cheese making up large parts of cultural life in Europe would be abandoned for the benefit of one cheese that met European standards. Supporters of unpasteurised cheese hence denied the idea of a more unified Europe that, in their view, provides little respect to the diverse cultural heritage of the European people. And indeed, although the health risks involved with raw milk cheese were evident, the law needed to change as such a strict requirement would not have found the support of the southern Member States of the EU. In other words: While robust scientific evidence requires regulation in order to counterbalance negative externalities to allow consumers to benefit from the efficiency gains of an internal market, the behaviour of people requires de-regulatory intervention in order to not endanger the whole concept of the internal market.

4.3.2 One Standard Fits All: Or How to Alienate Consumers

The first acts of consumer product safety regulation in the EU prescribed common European standards, enforced by classical command-and-control mechanisms, which regulated the product's lifecycle to different extents.[24] EU product safety law set detailed, obligatory substantial and procedural standards, which prescribed actions required by special target groups instead of setting performance standards, which had been the dominant governance mode in the EU for almost 30 years.[25]

[23] See Downes 2014, p. 113.

[24] See for a comprehensive study on the the regulative practice at that time Joerges et al. 1988, 252 et seqq.

[25] See Tricker 2000, p. 1; Hey, Jacob and Volkery 2007, p. 1861.

This classical harmonisation method via standard-setting in secondary law soon came under attack. The "Europeanisation"-approach resulted in the use of this command-and-control-regulation to an extent that had never been exercised before, not even in national law.[26] Consumers mourned about why Brussels needed to regulate the size and length of cucumbers and condoms, as well as the curvature of bananas. In short, this regulatory method "produced 'Europroducts', which alienated the consumer."[27]

These were largely in line with the classical free-trade-concept of EU internal market regulation, which was mainly concerned with erasing market barriers along the lines of national frontiers.[28] EU product safety law erased such market barriers by levelling the disparate laws in the Member States through the prescription of uniform standards. This was justifiable from an efficiency point of view, as these standards lower costs, increase trade between Member States and allow consumers to harvest these efficiency gains. In Europe, however, these experiences also show that consumers would rather accept a (more expensive) variety of products over the (cheaper) one-size-fits-all solution. They sometimes simply do not want to harvest such efficiency gains. In other words: while standards require regulation in order to allow consumers to benefit from the efficiency gains of an internal market, the behaviour of people requires de-regulatory intervention in order to not risk the whole internal market.

4.3.3 GMO Authorisation: Or Why Worry About New Technology?—A Very Short Comparative Analysis

Marketing of GMO products is a peculiar thing. As with any new technology, GMO products promise benefits to consumers. However, uncertainties with regards to the potential hazards of such new technologies may call for regulation.[29] Furthermore, regulators do not operate in a void at international level. Lax regulatory standards might attract businesses, but may also work against the international competition on global standards.[30] Like in any kind of product safety regulation, the main dilemma for policy makers is hence to find the optimal level of regulation in product safety.[31]

With regards to the regulation of GMO products, the USA has reacted to these concerns with reservation. The legal framework of GMO marketing is complicated and may only be sketched here.[32] While GMO products are indeed subject to

---

[26] McGee and Weatherill 1990, p. 583.

[27] McGee and Weatherill 1990, p. 582.

[28] Purnhagen 2014b, p. 318.

[29] See for further assessment into the challenges of regulation of new technology products van der Meulen et al. 2014, pp. 1–2.

[30] van der Meulen et al. 2014, pp. 1–2.

[31] van der Meulen et al. 2014, pp. 1–2.

[32] See for a more thorough analysis Grossman 2012.

authorisation most of the time, as a general policy, products of biotechnology are not treated fundamentally differently than conventional products.[33] This means that, for example, GMO foods require market authorisation (as additives) if they were not on the market prior to 1958 (and has not been included in a black list). An exception applies in case the product is Generally Recognized As Safe (GRAS). There are no special rules at federal level, which deviate from this general rationale for market authorisation of GMO food in the USA.[34]

In the EU, the picture is quite different. The USA and the EU share the fact that GMO regulation is complex and complicated. The approach to regulation, however, differs substantially.[35] While the EU similarly requires market authorisation (as novel foods) for products that were not on the market prior to 1997, GMO products require a special approval, depending on the intended use of the GMO product. And even if approved, Member States may still make use of a safeguard procedure to prohibit its marketing.

This very brief sketch shall suffice to make the following argument. While both regulatory regimes have comparable social prerequisites, the treatment of GMO products varies considerably. In my opinion, the most convincing argument for this divide is the difference of consumer perception. In the USA the majority of consumers is less critical towards new technologies and is hence readier to accept products such as those made from GMOs.[36] In the EU, consumers are much more sceptical in this respect, for various reasons.[37] Therefore, it is not because of scientific insights into efficiency that the EU regulates GMOs more harshly than the USA.[38] If it did not, the people's support of the European integration project would be at risk.[39]

4.3.4 Conclusion: Responsive Regulation and Legitimacy

The three short case studies brought to light why the EU should regulate responsively: If people do not subscribe to the project of the internal market any longer as they would have to accept negative effects, the whole project of the internal market is at risk. Elsewhere, research from political science has, for the same reason, already identified the need for such "input-legitimacy", which remedies the social failures that may originate from the traditional legality test applied by law or pure output-

[33] Office of Science and Technology Policy (OSTP), Coordinated Framework for Regulation of Biotechnology Products, 51 Fed. Reg. 23,302 (26 June 1986), p. 23.

[34] Some States such as Maine currently consider enacting special requirements of labelling law.

[35] See for an old (and therefore with regards to the legal regulations largely outdated), but on the substance still valid observation Lynch and Vogel 2001; for a more recent one Pollack and Shaffer 2009, pp. 45–77.

[36] Pollack and Shaffer 2009, pp. 45–52.

[37] Krystallis et al. 2007.

[38] See Valletta 2010.

[39] In political science, this has been investigated as a gap between input and output legitimacy, see Skogstad 2003, p. 321.

oriented legitimacy such as efficiency. If EU law would look at the proper function of the democratic legitimacy chain (legality) and the output of an efficient internal market only (output-legitimacy), it runs the risk of the people of Europe not subscribing to the actions of EU institutions any longer (input-legitimacy). Turned into the language of economics: If the EU integration process only targets macroeconomic efficiency, the results might create mistrust in the EU as a regulative entity and ultimately put the whole integration process at risk. This is not only a case of addressing negative externalities, as we are unsure most of the time whether harm is to be expected or whether market participants will be better off if the EU modifies this market failure. Regulatory intervention moreover happens to cure a "legitimacy market failure," as this is needed to ensure people's support of the European integration process.

4.4 Behavioural Research as Remedy: How Behavioural Research Contributes to Internal Market Integration

How to remedy such a "legitimacy market failure"? Regulating responsively can mean many things: Regulators could listen to intermediaries such as democratically elected representatives or interest groups, to polls or to media. I will argue that in the internal market context they should listen to the outcome of behavioural science. Acknowledging the imperfections of behavioural science research, it is nonetheless the most promising method to effectively integrate the internal market. As we have learned from research into the EU's regulatory dilemma, unlike nation-states EU regulation does not only need support of the citizenry, it also has to battle against Member States' protectionist agendas.[40]

Here, responsive and effective regulation are intertwined: In the absence of any *Kompetenz-Kompetenz,* the risk of a Member State's "selective exit"[41] is a steady companion of any regulatory attempt in EU law. In an EU market-state legal regime, where Member State's "voice" as the traditional safeguard mechanism to protect against "selective exit"[42] is fading away with the decreasing influence of Member States on the EU regulatory system,[43] the EU needs to find other means to gain Member States' trust in the EU legal order. Regulating responsively and systematically has the potential to ensure trust in the European institutions.[44] In order to ensure that the EU is able to argue soundly against the protectionist politics of Member States, hard data gained from behavioural research will be a much better fit to cut down Member States' opportunistic behaviour. Gaining knowledge about cultures, behaviours and wishes of consumers and entrepreneurs before regulatory interference allows Union institutions to base their intervention on not only

[40] Eberlein 2004, pp. 153–155.

[41] Weiler 2005.

[42] See Weiler 2005.

[43] Patterson and Afilalo 2008, pp. 148–160.

[44] Lenaerts 2004.

efficiency criteria, which are hard to grasp for most Europeans. Such intervention will have a much more solid ground to stand on if regulatory entities know about their behavioural impact and can illustrate it to Member States. EU entities can hence use such behavioural insights as ammunition for the daily battle over competences with the Member States, who, as we know from research on the regulatory dilemma of EU institutions,[45] each primarily follow their own protectionist agenda. This might also be an explanation why Art. 3 (3) subpara 4 TEU nowadays stipulates that the EU, when taking measures to establish the internal market, shall "respect its rich cultural and linguistic diversity, and shall ensure that Europe's cultural heritage is safeguarded and enhanced." If EU institutions present such data to Member States, they would have an incentive to find conflicting data that justifies their protectionist approach from a European perspective!

Such an approach risks putting the concept of efficiency gains from internal market harmonisation at risk. This is why the establishment of the internal market is still based, first and foremost, on classical arguments of efficiency. However, if these efficiency gains are or will not be accepted by society, whether right or wrong, they become detrimental to the idea of internal market establishment.

I will illustrate the application of these behavioural approaches in several areas of internal market regulation. With regard to Internet contract law, I will illustrate how behavioural studies have been used as a textbook example in order to remedy the "legitimacy market failure" (4.4.1). Subsequently, I will show how not taking into account behavioural insights may result in a legitimacy crisis of the EU in financial market regulation (4.4.2).

4.4.1 EU Contract Law: The Case of Internet Contract Law

The commercialization of the Internet has involved several advantages in view of enabling more efficient consumer purchase. However, every stage of the purchase process carries risks for consumers, which are specifically tied to the special circumstances triggered by the Internet.[46] When Internet sales took off in the early 1990s,[47] regulation of the Internet was primarily subject to classic national contract law. Academically, there were high-flying debates over whether "the cyberspace" needed regulation at all or whether it should be subject to self-regulation, where formally equal "netizens" organize their matters themselves.[48] In the shadow of these abstract debates, consumers faced fears such as whether shopping on the Internet could be trusted, whether they actually got what they ordered and whether the person they contracted with could be respected. Each of these questions concerned topics that traditional national law did not deal with. The result was that consumers were reluctant to shop using means of distant communication.

[45] Eberlein 2004, pp. 153–155.

[46] Binding and Purnhagen 2011, p. 187.

[47] By that time admittedly mainly preliminary forms of the Internet making use of distance communication such as Teletext existed.

[48] See for an overview over the debate Keller 2004, pp. 1, 10–16; Marsden 2011, pp. 47–50.

The lack of action on the part of the Member States provided a good reason to interfere for European institutions.[49] Taking the possible cross-border impact of such Internet-contracts as a justification, the EU started to regulate national contract law. The EU did not regulate in broad terms of vulnerability, but rather seem to have adopted insights from behavioural studies in its regulation. The major way of consumer protection in Internet contracts was a granting of a withdrawal right in Art. 6 of Directive 97/7/EC:[50]

> For any distance contract the consumer shall have a period of at least seven working days in which to withdraw from the contract without penalty and without giving any reason. The only charge that may be made to the consumer because of the exercise of his right of withdrawal is the direct cost of returning the goods.

> The granting of this right of withdrawal without having to prove any breach of duty of one of the contracting parties was new to national contract law all over Europe. There was no explanation of this right through traditional "fault-based" contract law theories.[51]

In order to understand this provision, one had to resort to the works of behavioural law and economics from across the Atlantic and bring them in line with European theories of contract law and the specific regulatory regime of the EU:

Traditional contract law theory is based on the concept of private autonomy. Private autonomy, however, demands quite a number of computing tasks from the contracting parties: Taken to extremes, it is up to the contracting party to discover everything it desires, the opponent's desires and the relevant price of the thing on the market in order to know when to enter into a contract or not.[52] This concept of private autonomy is what somehow equates to the economic model of the rational choice *homo oeconomicus*. This model assumes that decision-makers "know, or can know, all the feasible alternative actions open to them, that they know, or can easily discover, all relevant prices, and that they know their wants and desires."[53] Both models have limits. In contract law theory, it has been standard knowledge for a long time that certain flaws exist in the assumption of private autonomy. They have all been rooted in flaws from the formation of "will". Minors, for example, are systematically assumed to be unable to perform fully autonomously. It is for this reason that most national laws protect them. But also other forms influencing

---

[49] See on the relationship between Member State inaction and EU policy in the area of consumer protection, Micklitz 2001.

[50] Directive 97/7/EC has meanwhile been replaced by the Directive on Consumer Rights 2011/83/EC. As this argument draws from the historical right to withdrawal in Directive 97/7/EC, I will nonetheless build my argument on the outdated Directive.

[51] Recently, scholars start to investigate whether the withdrawal right could be justified under recourse of the classical free-will theory by relying on a failure in the formation of the contract, see Hoffmann 2012, p. 1156. I will not recall the reservations against classical free will theory here, it shall suffice to hint at J. Schapp's argument that "will" is legally only valid insofar as the law grants it validity, see Schapp 1986, p. 8 et seqq. To justify a legal provision with a will of the person is hence quite tautological.

[52] See Purnhagen 2013.

[53] Cooter 1989, pp. 385–386.

the free formation of will have been subject to scrutiny: If one party tricks another party into a contract by fraud or cheating, the other party is granted several rights to be freed from contract. It is these examples that show how under certain conditions, private autonomy needs regulative help in order to develop.[54] The model of private autonomy, however, is barely challenged.

In economic theory, the normative model of the *homo oeconomicus* has been the standard model for analysis for a long time. The most radical ones would leave the flaws from this normativity to the market: If a rational actor behaves irrationally, the market will punish such an irrational decision in the most efficient way.[55] Most economic scholars subscribe to the idea that there are nonetheless certain market-failures, which require regulative intervention. The normative model of *homo oeconomicus*, however, is not challenged. Especially under conditions of uncertainty (a regular condition in contractual relations), this theory demands (normatively!) quite some processing abilities from such a subject.[56]

This is the target point of behavioural contract law and economics: They introduce the premise that entering into a contract is first and foremost a decision of a human being with all its flaws and unstable desires, which can be hard to reconcile with static contracts. While the idea of private autonomy and efficiency is still a goal worth reaching, behavioural theories acknowledge and start from the premise that contract law emerges in a normative environment of rights and duties of individuals.[57] As this happens for regulatory purposes, only those biases that are systematic are of value. Game theory and behavioural studies have hence identified several occasions (usually termed "bias" in the respective jargon), where people systematically deviate from the idea of a rational acting agent, which have also been introduced into contract law theory.[58] Bluntly put behavioural law and economics try to align (microeconomic) individual rights and desires with (macroeconomic) welfare ideas in contract law.

Admittedly, the preparatory work of Directive 97/7/EC gave no indication about how this Directive in general and the right to withdrawal in particular came into being. It is an open secret that this Directive was drafted and put into being by one EU public official without any institutionalized prior impact assessments or publicly communicated reasons for the respective regulatory choices. However, the parallels to the behavioural discussion on the withdrawal right in the USA are just too evident to not assume that Directive 97/7/EC has not been influenced by this discussion. Indeed, it is easy to imagine how the behavioural concept was a welcome opportunity for the EU to remedy the market failure of output-oriented, macroeconomic efficiency-driven legitimacy. While having been a de-regulator in contract law for many years, acknowledging an individual's weaknesses in the newly emerging fields of Internet contract law opened up an opportunity for the

[54] See for a more developed analysis on rules of freedom from contract Ben-Shahar 2004.

[55] Schwartz 2008; Posner 1998.

[56] Cooter 1989, p. 386.

[57] Franck and Purnhagen 2014, p. 332.

[58] Eisenberg 1995.

EU to show that its cross-border regulative capacity can be used to remedy specific cross-border problems of individuals. This is a capacity that Member States do not have effectively available. Hence, it is not so much the protection of the individual that justifies regulatory intervention; rather it is primarily the need to convince the citizen of Europe of the internal market project by protecting and acknowledging their rights and privileges better than the Member States. The second need is to base EU regulation on sound scientific data which support the need for regulation. Such an approach makes it hard for Member States to argue against such regulatory intervention, at least in case they do not present supporting data themselves. It makes it more difficult to act opportunistically and to hide national protectionist arguments behind "cultural" beliefs.[59] As we could see in the example of GMO regulation, scientific evidence alone is not enough for legitimate intervention.

This is a convincing explanation why EU law introduced so-called cooling-off periods for consumer purchase in Internet sales. Before these rights were introduced, behavioural studies brought to light that under certain circumstances such as doorstep-selling arrangements and distance communication consumers are systematically prone to biases. If a doorstep-seller, for example, convinces the consumer of the unique quality of the product (which it in fact does not have), the doorstep-selling arrangement allows him to act like a monopolist. In such situational monopolies, consumers cannot compare qualities and prices and are willing to pay charges up to twice as high as they would regularly pay.[60] In Internet sales, on the contrary, consumers can compare prices. They are, however, not able to assess the quality of the desired product, as they are dependent on the information they get from a seller. There are several reasons why quality of information on the Internet is lower in quality than elsewhere. If consumers are unsure about quality but can discriminate prices, sellers with high quality standards are likely to be driven out of the market.[61] And not only that: consumers are also unsatisfied with buying a product that does not meet their quality expectations. For this reason, the withdrawal period of Art. 6 of Directive 97/7/EC will lower the risk of such a race to the bottom and consumer dissatisfaction. As business will have to internalize the prices of the right to withdraw in order to avoid a fall of its turnover, information and prices will correspond as much as possible with reality.[62]

The EU can and has made use of such insights of behavioural law and economics to justify consumer protection regulation in contract law. At a time when most national contract law in Europe was based on formal equality of the bourgeois ideal, the EU introduced the above-mentioned Directive on consumer protection in Internet sales. Before that, regulatory interference with Private law was reserved for absolute exceptional (and individual!) cases in most countries. Many perceived the horizontal intervention based on systematic biases (and not individual cases)

[59] See on this phenomenon Afilalo et al. 2014, p. 287.

[60] Eisenberg 1982, p. 773.

[61] Ogus 1994, p. 41.

[62] van den Bergh 2003, p. 83.

into contract law for the sake of consumer protection as a revolution.[63] Lawyers, in unity with businesses and politicians, have for a long time defended the bourgeois ideal of equal contracting without taking into account that the economic environments of mass production and communication meanwhile have triggered a change in these circumstances,[64] much to the dissatisfaction of consumers. The EU took advantage of this regulatory failure of national contact law, seemingly made sure that its regulation was backed up by sound behavioural research to ensure the support of consumers and took action.

Ever since, EU law has matured into a legal order that is not only perceived as a public legal order but also influences contract law by the creation of regulative private law.[65] This was only possible as the legitimacy market failure in this respect was properly backed up by the needs and demands of citizens as they speak through behavioural research. It is hence not so much the cure of information asymmetries that triggered regulation at Union level. It was also not so much the protection of the individual consumer, as the Union institutions continuously try to make us believe.[66] If it were, one could hardly explain why the Union did not leave this problem to the Member States' legal system. It was the legitimacy market failure, as the Union witnessed an opportunity to interfere with the "holy grail"[67] of national contract law by backing up the possibility for regulative interference with behavioural research.

4.4.2 Financial Markets Regulation: How the Neglect of Behavioural Studies in Regulation Triggered the Union's Legitimacy Crisis

The global financial crisis, which started in 2008, discovered threats and loopholes in European financial regulation. This is not the place to exhaustively write on what has been done in the past to remedy the situation.[68] In this piece, I will rather advance the argument that (unlike its US counterpart) Union securities regulation, in knowledge of the legitimacy failure, was required to take into account behavioural science in the black letter law relatively early. In action, however, it did not, as regulatory theory in these days relied heavily on the efficient market hypothesis, ignoring the legitimacy market failure, which ultimately led to distrust in the regulatory capacity of European institutions. That explains the hasty back and forth in the establishing of European financial market institutions after the crash, which, from a regulatory perspective, might also not be the most favourable option.[69] This

63 Flume 2000; Hammen 2010; Reich 2000, p. 261.

64 Patterson and Afilalo 2008, pp. 99–100.

65 Micklitz 2009, p. 3.

66 See recently Case C-508/12, 5. 12. 2013, *Vapenik v Thurner* [2014] ECR I-0000, para 26.

67 Reich 2000, p. 261.

68 See e.g. Avgouleas 2009, p. 440.

69 Tröger 2012; general Stigler 1971.

kind of activism will bring back trust in European regulatory capacity only in the very short term. In the long run, it has to be proven that it actually works in order to get the support of the people. There is evidence that such a long-run perspective needs to be responsive. Responsive regulation, which creates an enabling environment for behavioural research, is seen as the most promising way forward.[70] Only by doing so, one might be able to successfully outbalance the legitimacy market failure of Union law.

The blueprint for EU securities regulation has for a long time been US financial market regulation. The "disclosure, disclosure, disclosure!" paradigm that followed from Roosevelt's Securities Act 1933[71] and the Securities and Exchange Act 1934[72] have influenced also the early years of EU securities regulation.[73] The disclosure paradigm—based on the efficient market hypothesis which directly built upon the rational investor model[74]—has ever since been the backbone of financial market policy makers', analysts', and regulators' thinking.[75] Financial markets were perceived as

> an agglomeration of rational investors, who make optimal resource allocation and wealth maximization decisions, when provided with sufficient information and appropriately structured economic incentives. So all regulators had to do to safeguard efficient markets and help investors was to ensure that a vast volume of pertinent information entered the public domain in any given area of financial market activity. Provision of information to rational actors would then allow the market to self-regulate avoiding to large extent public intervention.[76]

Output-oriented efficiency, it seemed, was enough for legitimising action (or non-action) of authorities.

This disclosure paradigm has also been designed in a specific language of internal market regulation as an "information paradigm",[77] by which it secures the diversity of products.[78] It shall govern the EU's regulatory dilemma to establish a harmonized internal market on the one hand and secure cultural diversity on the other.[79]

The "information paradigm" from internal market regulation married with the disclosure requirement from modern finance theory seemed to be a good fit for interference with financial markets in the EU.[80] The Capital Markets Directive,[81]

---

[70] See e.g. Avgouleas 2009, p. 440.

[71] Securities Act of 1933, 15 U.S.C. § 77a to 77 mm (1994).

[72] Securities Exchange Act of 1934, 15 U.S.C. § 78a to 78mm (1994).

[73] Avgouleas 2009, p. 440.

[74] Samuelson 1965. In a little less draconic way Fama 1970, p. 383.

[75] Spindler 2011.

[76] Avgouleas 2009, p. 440.

[77] Purnhagen 2014a.

[78] See Usher 2001, p. 151 et seqq.; Steindorff 1996, p. 195.

[79] Steindorff 1996, pp. 195–196.

[80] See to the relations of both concepts Purnhagen 2014b.

[81] The consolidated Capital Requirements Directive comprises European Parliament and Council Directive (EC) 2006/48 for the Taking up and Pursuit of the Business of Credit Institutions [2006]

for example, fully endorsed the disclosure requirement without taking into account the consumer's limited means of processing them. However, not all regulation at EU level turned a blind eye on the consumer's limited cognition. The Markets in Financial Instruments Directive 2004/39/EC (MiFID) stipulates in its Art. 19 that information has to be presented to consumers "so that they are reasonably able to understand the nature and risks of the investment service and of the specific type of financial instrument that is being offered". That is a far cry from the initial "information paradigm" or "disclosure"—concept, which placed the whole burden of processing information on the consumer.[82] Especially, this passage could have opened up a leeway to design EU securities regulation right from the start in a behavioural way.

It did not. Policy makers, regulators and analysts, still trained in the fashion of the efficient market hypothesis, continued to act as if the MiFID did not provide any opportunity to accompany behavioural research. It is no surprise that in 2008, misaligned incentives and full disclosure were identified as the most salient problem of the financial crisis.[83] Since then, hectic reforms have been put into place. On the one hand, the findings of behavioural research shall be implemented into EU financial regulation, this time in a more effective way.[84] On the other, a supervisory structure of pan-European agencies for the financial market mushroomed from the regulatory table in Brussels. This all happened despite the knowledge of two obstacles: First, there being no or at least a very shaky competence norm at EU level for these reforms.[85] It was hence far from clear whether these measures would find support from the CJEU. Second, it is common knowledge from regulatory theory that the agency-models work rather to the detriment of consumers in nation-states.[86] Why shall they cure diseases at EU level if they could not already do that at national level?

The driving forces for these actions were neither legal commands nor protection of investors or markets per se. What Brussels regulators fear most are the Eurobarometer results. According to a Eurobarometer survey, trust in the European institutions has decreased significantly in the three largest Member States of the EU since the financial crisis (Fig. 4.1).[87]

In other words, after focussing for years on the output-legitimacy of financial market regulation, one realizes that the EU forgot to ask the people. This is the reason why input-legitimacy backed up with behavioural research is desperately needed, especially in the financial market sector. The "legitimacy market-failure" is, once again, the real reason for intervention.

OJ L 177/1 and European Parliament and Council Directive (EC) 2006/49 on the Capital Adequacy of Investment Firms and Credit Institutions [2006] OJ L 177/201.

[82] Franck and Purnhagen 2014, p. 336; Steindorff 1996, pp. 195–196.

[83] The President's Working Group on Financial Markets (PWGFM), Policy Statement on Financial Market Developments', March 2008.

[84] Avgouleas 2009.

[85] See in respect of the financial architecture Van Gestel and van Golen 2014.

[86] Stigler 1971.

[87] See with an assessment Torreblanca et al. 2013.

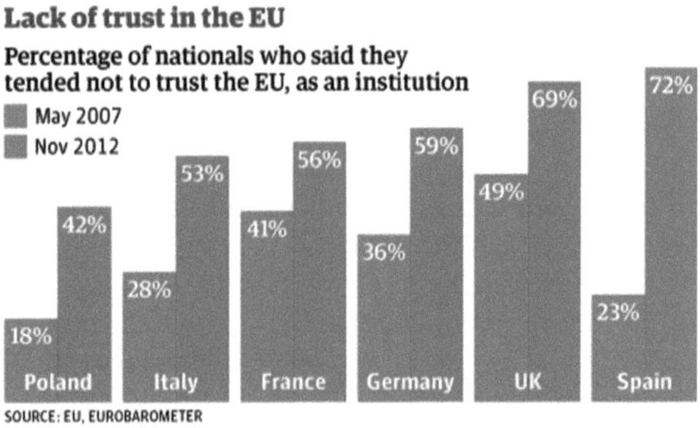

Fig. 4.1 Ian Traynor, Crisis for Europe as trust hits record low, The Guardian, available at http://www.theguardian.com/world/2013/apr/24/trust-eu-falls-record-low

4.5 Conclusion

I hence conclude the following:

1. At EU level, market establishment requires taking into account a "legitimacy market failure", which takes account of the fact that negative externalities might hinder the integrating purpose of internal market regulation.
2. This "legitimacy market failure" is a specific EU-understanding of the desire to create a "highly competitive social market economy".
3. Data from behavioural science are the best fit to establish an internal market effectively.

Acknowledgement I would like to thank Hans Micklitz, Jeff Rachlinski, Harm Schepel, Anne-Lise Sibony, and Avishalom Tor for valuable comments on an earlier version of this piece.

Bibliography

Ackermann, Thomas. 2007. *Der schutz des negativen interesses*. Tübingen: Mohr Siebeck.

Afilalo, Ari, Dennis Patterson, and Kai Purnhagen. 2014. Statecraft, the market state and the development of European legal culture. In *Towards a European legal culture,* ed. Geneviève Helleringer and Kai Purnhagen, 277–302. Baden-Baden: C. H. Beck/Nomos.

Allio, Lorenzo. 2011. On the smartness of smart regulation—A brief comment on the future reform agenda. *European Journal of Risk Regulation* 2:19–20.

Avgouleas, Emilios. 2009. The global financial crisis and the disclosure paradigm on European financial regulation: The case for reform. *European Company and Financial Law Review* 6 (4): 440–475.

Bekkers, V., and A. Edwards. 2007. Legitimacy and democracy: A conceptual framework for assessing governance practices. In *Governance and the democratic deficit: Assessing the democratic legitimacy of governance practices,* eds. V. Bekkers, G. Dijkstra, A. Edwards, and M. Fenger, 35–60. Aldershot Hampshire: Ashgate.

Ben-Shahar, Omri. 2004. Freedom from contract. *Wisconsin Law Review* 261–270.

Binding, Jörg, and Kai Purnhagen. 2011. Regulations on e-commerce consumer protection rules in China and Europe compared—Same same but different? *Journal of Intellectual Property, Information Technology and E-Commerce Law* 2:186–194.

Bizer, Kilian, and Martin Führ. 2002. Responsive Regulierung. Anforderungen an die interdisziplinäre Gesetzesfolgenforschung. In *Responsive Regulierung,* eds. Kilian Bizer, Martin Führ, and Christoph Hütting, 5. Tübingen: Mohr Siebeck.

Black, Julia, and Robert Baldwin. 2010. Really responsive risk-based regulation. *Law & Policy* 32:181–213.

Cooter, Thomas. 1989. Cognitive imperfections and the economic analysis of law. *Hamline Law Review* 12:385.

Danielsson-Tham M. L., E. Eriksson, S. Helmersson, M. Leffler, L. Lüdtke, M. Steen, S. Sørgjerd, and W. Tham. 2004. Causes behind a human cheese-borne outbreak of gastrointestinal listeriosis. *Foodborne Pathogens and Disease* 1 (3): 153–159.

Downes, Chris. 2014. *The impact of WTO SPS Law on EU food regulations.* Dordrecht: Springer

Dyson, Matthew. 2014. Divide and conquer: Using legal domains in comparative legal studies. In *Towards a European legal culture,* eds. Geneviève Helleringer and Kai Purnhagen, 115–137. Baden-Baden: C. H. Beck/Nomos.

Easton, David. 1965. *A system analysis of political life.* New York: Wiley.

Eberlein, Burkard. 2004. Formal and informal governance in single market regulation. In *Informal governance in the European Union,* eds. Thomas Christiansen and Simona Piattoni, 150–172. Cheltenham: Edward Elgar.

Eisenberg, Melvin. 1982. The bargain principle and its limits. *Harvard Law Review* 773.

Eisenberg, Melvin. 1995. The limits of cognition and the limits of contract. *Stanford Law Review* 47:211–259.

Fama, Eugene. 1970. Efficient capital markets: A review of theory and empirical work. *Journal of Finance* 25:383.

Flume, Werner. 2000. Vom Beruf unserer Zeit für Gesetzgebung. *Zeitschrift für Wirtschaftsrecht* 1427.

Franck, Jens-Uwe, and Kai Purnhagen. 2014. Homo economicus, behavioural sciences, and economic regulation—On the concept of man in internal market regulation and its normative basis. In *Law and economics in Europe—Foundations and applications,* ed. Klaus Mathis, 329–365. Heidelberg: Springer.

Grossman, Margaret Rosso. 2012. Genetically modified crops and their products in the united states: A review of the regulatory system. In *Jahrbuch des Agrarrechts,* ed. José Martìnez, 69–95. Baden-Baden: Nomos.

Hammen, Horst. 2010. Zerschlagt unsere Gesetzestafeln nicht! *Zeitschrift für Wirtschafts- und Bankrecht* 1357.

Hoffmann, Jan F. 2012. Verbraucherwiderruf bei Stellvertretung. *Juristenzeitung,* 1156.

Hey, B., K. Jacob, and A. Volkery. 2007. Better regulation by new governance hybrids? Governance models and the reform of European chemicals policy. *Journal of Cleaner Production* 15:1861.

Joerges, Christian, Jürgen Falke, Hans-Wolfgang Micklitz, and Gert Brüggemeier. 1988. *Die Sicherheit von Konsumgütern und die Entwicklung der Europäischen Gemeinschaft.* Baden-Baden: Nomos.

Jolls, Christine, and Cass Sunstein. 2007. Debiasing through Law. *Journal of Legal Studies* 35:199.

Keller, Moritz. 2004. Lessons for the hague: Internet jurisdiction in contract and tort cases in the European community and the united states. *The John Marshall Journal of Information Technology and Privacy Law* 23:1–74.

Koch, J., R. Dworak, R. Prager, B. Becker, S. Brockmann, A. Wicke, H. Wichmann-Schauer, H. Hof, D. Werber, and K. Stark. 2010. Large listeriosis outbreak linked to cheese made from pasteurized milk, Germany 2006/2007. *Foodborne Pathogens and Disease* 7 (12): 1581–1584.

Krystallis, A., L. Frewer, G. Rowe, J. Houghton, O. Kehagia, and T. Perrea. 2007. A perceptual divide? Consumer and expert attitudes to food risk management in Europe. *Health Risks and Society* 9:407–424.

Leiter, Brian. 2013. Legal realism, old and new. *Valparaiso Law Review* 48. (Forthcoming).

Lenaerts, Koen. 2004. "In the union we trust": Trust-enhancing principles of community law. *Common Market Law Review* 41:317–343.

Lynch, Diahanna, and David Vogel. 2001. The regulation of GMOs in Europe and the United States: A case-study of contemporary European regulatory politics, council on foreign relations press. http://www.cfr.org/agricultural-policy/regulation-gmos-europe-united-states-case-study-contemporary-european-regulatory-politics/p8688. Accessed 13 Oct 2014.
Macneil, Ian. 2000. Other sociological approaches. In *Encyclopedia of law & economics*, eds. Boudewijn Bouckaert and Gerrit De Geest, 694 et seqq. Cheltenham: Edward Egar.
Mann, Dennis-Jonathan. 2009. Ein Gebilde sui generis? Die Debatte um das Wesen der Europäischen Union im Spiegel der „Nature of the Union"-Kontroverse in den USA. In *Die Verfassung Europas*, eds. Frank Decker and Marcus Höreth, 319. Wiesbaden: VS Verlag für Sozialwissenschaften.
Marsden, Christopher. 2011. *Internet co-regulation*. Cambridge: Cambridge University Press.
McColm, Helen. 2011. Smart regulation: The European commission's updated strategy. *European Journal of Risk Regulation* 2:9–11.
McGee, Andrew, and Stephen Weatherill. 1990. The evolution of the single market: Harmonisation or liberalisation. *The Modern Law Review* 53:578.
Micklitz, Hans-Wolfgang. 2001. A comment on party autonomy and consumer regulation in the European community—A plea for consistency. In *Party Autonomy and the Role of Information in the Internal Market*, eds. Stefan Grundmann, Wolfgang Kerber, and Stephen Weatherill, 197–204. Berlin: Walter de Gruyter.
Micklitz, Hans. 2009. The visible hand of European regulatory private law—The transformation of European private law from autonomy to functionalism in competition and regulation. *Yearbook of European Law 2010*, 3–59.
Miles, Thomas, and Cass Sunstein. 2008. The new legal realism. *The University of Chicago Law Review* 75:831–851.
Nourse, Victoria, and Gregory Shaffer. 2009. Varieties of new legal realism: Can a new world order prompt a new legal theory? *Cornell Law Review* 95:61–138.
Ogus, Anthony. 1994. *Legal form and economic theory*. Oxford: Clarendon Press.
Patterson, Dennis, and Ari Afilalo. 2008. *The new global trading order.* Cambridge: Cambridge University Press.
Pollack, Mark, and Gregory Shaffer. 2009. *When cooperation fails.* Oxford: Oxford University Press.
Posner, Richard. 1998. Rational choice, behavioral economics, and the law. *Stanford Law Review* 50:1551–1575.
Purnhagen, Kai. 2013. The Architecture of post-national European contract law from a phenomenological perspective—A question of comparative institutional analysis. *The Rabel Journal of Comparative and International Private Law* 77:592–619.
Purnhagen, Kai. 2014a. Never the twain shall meet?—A critical perspective on cultural limits between internal continental dogmatism and consequential us-style law and economics theory. In *Law and economics in Europe—Foundations and applications*, ed. Klaus Mathis, pp. 3–21. Dordrecht: Springer.
Purnhagen, Kai. 2014b. The virtue of cassis de Dijon 25 years later—It is not dead, it just smells funny. In *Varieties of European economic law and regulation*, ed. Kai Purnhagen and Peter Rott, pp. 315–342. Dordrecht: Springer.
Radaelli, Claudio. 2007. Whither better regulation for the Lisbon agenda? *Journal of European Public Policy* 14:190–207.
Reich, Norbert. 2000. Das Phantom "Verbraucher" (endlich!?) im Gral des BGB!, *Verbraucher und Recht* 261.
Samuelson, Paul. 1965. Proof that properly anticipated prices fluctuate randomly 6. *Industrial Management Review* 6:41
Schapp, Jan. 1986. *Grundfragen der Rechtsgeschäftslehre*. Tübingen: Mohr Siebeck.
Scharpf, Friedrich W. 1970. *Demokratietheorie zwischen Utopie und Anpassung*. Konstanz: Konstanzer Universitätsverlag.
Scharpf, Friedrich W. 1997. *Games real actors play. Actor-centered institutionalism in policy research*. Boulder: Westview.

Scharpf, Friedrich W. 1999. Governing in Europe: Effective and democratic? Oxford: Oxford University Press.
Schwartz, Allan. 2008. How much irrationality does the market permit? *Journal of Legal Studies* 37:131–159.
Simon, William. 2006. Toyota jurisprudence: Legal theory and rolling rule regimes. In *Law and new governance in the EU and the US*, eds. Grainne de Búrca and Joan Scott, 57. Oxford: Hart.
Skogstad. 2003. Legitimacy and/or policy effectiveness?: Network governance and GMO regulation in the European Union. *Journal of European Public Policy* 10:321–338.
Spindler, Gerald. 2011. Behavioural finance and investor protection regulations. *Journal of Consumer Policy* 34:315.
Steindorff, Ernst. 1996. *EG-Vertrag und Privatrecht*. Baden-Baden: Nomos.
Stigler, George. 1971. The theory of economic regulation. *Bell Journal of Economics and Management Science* 2:3–21.
Torreblanca, J. I., M. Leonard, H. Kudnani, U. Guéerot, and T. Klau. 2013. The remarkable rise of continental Euroscepticism, theguardian.com. http://www.theguardian.com/commentisfree/2013/apr/24/continental-euroscepticism-rise. Accessed 24 April 2013. (20.09 BST2013).
Tricker, Ray. 2000. *CE conformity marking and new approach directives*. Oxford: Butterworth-Heinemann.
Tröger, Tobias. 2012. Organizational choices of banks and the effective supervision of transnational financial institutions. *Texas International Law Journal* 48:177–221.
Usher, John. 2001. Disclosure rules (information) as a primary tool in the doctrine on measures having an equivalent effect. In *Party autonomy and the role of information in the internal market*, eds. Stefan Grundmann, Wolfgang Kerber, and Stephen Weatherill. Berlin: de Gruyter.
Valletta, Marco. 2010. Consumer perception and GMOs in the European Union, policy responses to societal concerns in food and agriculture: Proceedings of an OECD workshop. http://www.oecd.org/tad/agricultural-policies/46838061.pdf. Accessed 13 Oct 2014.
Van den Bergh, Roger. 2003. De richtlijn consumentenkoop in rechtseconomisch perspectief. In *De richtlijn consumentenkoop in perspectief*, ed. Jan Smits. Den Haag: Boom Juridische Uitgaven.
van der Meulen, Bernd, Harry Bremmers, Kai Purnhagen, Nidhi Gupta, Hans Bouwmeester, and Leon Geyer. 2014. *Governing nano foods*. New York: Academic Press.
Van Gestel, Rob, and Thomas van Golen. 2014. Enforcement by the new European supervisory agencies: Quis custodiet ipsos custodes? In *Varieties of European economic law and regulation*, eds. Kai Purnhagen and Peter Rott, pp. 757–780. Dordrecht: Springer.
Walker, Neil, and Grainne de Búrca. 2007. Reconceiving law & new governance. *Columbia Journal of European Law* 13:522.
Weiler, Joseph. 2005. The transformation of Europe. *Yale Law Journal* 100:2403.
Wiener, Jonathan. 2006. Better regulation in Europe. *Current Legal Problems* 9:447–518.

Prof. Dr. Kai Purnhagen Wageningen and Rotterdam. Assistant Professor of Law and Governance at Wageningen University and distinguished international visitor at the Law Faculty of Erasmus University of Rotterdam. Hollandseweg 16706, KN Wageningen, The Netherlands. Kai.purnhagen@wur.nl. Fields of Interest: European and International Economic Law and Policy, Trade Law, Risk Regulation, Legal Theory, Theory of Regulation, Insurance Law, Contract and Consumer Law, German and US American Law.

Chapter 5
Can EU Consumer Law Benefit From Behavioural Insights?

An Analysis of the Unfair Practices Directive

Anne-Lise Sibony

Abstract This chapter explores in what ways behavioural insights could be used to shape the interpretation of European law on unfair practices. It is argued that insights from social psychology on influencing techniques are relevant to the interpretation of the directive on unfair practices. These insights cut across national legal traditions and could therefore contribute to a uniform interpretation of EU law in the field of unfair commercial practices. Both conceptual and empirical insights from psychology are valuable from a legal point of view. In order for such insights to be put to actual legal use, it is important to address the question of how they should be used. In this regard, presumptions appear to be a very apt vehicle to incorporate behavioural teachings into the law.

5.1 Consumer Law and Behavioural Science: The European Divide

5.1.1 Why Is EU Consumer Law Resistant to Behavioural Insights?

At present, the legal system largely operates on implicit rationalist assumptions. Much like traditional economics, which does so explicitly, legal systems often implicitly assumes that people can be governed as though they were rational.

As published in the European Review of Private Law (ERPL) 6 (2014), p. 901–942. With thanks for the kind permission to reprint this article.

A.-L. Sibony (✉)
University of Liège, Boulevard du Rectorat, 3 Bât. B33, 4000 Liège, Belgium
e-mail: alsibony@ulg.ac.be

K. Mathis (ed.), *European Perspectives on Behavioural Law and Economics*,
Economic Analysis of Law in European Legal Scholarship 2,
DOI 10.1007/978-3-319-11635-8_5

European consumer law illustrates this relative blindness of the law to the complexity of actual behaviour of humans in at least two different ways.

First, it contains a very large number of information requirements[1] and more generally rests on what has come to be called an "informational paradigm".[2] Information requirements make a lot of sense if consumers are rational and have a lot of available processing capacity. Such requirements make it mandatory for traders to gather all the information deemed relevant, thus decreasing search costs for consumers. If consumers had any inclination to read food labels, terms of services or consumer contracts and tended to rely on the information given in the manner in order to make "informed choices", then EU law as it stands would be doing a wonderful job at helping them. By and large, European laws in the field of consumer protection are still drafted as though scarcity of information were the issue. The problem is that the scarce resource is not information but attention.[3]

Second, EU consumer law still largely relies on the fiction that consumers are "reasonably well-informed and reasonably observant and circumspect".[4] The figure of the average consumer created by the Court is a not so distant cousin of *homo oeconomicus*.[5] Using such a heroic consumer as a standard for the appraisal of unfair practices makes sense if the aim is to unify the internal market. To traders, national provisions protecting consumers often represent obstacles to trade. For example, when Belgian law required margarine to be packaged in cubic form so as to avoid confusing consumers between butter and margarine, margarine producers from other Member States would have had to repackage their product if they wanted to sell in Belgium.[6] Faced with such rules, the Court of Justice is called to decide whether they can be justified. This involves a balancing exercise between free movement and Member States domestic policy goals. The proportionality test provides the legal framework for reasoning this trade-off. It requires the courts to assess whether

[1] The directive on consumer rights consolidates many of these requirements. Directive 2011/83/EU on consumer rights, OJ L 304, 22/11/2011, pp. 64–88, spec. Article 5 "Information requirements for contracts other than distance or off-premises contracts" contains 8 informational requirements, making it mandatory for traders to disclose such information as the main characteristics of the goods or services, the business address of the seller and telephone number (but not email), total price of the goods or services, arrangements for payment, delivery, etc. Article 6 "Information requirements for distance and off-premises contracts" lists 20 different items of information whose provision is mandatory. The services directive also emphasizes the information dimension. Chapter V of the directive, entitled "Quality of Services" contains in article 22 a long list of information that Providers must make available. Directive 2006/123/EC of the European Parliament and of the Council of 12 December 2006 on services in the internal market, OJ L 376, 27/12/2006, pp. 36–68.

[2] Reich and Micklitz 2014, p. 21; Stuyck et al. 2006, p. 108 and references cited; Weatherill 2013, Chap. 4; Franck and Purnhagen 2014, pp. 334 et seq.

[3] On the failure of information requirements more generally, see Ben-Shahar and Schneider 2011; Ben-Shahar and Schneider 2014. For a study on smarter disclosure requirements, see Bar-Gill 2012.

[4] Established case law since Case C-210/96 *Gut Springerheide* [1998] ECR I-4657, para. 31.

[5] *Homo oeconomicus* is presumably even more heroic and lives in a world where there is no need for consumer protection.

[6] Such a regulation was at hand in Case 261/81, *Rau* [1982] ECR 3961.

a national measure is (i) *apt* to achieve its stated goal and, (ii) if it is *necessary* to do so. If less restrictive measures can achieve the stated goal, the national measure is incompatible with the internal market. In order to conduct the necessity assessment of domestic consumer protection rules, the Court needed a standard. It chose to answer the question "when is a measure necessary to protect consumers?" by holding that it is only necessary when a reasonably well-informed and reasonably observant and circumspect consumer needs it. This standard makes it easy to strike down national measures that adopt a protective stance and is therefore particularly suited to the task of removing obstacles to trade. As Micklitz puts it, the 'normatively determined reasonable consumer (…) [is] a vehicle [for] realising the internal market'.[7] As a standard for consumer protection, the average consumer standard may score less well as, the real average consumer might more aptly be described as reasonably overwhelmed, distracted and impatient.[8]

At first sight, the heritage of EU consumer law does not appear particularly welcoming to insights from behavioural sciences. Surely, the drafters or EU laws and judges of the Court of justice know that consumers more often than not do not read the information they are given (after all, drafters and judges too are consumers), but they had reasons to craft a fiction. In addition to being useful for the all-important task of achieving a single market, it seemed a clever compromise between diverging interests. Firms were not overburdened with compliance costs and the EU appeared to take consumers interests at heart.

5.1.2 Reasons to Change

Up until the recent spread of behavioural wisdom,[9] EU Consumer law could be viewed as expressing a liberal philosophy, in the (European) sense that individuals, also in their capacity as consumers, were in charge of their own well-being. The role of law was only to ensure fairness and transparency in order to protect individual autonomy.[10] In this perspective, the degree of protection can be apprehended with a cursor analogy. The task of the law is to position the cursor on an axis between under-protection and over-protection. When arguing that over-protection is

---

[7] Micklitz 2014, p. 101. On internal market considerations in the UCPD more generally, see 77 et seq. in the same chapter.

[8] Without using this particular formula, many commentators agree. For a critique of the average consumer from a behavioural angle:Incardona and Poncibó 2007; Trzaskowski 2011; Scholes 2012. From a more legal perspective: Mak 2011. Weatherill, for his part, argues that, while the average consumer standard on its face expresses unrealistic behavioural assumptions, the case law of the Court still leaves room for relevant and substantiated behavioural arguments. Weatherill 2007, p. 133.

[9] Many books in recent years have popularized the teachings of behavioural studies Thaler and Sunstein 2008; Ariely 2008; Lehrer 2010; Kahneman 2011; Mullainathan and Shafir 2013.

[10] As Micklitz argues, this philosophy is apparent in the UCPD test for unfair practices ("to appreciably impair the consumer's ability to make an informed decision, thereby causing the consumer to take a transactional decision that he would not have taken otherwise" (art. 2 e)): Micklitz 2014, p. 92.

a dangerous zone, the figure of the "idiot" serves an important rhetorical function. The role of the legal system, it can be argued, is not to protect idiots, but normal people. If normal people want to behave like idiots, it is not for a nanny state—and far less for a nanny Europe—to look after them, it is their choice and they should live with the consequences.

Behavioural studies show that we are all "idiots" or, rather, they explain how easily people who are not at all idiotic can be fooled and why. The behavioural perspective on human decision-making dispels—or at least should dispel—any negative judgement or rhetoric on "irrational" behaviour.[11] Insights from behavioural studies also allow a more reasoned and a more radical critique of the "average consumer" standard.[12] As it becomes clear that the implicit behavioural assumptions imbedded in consumer law do not survive the confrontation with science, both the effectiveness and the legitimacy existing instruments are challenged.[13] Indeed, from an effectiveness point of view, it does not make sense for the law to ignore what is known on how people really behave.[14] In turn, laws that are known to be ineffective are not legitimate. Understandably, they tend to be perceived as hypocritical.

5.1.3 Time to Change

Times seem ripe for a change. Indeed, in recent years, several governments and regulatory agencies have shown a growing interest for the use of behavioural insights in policy making.[15] At European level, this is particularly true in the field of consumer protection. Directorate-General for Health and Consumers (DG Sanco) of the European Commission has commissioned several studies and experiments on discrete questions regarding consumer choice (such as impact of labelling) in various markets (e.g., energy, financial services, healthcare, gambling).[16] The European Occupation and Pensions Authority (EOPA) also shows interest in designing information requirements that are more behaviourally informed, paying close attention to how and when information is presented.[17]

---

[11] This idea is aptly captured in the title of Ariely 2010.

[12] Incardona and Poncibó 2007 and Trzaskowski 2011.

[13] On this issue, albeit in a different field of law, see Quigley and Stokes 2014.

[14] Tor 2008, pp. 240–241; Shafir 2013, p. 1.

[15] For a direct account of the US experience, see Sunstein 2013. In the UK, a Behavioural Insights Team, better known as the 'Nudge Unit' has been created within the Cabinet Office: https://www.gov.uk/government/organisations/behavioural-insights-team/. The French Government commissioned an expert report on the use of behavioural economics. Several regulatory agencies, in particular in the financial sector, experiment with the use of behavioural tools. More recently OECD has shown interest in the potential of behaviourally informed regulation. Lunn 2014.

[16] Ciriolo 2011; DG Sanco publicises its use of behavioural economics on a dedicated webpage: http://ec.europa.eu/consumers/behavioural_economics/ (last visited on March 2, 2014).

[17] See for example the report by the European Insurance and Occupational Pensions Authority (EIOPA).

5.1.4 Change Must Happen at EU Level

So far, the internal market imperative has led the Court to erect a barrier to behavioural insights. No particular hostility of the Court should be read into this state of the law. Indeed, at the time when the Court crafted the character of the average consumer, the behavioural approach to law was not part of the conversation. The Court did not reject behavioural arguments; it was not presented with any. Even in recent years, there is no visible sign in the case law that litigants use behavioural arguments.[18] The closure of the Court's reasoning to behavioural insights can therefore be viewed as more accidental than intentional. In addition, the price to pay for the purely normative approach it embraced when designed the average consumer may not have been immediately apparent, for at least two reasons. First, the Court may have displayed a 'present bias':[19] the benefits for the single market were immediate, while the cost were deferred and thus underestimated. Second, this effect may have been strengthened by the fact that the cost of imbedding behaviourally erroneous premises in the law was not clearly spelt out. The Court did not have to make an explicit choice between winning a prize now or a larger prize later or buying something now and pay it later with interest on a credit card bill later. The true cost of behavioural inaccuracy in the law could not and, in fairness, still cannot be calculated.[20] Indeed, the benefits of a more behaviourally-informed consumer law are also very difficult to evaluate, if only because of incorporating behavioural insights into the law involves trade-offs.[21]

What can be determined with certainty is that, if behavioural insights have a future in consumer law in Europe, it must be at EU level. The national level would be the wrong place to instil behavioural wisdom into the law because the internal market arguments against diversity of consumer protection measures apply exactly in the same way irrespective of whether these measures are behaviourally informed or not. Had the Belgian measure regarding the packaging of margarine been backed up by hard evidence from the physiology of perception, it would not have hindered trade any less. Science might have helped the government prove that its measure was justified, but it is clear that if governments from the various Member State each focus on different aspects of consumer protection, adopt different measures, the fact that such measures may be adopted to counteract a behaviourally plausible

[18] For an analysis of one typical judgment of the Court from a behavioural angle, see Sibony 2013.

[19] The 'present bias' describe a common tendency to opt for a course of action that will result in immediate gratification even if this will entail a high cost at a later point in time. This tendency is at the root of procrastination. Economists who are interested in measuring the discounting rate people apply to future rewards when they choose a more immediate reward call this bias 'hyperbolic discounting'. See e.g. Laibson 1997. Several studies conducted on students over the past decade show that the proportion of procrastinators is between 40 and 60 %. Bisin and Hyndman 2014, 27 and references cited.

[20] On the political price for ignoring the reality of consumer/citizen's preferences, see Purnhagen 2014.

[21] Tor 2013, pp. 17–18 (explaining that prohibiting practices that are misleading for some but not all consumer may favor gullible consumers over more rational ones).

risk will not make regulatory diversity any less costly for traders. In various areas of EU law, the Court has developed effective techniques to avoid engaging with scientific evidence[22] and, in its balancing exercise, it could very well be inclined to accord more weight to free movement than to relevant evidence on how prone to errors consumers are.

If behavioural insights are worked into the law at European level, the tension between diversity and accuracy disappears. Behavioural wisdom is given a better chance to make the law more efficient because the efforts required to elaborate on legally meaningful uses of empirical data have a higher probability of yielding results that will actually serve consumer protection, rather than feeding arguments between Member States and the EU institutions. Choosing the EU level to analyse whether and how behavioural insights could help improve the law also makes sense from a purely legal perspective. In EU consumer law, the current trend is towards maximum harmonisation. There is therefore less room than in the past for national regulatory experiments in the field of consumer protection. For all these reasons, behaviourally-informed regulatory innovation should happen at EU level. Regulatory innovation can occur by way of new instruments, but also new ways to interpret and enforce existing legislation. In this regard, the Unfair Commercial Practices Directive ("UCPD")[23] is an instrument of choice to explore the possibility of making a meaningful use of what psychology teaches us about consumer behaviour. This, however, is no easy task.

5.1.5 Challenges

Interpreting and applying the UCPD in a behaviourally-informed manner faces two major challenges, which Tor calls 'the material distortion challenge' and the 'average consumer challenge'.[24] The first is a baseline problem, which is inherent to the test contained in the directive. Article 5 prohibits practices that are contrary to professional diligence and 'materially distort the economic behaviour of consumers'. According to article 2, 'to materially distort the economic behaviour of consumers' means using a commercial practice to appreciably impair the consumer's ability to make an informed decision, thereby causing the consumer to take a transactional decision that he would not have taken otherwise'. As Tor notes, this is at first glance an extremely broad test. In a free market economy, it would be against the widely shared normative intuition to even consider prohibiting many practices that are known to influence choice, such as the way in which options are displayed in a store or on a menu. It is therefore necessary to find a reasonable interpretation of the 'material distortion' requirement. While this is clearly a challenge, it is by no means

[22] Sibony 2012a.

[23] Directive 2005/29/EC of the European Parliament and of the Council of 11 May 2005 concerning unfair business-to-consumer commercial practices in the internal market, OJ 2005 L 149/22, "UCPD".

[24] Tor 2013, p. 15 sq.

specific to a behaviourally-informed perspective on the directive. The difficulty of articulating sound normative principles is inherent to the directive itself. The reason why it must be borne in mind with particular vigilance when revisiting the directive from a behavioural standpoint is because behavioural studies show that many techniques, that no one ever intended to prohibit, do in fact impact behaviour and possibly do so in a significant manner. The risk is therefore that a behaviourally-informed but normatively naïve reading of the directive would result in overbroad interpretation of the prohibition. In this regard, it is useful to read the two-pronged test of article 5 as containing one criterion that expresses a normative judgement on what practices are acceptable (the 'professional diligence' criterion) and another one that is open to an empirical appraisal of the efficacy of the commercial practice ('material distortion' criterion). In other words the directive provides a mechanism for refusing on purely normative grounds to extend the prohibition to commercial practices that are considered acceptable, irrespective of how much they may influence consumer's decision.

The second challenge Tor identifies is posed by the central notion of the 'average consumer'. The average consumer standard is truly in tension with empirical evidence because of its inherent simplificatory function. Behavioural studies show that not all consumers are prone to fall into the same traps, not to the same degree and not in all circumstances. Meanwhile, the law as it stands requires courts to assess whether a given practice distorts the choice pattern of the (unitary) average consumer. In line with the case law of the Court, the directive states that the average consumer test 'is not a statistical test'.[25] Empirical data could in principle shed light on how many consumers display certain behavioural traits, such as sensitivity to framing effects or present bias. The statement that the average consumer is a 'typical' consumer rather than a statistical construct does not make such data completely irrelevant, as they could be taken into account to assess what is typical, but does create uncertainty, as the relevance of empirical data on consumer behaviour will be a matter for courts to decide. No guidance is provided on this difficult issue. Courts are simply invited to 'exercise their own faculty of judgement'.[26] In particular, courts may not be fully aware of the trade-offs that their decisions will entail. As Tor points out, deciding that the average consumer needs protection against certain practices may result in imposing costs not only on traders but also on those consumers who would not have been misled by the practice at issue.[27] At this stage, the distributive aspects of consumer protection are in need of more elaboration.

The substantive test contained in the directive presents several levels of normative indeterminacy (what is 'material distortion', what is 'typical'). In other words, it is a hard test to apply. When faced with a hard question, humans tend to substitute an easier one, which they can more readily answer, and (mistakenly) consider they have answered the initial hard question. For example, if asked how dangerous the crossing near her home is, a person might answer on the basis of her recollection of

[25] UCPD, recital 18.

[26] UCPD, recital 18.

[27] Tor 2013, p. 18.

accidents at that location.[28] Attribute substitution is a very common phenomenon. It is tough to explain why beautiful faces are perceived as more familiar than less aesthetically perfect ones (likability is substituted for familiarity).[29] The same mechanism underlies prejudices: if a person has preconceived ideas about intelligence or honesty characterising different races, she is likely to judge these attributes based on physical appearance.[30] In the context of judging whether a commercial practice is unfair within the meaning of UCPD, one cannot rule out that the conditions for attribute substitution are met: it is hard to assess whether a practice materially distorts the average consumer's behaviour and it is easy to substitute a different question, one more familiar to courts on the basis of their respective legal tradition on unfair competition. If judges were prone to the heuristics just described when applying the general clause of UCPD, it could result in courts answering the purely normative question "is the practice 'contrary to professional diligence'—or 'in accordance with good business practices'"—and (implicitly) infer that, if it is, then it must also be likely to distort the economic behaviour of the average consumer. Because material distortion is difficult to assess, courts might appraise acceptability instead. Such a shortcut would collapse the two-pronged test of article 5 into a single overall assessment of unfairness. It would also constitute yet another way of keeping empirical insights at bay.

5.1.6 Aims and Scope of this Chapter

The UCPD is a central piece in EU consumer law. It is therefore a good place to start investigating if and how behavioural insights impact the existing EU legal framework. While other studies have focussed on how to change the legal framework in order to make it more behaviourally informed,[31] this analysis considers how behavioural insights could be incorporated by way of judicial interpretation into the existing legal framework. Open textured rules invite interpretation and there is evidence from other areas of law, singularly competition law, that judicial interpretation can incorporate ideas from relevant scientific discourses. As I have argued elsewhere, there are only a limited number of legal techniques that can be used to incorporate science into judge-made law.[32] Could these same incorporating mechanisms that are at work with economics in the field of competition law help with making consumer law behaviourally wiser? This is the question I endeavour to answer in this paper.

From the perspective of legal theory, this exploration is linked to the general question of how science is used in the law.[33] If psychology can contribute to

[28] Tor 2008, p. 245 (citation omitted).

[29] Monin 2003.

[30] Kahneman and Shane 2002.

[31] In particular disclosure requirements and rules on consumer contracts. See Luth 2010 and references cited at footnote 3.

[32] Sibony 2012b.

[33] Feldman 2009.

consumer law in similar ways as economics contributes to competition law, this would be an indication—certainly short from a general proof, but nevertheless an indication—that there are invariants in the legal techniques through which science is incorporated into the legal discourse. I think there is a good reason to believe that such invariants exist, simply because law is low tech: there are only a limited number of legal techniques that can serve as vehicle for importing science into the law.[34] This in particular is true of judge-made law, which—understandably if one considers how much black-letter law there is to study—has not so far been the focus of studies on use of behavioural sciences in consumer law.

From the perspective of European law, a further implication would deserve to be explored. It is linked to the much-discussed question of intensity of harmonisation.[35] The directive on unfair practices is a directive of full harmonisation.[36] Yet, as is often the case when the language of a directive uses broad concepts such as "unfair", "material distortion" or "undue influence", even meticulous transposition into national legal orders will not prevent such phrases from having different meanings or from prompting a different set of associations in various national legal contexts.[37] Uniform definitions such as those given in the directive, do not really alleviate this problem, because they are themselves framed in very broad terms.[38]

Against this background, might incorporating psychological insights have the added benefit of helping to unify the interpretation of the directive? This would

---

[34] This idea emerged from my research on how insights from economics are integrated in case law in the field of competition law: Sibony 2008. For a concise exposition in plain French, Sibony 2010.

[35] See *inter alia*: Micklitz 2014; Smits 2006.

[36] The Court made this extremely clear in joined cases C-261/07 and C-299/07, *VTB-VAB and others*, [2009] ECR I-2949, paragraph 52. In this judgment, the Court ruled that Belgian law prohibiting joint selling *per se* was contrary to the directive, whose annex "exhaustively lists the only commercial practices which are prohibited in all circumstances and accordingly do not have to be assessed on a case-by-case basis" (paragraph 61). A string of cases applied the same reasoning to hold that various other national *per se* prohibitions of certain commercial practices violated the directive: Case C-304/08 *Plus Warenhandelsgesellschaft* [2010] ECR 217 (prohibition of commercial practices which make the participation of consumers in a lottery conditional on the purchase of goods or the use of services); Case C-522/08 *Telekommunikacja Polska* [2010] ECR I-2079 (prohibition of joint selling); Case C-540/08 *Mediaprint Zeitungs- und Zeitschriftenverlag* [2010] ECR I-10909 (prohibition on commercial practices making the offer of bonuses to consumers subject to the purchase of goods or services); Case C-288/10, *Wamo* [2011] ECR I-5835 and Case C-126/11, *Inno* (summary publication) (prohibition of announcements of price reductions during the weeks preceding the official sales period); Case C-343/12, *Euronics Belgium* (summary publication) (prohibition of selling goods at a loss).

[37] As pointed out by the Office of Fair Trading during the transposition of the UCPD, the directive introduced several new concepts in UK Law. The OFT Guidance (2007), p. 4. The same holds true for most if not all member states. The intended novelty of autonomous EU law concepts carries the message that harmonised rules are different from previous national regimes. Micklitz 2014, p. 89 but it cannot de-activate national reasoning patterns.

[38] For example, art. 2 e) provides that "'to materially distort the economic behaviour of consumers' means using a commercial practice to appreciably impair the consumer's ability to make an informed decision, thereby causing the consumer to take a transactional decision that he would not have taken otherwise".

call for careful exploration, which is beyond the scope of this paper. The issue is complex, as different lines of argument seem to pull in different directions. At a conceptual level, a more precise analytical framework for appraising unfair practices would in itself have a much needed unifying potential, as it would cut across national differences in legal cultures.[39] Yet, it would remain to be seen whether that would lead to uniform application of the directive across Europe. At a normative level, the directive recognizes that cultural norms have a bearing on the appraisal of unfair practices.[40] At an empirical level, there may be a need to distinguish between commercial practices that leverage basic cognitive or emotional mechanisms that are similar for Spanish, Danish and Polish consumers,[41] the so-called "marketing universals",[42] and those that reply on more elaborate processes that are influenced by culture.[43] Such an investigation, however, will only become useful if it is first established that EU Consumer law could and should incorporate insights from psychology, which is the task of this paper.

5.1.7 *Why Psychology?*

Before turning to the enquiry, a word of explanation on the interdisciplinary choice made in this article may be necessary. Behavioural economics is much more prominent than psychology in the current discourse on behaviourally informed policy making.[44] The irony of this state of the interdisciplinary conversation must be recalled. For a long time—about 50 years –, economists embraced the rationality

[39] On the risk of divergence between national interpretations, see Weatherill 2013, p. 239.

[40] 'The Directive takes as a benchmark the average consumer, who is reasonably well-informed and reasonably observant and circumspect, *taking into account social, cultural and linguistic factors*, as interpreted by the Court of Justice' (emphasis added).

[41] The phenomena addressed by Kahneman in his Nobel Prize lecture would probably be considered basic mechanisms, as would loss aversion. Kahneman 2002. One example of the relevance of hard-wired neural circuits for the effectiveness of commercial practices is 'magic prices' (prices that end in 9). Schindler and Wiman explain the fact that we tend to underestimate prices ending in 9 by the fact that, when storing numbers in our long term memory, we pay less attention to digits that are on the right hand side than to those on the left hand side. See also Guéguen 2009, 11–26. For a more general study, see Knutson et al. 2007.

[42] Dawar and Parker 1994.

[43] Most research on cultural differences deals with the individualism-collectivism distinction. For a summary, see Maheswaran and Shavitt 2000. Cultural difference are shown to exist in relation with commercial behaviour of consumers that could be relevant for the application of the UCPD, e.g., on impulsive buying: Kacen and Lee 2002. National courts appear to have a different perception of certain practices, in particular 'aggressive practices': Micklitz 2014, p. 113.

[44] See. e.g. Lissowska 2011; Lunn 2014; Oliver 2013 (throughout the book). See also conference organised by DG Sanco on Sept 30 2013, *Applying Behavioural Insights To Policy-Making: Results, Promises and Limitations*. In the field of consumer law, see Bar-Gill 2012, p. 6 et sEq. ; Luth 2010, e.g., 66; Incardona and Poncibó 2007; Trzaskowski 2011; Scholes 2012. From a more legal perspective: Mak 2011. Weatherill, for his part, argues that, while the average consumer standard on its face expresses unrealistic behavioural assumptions, the case law of the Court still leaves room for relevant and substantiated behavioural arguments. Weatherill 2007, p. 133.

hypothesis as a matter of professional identity.[45] It is never easy to call one's identity into question and the reluctance of the guardians of the economic temple against empirical assaults on the very foundations of the edifice was understandable. Nonetheless, it is a paradox that the current research efforts towards making policies and laws more behaviourally-informed should be labelled as law and behavioural *economics*.[46] As Daniel Kahneman writes "Labels matter, and the mislabelling of applied behavioural sciences as behavioural economics has consequences".[47] The consequences Kahneman points to are, first, that "important contributions of psychology to public policy are not recognized as such" and, second, that this unfairness drives young psychologists away from applied research that could be useful to policy making.[48]

It is fair to confess, however, that the research presented in this paper was not undertaken as an attempt to redress a wrong done to psychologists. My realisation of the relevance of psychology for consumer law was rather fortuitous. It stemmed from the impulse buy of a pop-science book on social psychology, which had been a bestseller in France, and which I was lured to buy by its colourful cover and amusing title.[49] To a lawyer trying to make sense of the unfair commercial practices directive, there is a striking proximity between what psychologists call "manipulation" or "influence" and what this directive seems to mean when it defines prohibited commercial practices in terms of "material distortion" of choice patterns or "undue influence". Such proximity between words at least justified the hypothesis that psychological insights may be relevant for the interpretation of the legal rule.

Anecdote apart, there is a substantive reason why lawyers may want to borrow specifically from psychology, in particular in the field of consumer law. Most behavioural economics studies do not deal with interpersonal relations[50] and, when it comes to regulating marketing practices, the inter-personal dimension is significant, at least for some practices. The psychological insights reviewed in this article all come from social psychology and relate to interpersonal relations. These insights are typically not incorporated in a behavioural economic approach and yet they are worth exploring in their own right.

---

[45] Oliver 2013, p. 13.

[46] A better name is Law and Behavioural Sciences or 'Behavioural Analysis of Law', see Tor 2008 and his discussion on names for this approach at footnote 13. An important nuance between the two names is that 'Behavioural Analysis of Law' suggests that the law is the object of the behavioural analysis while the more neutral 'Law and Behavioural Sciences' allows for the possibility that the function of behavioural sciences may be to shed light on facts (rather than law), leaving it to legal analysis to decide whether and how this knowledge on facts could and should be incorporated. In my view, the part of the analysis consisting in connecting (any) scientific insights about facts to the law is not specifically behavioural.

[47] Hahneman, foreword to Mullainathan and Shafir, IX.

[48] ibid.

[49] Joule and Beauvois 2002. The book sold so well that it is reported to have saved Grenoble University Press from bankruptcy. Its title translates as 'Little Treatise of Manipulation for the Use of Honest People'.

[50] Micklitz et al. 2011, p. 273.

From a methodological standpoint, there is an additional reason to give precedence to psychology over behavioural economics.[51] Consider a legal scholar endowed with some rationality and who embraces a utilitarian perspective: she is willing to get acquainted with other disciplines but wishes to choose the path of her interdisciplinary excursion with care, so as to maximize the expected legal return of her journey. From such a vantage point, behavioural economics and psychology are competing destinations. For the consumer lawyer, they constitute imperfectly substitutable sources of wisdom on consumer behaviour. In this context, psychology appears to have one advantage over behavioural economics: it attempts to describe and explain cognitive and emotional processes that affect our choices, not to *model* behaviour. Because behavioural economics is a branch of economics and because contemporary economists are mostly in the business of modelling, behavioural economists can only relax the heroic hypotheses of neo-classical economics (the well-known rational consumer model) one by one.[52] If they drew simultaneously on all insights of psychology relating to how we actually behave, too many hypotheses needed for equations to "behave" would have to be relaxed at the same time and modelling would become impossible. Among economists—and some economically minded lawyers—this leads to the perception that behavioural economics is a "weak" theory, because it cannot produce an overarching framework of analysis comparable to that of general equilibrium. In other words, disciplinary identity affects the way in which economists borrow from the original source of wisdom about behaviour, i.e. psychology.

Lawyers in general and judges in particular are not concerned with modelling, hence they do not have a good reason to limit themselves to those insights of psychology, which are digestible by economists. This does not mean that the law can incorporate all the fine-grained analyses from psychology and, in particular, the full richness of studies on the context-dependent character of decision-making. Law also has a limited capacity to absorb external knowledge, but it has its own limitations, which are not the same as those of economics. Lawyers, therefore, should go shopping for science on their own and see for themselves what psychology has in store that could be of use to them.

5.1.8 Word Choice

The word "bias" is initially a statistical and value-neutral term, but, as psychological wisdom filtered through a layer of economics before reaching a wider audience, this word acquired a different connotation and an unpleasant normative undertone. It

---

[51] Thanks to Roberto Galbiati (an economist) for drawing my attention to this point by expressing so clearly his doubts about the wisdom of my choice.

[52] That behavioural economics is about modelling appears consensual. Altman 2012. The book opens with this sentence: "Behavioural economics is all about making our *economic models* [...] more rigorous and realistic, by building them on solid empirical foundations" (emphasis in the original). For an illustration of rewriting a branch of economic theory (industrial organization) relaxing the rationality hypothesis, see Spiegler 2011.

suggests—wrongly—that the norm from which reality deviates is the *homo oeconomicus*, the fiction neoclassical economists have invented to serve the mathematical needs of a science then in infancy.[53] It would make more sense to take humans rather than "econs" as a point of reference and acknowledge it in the words we use.[54] So-called "biases" are deviations to economists but, to the rest of the world, they constitute deeply rooted psychological realities that are best acknowledged as facts of life rather than judged harshly. It is hard to go against prevailing word use, but perhaps the more value-neutral "behavioural trait" or simply "trait" could be given a chance.

5.1.9 *Structure of this Paper*

Section 2 explains why psychology studies on social influence are relevant to EU consumer law on unfair practices. Section 3 deals with one channel of influence, which is of particular interest for legal purposes and which psychologists call "commitment". Section 4 envisages possible objections to importing psychological insights into legal decision-making processes, in particular court adjudication. Section 5 confronts legal typology of unfair practices to categories of psychology and finds that the partial mismatch opens interesting avenues for reasoning by analogy. Section 6 reflects on other possible legal uses of psychological insights in consumer law and finds that critical use and evidentiary use do not seem as valuable as the main interpretative use described in the previous sections. Finally, Section 7 contains concluding remarks.

5.2 Relevance of Social Psychology for EU Law on Unfair Practices

5.2.1 *Marketers Rely on Insights from Psychology and so Should Regulation of Marketing Practices*

Influence is the generic term used by psychologists to refer to all techniques that impact on someone's behaviour. The study of influencing techniques and of the different channels through which they work is part of social psychology, of which

[53] As Hausman explains, it is not because economics truly believed that humans were rational in the narrow sense they defined that they chose to base their theory on *homo oeconomicus*. Rather, it is because they wanted their science to be 'separate' and formalised that needed consumers preference to have certain properties, failing which the utility functions would not be (mathematically) 'well behaved' and it would be impossible to calculate an equilibrium. In particular, that they needed preference to be convex (which translates as diminishing marginal utility or 'the more apples you eat, the less pleasure you derive from an additional apple) and transitive (which translates as 'if you prefer pears to apples and apples to oranges, you prefer pear to oranges'). Hausman 1992, Chaps. 1 and 2.

[54] The phrase was coined by Thaler and Sunstein 2008, p. 6.

consumer psychology is a sub-branch. Because most of these mechanisms are unconscious, the subject under influence does not readily detect influencing techniques. This is why psychologists use the phrase "compliance without pressure".[55] Subjects under influence do not consciously feel manipulated because the succession of the two (or more) actions obeys a natural internal logic. Manipulation uses natural human tendencies by carefully choosing stimuli, which will, as a rule, induce predictable reactions. The sub-conscious nature of influence is the very reason why these techniques are so useful to marketers.[56] A refined understanding of emotional and cognitive processes makes it possible for marketers to devise more subtle, clever and effective ways to influence consumers. If, on the other hand, the law stays blind to the underlying logic of the very practices it seeks to regulate, it puts regulation of commercial practices at a cognitive disadvantage compared to regulatees. In fairness, the law as it stands cannot be described as completely blind to psychological mechanisms, but it is possibly short-sighted, because it relies on folk psychology rather than science.

5.2.2 Where Psychology Will not Help: Normative Indeterminacy in the UCPD

There is one aspect in the directive on unfair commercial practices with which psychology is unlikely to help: this is its normative indeterminacy.

The UCPD regulates marketing practices by way of both general and specific prohibitions. Article 5 gives a general definition of unfair practices (discussed below). Then articles 6 to 9 give definitions of particular categories of unfair practices: misleading practices (articles 6 and 7) and aggressive practices (Articles 8 and 9). The annex of the directive gives a list of 31 commercial practices deemed abusive in all circumstances. For these listed practices, there is no need to apply the general or semi-general definitions: they are prohibited *per se*. As explained by Advocate General Wals in his opinion in the *CHS* case, the structure of the directive favours an approach he calls "top-down", in fact one that starts with the most specific rules (black list) and then progresses as necessary towards the more general rules (provisions on misleading or aggressive practices) or, if they do not apply, to the general clause (article 5).[57]

---

[55] See e.g. Freedman and Fraser 1966.

[56] A number of studies on influencing techniques in commercial contexts have appeared in marketing journals rather than psychology journals. See e.g Anderson and Simester 2003. Studies published in psychology journals sometimes have a distinct marketing angle. See e.g. Aggarwal and Vaidyanathan 2002 or studies on effect of touching cited at footnote 70. Several authors quoted throughout this article work in marketing rather than psychology departments.Sub-conscious nature of influence does not mean of course that in cannot be observed. Indeed, neuromarketing, which has been developing in recent years, takes the study of purchasing decision a step further by literally observing, with the help of brain imaging techniques, how we react to different stimuli. For a good introduction to neuromarketing, see Lindstom 2008; Renvoisé and Morin 2007.

[57] Opinion in Case C-435/11, *CHS Tour*, NYR, para. 29. I am not sure if naming this approach "top down" is very evocative, but the description of the approach is clearly accurate and consensual.

Given this general structure of the assessment of commercial practices under the UCPD, it is particularly interesting to confront the notion of influence, as defined in psychology, with the general and semi-general legal definitions of unfair practices. The list of commercial practices that are prohibited *per se* can more profitably be read in connection with specific empirical studies (see below).

When reading the general legal definition, it is hard to understand which influencing techniques come within the scope of the general prohibition of unfair practices. Indeed, this definition is quite vague.[58] It reads as follows:[59]

> A commercial practice shall be unfair if:
> (a) it is contrary to the requirements of professional diligence, and
> (b) it materially distorts or is likely to materially distort the economic behaviour with regard to the product of the average consumer whom it reaches or to whom it is addressed, or of the average member of the group when a commercial practice is directed to a particular group of consumers.[60]

The second criterion used in this definition (material distortion of consumer behaviour in relation to a product) is clearly reminiscent of the notion of influence used in psychology. It should be stressed, however, that not all influence is prohibited, since influence is only one of two criteria for defining prohibited unfair practices. The other is that the commercial practice must be "contrary to professional diligence". The meaning of "professional diligence" remains unclear and may give rise to slightly divergent interpretation depending on the meaning of the closest notion under national law,[61] but the function assigned to this notion in the definition of unfair commercial practices is that of a limiting factor: only practices that are contrary to the standard of professional diligence are prohibited. If a trader acts "diligently", what he does to influence consumers is not unfair even if it is effective. Definitions and interpretive guidance given both at EU and at national level do not—and cannot—suppress the open-endedness of the concept.[62] "Professional diligence" is the locus of a largely indeterminate—normative judgement.

See UK guidance document: Department for Business Enterprise and Regulatory Reform (2008), p. 12.

[58] (Perceived) vagueness in the law is a feature that is conducive to imports from science—or extra-legal knowledge generally—into the law. On vagueness as a perceived (as opposed to intrinsic) feature of a text, see Black 1997, Chap. 1 (building on H.L.A. Hart). On vagueness as a pre-condition for porousness of the law, see Sibony 2010.

[59] UCPD, art. 2 paragraph 2.

[60] Emphasis added.

[61] Micklitz 2014, p. 91.

[62] Article 2 (h) of UCPD defines "professional diligence" as "the standard of special skill and care which a trader may reasonably be expected to exercise towards consumers which is commensurate with either—(a) honest market practice in the trader's field of activity, or (b) the general principle of good faith in the trader's field of activity". Commission Staff Working Document—Guidance on the Implementation/Application of Directive 2005/29/EC on Unfair Commercial Practices. In the UK, the OFT Guidance (cited at footnote 38) explains that "the word 'special' is not intended to require more than would reasonably be expected of a trader in their field of activity". The Commission' guidance notice does not attempt to further define or explain the standard of "professional diligence".

In a way, article 5 UCPD is a puzzling text: do diligent marketers not use the most apt and subtle techniques to influence consumers? Is it not the very purpose of their job to find ways to make us buy what we neither need nor want? On the other hand, is it not the very purpose of the directive to assert that not everything zealous marketers do is acceptable? Conceptually, "diligence" is a strange choice for expressing a normative judgement on commercial practices because it seems to refer to a norm for good and bad practices shared by a professional community. If, however, a business community is made up of professional manipulators, it is clear that the EU legislator should not embrace its norms in a consumer protection directive. In fact, the definition of "professional diligence" in the directive only makes sense in conjunction with European Codes of Conduct defining good practices. This was the original project of the Commission but the codes were never adopted.[63]

One way out of the normative conundrum posed by this incomplete text is to adopt a different reading of Article 5. Instead of reading "professional diligence" as meaning "diligence as understood by the professionals", one can hold it to mean "fairness as commonly understood". This is in essence how the OFT guidance recommends interpreting the provision: "poor current practice that is widespread in an industry/sector cannot amount to an acceptable objective standard. That is because this is not what a reasonable person would expect from a trader who is acting in accordance with honest market practice or good faith".[64] This certainly adds yet more indeterminacy to the law; it also makes the definition circular, as, under this reading, an unfair practice would essentially be defined as one that (a) is unfair and (b) effective. Circularity is not a very satisfying feature in a legal rule. Yet, at the same time, it accords with normative intuition better and allows courts to exclude from the scope of the prohibition a wide range of techniques often used in the commercial sphere and which are shown to materially influence consumers, but could not be said to be unfair in any socially acceptable sense. Such techniques presumably include (at least) smiling,[65] being polite with a consumer[66] and asking a consumer how she is doing.[67]

For many techniques, however, common sense and ordinary meaning of words are not sufficient guides.[68] Take, for example, the technique that consists in touching

[63] Micklitz 2014, p. 91.

[64] OFT Guidance, § 10.4, 47.

[65] Effect of smile has long been established. Tidd and Lockard 1978 (effect of smile of the waitress on tips). Outside of a commercial context, effect of smile on submission has also been documented. See Guéguen and Fischer-Lokou 2004. More recently, the effect of smile in online communication has also been explored (and found positive): Guéguen 2009, pp. 210–212.

[66] On this point, see Guéguen 2009, pp. 35–39.

[67] Just asking "how are you doing?" has a significant effect on response to a subsequent request. For an account of experiment on this "trick question", see Guéguen 2009, pp. 75–78.

[68] Referring to ordinary meaning of words is a classical technique of legal interpretation. However, when European law is at stake, the use of this technique is more difficult because of the plurality of languages in which the law (here the directive) is translated. Some words or phrases (here "professional diligence") may carry different connotations in different languages as well as different associations in different legal systems.

(barely) a consumer. Its use is surprisingly effective,[69] but is it "contrary to professional diligence" to instruct sales personnel to touch customers? Marketing ethics rather than psychology would probably be the appropriate source to turn to on these and similar issues. Whether it can provide precise guidance however is not clear,[70] nor is it obvious that it would be legitimate for enforcement authorities and courts to turn to marketers themselves as a source of knowledge on how to best regulate their conduct.

Psychology cannot readily help with normative issues, nor should it: outsourcing normative issues to science is not a commendable way for lawyers to use science.[71] This does not mean that behavioural studies could not play any role regarding difficult normative issues in the field of unfair commercial practices. Indeed, empirical studies could help identify what practices are *perceived* as unfair, but it would still be for courts, 'exercising their own faculty of judgement'[72] to determine whether and when they want to rely on the knowledge accumulated on normative judgements. What psychology, however, can help with at present is with the interpretation of the second criterion in the two-pronged test of article 5 UCPD, which require courts to assess whether a practice "materially distorts" the behaviour of the average consumer.

5.2.3 What Psychology Can Help With: 'Material Distortion of Consumer Behaviour' and 'Misleading Practices'

The UCPD is porous to insights from psychology because of three provisions in particular, all of which contain clear references to what psychologists call "influence". The first one has already been discussed: the general definition of unfair practices, in article 5 requires that practices "materially distorts" the behaviour of the average consumer in relation to a product. The second and third provision whose interpretation could benefit from psychological insights are the prohibition of "misleading actions" and "misleading omissions" (respectively articles 6 and 7 UCPD). It is clear from the wording of the definition of misleading actions that, through the criterion of deception, which is central, the EU legislator was trying to address a form of influence. The definition reads as follows:

[69] Several experiments have shown the influence of touch on consumer behaviour. In one experiment, consumers in a supermarket were offered slices of pizza to taste. If they took one, they were given a coupon and shown where the pizza could be found in the supermarket. The consumers who were touched were more likely to take the pizza and to purchase it than those who were only addressed verbally. Smithet al. 1982. In another experiment, waiters in a restaurant touched some of the consumers who were dining. Couples where one person was touched gave significantly higher tips than those were neither was touched. The effect of touch varied only very slightly according to sex (both of the diner and of the waiter). Hornik 1992.

[70] See Brenkert 2008, 27 et seq.

[71] Feldman 2009, pp. 13–14, 119.

[72] UCPD, recital 18.

> A commercial practice shall be regarded as misleading if it contains false information and is therefore untruthful or in any way, including overall presentation, deceives or is likely to deceive the average consumer, even if the information is factually correct, in relation to one or more of the following elements, and in either case causes or is likely to cause him to take a transactional decision that he would not have taken otherwise.[73]

In defining misleading practices, the directive also deals with influence caused by contextual factors, albeit only in two specific cases (confusion and violation of a code of conduct):

> A commercial practice shall also be regarded as misleading if, in its factual context, taking account of all its features and circumstances, it causes or is likely to cause the average consumer to take a transactional decision that he would not have taken otherwise, and it involves:
>
> (a) any marketing of a product, including comparative advertising, which creates confusion with any products, trademarks, trade names or other distinguishing marks of a competitor;
>
> (b) non-compliance by the trader with commitments contained in codes of conduct by which the trader has undertaken to be bound, where:
>
> (i) the commitment is not aspirational but is firm and is capable of being verified, and
>
> (ii) the trader indicates in a commercial practice that he is bound by the code.[74]

Even if contextual factors are explicitly referred to in connection with two rather specific hypotheses, this paragraph is interesting in that it invites courts to consider "all features and circumstances" of the factual context. This is precisely why this open-textured definition lends itself to taking insights from psychology into account. Though the Commission refers to behavioural economics rather than psychology,[75] this is recognized by its guidance notice, which reads: "The definition of a misleading action used in the Directive has taken into account the current state of knowledge of how consumers take decisions in the market space. For example, new insights from behavioural economics show that not only the content of the information provided, but also the way the information is presented can have a serious impact on how consumers respond to it. [...] It is then for the national courts and administrative authorities to assess the misleading character of commercial practices by reference, among other considerations, to the current state of scientific knowledge, including the most recent findings of behavioural economics".[76]

In line with this opening to behavioural insights, the directive contains explicit provisions to cover situations of practices, which are capable of deceiving

[73] Art. 6, paragraph 1. Emphasis added. This paragraph is followed by a list of items in relation to which information given to the consumer can be misleading: (a) the existence or nature of the product; (b) the main characteristics of the product [...], (c) the extent of the trader's commitments [...], (d) the price or the manner in which the price is calculated, or the existence of a specific price advantage; (e) the need for a service, part, replacement or repair; (f) the nature, attributes and rights of the trader [...]; (g) the consumer's rights [...] or the risks he may face.

[74] Art. 6, paragraph 2.

[75] See above Sect. 2.2.

[76] Commission Staff Working Document—Guidance on the Implementation/Application of Directive 2005/29/EC on Unfair Commercial Practices SEC (2009) 1666, hereinafter 'Guidance notice', 32.

consumers "in any way, including overall presentation", even if the information provided is factually correct. The examples given in the notice are default options, provision of unnecessarily complex information,[77] certain price comparisons,[78] "copycat packaging"[79] and misleading environmental claims.[80]

The directive further defines "misleading omissions", and, in this definition too, the key legal criterion is influence. The drafters of the directive used a somewhat more complex wording, requiring that the omission "causes the average consumer to take a transactional decision that he would not have taken otherwise". Yet, there seems to be no difference in meaning with article 6 or the notion of influence. However, the wording of article 7, unlike the previously quoted passages of article 6, contains an implicit reference to the model of a rational consumer. It is apparently assumed that the average consumer can process correctly information that is given to him. The definition of misleading omission reads as follows:

> A commercial practice shall be regarded as misleading if, in its factual context, taking account of all its features and circumstances and the limitations of the communication medium, it omits material information that the average consumer needs, according to the context, to take an informed transactional decision and thereby causes or is likely to cause the average consumer to take a transactional decision that he would not have taken otherwise.[81]

The provisions on misleading practices (articles 6 and 7) appear as a mix of pre-behavioural focus on the content of information and openness to behavioural insights on the context of information provision.[82] Although the guidance notice does not comment on this point, this provision also seems permeable to insights on circumstances in which missing information is likely to distort consumer behaviour.[83] This is true in particular of Article 7(2), which provides that information given "in an untimely manner", rather than omitted, can also be misleading.[84] The behavioural wisdom of this addition is beyond doubt as many influencing techniques crucially rely on the sequence in which information is given.[85] Some studies also show that timing, irrespective of sequence, may have an influence.[86]

---

[77] Guidance notice, 32.

[78] Guidance notice, 34.

[79] Guidance notice, 36.

[80] Guidance notice, 36.

[81] Art. 7, paragraph 1. Emphasis added.

[82] On the first aspect, see Micklitz 2014, p. 102.

[83] In this respect, we read the text of the directive as being more permeable to insights from psychology than Incardona and Poncibò indicate Incardona and Poncibò 2007, p. 33, referring to recital 18 of the directive and asking whether the admission that the average consumer must be appraised taking into account social, cultural and linguistic factors might allow courts to consider the average consumer as an emotional consumer rather than just a "reasonably well informed and reasonably observant and circumspect" consumer (the classical Court formula since case C210/996, *Gut Springenheide*, ECR[1998] I-4757, para. 31).

[84] Article 7, paragraph 2.

[85] These techniques, to which we return below in detail, include: low-ball, lure, "that's-not-all", foot-in-the-door, foot-in-the-mouth, fear and relief.

[86] Yoon and Danziger 2007.

Article 8 and 9 of the directive define "aggressive practices". Psychology may also be relevant to the application of those provisions, which centrally refer to "undue influence", but it is apparent that aggressive commercial practices are outside the scope of "compliance without pressure",[87] because they are precisely about exerting pressure on consumers. This is the reason why they will be left out of the present analysis, which is restricted to soft influence.

It is possible to conclude from the above cursory reading of the main definitions contained in the directive that there is substantive conceptual convergence between what the European legislator is trying to prohibit—practices that "causes the average consumer to take a transactional decision that he would not have taken otherwise"—and social influence, as studied by psychologists. Influence seems to be just another word for the type of conduct the directive is trying to catch, and this other word carries with it a wealth of accumulated empirical knowledge about what does influence people, including consumers. Studies on influencing techniques should therefore retain the attention of anyone trying to interpret or apply the directive on unfair practices. Psychological studies on influence, at least those which relate to a commercial context, are therefore relevant to help identify conducts which could fall under the general definition of an unfair practice.

5.2.4 How Can Psychology Help? An Analytical Guide to Influence

Psychology can help with understanding how influence works. Psychologists have identified several channels of influence. Cialdini classifies them in six categories.[88] First, there is reciprocation. According to a seemingly universal norm, we want to repay others for what they give to us (also if only apparent concessions).[89] Second, there is what psychologist call "commitment". This category is of particular interest for legal purposes and will be further developed in Section 4. The bottom line of commitment is that we have a nearly obsessive desire to be—and to appear—consistent with what we have already done. This tendency can easily be exploited because once we have chosen to behave in a certain way, we will experience personal and interpersonal pressures to behave consistently.[90] Third, "social proof" acts as a means of influence. This principle states that one means we use to determine what is an appropriate course of conduct is to find out what other people think is appropriate (e.g. laughing at a poor joke in a TV show).[91] Fourth, liking is a powerful influence channel. We simply prefer to accept requests when they come from someone

[87] This phrase is borrowed from Freedman and Fraser 1966.

[88] For a clear account, see Cialdini 2007 or Cialdini 2009, respectively at 18 et seq., 51 et seq., 97 et seq., 141 et seq., 174 et seq., 198 et seq.

[89] Cialdini 2007, pp. 17–21; Cialdini 2009, pp. 18–50.

[90] Cialdini 2007, pp. 57; Cialdini 2009, pp. 51–96.

[91] Cialdini 2007, pp. 116; Cialdini 2009, pp. 97–140.

we know and like. This principle may be used by strangers in a variety of ways to get us to comply with their requests (we tend to like physically attractive people, people which appear as similar to us).[92] Fifth, authority (or the mere appearance of authority) is also a channel of influence. It seems to be more difficult to refuse to do something when asked by someone displaying a form of authority (whether based on specialized knowledge, title, cloths) than to say no to someone who is not vested with particular authority (e.g., nurse as opposed to doctor, student as opposed to professor).[93] Finally, scarcity seems to be another thing that makes us tick. Offers seem more valuable to us when their availability is—or artificially seems to be—limited (e.g. "limited stock", "two-day special offer")[94] than when the same offer appears to be lasting.

We will return in Sect. 5 to the usefulness of this typology as a conceptual framework but before doing so, it is useful to illustrate in some detail the particular value of one item in this typology. The notion of commitment is of interest because it underlies several different influencing techniques, which may be used in a commercial context.

5.3 Commitment: A Notion Worth Borrowing from Psychology

5.3.1 The Notion

As is clear from the above, "commitment" is a *faux ami*: the word has a different meaning in psychologese and in legalese. For psychologists, it refers to the link between an individual and his/her acts,[95] not to an agreement or promise to do something in the future. More precisely, commitment is shaped by our internal drive for consistency. If we act in a certain way, we tend to prefer subsequent courses of actions that are consistent with this particular action.[96] This is why commitment is one powerful channel through which influence works: many influencing techniques induce internal commitment by first requiring from the subject an action, which has no other purpose than committing her and will therefore increase the likelihood of subsequently obtaining from her a target behaviour, which is consistent with the initial action.

[92] Cialdini 2007, pp. 167; Cialdini 2009, pp. 141–173.

[93] Cialdini 2007, pp. 208–220; Cialdini 2009, pp. 174–197.

[94] Cialdini 2007, pp. 238; Cialdini 2009, pp. 198–226.

[95] This definition was originally proposed by Kiesler in Kiesler 1971. See Joule and Beauvois 2002, pp. 74; Guéguen 2004, pp. 141.

[96] Cialdini 2007, at 67 writes: "Each of the strategies is intended to get us to take some action or make some statement that will trap us into later compliance through consistency pressure".

Psychologists have found that it is amazingly easy to induce commitment. It often takes only one act for a subject to feel committed. This act can be as apparently harmless as answering a short questionnaire, trying or tasting something for free or clicking on a web link.[97] A variety of circumstances have been shown to be conducive to commitment. Cialdini cites four influencing factors, not all of which need to be present for commitment to happen, but each of which facilitates commitment.[98] First, a "magical act" is helpful for the subject to feel internally committed. An example is where a consumer is asked to fill a form. Second, "the public eye" seems to be particularly important. We feel more committed by an act and for a longer time if we have performed it in the presence of at least one other person. Third, the cost of the initial act seems positively correlated to the intensity of commitment: the more costly (in time, attention or money) the initial conduct, the more we tend to stick to it (thus making mistakes more costly).[99] Fourth, we feel more committed if we perceive (even mistakenly) our initial behaviour as freely chosen. According to empirical studies, it is disarmingly easy to reinforce this feeling of freedom for the purposes of inducing commitment. It is enough to add "but of course, you are free to do otherwise" to enhance significantly your chances of obtaining what you want.[100] This mechanism seems to be so universal it even works over the internet, without face-to-face interaction.[101]

Besides these four factors highlighted by Cialdini, other authors point to further factors conducive to commitment: the number of occurences of the preliminary conduct (the more we have acted in a certain way, the more likely we are to want to act in a manner consistent with this series of acts), its irrevocable character, the subjective importance of the behaviour to the subject (we feel less committed if the act is unimportant to us), the feeling of responsibility (we feel more committed if we are personally responsible for setting a standard of conduct).[102]

---

[97] Joule and Beauvois 2002; Freedman and Fraser 1966.

[98] Cialdini 2007, pp. 67–103.

[99] A classical experiment in this regard is that of Arkes and Blumer 1985. In this experiment, students could sign up for two different week-end trips. For the first one, they had to pay $ 100 and only $ 50 for the second one, which was more appealing. It turns out that they have to choose between the two as both trips will be organized the same week-end. Having paid the non-refundable sum of $ 150, students should rationally choose the more appealing week-end. Yet, the majority chooses the more expensive trip. Joule and Beauvois 2002, at 41 generalize this result and explain that, in order to effectively trap someone in a spending spiral (what they call "abstruse trap" ("piège abscons" in the French original), the following conditions have to be met: (i) the subject must have decided to engage in some form of spending in order to reach a certain goal (e.g. wait for the night bus in order to get home); (ii) she must be uncertain as to whether the goal may be reached in this way (there may be no more busses tonight); (iii) the individual must feel that each additional spending (e.g. waiting longer rather than hailing a passing cab) will increase the probability of reaching the goal through the preferred means and (iv) the subject must not have initially set a limit to her spending (how long she would be ready to wait).

[100] Guéguen and Pascual 2000, 2002, 2005.

[101] Jacob et al. 2003.

[102] See e.g Joule and Beauvois 2002, pp. 74–78; Guéguen 2004, p. 168.

5.3.2 *Influencing Techniques Based on Commitment*

Several influencing techniques rely on commitment. Three of them have been extensively studied. In the jargon of social psychology, they are called "foot-in-the door", "low ball" and "lure".[103]

Foot-in-the door was initially shown to be effective by Freedman and Fraser in a seminal article of 1966.[104] This technique is sequential: in the first stage (priming), a small request is presented. Only after the request has been accepted and completed a second—larger request is made. In the initial experiment, American housewives were asked to answer a few questions about which soaps they used. A few days after they had agreed to answer the questionnaire, they were asked to allow a survey team of six men to come to their house and classify all cleaning products for two hours. This large request was accepted significantly more often if it had been preceded by the small request than if not.[105]

Low-ball is another sequential compliance technique. Here, a requester induces a subject to accept a request and only then reveals hidden costs of performing this behaviour. Experiments show that a requester who uses this technique obtains greater final compliance than a requester who informs directly subjects of the full costs of the target behaviour. In the experiment that gave rise to the seminal article on low ball, students were asked to participate in an experiment.[106] Some (control group) were told initially that this experiment would require their presence at the lab at 7 am. Others were told about this inconvenient time only after they had accepted to take part (low-ball condition). The result was that members of the second group generally did not take their word back, even though they might not have accepted if they had initially been informed that they would have to get up so early. In a more recent study on the same technique, authors have carried out a field experiment (i.e. they did not stage the experiment in a campus setting, which is practical for academics running the experiments but where there may be biases due to the fact that subjects are all students). People at the entrance of a hospital building were asked if they could mind a dog while the dog owner visited a patient. Only after they had accepted were they told that the visit would take about half-an-hour.[107] Again, it was shown that using the low ball technique was much more effective than asking people directly if they would mind a dog for half-an hour. The low-ball technique has also been studied in a commercial context, but, somewhat surprisingly, the study did not show it to be effective.[108] This, however, could be due to experimental design

[103] It should be noted here that one (isolated) study shed doubt on whether the efficacy of low ball actually rests on commitment: Burger and Petty 1981.

[104] Freedman and Fraser 1966.

[105] The study controlled for several factors and there were several variants in the scenarios used.

[106] Cialdini et al. 1978.

[107] Guéguen et al. 2002. In this study, as in the initial 1978 article, the authors controlled for gender effect and showed that there is none.

[108] Motes and Woodside 1979. Motes and Woodside used a promotional offer on nail polish bottles. Variations of a special offer were presented to female buyers in a department store (reduced price/reduced price for two/three bottles) and clients were then told that the reduced price was

and other experiments are needed before any conclusions can be drawn on the basis of only one study.

A third technique based on commitment is called lure. It consists in, firstly, leading a person to take the decision to engage in an advantageous behaviour and, then, informing her that circumstances have changed and the planned action can thus no longer take place. At this stage, an alternative, less advantageous course of action is suggested. This technique is similar to the low-ball technique in that both involve two decisions, one made before knowing the real cost of the target behaviour, and one after being informed of the same. The difference lies in the fact that, in low-ball, both decisions concern the same behaviour, which is made more costly, while in the lure technique, the decisions involve two distinct behaviours. Lure has been shown to be effective, initially in a non-commercial context,[109] and then in field experiments in a commercial context.[110]

5.3.3 Legal Relevance: Psychological Concepts as Building Material for Legal Tests

The above examples of manipulation techniques based on commitment show how versatile this influence channel is. This is precisely why the notion of commitment is valuable for the purposes of interpreting and applying the general clause of the unfair practices directive.[111] It has been pointed out that this general clause will rarely be needed because most common practices are dealt with under the list in the annex of the directive.[112] While this may be the case, it remains that rational marketers confronted with a *per se* prohibition of 31 commercial practices can reasonably be expected to design new techniques, which will not fall foul of the prohibition but will have a similar effect. Therefore, the broad and open textured definition of unfair practices contained in article 5 may be viewed as the safety net of consumer protection against manipulative commercial creativity. Because open textured notions are, as such, inherently hard to apply to facts directly, they call for intermediary

---

higher than initially announced. Clients did not buy significantly more nail polish than in the control condition, i.e. when initially informed about the correct promotional price.

[109] Joule et al. 1989. In this study, students are recruited to participate in a rather interesting and well-paid experiment. Once they have accepted, they are asked to come to the laboratory. There, they are informed that the interesting research has been completed, but that they can participate in another experiment, for which they will not be paid. The results show that subjects accept more often to take part in the unpaid experiment when this technique is used than when it is not.

[110] Guéguen and Jacob 2006. The authors placed a pair of shoes at a promotional price in a shoe shop window. When a consumer enters the shop and asks for her size, a salesperson explains that this size is no longer available, but presents a similar model, which is sold at the normal tag price. Using this technique, more pair of shoes are sold than in the absence of lure.

[111] European legal commentators commonly refer to the general definition of unfair practices contained in article 5 of the directive as the "general clause".

[112] Collins 2010, p. 97. According to Micklitz, the general clause only applies in 'extreme and obvious cases', Micklitz 2014, p. 95.

steps to be defined. Where statutory language is vague, notions borrowed from extra-legal sources of knowledge may be used to frame legal tests or sub-tests.[113] In antitrust law, economics serves as a source of such intermediary notions, which are then woven by courts into legal tests.[114] In the field of consumer law, psychology could, in much the same way as economics in the field of antitrust, be a source of inspiration for courts at the stage of designing legal sub-tests for the purposes of assessing whether a practice "materially distorts or is likely to materially distort the economic behaviour with regard to the product of the average consumer".

"Commitment"—as defined by psychologists—is a useful intermediary notion, because it may be helpful to ask "does this practice induce commitment"?—rather than "is this practice likely to materially distort the economic behaviour of the average consumer?" The first question seems somewhat less difficult to answer than the second one if one considers that there is a body of available knowledge on which it is possible to draw in order to identify relevant facts, namely the various factors which have been shown to be conducive to commitment.[115] Drawing on the insights from social psychology, courts could in particular consider whether a practice is sequential. Indeed, this is a common trait to all practices based on commitment, and seemingly a necessary one, as the priming phase is the one inducing commitment in view of the second phase. Courts may further ask if any commitment-inducing factors are present, such as leading the consumer to accept a request in the presence of others, stressing her freedom to say no, or somehow requiring her to incur a sunk cost, which is likely to lead to perseverance. In other words, what courts may borrow from psychology on commitment is an analytical grid.

It follows from the above that there are certainly contact points between the legal definitions of unfair practices under EU law and the notion of commitment used by psychologists to study manipulation. This proximity suggests that imports from psychology may be put to some meaningful legal use. It is however necessary to consider possible objections and to state a more precisely *how* notions such as commitment may be useful in the legal sphere.

5.4 The Value of Psychological Concepts for the Interpretation of Consumer Law

It could be objected that social psychology as a science is not robust enough to warrant legal use. This however does not seem a valid objection. The fact that research in social psychology may still progress and unveil other factors or add nuances

[113] We call "sub-tests" tests designed by courts in order to apply a broad legal test, such as that of article 5 of the directive. A sub-test in this context could be a criterion or an articulated series of criteria which courts would hold relevant for the purposes of appraising whether a commercial practice is misleading or otherwise unfair.

[114] Vesterdorf 2006 and Sibony 2008, p. 446 et seq.

[115] See Sect. 4.1.

to the relevance of certain factors which have as yet been shown to play a role in inducing commitment is not a reason to turn away from this source of wisdom on consumer behaviour. Four reasons support this claim.

Firstly, imperfect guidance is better than no guidance at all. Secondly, courts, by their very nature, have to adjudicate cases; they cannot wait for relevant science to be complete and have to take into account best available knowledge. Thirdly, science used in other fields of law where a need for external input is felt is not necessarily more robust than psychology. Indeed, economics, which is rather widely used in interpreting antitrust law, is well known for its fast pace of scientific innovations. It also has little claim to empirical validity.[116] From the point of view of view of scientific validity, psychology would certainly stand the comparison. Fourthly, scientific refinements, which constitute the substance of conversation within a scientific community, may simply not matter from the point of view of law. An example will help illustrate this point. A thorough study was conducted on a technique eloquently called "and-that's not-all".[117] As the name suggests, this technique consists in presenting an initial offer and then, without waiting for the addressee of the offer to accept or reject it, topping it up and offering an additional advantage (extra quantity of the same good or free item) or a reduced price. This technique is shown to be effective in various contexts, i.e. the second offer is significantly more often accepted when this technique is used than when presented directly. However, why this technique is effective was not clear. A series of seven experiments was designed to appraise competing explanations. This type of questioning about causality is certainly very interesting from a scientific point of view, but the results do not matter from a legal point of view. For a court of law, it does not matter *why* a commercial practice distorts behavioural patterns of consumers subjected to it, it suffices that the technique does significantly distort the average consumer's choice patterns.[118]

The same remark applies to other techniques. For example, the so called "door-in-the-face" technique, which is the opposite of "foot-in-the-door" in that it consists in first presenting a large request followed by a small one. When the first request is so costly that subjects are very likely to refuse, and do refuse before being presented with a smaller request, this technique has been shown to be effective. Yet, competing explanations have been presented: reciprocity was initially thought to be the underlying mechanism[119] and this is consistent with subsequent studies both in

[116] This deliberate choice is part of the disciplinary identity of modern economics. See Hausman 1992, Chap. 6 "The structure and strategy of economics".

[117] Burger 1986.

[118] This presupposes that experimental results may translate as a statement about how the "average consumer" behaves. At first sight, this transfer seems plausible, but this point may need further elaboration.

[119] Cialdini et al. 1975. In this study, the large request consisted asking the subject to volunteer to help delinquent juveniles for two years, the small request was to chaperon a group of underprivileged children for one visit to a zoo.

non-commercial[120] and in commercial context,[121] but scholars have also found that natural inclination to reciprocity does not explain the full effect of the door-in-the face technique and that additional explanations need to be considered.[122] One study finds results inconsistent with the reciprocity hypothesis.[123] Such debates are the essence of science. They do not mean that science is useless neither in general, nor for legal use in particular. This is because of the type of uses law can make of scientific insights. Again, for the purposes of appraising allegedly unfair commercial practices in the light of the general clause, judges need to know what influencing technique work, not why they work.

This remark is not in contradiction with the proposition that notions such as commitment, which name a causal mechanism, may be useful for courts. In fact, courts may use empirical and conceptual knowledge distributively. When there are convincing reasons, based on empirical studies, to believe that a given commercial practice does influence consumers, courts will not need to explore why this is the case and will be able to defer to scientific knowledge, provided it is considered robust enough, bearing in mind that the alternative is judges' own account of folk psychology. When this is not the case, effectiveness will not be presumed and will have to be established on the facts of the case. This is where having an analytical grid for factual appraisal will be helpful.

It remains of course to be seen whether European courts, who will have to interpret and apply the broad definition of unfair practices 'making use of their own wisdom'[124] will find insights from psychology worthy of consideration. It may be some time before it is possible to find out, because most cases will probably be dealt with under the *per se* prohibitions. Nevertheless, the conceptual delineation of channels of influence, and especially the analysis conducted under the heading of commitment seems a valuable input to structure judicial appraisal of complex facts where a practice is purported to be unfair under the general clause. Courts may also use empirical knowledge relating to effectiveness of various techniques, when it is robust enough, to justify a presumption of effectiveness of a given technique, whether or not causality is clear.

120 Pascual and Guéguen 2006. This study was staged in bars. A girl asked other consumers if they could pay for the drink her boyfriend had not paid before leaving the bar (explaining she didn't have enough money to pay his drink). After the subject refused, the girl asked for some change to contribute to the unpaid bill. The study showed that this works better than directly asking for change.

121 Mowen and Cialdini 1980. In this study, subjects were initially asked to participate in a survey and answer a long questionnaire (for up to two hours). After the subject had declined, the experimenter would make the second request (target behaviour), which consisted in completing a short survey of 15 min; Ebster and Neumayr 2008. This study took place in a mountain hut. When subjects passed by the entrance, they were approached by a female experimenter who invited them to buy some home-made cheese. Subjects were first asked to buy a piece of cheese weighing about two pounds and, after they declined, were proposed a piece of one pound.

122 Such as self-perception or authority of the person making the offer.

123 Millar 2002.

124 UCPD, recital 18.

As the majority of cases will be dealt with not under the general clause but under the list of *per se* prohibitions contained in the annex or under semi-general clauses (defining misleading and aggressive practices), it is necessary to turn to how psychological and legal typologies of influencing techniques relate to one another.

5.5 Unfair Practices Between Legal and Psychological Categorization: The Contribution of Psychology to Legally Valid Analogies

The directive distinguishes two categories of unfair practices: misleading and aggressive commercial practices. There is no indication that this is a complete typology. Indeed, paragraph 4 in article 5 states

> [i]n particular, commercial practices shall be unfair which:
> (a) are misleading as set out in Articles 6 and 7, or
> (b) are aggressive as set out in Articles 8 and 9.[125]

The text thus leaves open the possibility that a practice may be found unfair under the general clause even if it is neither misleading nor aggressive. Other categories of unfair practices could conceivably be recognized and this is an opening in the law to other categorisation emanating from psychology.

The legal classification is nevertheless structuring in the directive. The 31 practices listed in annex I of the directive, which are prohibited *per se*, are classified according to these categories. Out of 31, 23 are labelled misleading and eight fall under the category of aggressive practices.

Overall, the list of misleading practices displays a good fit with psychological categories. The prohibitions of bait advertising,[126] false allegation that a product will only be available for a short time[127] and false allegation that commercial premises are about to close[128] are entirely consistent with findings on the effect of perceived scarcity.[129] "Bait and switch",[130] which is also prohibited appears as a particular case of the broader category of "lure". Unannounced language switch (when after-sale service is only available in a language other than the language used to conclude the transaction) [131] is a hidden cost and therefore appears to resort to the category

125 Emphasis added.

126 Point 5 of the annex.

127 Point 7 of the annex.

128 Point 15 of the annex.

129 Cialdini 2007, p. 238; Cialdini 2009, pp. 198–226. The practice prohibited under point 18 of the annex could possibly also be linked to artificial creation of an impression of scarcity, but it is less clear.

130 Point 6 of the annex.

131 Prohibited under point 8 in the annex.

of low ball. The same may be said of the prohibition of false gifts (where the consumer must in fact incur a cost to retrieve the gift).[132] In all of these cases, specific prohibitions contained in the annex appear to relate to particular instances of what is understood (by psychologists) to be a single broader influencing mechanism. In all such cases, there is room for arguments such as "why forbid lure only in particular instances?". In other words, there is room for courts to reason by analogy and infer that other avatars of the same mechanism should fall under the general clause.

It should be noted that not all practices that are prohibited *per se* can be linked to influencing technique studied by psychologists. This is in particular true of practices, which were previously dealt with under the misleading advertising directive and consist in outright lies.[133] It also applies to other practices mentioned in the annex.[134] This does not detract from our point, which is not to assert that everything in the law of unfair practices is explained or justified by the findings of psychology. Rather, the point is that there are some instances of correspondence between legal and extra-legal categories. Indeed, it is because the fit is only partial that it is interesting from the point of view of enriching the law. Using the categories of psychology helps suggest analogies.[135] Of course, it remains for courts to decide whether an analogy is good enough to warrant extension of the prohibition from the black list to a prohibition under the general clause of article 5 or under the definition of misleading practices under article 6 or 7. In principle, this extension should not be automatic, as courts would need to check, under article 5, if the practice is "contrary to professional diligence". Under article 6 or 7 however, reasoning by analogy would seem to flow smoothly, as the conditions the court would need to assess in addition to the misleading effect are scope-defining (e.g. the prohibition is restricted to missing or misleading information *on certain aspects* of the transaction), but do not contain another substantive criterion.[136] There is therefore, under these provisions, a large room for reasoning by analogy with prohibited practices from the black list. Psychology provides the categories with regard to which the analogies may be made and this qualifies as an important contribution to the possible developments of the law.

---

[132] Point 20 of the annex.

[133] Council Directive 84/450/EEC concerning misleading and comparative advertising, OJ L 250, 19.9.1984, p. 17, amended by Directive 97/55/EC of the European Parliament and of the Council, OJ L 290, 23.10.1997, p. 18. These practices are listed under number 1 to 4 in the annex.

[134] Practices listed under points 9–14, 16, 17, 19 and 21–23.

[135] On the fundamental role of analogies in thought in general, see Hofstadter and Sander 2011.

[136] This point was already quite clear from the text of the directive, but was confirmed by the Court in *CHS Tour*. Case C-435/11, *CHS Tour*, NYR. In this case, Team 4 Travel, a tour operator who organized skiing trips in Austria had entered exclusive contracts with several accommodation providers. In its brochure, it mentioned that these accommodations were "exclusive" and explained the meaning of the term. In breach of the contracts with Team 4 Travel, some of the accommodation providers rented out rooms to a competing operator (CHS) during the exclusivity periods. This resulted in the brochure containing inaccurate information unbeknownst to Team 4 Travel. Before the Austrian courts, the question arose whether it could rely on its compliance with professional diligence to escape the prohibition of misleading practices under article 6 of the directive.

5.6 Insights from Psychology and Evidence

The legal uses of psychology discussed so far relate to interpretation of the law. In this type of use, concepts, distinctions, typologies are what the law borrows from psychology. The law, however, does not only need to be interpreted, it also needs to be applied. Psychology, for its part, offers countless empirical studies. Could it, then, be useful to the enforcement of consumer law not only at the conceptual/interpretive level but also at the factual/evidentiary level? To answer this question, two different types of evidentiary uses need to be distinguished: direct case-specific evidence and presumptions. While the first seems impractical and often unnecessary, the second appears worthy of courts' attention.

5.6.1 Direct Evidentiary Use of Psychology Studies

There are two reasons why it is not likely that empirical studies from psychology will be used as evidence in a specific case. The first is financial and the second pertains to the abstract type of appraisal favoured by the courts.

Consumer law cases are often small stake cases. This explains why they are not often litigated before courts. When they are, the party who wants to establish that a commercial practice is unfair, generally a consumer or a consumer association, bears the burden of proof.[137] These litigants will typically not have the necessary resources to hire and expert psychologist. This constraint is independent from the potential usefulness of expert testimony for the case. In this respect, use of psychology in consumer law litigation is very different from use of economics in antitrust litigation, where large corporations have the means and the incentives to hire experts. The lack of demand probably explains the lack of supply of specialized psychological experts in the field of consumer law. This is reinforced by the lack of demand for case-specific psychological expert evidence emanating from courts.

Courts are unlikely to need case-specific expert evidence for two related reasons. First, the standards they have to apply—be it the average consumer in general, the average consumer of a target group or of a group of vulnerable consumers[138]—all call for a rather abstract appraisal. Second, the legal test is not whether a commercial practice has in fact led a consumer to take a decision she would not otherwise

[137] In consumer law, the burden of proof is sometimes reversed, but it is not the case here. See Micklitz 2014, p. 121.

[138] Under article 5 (b), the test is whether a practice "materially distorts or is likely to materially distort the economic behaviour with regard to the product of the average consumer whom it reaches or to whom it is addressed, or of the *average member of the group* when a commercial practice is directed to a *particular group of consumers*". Under article 5(3), "Commercial practices which are likely to materially distort the economic behaviour only *of a clearly identifiable group of consumers who are particularly vulnerable* to the practice or the underlying product because of their mental or physical infirmity, age or credulity in a way which the trader could reasonably be expected to foresee, shall be assessed from the perspective of the average member of that group."

have taken; rather it is whether the practice has the potential to do so. How concretely should this potential be appraised? The guidance which can be derived from the case law of the Court of justice on this point is not entirely clear. On several occasions, the Court ruled out that a practice could be misleading for the average consumer based not on evidence but on its normative judgement.[139] When the Court does not rule out that a practice could be misleading, it leaves it to the national courts to obtain concrete evidence by way of survey or expert opinion.[140]

It is therefore possible that national courts will want data to help them appraise the effect of a given commercial practice on consumers. In such a case, it would seem both impractical and expensive to launch an empirical study. It seems more reasonable for a court to appoint an expert who can explain what can be inferred from the abundant existing literature that could be relevant to the court's appraisal. This seems a better course of action both practically and from the perspective of a sound use of science in legal proceedings. On any particular question regarding the effect of a practice, a serious psychologist is likely to explain that it depends from a variety of contextual factors. The Court will need a general answer. The finesse gap between the level of granularity common in empirical studies published in peer-reviewed psychology journals and the coarseness of the statement that will be helpful to a court of law will never be bridged by more empirical studies. The only sensible way to deal with it is to acknowledge the existence of this gap, discuss the relevance of scientific insights and decide what a legally acceptable generalisation is. A dialogue between the court and an expert or *amicus curiae* presenting a meta study based on existing science is much more apt to help the court than a case-specific empirical study even if one could be designed and paid for. In other words the evidentiary use of psychology (or any other behavioural science) that can meaningfully be contemplated is the admission of presumptions.

5.6.2 *Presumptions*

The first and foremost evidentiary use of psychology in unfair practices cases consists of presumptions. As outlined above, empirical evidence from psychology may serve as authority for courts to presume the distorting power of a commercial practice on consumer behaviour. However, for the reasons explained, it is unlikely that empirical studies will be used as evidence adduced by the parties to a trial. Rather,

[139] See the discussion in Micklitz 2014, pp. 98–100.

[140] See e.g. Case C-220/98, *Estée Lauder* [2000] ECR I-117, pp. 30–31: "Although, at first sight, the average consumer—reasonably well informed and reasonably observant and circumspect—ought not to expect a cream whose name incorporates the term 'lifting' to produce enduring effects, it nevertheless remains for the national court to determine, in the light of all the relevant factors, whether that is the position in this case. [...] it is for the national court—which may consider it necessary to commission an expert opinion or a survey of public opinion in order to clarify whether or not a promotional description or statement is misleading—to determine, in the light of its own national law, the percentage of consumers misled by that description or statement which would appear to it sufficiently significant to justify prohibiting its use".

courts could use the gist of such studies independently from whether parties rely on psychology to argue their case to inform their appraisal of what is the predictible effect of a given commercial practice on consumers. Presumptions are rebuttable, so that, if the science evolves in such a way as to show that a science-based presumption has become inacurate, it will be possible to rebut it.

The practical question is of course how courts might learn about insights from psychology that are relevant to the interpretation of UCPD. There are only two avenues for such transfer of knowledge to occur: parties' submissions and judges training. Parties could invoke psychology in their argument, in a general way, which is not the same as commissionning a case-specific study (the hypothesis considered in section 6.1) and is much less costly. It does not seem completely irrealistic to imagine such a development in the future. For example, BEUC, the federation of consumer associations at EU level, is showing a keen interest in behavioural sciences.[141] Alternatively or—preferably—cumulatively, Courts could be made more aware of the relevance of psychology for consumer law if specific trainings were organised. Such trainings exist in all Member States, sometimes with the involvement of EU institutions, such as Commission's programme for training sessions for judges applying competition law. In the same way as such continuing education progammes include elements of economics, relevant elements of psychology could be included in training modules on consumer law.

If courts were more aware of the relevance of consumer psychology for the interpretation and application of UCPD in particular and, possibly, of consumer law more generally, one question would still remain. While judge-made presumption constitutes a reasonable use of psychology, such use of science is not always transparent. In some European jurisdictions—as well as before the ECJ—[142] there is no procedural obligations for courts to hear an amicus curiae when they plan of relying on scientific input to inform their judgement. This is certainly regrettable as it is to be feared that, without appropriate procedures for bringing science into the courtroom, courts will either ignore science or rely on inadequate accounts of scientific findings. Procedures to check for good science are needed generally and will be needed in consumer law as well if the suggestions made in this article are to be followed.

Bibliography

Aggarwal, Praveen, and Rajiv Vaidyanathan. 2002. Use it or lose it: Purchase acceleration effects of time-limited promotions. *Journal of Consumer Behaviour* 2 (4): 393–403.

Altman, Morris. 2012. *Behavioural economics for dummies*. New York: Wiley.

[141] N. Helberger, Forms matter: Informing consumers effectively (report for BEUC), sept. 2013, http://www.beuc.org/publications/x2013_089_upa_form_matters_september_2013.pdf (last visited nov 3 2014)

[142] E. BARBIER DE LA SERRE & A.-L. SIBONY, 'Expert Evidence before the EC Courts', *Common Market Law Review*, 2008, 45(4), 941–985.

Anderson, E. T., and D. I. Simester. 2003. Effects of $9 price endings on retail sales: Evidence from field experiments. *Quantitative Marketing and Economics* 1:93–110.
Ariely, Dan. 2008. *Predictably irrational: The hidden forces that shape our decisions*. New York: Harper Perennial.
Ariely, Dan. 2010. *The upside of irrationality: The unexpected benefits of defying logic*. New York: Harper Collins.
Arkes, H. R., and Catherine Blumer. 1985. The psychology of sunk cost. *Organizational Behaviour and Human Decision Processes* 35:124–140.
Bar-Gill, Oren. 2012. *Seduction by contract: Law, economics and psychology in consumer markets*. Oxford: Oxford University Press.
Ben-Shahar, Omri, and C. E. Schneider. 2011. The failure of mandated disclosure. *University of Pennsylvania Law Review* 159:646–749.
Ben-Shahar, Omri, and C. E. Schneider. 2014. More than you wanted to know: The Failure of Mandated Disclosure. Princeton University Press.
Bisin, Alberto, and Kyle Hyndman. 2014. Present-bias, procrastination and deadlines in a field experiment, NBER Working Paper No. 19874.
Black, Julia. 1997. *Rules and regulators*. Oxford: Clarendon Press.
Brenkert, G. G. 2008. *Marketing ethics*. Boston: Blackwell.
Burger, J. M. 1986. Increasing compliance by improving the deal: The that's-not-all technique. *Journal of Personality and Social Psychology* 51 (2): 277–283.
Burger, J. M., and R. E. Petty. 1981. The low-ball compliance technique: Task or person commitment? *Journal of Personality and Social Psychology* 40 (3): 492–500.
Cialdini, R. B. 2007. *Influence: The psychology of persuasion*. New York: Harper Business.
Cialdini, R. B. 2009. *Influence: Science and practice*. London: Pearson International.
Cialdini, R. B., J. E. Vincent, S. K. Lewis, Jose Catalan, Diane Wheeler, and Betty Lee Darby. 1975. Reciprocal concessions procedure for inducing compliance: The door-in-the-face technique. *Journal of Personality and Social Psychology* 31 (2): 206–215.
Cialdini, R. B., J. T. Cacioppo, Rodney Bassett, and J. A. Miller. 1978. Low-ball procedure for producing compliance: Commitment then cost. *Journal of personality and Social Psychology* 36 (5): 463–476.
Ciriolo, Emanuele. 2011. Behavioural economics at the European Commission: Past, present and future. Oxera Agenda, 1–5.
Collins, Hugh. 2010. Harmonisation by example: European laws against unfair commercial practices. *Modern Law Review* 73:89–118.
Commission, *Guidance on the Implementation/Application of Directive 2005/29/EC on Unfair Commercial Practices*, Commission Staff Working Document, SEC (2009) 1666 ("Commission Guidance"). http://ec.europa.eu/justice/consumer-marketing/files/ucp_guidance_en.pdf.
Commission, *Applying Behavioural Insights To Policy-Making: Results, Promises and Limitations,* conference organised by DG SANCO on Sept 30 2013. http://ec.europa.eu/dgs/health_consumer/information_sources/consumer_affairs_events_en.htm. Accessed 12 Nov 2013.
Dawar, Niraj, and Philip Parker. 1994. Marketing universals: Consumers' use of brand name, price, physical appearance, and retailer reputation as signals of product quality. *The Journal of Marketing* 58:81–95.
Ebster, Claus, and Birgit Neumayr. 2008. Applying the door in the face compliance technique to retailing. *International Review of Retail, Distribution and Consumer Research* 18 (1): 121–128.
European Insurance and Occupational Pensions Authority (EIOPA). 24 January 2013. *Good practices on information provision for DC schemes—Enabling occupational DC scheme members to plan for retirement*, report, EIOPA—BoS 13/010. https://eiopa.europa.eu/publications/reports/index.html. Accessed 12 Nov 2013.
Feldman, Robin. 2009. *The role of science in law*. Oxford: Oxford University Press.
Franck, Jens-Uwe, and Kai Peter Purnhagen. 2014. Homo economicus, behavioural sciences, and economic regulation: On the concept of man in internal market regulation and its normative basis. In *Law and economics in Europe—Foundations and applications,* ed. Klaus Mathis, 329–362. Dordrecht: Springer.

Freedman, J. L., and S. C. Fraser. 1966. Compliance without pressure: The foot-in-the-door technique. *Journal of Personality and Social Psychology* 4:195–202.
Guéguen, Nicolas. 2004. *Psychologie de la manipulation et de la soumission*. Paris: Dunod.
Guéguen, Nicolas. 2009. *Psychologie du consommateur: Pour mieux comprendre comment on vous influence*. Paris: Dunod.
Guéguen, Nicolas, and Jacques Fischer-Lokou. 2004. Hitchhikerss' smiles and receipt of help. *Psychological reports* 94 (3): 756–760.
Guéguen, Nicolas, and Céline Jacob. 2006. La chaussure-leurre: Une application de la technique du leurre sur le comportement du consommateur, *12th AFM congress*, Nantes (France).
Guéguen, Nicolas, and Alexandre Pascual. 2000. Evocation of freedom and compliance: The 'but you are free of…' technique. *Current research in social psychology* 5 (18): 56–59.
Guéguen, Nicolas, and Alexandre Pascual. 2002. La technique du 'vous êtes libre de…': induction d'un sentiment de liberté et soumission à une requête ou le paradoxe d'une liberté manipulatrice. *Revue Internationale de Psychologie Sociale* 15:51–80.
Guéguen, Nicolas, and Alexandre Pascual. 2005. Improving the response rate to a street survey: An evaluation of the 'but you are free to accept or to refuse' technique. *The Psychological Record* 55:297–303.
Guéguen, Nicolas, Alexandre Pascual, and Lionel Dagot. 2002. Low-ball and compliance to a request: An application in a field setting. *Psychological Reports* 91:81–84.
Hausman, D. M. 1992. *The inexact and separate science of economics*. Cambridge: Cambridge University Press.
Hofstadter, D. R., and Emmanuel Sander. 2011. *Surface and essences*. New York: Basic Books.
Hornik, Jacob. 1992. Tactile stimulation and consumer response. *Journal of Consumer Research* 19:449–458.
Incardona, Rossella, and Cristina Poncibó. 2007. The average consumer, the unfair commercial practices directive, and the cognitive revolution. *Consum Policy* 30:21–38.
Jacob, Céline, Nicolas Guéguen, and Alexandre Pascual. 2003. Évocation sémantique de la liberté et sollicitation d'une requête sur internet: Analyse d'une nouvelle procédure d'influence du comportement de l'internaute. *Revue des Sciences de Gestion* 201–202:33–41.
Joule, Robert-Vincent, and Jean-Léon Beauvois. 2002. *Petit traité de manipulation à l'usage des honnêtes gens*. Grenoble: Presses Universitaires de Grenoble.
Joule, Robert-Vincent, Fabienne Gouilloux, and Florent Weber. 1989. The lure: A new compliance procedure. *Journal of Social Psychology* 129 (6): 741–749.
Kacen, J. J., and Julie Anne Lee. 2002. The influence of culture on consumer impulsive buying behaviour. *Journal of Consumer Psychology* 12 (2): 163–176.
Kahneman, Daniel. 2002. Maps of bounded rationality: A perspective on intuitive judgment and choice. http://www.nobelprize.org/nobel_prizes/economic-sciences/laureates/2002/kahneman-lecture.html (Accessed 15 Oct 2014) (Published as 'A perspective on judgment and choice: Mapping bounded rationality'. *American Psychologist* 58 (9): 697–720).
Kahneman, Daniel. 2011. *Thinking, fast and slow*. New York: Farrar, Strauss, Giroux.
Kahneman, Daniel, and Frederick Shane. 2002. Representativeness revisited: Attribute substitution in intuitive judgment. In *Heuristics and biases: The psychology of intuitive judgment*, ed. Thomas Gilovich, Dale Griffin, and Daniel Kahneman, 49–81. Cambridge: Cambridge University Press.
Kahneman, Daniel, and Amos Tversky. 1979. Prospect theory: An analysis of decision under risk. *Econometrica* 47:263–291.
Kiesler, C. A. 1971. *The psychology of commitment; experiments linking behaviour to belief*. Waltham: Academic.
Knutson, Brian, Scott Rick, G. E. Wimmer, Drazen Prelec, and George Loewenstein. 2007. Neural predictors of purchases. *Neuron* 53:147–156.
Laibson, David. 1997. Golden eggs and hyperbolic discounting. *Quarterly Journal of Economics* 112:443–477.
Lehrer, Jonah. 2010. *How we decide*. Boston: Mariner Books.
Lindstrom, Martin. 2008. *Buyology*. New York: Broadway Books.

Lissowska, Maria. 2011. Overview of behavioural economics elements in the OECD consumer policy toolkit'. *Journal of Consumer Policy* 34:393–398.
Lunn, Pete. 2014. *Regulatory policy and behavioural economics*. OECD Publishing: Paris.
Luth, Hanneke. 2010. *Behavioural economics in consumer policy: The economic analysis of standard terms in consumer contracts revisited*. Antwerp: Intersentia.
Maheswaran, Durairaj, and Sharon Shavitt. 2000. Issues and new directions in global consumer psychology. *Journal of Consumer Psychology* 9 (2): 59–66.
Mak, Vanessa. 2011. Standards of protection: In search of the 'average consumer' of EU law in the Proposal for a Consumer Rights Directive. *European Review of Private Law* 19:25–42.
Micklitz, Hans-Wolfgang. 2014. Unfair commercial practices and misleading advertising. In *European consumer law*, ed. Norbert Reich, Hans-Wolfgang Micklitz, Peter Rott, and Klaus Tonner, 67–123. Cambridge: Intersentia.
Micklitz, Hans-Wolfgang, L. A. Reisch, and Kornelia Hagen. 2011. An introduction to the special issue on "behavioural economics, consumer policy, and consumer law". *Journal of Consumer Policy* 34:271–276.
Millar, M. G. 2002. The effectiveness of the door-in-the-face compliance strategy on friends and stranger. *Journal of Social Psychology* 142 (3): 295–304.
Monin, Benoît. 2003. The warm glow heuristic: When liking leads to familiarity. *Journal of Personality and Social Psychology* 85 (6): 1035–1048.
Motes, W. H., and A. G. Woodside. 1979. Influence of low-balling on buyers compliance. *The Journal of Psychology* 101:219–221.
Mowen, J. C., and R. B. Cialdini. 1980. On implementing the door-in-the-face compliance technique in a business context. *Journal of Marketing Research* 17:253–258.
Mullainathan, Sendhil, and Eldar Shafir. 2013. *Scarcity: Why having too little means so much*. Times Books: New York.
Office of Fair Trading (OFT). 2007. Consumer protection from unfair trading regulations 2007 guidance—Draft guidance on the UK implementation of the Unfair Commercial Practices Directive, OFT931con. http://webarchive.nationalarchives.gov.uk/20140402142426/. Accessed 15 Oct 2014.
Oliver, Adam. 2013. *Behavioural public policy*. Cambridge: Cambridge University Press.
Pascual, Alexandre, and Nicolas Guéguen. 2006. Door-in-the-face technique and monetary solicitation: An evaluation in a field setting. *Perceptual and Motor Skills* 103:974–978.
Purnhagen, Kai Peter. 2014. Social market economy is not an oxymoron: Why EU internal market law has always been behavioural. In *European perspectives on behavioural law and economics*, ed. Klaus Mathis. Dordrecht: Springer. (In this volume).
Quigley, Murieann, and Elen Stokes. 2014. Nudging and evidence-based policy in Europe: On normative legitimacy and effectiveness. In *Nudging and the law: A European perspective*, eds. Alberto Alemanno and Anne-Lise Sibony. Oxford University Press. (Forthcoming).
Reich, Norbert, and Hans-Wolfgang Micklitz. 2014. Economic law, consumer interests and EU integration. In *European consumer law*, eds. Norbert Reich, Hans-Wolfgang Micklitz, Peter Rott, and Klaus Tonner, 1–65. Cambridge: Intersentia.
Renvoisé, Patrick, and Christophe Morin. 2007. *Neuromarketing: Understanding the "buy button" in your consumer's brain*. Nashville: T. Nelson.
Scholes, Annette Nordhausen. 2012. Behavioural economics and the autonomous consumer. *Cambridge Yearbook of European Legal Studies* 14:297–324.
Shafir, Eldar. 2013. Introduction. In *The behavioural foundations of public policy*, ed. Shafir Eldar. Princeton: Princeton University Press.
Sibony, Anne-Lise. 2008. *Le juge et le raisonnement économique en droit de la concurrence*. Paris: LGDJ, coll. Droit et économie.
Sibony, Anne-Lise. 2010. La porosité du droit: À propos des relations du droit avec d'autres disciplines, *Revue de la Faculté de Droit de l'Université de Liège*, 271–278. http://hdl.handle.net/2268/34788.

Sibony, Anne-Lise. 2012a. La preuve scientifique évitée: Inventaire de quelques techniques judiciaires. In *Preuve scientifique, preuve juridique,* ed. Eve Thruilhé-Marengo, 161–180. De Boeck & Larcier: Bruxelles. http://hdl.handle.net/2268/142713. Accessed 15 Oct 2014.
Sibony, Anne-Lise. 2012b. Limits of imports from economics into competition law. In *The global limits of competition law,* eds. Ioannis Lianos and D. D. Sokol, 39–53. Stanford: Stanford University Press. http://hdl.handle.net/2268/122755. Accessed 15 Oct 2014.
Sibony, Anne-Lise. 2013. Ving Sverge. In *Landmark cases of EU consumer law—In honour of Jules Stuyck,* ed. Terryn Evelyn, Colaert Veerle, and Straetmans Gert, 471–492. Antwerp: Intersentia.
Smits, J. M. 2006. European private law: A plea for a spontaneous legal order. In *European integration and law,* eds. M. C. Deirdre, M. S. Jan, Klip Andre, and J. A. McCahery, 55–107. Antwerpen: Intersentia.
Smith, D. E., J. A. Gier, and F. N. Willis. 1982. Interpersonal touch and compliance with a marketing request. *Basic and Applied Social Psychology* 3:35–38.
Spiegler, Ran, 2011. *Bounded rationality and industrial organization.* Oxford: Oxford University Press.
Stuyck, Jules, Evelyn Terryn, and Tom van Dyck. 2006. Confidence through fairness? The new directive on unfair business-to-consumer practices in the internal market. *CMLRev* 43:107.
Sunstein, C. R. 2013. *Simpler: The future of government.* New York: Simon and Schuster.
Thaler, R. H., and C. R. Sunstein. 2008. *Nudge: Improving decisions about health, wealth, and happiness.* London: Yale University Press.
Tidd, K. L., and J. S. Lockard. 1978. Monetary significance of the affiliative smile: A case of reciprocal altruism. *Bulletin of the Psychonomic Society* 11 (6): 344–346.
Tor, Avishalom. 2008. The methodology of the behavioral analysis of law. *Haifa Law Review* 4:237.
Tor, Avishalom. 2013. Some challenges facing a behaviorally-informed approach to the directive on unfair commercial practices. In *Unfair commercial practices: The long road to harmonized law enforcement,* ed. Tihamér Tóth. Pázmány Press: Budapest.
Trzaskowski, Jan. 2011. Behavioural economics, neuroscience, and the unfair commercial practises (sic.) Directive. *Journal of Consumer Policy* 34:377–392.
UK guidance document: Department for Business Enterprise and Regulatory Reform. (2008). Guidance on the UK Regulations (May 2008) implementing the Unfair Commercial Practices Directive ("OFT Guidance"). https://www.gov.uk/government/uploads/system/uploads/attachment_data/file/284442/oft1008.pdf. Accessed 15 Oct 2014.
Vesterdorf, Bo. 2006 Economics in courts: Reflections on the role of judges in assessing economic theories and evidence in the modernised competition law regime. In *Liber Amicorum in Honour of Sven Norberg: A European for all seasons*, eds. Martin Johansson, Nils Wahl, and Ulf Bernitz, 505–524. Bruxelles: Bruylant.
Weatherill, Stephen. 2007. Who is the average consumer? In *The regulation of unfair commercial practices under EC Directive 2005/29,* eds. Stephen Weatherill and Ulf Bernitz, 115–138. Oxford: Hart Publishing.
Weatherill, Stephen. 2013. *EU consumer law and policy.* Cheltenham: Edward Elgar Publishing.
Yoon, Carolyn, M. P. Lee, and Shai Danziger. 2007. The effects of optimal time of day on persuasion processes in older adults. *Psychology and Marketing* 24 (5): 475–495.

Anne-Lise Sibony Liège. Professor of European Law at the University of Liège. Director of Institut d'Etudes Juridiques Européennes (IEJE). Boulevard du Rectorat, 3, Bât. B33, B-4000 Liège, Belgium. Tel: +32 4 366 30 25; Fax: +32 4 366 31 55. alsibony@ulg.ac.be. Fields of Interest: EU Law (Competition Law, Consumer Law, Internal Market), Law and Behavioural Sciences.

Chapter 6
Buttons, Boxes, Ticks, and Trust

On the Narrow Limits of Consumer Choice

Martin Engel and Johanna Stark

Abstract Consumers shall be considerate and responsible, have the necessary information available and choose from a vast array of goods whatever best satisfies their needs. The ideal understanding of the European consumer relies on splendid supply and sound choice. Whereas the supply of goods and services in the Union as well as in most Member States is impressive, consumer choice in form of B2C contracts is a weak point. Sure enough, choosing contractual options and agreeing to proposed conditions has definitely become fancier in the digital age. Customers tick appealing boxes with green checkmarks and hit stylish buttons to plot a way through the conclusion of a contract. At the same time, choices have not become easier at all as traders and legislators have come to know how to expertly strike the keys of choice architecture. Thus, how much of contemporary consumer choice does in fact match the ideal of considerate and responsible decisions? Examining three examples of how relevant information is presented to consumers in order to contribute to their "empowerment", we come to the conclusion that the current EU consumer policies fail, at least occasionally, to take into account key lessons that cognitive psychology and behavioural law and economics have taught us over the past decades. We conclude by giving an outline of how the current strategies could be amended so as to make them more effective towards the overall goals of consumer empowerment and consumer confidence.

M. Engel (✉) · J. Stark
Center for International Law, University of Munich, Veterinaerstrasse, 5
80539 Munich, Germany
e-mail: martin.engel@jura.uni-muenchen.de

J. Stark
e-mail: johanna.stark@jura.uni-muenchen.de

K. Mathis (ed.), *European Perspectives on Behavioural Law and Economics*,
Economic Analysis of Law in European Legal Scholarship 2,
DOI 10.1007/978-3-319-11635-8_6

6.1 Introduction

Within the last decade, European consumer law has changed fundamentally. Initiated by the European Union, Member States have widely harmonized their consumer contract laws and introduced a number of new rights guarding consumers against undue influence on their contractual decisions. The right to withdraw from a distance selling contract is one of the most visible aspects of this development, which eventually aims at strengthening consumer confidence in a reliable single market.[1] Correspondingly, the EU obliges traders to provide comprehensive information on the condition and structure of traded goods, on applicable consumer rights, and lately even on consumer rights enforcement.[2]

Whereas consumer law, particularly in Germany, traditionally leaned towards protecting the vulnerable consumer[3], recent legislative strategies prescribed by the European Union have taken the approach of so-called *consumer empowerment*.[4] Consumers are perceived as responsible people, who lack information but are otherwise well able to decide on their own. The EU envisions a truly well-informed, responsible, and confident consumer.[5] In this vein, it is thought to be appropriate to establish mandatory information duties for traders and choice mechanisms for consumers aiming at enabling consumers to make well-informed and thus better decisions. The focus is on building an adequate basis for consumer decision-making while imposing information costs unilaterally on the trader.

Behavioural economics tell us that the marginal value of information is descending—and in fact is doing so quite rapidly, eventually even turning negative.[6] This sets factual boundaries to the concept of consumer empowerment: The ideal of a consumer prudently deciding on the basis of complete information comes with costs that are prohibitively high. The real consumer is not a trained lawyer, and even

[1] See Recital (6) of the Consumer Rights Directive 2011/83/EU.

[2] See, e.g., Chapters II and III of the Consumer Rights Directive 2011/83/EU and Art. 13 of the Directive 2013/11/EU on consumer ADR.

[3] As Howells 2005, p. 359 points out, "[v]ulnerable consumers are seen as atypical consumers ... whose needs should not get in the way of deregulation and liberalization to benefit the 'average' consumer". See Waddington 2013 on the tension between vulnerable consumers and EU consumer law.

[4] See the Commission Staff Working Paper "Consumer Empowerment in the EU", SEC(2011) 469 final, Art. 2 of the proposed Regulation on a Consumer Programme 2014–2020 (COM(2011) 707 final), and the EU agenda at http://ec.europa.eu/consumers/consumer_empowerment/index_en.htm: „The main objective of the EU Consumer Policy Strategy is to empower EU consumers through: Choice; Information; Awareness of consumer rights and means of redress.“ Consumer Empowerment in the Member States is even measured by a "Consumer Empowerment Index"; Nardo et al. 2011. See also de Hoon and Mak 2011.

[5] E.g., COM (2007) 99, 4: „Europe's consumers are the lifeblood of the European economy. Confident, informed and empowered consumers are the motor of economic evolution. "The three main goals of EU consumer policy articulated on the same page are: (1) empowerment through information and market transparency; (2) enhancing consumer welfare regarding price, choice, quality and safety of products; (3) effective protection from serious risks and threats.

[6] Nelson 1970; Wein 2001, p. 81.

lawyers are challenged with the complexity of their contractual decisions. Hence, it is crucial for legislators to develop coherent strategies on how to deal with the factual limitations of consumer information.

This paper gives three examples of how consumer empowerment is taking place today and assesses whether the current strategies stand any chance of reaching their professed goals. The first example deals with information on issues such as Terms and Conditions, which consumers have to confirm attention of before being able to proceed with a particular transaction. The second policy to be discussed is the provision of multiple contractual options, e.g., with regard to the applicable law. The last example is about consumer decisions on complex contracts involving prior advice originating from the trader's side. We conclude with a short sketch of the advantages to be gained from a consumer law that takes into account where consumers actually stand and what their capacities and limitations are.

6.2 Ticking Boxes

One of the most common ways to provide the consumer with information on the legal conditions of a distance selling contract is to provide a link to a lengthy document or webpage and let customers confirm that they have read it and agree to it.

6.2.1 Coping with Contract Complexity

The average European online shopper has probably ticked off several hundreds, if not thousands of checkboxes throughout his life. Only few contracts go without these extra boxes. One particular type of tickmark has recently been addressed in the Consumer Rights Directive 2011/83/EU: For any add-ons to the core contract matter that trigger additional costs—travel insurance, snow tyres for a rental car, or a seat reservation in a train–traders need the express consent of the consumer. This consent is only binding if it was not inferred by using default options which the consumer would have been required to reject in order to avoid the additional payment. Thus, in the future, "no add-on" will be the default switch.[7]

Whereas this ticking payment bomb has now been defused by the EU, another checkbox problem has not been solved, namely boxes consumers have to check in order to confirm they have taken notice of information on extra conditions of the contract. Consumers are regularly asked to actively confirm that they accept the General Terms and Conditions of a trader or a trading platform. They have to sign off that they are aware of the risks of their investment or the product they are about to buy.

[7] Art. 22 of the Consumer Rights Directive 2011/83/EU. See also the new EU nudging policy, announced by the Directorate General for Health and Consumers; http://ec.europa.eu/consumers/behavioural_economics/index_en.htm.

To check the respective box or provide a confirming signature is an absolute condition to entering into the contract. The terms are non-negotiable;[8] the only alternative for the consumer is to walk away and contract with someone else—most likely under similar conditions. The phenomenon of squeezing a huge load of terms or disclosures into a small "tickable" box is a means of coping with contract complexity arising out of the trader's—perfectly rational—wish to fulfil his information duties as well as enjoy minimal obligations against his counterpart.

6.2.2 *Blind Ticking*

Judging from formalities alone, agreement on contract conditions by checkbox confirmation makes provisions for future impairments and gets the approval of both parties. However, from the confirmation tick alone one should not jump to the conclusion that consumers actually know the content of these provisions and positively agree to them. Instead, they only agree not to stand a chance in negotiating them. What in fact happens is that traders pull the terms as much in their direction as they can, anticipating that—as opposed to altering the price of the product or shipping costs, for example—this will not hurt the chances of consumers concluding the contract.[9]

Given that consumers know it will require a substantial investment of their time and energy to understand the "small print"[10] and that there is no way to negotiate it, they will not even waste their time to read it. Instead, they tick off the box and deliberately rely on the legislator to save them at least from the most unfortunate and inappropriate terms. Of course, if at least a few consumers read the small print and succeed to raise the awareness of many others, consumers in general may profit.[11] However, other than very few large players like Facebook or Instagram, the vast majority of traders will never see their terms be publicly contested: public control widely fails.[12]

The information level of the consumer thus remains low as he is rationally apathetic as to the legal conditions the trader has unilaterally laid down: In most cases, he will rather ignore disadvantageous terms and buy the item than worry about them. The box he has to check in passing may only take a second at the time, but in sum for all transactions carried out, these boxes will be worth a couple of hours, if

[8] The authors of this contribution once tried to negotiate on the applicable law to an Amazon purchase; an attempt that had to fail and indeed failed.

[9] Korobkin 2003, pp. 1205–1206, 1217–1244; Becher 2007, pp. 170–173.

[10] Hadfield et al. 1998, p. 146.

[11] Howells 2005, pp. 356–357.

[12] Ayres and Schwartz 2014, p. 547 report several telling (and humorous) examples of the extent to which standard contract terms go unnoticed, such as: A company named Gamestation in 2010 included in its terms and condition a clause committing consumers to "sell their souls", with 700 people checking the respective tickbox, having noticed nothing.

not a working day—simply for confirming knowledge and understanding of something that will never be read, understood, or questioned.

6.2.3 *Limits of Information Processing*

The view of the mechanically ticking consumer furnishes a vivid example how limited consumers' capacity to proceed information indeed is. The point where the value of information becomes negative is reached as soon as this information goes beyond the very core subject matter of the contract. The consumer is certainly interested in which piece of furniture he is about to buy. Most likely, he will also give thought to shipping expenses and may even consider to buy an add-on like a wood care product or a cleaning cloth. But as long as he can evade to be convened with contract conditions such as details of cancellation or statutes of limitation he will squander nary a thought on any of those issues. The problem is thus not only about information the average consumer *cannot* process,[13] but about information the average consumer *reasonably does not* process.

Admittedly, the European Union does not ask Member States to make consumers explicitly agree to standard terms of traders. Unlike a common belief, the tick boxes are not directly required by law but only used by traders to preserve evidence of the consumer having considered the respective terms or cancellation conditions.[14] However, by burdening the trader with immense information duties[15] and by allowing her to unilaterally set contractual terms within a certain corridor the legislator sets large requirements and notable incentives to increase contract complexity.

The ideal of a consumer prudently deciding on the basis of complete information thus comes along with costs that are prohibitively high. This sets narrow factual boundaries to the concept of consumer empowerment. Even though this is not a particularly new finding, the EU still follows a policy of excessive consumer information that unfortunately confuses consumer confirmation with considerate consumer decision.

6.3 Hitting Buttons

Sometimes, consumers do not face a Hobson's choice as is the case with sellers' standard terms that are in fact unnegotiable. There are contracts concluding which consumers may have two or more real alternatives to choose from.

[13] See, among many others, Malhotra 1982 as well as Howells 2005, pp. 359–360.

[14] For example, in German civil law, § 305 (2) BGB requires traders to clearly display their terms and conditions but does not require any form of express consent by the consumer.

[15] Art. 6 Consumer Rights Directive 2011/83/EU.

6.3.1 Creating Alternatives

When alternatives or variations are provided as *add-ons* to the contract this is mostly accomplished with checkable boxes.[16] In contrast, choice options which relate to *contract conditions* are increasingly provided for by buttons. The latter ones turn out to be far more problematic as they materialize only in the future and the rational consumer thus often does not care about them.[17] The first example of such a button choice in online sales was introduced by the eBay starbust PayPal advertising their payment system with a pretty PayPal button. This button is still in place and it is indeed harmless as the fees charged by PayPal are already taken into account by the trader.[18] There are other cases, however, where hitting one or the other button involves costs or other consequences that the consumer cannot assess at all.

One of them is the blue button that has been proposed as an "entrance gate" for the application of the envisioned Common European Sales Law (CESL).[19] In late 2011, the European Commission presented a draft version of a so-called optional instrument—intended to be an optional alternative to the national sales laws of the Member States, which consumers would choose by pushing a fancy[20] blue button with yellow stars before closing the contract.[21] A similar choice is subject to the proposed optional instrument in European Insurance Contract Law.[22]

6.3.2 Consumer Choice as the New Paradigm of EU Consumer Law

In a way, the draft CESL was an attempt to "paypalize" European contract law.[23] However, details of how the CESL would be chosen by whom were left unclear by the Commission's proposal, particularly by the "chapeau rules" on the CESL's application.[24] Open questions are whether traders would be required to offer the "blue

[16] See Sect. 6.2.1 above.

[17] The fact that the consumer does not care is a consequence of the behavioural phenomenon of hyperbolic discounting; see Strotz 1955–1956, p. 165; Laibson 1997.

[18] Indirectly, they are, of course, passed on to and taken into account by the consumer via the pricing mechanism; however, the PayPal button is unobjectionable even under Art. 22 of the Consumer Rights Directive as even the consumer has budgeted the passed-on PayPal fee when hitting the button.

[19] COM(2011) 635 final, following Schulte-Nölke 2007, pp. 348–349.

[20] The nattiness of the button is not to be underestimated: Bagchi and Cheema 2013, p. 948 have found out that blue background colour makes a buyer rather agree to a contract than red background colour; the study has indeed not tested the effects of confirmation buttons, however, a similar correlation is plausible. See also Bellizzi and Hite 1992, p. 347.

[21] See Sect. 6.2.1 above.

[22] Basedow 2014; Heiss and Lakhan 2011.

[23] Engel and Stark 2013, p. 337.

[24] Micklitz 2012, p. 290 convincingly argues that the choice would be rather the seller's.

button"[25] and thus to contract on the basis of the CESL, and what would happen in case a consumer declines to opt into the European regime.[26] What would be the default solution? The contract law stated in the trader's Terms and Conditions? The contract law of the consumer's place of residence? No contract at all?

Only in the third case could the CESL contribute to one of the paramount goals professed in the preparatory documents, i.e., reconciling a high level of consumer protection with reduced transaction costs particularly for small and medium enterprises engaged in cross-border distance selling. Transaction costs in a scenario in which the trader would have to offer the CESL option but could not deny to contract with a consumer that does not take him up on this offer would be significant: He would have to be prepared to contract on at least two different legal bases at any time—hardly a cost-saving situation.

In the alternative scenario in which no opt-in into the CESL regime would also mean no contract, talk of the consumer having a real choice appears euphemistic at best. Opt-in would then be as unavoidable as agreeing to Terms and Conditions is now. To sum up: If the CESL is meant to contribute to consumer empowerment by increasing meaningful consumer choices, the rules determining when and how it would come to be applied must be designed so as to reflect this goal (i.e. conclusion of contract not dependent on opt-in). Competing objectives, such as saving transaction costs for businesses, should be treated as such. Pretending to achieve both by offering consumers a choice not worth the name does not advance consumer empowerment at all.

6.3.3 Choice Overload and Rational Incompetence

Just as consumers can be overloaded and eventually confused by too much information that cannot be properly processed, a similar situation can arise when they are given more choice options than they can competently assess and compare or when the complexity of the available options is overwhelming. Such "choice overload" may even lead to consumers trying to avoid a then complicated choice situation altogether or making a random move.[27] This is one of the reasons that explain and intensify the phenomenon of "sticky defaults"[28]—people tending to not depart from a default choice situation, for fear of making a worse choice on their own.[29] Means

---

[25] For the marketing effect of European symbols see MPI for Comparative and International Law 2011, p. 404.

[26] Eidenmüller, Jansen, Kieninger, Wagner and Zimmermann 2012, p. 321, advocating a choice in favour of the CESL to be allowed in standard terms.

[27] See Shafir 2008, p. 304 as well as Iyengar and Lepper 2000, describing a study in which shoppers were offered to try either 6 or 24 different kinds of jam in a supermarket. Of those who tasted one of the 6 jams offered, 30 % continued to buy one, as opposed to only 3 % of those who chose between 24 jams.

[28] Ayres 1999, p. 907.

[29] Ben-Shahar and Pottow 2006, p. 651; Ayres 2012, pp. 2084–2095.

could be found, of course, to not let consumers stick to a "default choice of law" when presented with the CESL option, e.g. by requiring them to hit one button or the other, or otherwise not to be able to conclude the contract. This would raise costs for consumers to completely avoid the choice (having to find another trader who offers a deal without a choice requirement), but it would not solve the problem of choice overload itself.

The button solution aims at "nudging"[30] consumers to choose a reliable sales law, uniformly applicable throughout the whole European Union and offering a relatively high level of consumer protection. It is unlikely that the average consumer will rudimentarily comprehend the difference between various sales laws,[31] as even lawyers struggle to name the advantages and disadvantages of one or the other. Relying on the fact that consumers would "decide" on the CESL by pushing the button would amount to taking this choice for what it is not. Rather than being based on the qualitative merits of the chosen contract law regime, the decision would be influenced by the layout of the button,[32] the success of the Commission's marketing strategies, or the lack of alternatives to conclude a contract with the particular seller (see 3.2 above).

As in the PayPal case, the EU plans to actually advertise its own law against the respective national law of the trader. However, together with the unpredictable costs, the advertisement mechanism results in consumer selection now being a significantly influenced choice.[33] Without question, the idea behind the button is noble: Consumers shall have more options to choose from, make responsible choices and be better off. They shall step up from the weak to the empowered person. In the eyes of the Commission, the CESL could even work as a role model for other fields of law: Thoughts on an optional instrument in European insurance contract law are already underway.[34] Other fields of law might follow. However, as long as the people making such choices lack an adequate understanding of what they are doing, the fairer policy would be to rule on the subject so that consumers are neither squeezed by traders nor by their own arbitrary choices.

---

[30] To borrow a term from Thaler and Sunstein 2009.

[31] Sefton-Green 2011, pp. 143–144.

[32] See above sect. 2.

[33] The EU strategy also fails to take into account the details of who is making which choices in this process: Leaving aside the until now unsolved questions of how exactly the CESL would be chosen, it will presumably always come down to the fact that the seller will first decide whether he offers to contract on that basis and if he does, it will be worth it for him only if the consumer agrees to that offer, which he will probably do because he expects he cannot bargain with the distant seller about this aspect of the contract.

[34] See above sect. 2.

6.4 Sales and Advice

The first two examples have dealt with problems of consumer empowerment strategies particularly in the legal rules on distance selling. The last example deals with the possibilities of consumer empowerment by information, especially in situations of personal interaction between consumer and trader and his representatives, regarding not primarily the quantity and presentation of information, but the trustworthiness of its sources.

6.4.1 Making the Consumer Understand

Many contractual decisions by consumers are complex—which product is most suitable to their set of preferences depends on many parameters. When contracting on private pension provisions, for example, the best choice for consumers depends on how much money they will need to be paid by the pension, how much money they will be able to put into the scheme over the next years, how much flexibility or security is needed, etc. All these questions may best be answered by someone who has expert knowledge on the options available, comparative chances and risks associated with these options, and is able to guard consumers against falling prey to cognitive biases such as overconfidence regarding their future financial capacities.

In order to cope with this situation, complex consumer contracts often integrate a product sales component with some form of pre-contractual advice from the seller. Ideally, when the contractual decision—whether on a financial investment or a new family car—is rather complex in its structure, the trader first honestly advises on which product best fits the needs of the consumer and then sells the product. In the best of cases, the consumer thus understands which product he prefers and subsequently makes an informed choice.

However, it is only in an ideal world that such advice is given by someone with nothing but the consumer's best interest in mind, who has no self-interest in whatever follows from the advice given.

6.4.2 Advising vs. Advertising

In reality, bank counsellors, car dealers, insurance agents, and other sellers and their representatives are quite keen on the subject matter they advise on because of remuneration mechanisms: The more expensive the product they recommend the more advantageous a contract will be for them. As a result, pre-contractual advice will not be directed towards the best interests of the principal, but will at least partially be driven by the interests of the advising agent. The proper name for such activity, however, is not advice, but advertising. In that case, information given to the consumer does not aim at impartially weighing advantages and risks of a contract against one another and relating them to the preferences and circumstances of the particular consumer.

Sure enough, sellers have and shall have every right to advertise their products. It is necessary and perfectly legitimate for them to try to be as successful as possible. The problem is that, in many cases, the advertising component comes in the disguise of impartial advice and that consumers tend to misunderstand it as such. By calling themselves "advisors" instead of "sellers", traders further complicate the problem. The result is that with regard to some complex products, consumers tend to not anecdotally but systematically end up with contracts that, in hindsight, prove not to match their interests very well. This is the case, for example, with financial products such as private pension and insurance schemes with long-term consequences for consumers.[35]

6.4.3 Contextuality and Reciprocity

The insight that whoever gives information on or about something usually has their own interests in mind and that this is relevant in the context of pre-contractual dealings between consumers and traders is neither new nor revolutionary nor has it been originally discovered by cognitive psychologists. However, behavioural economics based on cognitive psychology demonstrate how this problem is aggravated when consumer empowerment is crucially based on the idea of the reasonable, well-informed, or at least easily informable consumer with stable preferences. Acting as a source of information before the conclusion of a contract enables sellers to actively utilize consumers' behavioural tendencies to perceive and process information in their favour.

Such behavioural tendencies are manifold and for sellers quite easy to predict: We tend to place high weight on the short-term dimension of our decisions and relatively low weight on their long-term consequences.[36] Thus, when being advised on financial products, progressive payment plans that place large shares of the overall financial commitment in the rather distant future will often meet with open ears of consumers concentrating on relatively low immediate obligations.[37] With such overconfidence in their future financial abilities, consumers may end up entering into contracts they do not need and later have to sell or terminate at significant cost.[38]

Framing and anchoring effects are names for the fact that we perceive information about a product depending on the way it is presented to us, for example in comparison to other products, contractual options, or even other random numbers.[39]

[35] Mak 2012, pp. 262–263 thus argues for more differentiation in consumer law: Whether consumers should be allowed to conclude complex financial contracts should depend on their financial literacy.

[36] See e.g. Laibson 1997.

[37] On the example of mobile phone pricing plans marketed to (US) consumers Grubb 2009, thus explaining the use of proportionately high "late fees" and "teaser rates".

[38] Ulen 2001, p 117, 128.

[39] Tversky and Kahneman 1974, pp. 1128–1130.

By comparing a product to alternatives that are much more expensive, for example, it is easy to create the impression that it has a rather reasonable price. Clever traders, quite understandably, will not begin advising a customer by informing him about the standard model of a product with a comparatively low price. These behavioural tendencies do not arise out of our inability to process a sheer amount of information, but of distortive influences on how we perceive information and what we make of it.

Another problem is that we are also subject to biases that involve what may be termed a "social" component and that influence our behaviour particularly in situations of personal interaction with others. Behavioural studies have, for example, well documented a tendency of people to behave reciprocally to a counterpart.[40] Thus, the car-dealer who is offering you some coffee or a toy to your children rarely does so out of altruism. He knows perfectly well that when given something, people tend to feel that it is adequate to give something in return, whatever that may be. In the middle of the decision process whether to buy the new car at this dealer, now or at some later time, the reciprocity effect just described may work to his favour. Unconsciously, it may add that little bit of an incentive needed to make someone sign the contract immediately instead of disappointing perceived expectations of reciprocity by taking a few more days to think about it.

The upshot of our tendency to behave reciprocally is that when consumers and traders interact personally, the effects are rarely limited to exchange of information and communication of preferences. The stage of pre-contractual advice, be it deserving of the name or not, is crucial as it bears a chance for the trader to offer a kind of advance service, in the hope that his efforts will be recognized reciprocally by the consumer. Of course, no one will buy a car or an insurance he does not want at all simply because he was offered a free cup of coffee.

Whether traders' practices that play on the above described biases and the tendency to meet (perceived) social expectations of reciprocity deserve to be described as manipulative depends on how extensive and with what motives in mind they are applied. It may also help to distinguish between two ways in which traders can utilize the reciprocity mechanism: First, offering advice to the consumer serves as a trigger of the reciprocity mechanism; second, seemingly small favours such as a coffee or other drink are intensifiers, blurring the adversary characteristics of the B2C-relationship and emphasising advisory features instead. Whereas the average consumer will at least occasionally be able to identify the coffee as a reciprocity trigger, the trigger of a sales commission which turns advice to advertising will normally be overlooked. It may thus depend on the visibility of the reciprocity trigger whether we perceive a certain sales activity as tolerable advertisement or unfair[41] trick.

---

[40] See Cialdini 2006, Ch. 2; Falk and Fischbacher 2006; Fehr and Gächter 2000.

[41] Speaking of fairness invites thinking of Rawls 1999 [1975]: When trying to decide whether a social practice is unfair enough as to warrant a legislative reaction, the veil of ignorance may be put to good use. The idea, put very simply, is that if behind such a veil—i.e., without information as to what role one would play in the scenario in question—we would have reason to object on grounds of fairness, we have reason to try to prevent such practices in the real world as well.

6.5 Complexity Reduced, Confidence Increased

In the end, the problems with the strategies of consumer empowerment that we have illustrated all come down to the fact that consumers are far less able to cope with the complexity of their contractual decisions than the law currently presupposes: They are unable to process the sheer amount of information they are presented with (Section 6.2), they are incompetent with regard to many of the choices that the law expects them to make to their own benefit (Section 6.3), and they tend to fall prey to social biases in situations where advisory and sales components of a complex contract are not clearly separated (Section 6.4). As discussed above, consumers' behavioural propensities hinder the satisfaction of their preferences. Ignoring information offered to them leads to consumers blindly accepting Terms and Conditions that may not reflect their preferences at all. Relying on advice while failing to acknowledge the preferences and incentives informing such advice as well as the social biases that influence our interactions with others has similar effects.

It cannot be expected that modelling consumer empowerment strategies along the lines of the behavioural sciences would lead to perfectly well informed consumers with optimal decisions over night. Nevertheless, taking these findings into account may help alleviate the above described problems, at least to some extent. What would a behavioural law and economics approach to consumer law require of the European legislator? Three examples shall be sketched shortly in the following.

6.5.1 Less Individual Information, More Mandatory Law

With regard to the countless boxes ticked by consumers rather in passing than with the effect of increasing their state of information, the legislator might consider an alternative in order to not only save tick time but also simplify the legal situation in case of impairment of performance.[42] This might be done by largely voiding terms and conditions in consumer contracts and instead referring the contracting parties to the mandatory rules of the applicable substantive law.[43]

This would lessen complexity by leaving less room for individual arrangements, thereby reducing the need for individualized information. If the consumer's and seller's rights were always the same, consumers might eventually come to know and understand this sole catalogue of basic rights and duties. In case a certain industrial sector needs special rules this could be provided for in special statutes. Such an approach would supersede the explication of cancellation and liability policies

[42] Thus, legal policy should not only moderate expectations on information strategies, as Howell 2005, pp. 362–364, suggests. Policy makers rather have to be aware of the fact that information overkill may actually materially disadvantage the consumer. This calls for more than cautious information policies, i.e. it argues for an active policy of information reduction.

[43] Howells 2005, p. 356 follows a similar but more cautious argumentation stating that information will at least not hurt the consumer. In favor of mandatory law as a response to consumers' bounded rationality also Korobkin 2003(fn. 9), pp. 1244–1247.

because they would then be widely the same, e.g., for all consumer distance selling contracts. It would also free significant resources on the part of the traders as they could save a lot of time and legal efforts which are spent preparing terms and conditions valid under the current law today. And for what it is worth, it would also be more honest as to the policy instruments the EU is using to eventually harmonize the substantive sales laws of its Member States.[44]

An important caveat is in place here: By saying that the issue of complex terms and conditions may be solved in part by creating uniformly applicable mandatory law, of course, nothing is said about the appropriate level of protection that these mandatory laws should provide. This is an entirely different question.

It would be unfair to accuse the EU of entirely neglecting the potential of the behavioural sciences as a tool for making regulation of consumer affairs more effective. In fact, behavioural law and economics has been taken up as a subject by the Directorate General for Health and Consumers, as acclaimed on its website and evidenced by major conferences held every two years.[45] A closer look at the activities, however, raises doubts as to whether the Directorate's claim to be "incorporating behavioural economics in [its] policy work" is as realistic as it prima facie sounds. This may be illustrated by Article 6 of the Consumer Rights Directive[46] in which traders' duties of information are stated. The norm in itself counts more than 1000 words, divided into 30 (sub)sections. Among these is Art. 6 No. 1 (i) stating that the consumer is to be informed that he will have to bear shipping costs in case of withdrawal. If the trader fails to inform on this, he will have to bear shipping costs himself. Details as to how this information is to be presented to the consumer are not given except that it must be "in a clear and comprehensible manner" (Art. 6 No. 1), in practice most likely hidden behind another ticking box. With the above discussion of consumers' behavioural tendency to not even read, let alone understand such information, the norm does not make much sense. If traders shall be exempt from having to bear return shipping costs, the behaviourally informed solution

[44] This is especially true for the CESL: Instead of proposing an optional instrument to bring the consumer into power the EU could also have aimed for the harmonization of the 28 sales laws of its member states. The Commission indeed considered this alternative but eventually rejected it because of the unanimity requirement of Art. 352 TFEU. As most of the member states' sales laws stand in a long legal tradition it was highly unlikely that an agreement on their total harmonization resulting in a unified European sales law or even civil code could be achieved in the near future. Thus, the creation of the optional instrument was a trick to pass by the TFEU process of considerate harmonization by "sneaking in" a 29th sales law through the back door of vertical regulatory competition, fancily advertise the European competitor it with a posh button, and operate for factual harmonization by consumers always "choosing" the European law. What seems like a smart political move, however, turns out as a circumvention of the principle of conferral. The genuine process here would be either to change the unanimity requirement laid down in Art. 352 TFEU or campaign for unanimity.

[45] See http://ec.europa.eu/consumers/behavioural_economics/index_en.htm with additional information on the conferences in 2008, 2010 and 2013. A look at the list of participants, however, creates the impression that the purpose of these gatherings is rather for representatives of EU institutions to meet and greet with industry and lobby groups.

[46] 2011/83/EU, to be implemented by 13.6.2014.

would have been a straightforward rule to this effect, instead of again adding to the excessive pile of information duties that have shown to be ineffective.

6.5.2 Less Choice of Law, More Enforcement of Rights

The idea that the consumer should make an informed decision on the substantial law best suited for his interests is riddled with problems.[47] The average consumer is not a trained lawyer, and treating him as one does not help his empowerment at all.

If the goal is to help consumers by creating a legal environment that is worth for them to be familiar with, it would be more promising to concentrate not on modifications of substantive law or even choice between different substantive law regimes, but on easing the enforcement of whatever consumer rights there are by creating simple and fast procedures for small consumer claims. This is something that consumers do in fact pay attention to and that they take into account when deciding where to buy, according to which legal conditions. The new EU regulation on online dispute resolution for consumer disputes[48], for example, is a step in the right direction.

If the EU really aims at advancing competent consumer decisions the Commission would be well advised to reduce optionalities to cases consumers can entirely comprehend. Consumer attention regularly stops right beyond the product being purchased. Consumers have no interest whatsoever in Terms, Conditions, the applicable law, or future contingencies. Thus, options for the product or service itself can be regarded as perfectly suitable but any other option will not be seriously considered.

6.5.3 Less Bundling, More Incentive Transparency

Considering the biases in information processing and the influence of social norms that partly determine consumer decisions, the legislator would do better to legally separate sales and advice, thereby supporting incentive transparency. Given that advice to consumers has to come from somewhere, it would be prudent to significantly strengthen the financial, legal, and political capacities of information intermediaries such as consumer organizations and their impartial advice services.

This being a rather political decision on the allocation of resources and competences to these intermediaries, attention should also be paid to what can be achieved by regulating the interaction of trader and consumer when the contractual setting calls for advice. Measures aimed at incentive transparency include a mandatory

[47] See Section 3.3 above.

[48] Regulation (EU) No 524/2013. The accompanying Directive 2013/11/EU on consumer ADR, however, raises serious doubts as to the efficiency of rights enforcement and consumer access to justice; see Eidenmüller and Engel 2014.

grammatical separation of sales and advice, i.e., not calling insurance agents "advisors".[49] Appearing to be a minimal change at first, the behavioural implications of such labelling should not be underestimated.

Furthermore, indirect remuneration schemes (i.e. commissions, bonuses, and other incentives) should have to be disclosed and mixed forms of remuneration that supplement direct fee arrangements with commissions should be prohibited.

6.6 Conclusion

We have sketched several ways in which the law could be revised so as to better account for the cognitive limitations and consequent behavioural tendencies of consumers, by reducing complexity or by helping them deal with it more effectively, e.g., by making incentives of their counterparts more transparent. Summing up the lessons from the examples and coping strategies discussed above: What is to be gained from paying more attention to the findings of the behavioural sciences of the last decades when drafting and revising EU consumer regulation?

The idea is that the rationales behind the goal of consumer empowerment are not just to make life easier for consumers and harder for traders, but that empowered consumers will be more confident consumers, eventually to the benefit of both sides. Such confidence, in turn, may lead to consumers more actively contributing to a well-functioning internal market as their confidence ideally bridges the spatial distance between both contracting parties.[50]

While asking the European legislator not to neglect the numerous insights of the behavioural sciences, it is important not to overestimate their significance as well. Behavioural economics tell us how people tend to react in particular situations, how they typically deal with information, and in which ways their behaviour departs from the assumptions of neoclassical economics. These findings thus enable impact assessments in the field of consumer law to be more precise, and consumer regulation to be more effective in reaching its professed goals. These goals, however, such as the overall objective of consumer empowerment or the level of protection arising out of this objective, are political in nature, not behavioural.

Bibliography

Ayres, Ian. 1999. Empire or residue: Competing visions of the contractual canon. *Florida State University Law Review* 26 (4): 897–912.

Ayres, Ian. 2012. Regulating opt-out: An economic theory of altering rules. *Yale Law Journal* 121 (8): 2032–2116.

[49] Similar suggestions were made by Rehberg 2005, p. 1015.

[50] Eurostat 2009, pp. 50–54; Flash Eurobarometer 358, pp. 23–32.

Ayres, Ian, and Alan Schwartz. 2014. The no-reading problem in consumer contract law. *Stanford Law Review* 66 (3): 545–610.

Bagchi, Rajesh, and Amar Cheema. 2013. The effect of red background color on willingness-to-pay: The moderating role of selling mechanism. *Journal of Consumer Research* 39 (5): 947–960.

Basedow, Jürgen. 2014. Versicherungsvertragsrecht als Markthindernis. *Europäische Zeitschrift für Wirtschaftsrecht* 25 (1): 1–2.

Becher, Shmuel I. 2007. Behavioral science and consumer standard form contracts. *Louisiana Law Review* 68 (1): 117–179.

Bellizzi, Joseph A., and Robert E. Hite. 1992. Environmental color, consumer feelings, and purchase likelihood. *Psychology & Marketing* 9 (5): 347–363.

Ben-Shahar, Omri, and John A. E. Pottow. 2006. On the stickiness of default rules. *Florida State University Law Review* 33 (3): 651–682.

de Hoon, Machteld, and Vanessa Mak. 2011. Consumer empowerment strategies—a rights-oriented versus a needs-oriented approach. *Zeitschrift für Europäisches Privatrecht* 22 (3): 518–532.

Eidenmüller, Horst, and Martin Engel. 2014. Against false settlement: Designing efficient consumer rights enforcement systems in Europe. *Ohio State Journal on Dispute Resolution* 29 (3), 261–297.

Eidenmüller, Horst, Nils Jansen, Eva-Maria Kieninger, Gerhard Wagner, and Reinhard Zimmermann. 2012. The proposal for a regulation on a common European sales law: Deficits of the most recent textual layer of European contract law. *Edinburgh Law Review* 16 (3): 301–357.

Engel, Martin, and Johanna Stark. 2013. The CESL as a European brand—PayPalizing European contract law. In *Regulatory competition in contract law and dispute resolution*, ed. Horst Eidenmüller, 337–346. Munich: Beck.

European Commission. 2013. *Flash eurobarometer 358–consumer attitudes towards cross-border trade and consumer protection*. Brussels: European Union.

Eurostat. 2009. *Consumers in Europe*. Luxemburg: European Communities.

Falk, Armin, and Urs Fischbacher. 2006. A theory of reciprocity. *Games and Economic Behavior* 54 (2): 293–315.

Fehr, Ernst, and Simon Gächter. 2000. Fairness and retaliation: The economics of reciprocity. *Journal of Economic Perspectives* 14 (3): 159–181.

Grubb, Michael D. 2009. Selling to overconfident consumers. *American Economic Review* 99 (5): 1770–1807.

Hadfield, Gillian K., Robert Howse, and Michael J. Trebilcock. 1998. Information-based principles for rethinking consumer protection policy. *Journal of Consumer Policy* 21 (2): 131–169.

Heiss, Helmut, and Mandeep Lakhan, eds. 2011. *Principles of European insurance contract law: A model optional instrument*. Munich: Sellier.

Howells, Geraint. 2005. The potential and limits of consumer empowerment by information. *Journal of Law and Society* 32 (3): 349–370.

Iyengar, Sheena S., and Mark R. Lepper. 2000. When choice is demotivating: Can one desire too much of a good thing? *Journal of Personality and Social Psychology* 79 (6): 995–1006.

Korobkin, Russell. 2003. Bounded rationality, standard form contracts, and unscionability. *University of Chicago Law Review* 70 (4): 1203–1295.

Laibson, David. 1997. Golden eggs and hyperbolic discounting. *The Quarterly Journal of Economics* 112 (2): 443–477.

Max Planck Institute for Comparative and International Private Law. 2011. Policy options for progress towards a european contract law. comments on the issues raised in the green paper from the commission of 1 July 2010, COM (2010) 348 final. *RabelsZ* 75 (2): 371–438.

Mak, Vanessa. 2012. The myth of the 'Empowered Consumer': Lessons from financial literacy studies. *Journal of European Consumer and Market Law* 1 (4): 254–263.

Malhotra, Naresh K. 1982. Information load and consumer decision making. *Journal of Consumer Research* 8 (4): 419–430.

Micklitz, Hans-Wolfgang. 2012. The expulsion of the concept of protection from the consumer law and the return of social elements in the civil law: A bittersweet polemic. *Journal of Consumer Policy* 35 (3): 283–296.
Nardo, Michela, Massimo Loi, Rossana Rosati, and Anna Manca. 2011. *The consumer empowerment index*. Luxembourg: European Union.
Nelson, Phillip. 1970. Information and consumer behavior. *Journal of Political Economy* 78 (2): 311–329.
Rawls, John. 1999 [1975]. *A theory of justice*. Cambridge: Harvard University Press.
Rehberg, Markus. 2005. Transparenz beim Vertrieb von Finanzprodukten—Das Konzept der Kompensation mangelnder Produkt-durch Statustransparenz vor dem Hintergrund der aktuellen europäischen Rechtsentwicklung. *WM Zeitschrift für Wirtschafts-und Bankrecht* 68 (22): 1011–1019.
Schulte-Nölke, Hans. 2007. EC law on the formation of contract—from the common frame of reference to the 'Blue Button'. *European Review of Contract Law* 3 (3): 332–349.
Sefton-Green, Ruth. 2011. Choice, certainty and diversity: Why more is less. *European Review of Contract Law* 7 (2): 134–150.
Shafir, Eldar. 2008. A behavioural perspective on consumer protection. *Competition & Consumer Law Journal* 15 (3): 302–317.
Strotz, Robert H. 1955–1956. Myopia and inconsistency in dynamic utility maximization. *The Review of Economic Studies* 23 (3): 165–180.
Thaler, Richard H., and Cass R. Sunstein. 2009. *Nudge. Improving decisions about health, wealth, and happiness*. New York: Penguin.
Tversky, Amos, and Daniel Kahneman. 1974. Judgment under uncertainty: Heuristics and biases. *Science* 185: 1124–1131.
Ulen, Thomas S. 2001. Information in the market economy—cognitive errors and legal correctives. In *Party autonomy and the role of information in the internal market*, eds. Stefan Grundmann, Wolfgang Kerber, and Stephen Weatherill. 98–129. Berlin: de Gruyter.
Waddington, Lisa. 2013. Vulnerable and confused: The protection of "Vulnerable" consumers under EU law. *European Law Review* 38 (6): 757–782.
Wein, Thomas. 2001. Information problems and market failure: The perspective of economics. In *Party autonomy and the role of information in the internal market*, eds. Stefan Grundmann, Wolfgang Kerber, and Stephen Weatherill. 80–97. Berlin: de Gruyter.

Dr. Martin Engel. Munich. Post-doctoral researcher, Center for International Law, University of Munich. D-80539 Munich, Veterinaerstrasse 5, Tel. +49 (0)89 21 80-20 23. martin.engel@jura.uni-muenchen.de. Fields of Interest: Law of Civil Procedure, Consumer Law, Law and Economics, Legal Profession.

M.Phil. Johanna Stark Munich. Ph.D. Candidate. Center for International Law, University of Munich. D-80539 Munich, Veterinaerstrasse 5, Tel. +49 (0)89 21 80-20 23. johanna.stark@jura.uni-muenchen.de. Fields of Interest: Legal Theory and Philosophy, Law and Economics, European Private Law, Consumer Law.

Chapter 7
Loss Aversion, Omission Bias and the Civil Standard of Proof

Mark Schweizer

Abstract This article shows how insights from cognitive psychology, namely loss aversion, omission bias and status quo bias, explain the intuitive appeal of a standard of proof in civil cases that is considerably higher than the "preponderance of the evidence" or "balance of probabilities" standard employed by Common Law. These insights may explain the almost visceral rejection any suggestions lowering the standard of proof in civil matters have received in Germany. They do not, however, provide a normative basis for a standard of proof higher than 50% posterior subjective probability in civil cases.

7.1 Introduction

While Common Law knows at least two different standards of proof, the "preponderance of the evidence" (or "balance of probabilities" in English law) for civil cases and the "proof beyond reasonable doubt" in criminal cases,[1] continental European Civil Law generally does not distinguish between standards of proof in civil and criminal matters.[2] This is one of the most fundamental differences between Common Law and Continental European Civil Law.[3]

Under the "preponderance of the evidence" standard of US law and the "balance of probabilities" standard of English law, the plaintiff has discharged his burden of persuasion if the fact finder is convinced that the allegations in support of the claim are more likely true than not.[4] If the fact finder is inclined to believe the plaintiff

[1] See *Addington vs. Texas,* 441 U.S. 418 (1979), 422, 423; for English law *In Re H & Others* (minors) UKHL 16, AC 563 (1995), sect. 76; Wright 2009, 80.

[2] Engel 2009, 435; Motsch 2009, 242.

[3] Paulus 1997, 750; Kokott 1998, 18; Clermont and Sherwin 2002, 262 et seq.; Engel 2009, 435; Motsch 2009, 242; but see Gottwald 2000, 175; Brinkmann 2005, 3.

[4] For US law O'Malley et al. 2001, § 166.51; for English law *Miller vs. Minister of Pensions,* 3 All ER 372 (1947), 373 et seq.

M. Schweizer (✉)
University of St. Gallen, Huttenstrasse 40, 8006 Zurich, Switzerland
e-mail: mark.schweizer@gmail.com

K. Mathis (ed.), *European Perspectives on Behavioural Law and Economics,* Economic Analysis of Law in European Legal Scholarship 2,
DOI 10.1007/978-3-319-11635-8_7

more than the defendant, even to the slightest degree, then he or she must find for the plaintiff.[5]

The standard of proof under Continental Civil Law, on the other hand, always requires the (full) conviction of the judge, be it a "conviction intime" or a "conviction raisonnée", a reasoned or reasonable conviction meaning that the judge must justify his or her decision by valid arguments.[6] This standard is described in the leading case of the German Federal Supreme Court (Bundesgerichtshof) as a

> personal conviction [...] in doubtful cases, the judge may and must be content with a degree of certainty useful for practical life that silences doubt without completely excluding it.[7]

Neither German nor Swiss courts have ever expressed the decision threshold as a quantified subjective probability. The traditional doctrine is also reluctant to do so, but when it does quantify the standard of proof, the decision threshold is said to be above 90 %;[8] sometimes even figures of 95 %[9] or 99.8 %[10] are given.

There are certainly many exceptions to the standard of full conviction in civil cases, namely for allegations that are notoriously difficult to prove, such as causality in medical malpractice or the theft of an insured item to be proven by the policy holder.[11] But the exceptions—and the considerable doctrinal effort required for their justification—prove the rule.[12] It can hardly be doubted that the standard of proof demanded by doctrine and case law for civil matters in Germany and Switzerland is much higher than the "balance of probabilities" required by Common Law.[13] This became most evident with the harsh rejection any suggestions for a lower standard of proof have been met with in Germany in the 1970s and 1980s.[14]

This has "puzzled" Common Law scholars,[15] as normative decision theory provides an elegant explanation for the preponderance of the evidence standard (as will

[5] For English law Redmayne 1999, 172; for US law *Livanovitch v. Livanovitch,* 131 A. 799, 800 (Vt. 1926) ("If [...] you are more inclined to believe from the evidence that he did so deliver the bonds to the defendant, even though your belief is only the slightest degree greater than that he did not, your verdict should be for the plaintiff" (quoting the jury instructions).

[6] The standard of proof in Germany is better described as a "conviction raisonnée" rather than the French "conviction intime"; see Deppenkemper 2004, 208 et seq., 421 and the references cited therein.

[7] BGHZ 53, 245 = BGH NJW 1970, 946 (translation from German by the author); for Swiss law BGE 130 III 321 sect. 3.2.

[8] For German law Kadner Graziano 2011, 189; for Swiss law Berger-Steiner 2008, sect. 6.81; Walter 2009, 53; Bühler 2010, sect. 9.

[9] For German law Greger 1978, 110; for Swiss law Summermatter and Jacober 2012, 142.

[10] For German law Bender 1981, 258; Fuchs 2005, 80.

[11] See, e.g., for German law BGH NJW 1995, 2169; NJW 2004, 777; for Swiss law BGE 130 III 321 sect. 3.3; 132 III 715 sect. 3.2.

[12] Walter 1979, 184.

[13] But see Gottwald 2000, 175; Brinkmann 2005, 3, who argue against any difference in principle between the German and the Common Law's standard of proof in civil cases.

[14] Prütting 2010, 142.

[15] Clermont and Sherwin 2002, 244.

be explained in detail below).[16] In this article, I seek to demonstrate how insights from cognitive psychology can explain the intuitive appeal of a standard of proof considerably higher than 50 % posterior subjective probability in Civil matters. I shall argue, however, that the psychological insights cannot provide a normative basis for the Civil Law's higher standard of proof in civil cases.

The article is structured as follows: First, the standard of proof is defined and distinguished from the related concept of burden of proof. Secondly, the theoretic justification for the balance of probabilities standard is explained in some detail. Despite the elegant justification provided by normative decision theory, the lower standard has been viscerally rejected by German doctrine, as will be explained next. Then, the insights from cognitive psychology that explain the intuitive appeal of a higher standard of proof, namely loss aversion, omission bias and status quo bias, and their empirical support, are summarized. In a final section, it is examined whether these insights can provide a normative basis for a higher standard of proof, and it will finally be argued that they cannot.

7.2 Standard of Proof Defined

In the following, the standard of proof will be understood as the decision threshold of the fact finder that allows him to find in favour of the party bearing the burden of persuasion (generally the plaintiff in civil cases—although it is well understood that burden of persuasion does not depend on the role of the party—and the state in criminal cases). It is assumed that this decision threshold can be expressed as a subjective probability, or as a degree of conviction, that the factual statements supporting the claim (or accusation) are true.

In a fully Bayesian account of the judicial fact finding and decision-making process, the fact finder starts with some prior probability for the truth of the relevant factual statements, then updates this probability in light of the evidence presented to her during the trial using Bayes rule, and ultimately arrives at a posterior subjective probability for the truth of those statements.[17] She then compares this posterior subjective probability to a pre-determined decision threshold—the standard of proof—and decides for the party bearing the burden of proof if her degree of belief exceeds the decision threshold, and against that party if her degree of conviction does not exceed the threshold (some tie-breaking rule is needed if the posterior subjective probability is exactly equal to the decision threshold; the majority view being that in this case, the decision goes against the party bearing the burden of proof[18]).

[16] The seminal papers are Kaplan 1968 and Cullison 1969.

[17] The use of the plural for "statements" is deliberate. In my view, the Bayesian posterior probability must be for the joint probability of all relevant factual statements being true. This avoids the much debated "conjunction paradox" at the potential cost of defining standard of proof differently than current law.

[18] Kegel 1967, 337; Maassen 1975, 10; Redmayne 1999, 172; Posner 2007, 647, but see Motsch 1983, 83.

Whether the Bayesian analysis of evidence evaluation is insightful or misleading has been debated for over 40 years.[19] For the behavioural analysis presented in this contribution however, it is not necessary that one fully embrace the Bayesian approach. It is sufficient if one accepts that conviction comes in degrees, rather than in the dichotomous categories of "I'm convinced" and "I'm not convinced". It is difficult to make an argument for this other than pointing out that people behave as if their convictions had degrees (usually, betting is pointed out as a prime example, but some lawyers take exception to the comparison of judicial decision-making and betting, so it is probably best avoided). One further has to accept that different standards of proof can be expressed as different degrees of belief or conviction. One does not, however, have to accept that the different standards can be expressed as exact numbers on a scale from 0 to 1 (or more often, in the legal literature, on a scale from 0 to 100 %). The latter claim is highly controversial, at least for the criminal standard of "proof beyond any reasonable doubt".[20]

Finally, it is best to avoid the term "burden of proof" for the standard of proof. "Burden of proof" should be reserved for the procedural obligation to persuade the fact finder ("burden of persuasion" or "objektive Beweislast" in German terminology) and to adduce evidence ("burden of production" or "subjektive Beweislast"[21] in German terminology). The burden of persuasion determines which party suffers (by losing his or her case) when the conviction of the fact finder does not reach the pre-determined decision threshold.[22] It is fixed—according to German doctrine by substantive law—and stays constant during litigation. The burden of production, or burden of producing evidence, on the other hand can shift during litigation.[23] It initially lies with the party bearing the burden of persuasion, but once that party has adduced sufficient evidence to create a degree of belief in the mind of the fact finder that exceeds the decision threshold, it shifts to the other party, who is now obliged to adduce evidence to the contrary at the pain of losing the case.

7.3 Standards of Proof in a Decision Theoretic Framework

The decision theoretic model is the oldest and still, certainly in the legal literature, the most widely used analytic framework for the analysis of standards of proof. Its appeal lies in that it is both simpler than more recent game-theoretic and mechanism design approaches and that it maps relatively well to positive Common law.

---

[19] See Park et al. 2010, for an overview. The debate started with Finkelstein and Fairley 1970 and the answer came from Tribe 1971. The collection of essays by Tillers 1988 provides an overview of the debate up to that time, and Tillers 2011 a summary of the debate since.

[20] See the references cited in Tillers and Gottfried 2007.

[21] Rosenberg 1965, 16.

[22] Baumgärtel 1996, n. 9.

[23] Musielak 1975, 49.

Table 7.1 Potential errors in hypothesis testing

	True state is H_0	True state is H_1
Decision for H_0	Correct	Type II error
Decision for H_1	Type I error	Correct

> Bayesian decision theory seems to provide a pleasing and harmonious interpretation of civil litigation's usual requirement of proof by a preponderance of the evidence.[24]

Under the decision theoretic framework, which was first used independently by Kaplan and Cullison, the focus is exclusively on the decision problem facing the fact finder, who has to make his decision about the true state of the world under uncertainty. The fact finder is treated like a welfare-minded social planner, trying to make the decision that maximizes social utility (or minimizes social cost; like most legal scholars, I use the cost minimization paradigm in the following).

When deciding whether a hypothesis—such as the factual statements made by the plaintiff—is true, the decision-maker can fall victim to two errors: accepting the hypothesis as true although it is actually false, and rejecting the hypothesis as false although it is actually true. These two mistakes are often referred to as type I, or α-error, and type II, or β-error.[25] "Error" here means simply that the accepted factual statements and reality do not correspond; "error" does not mean the decision maker is at fault in any way. (Table 7.1)

If the social costs of the different types of errors are not equal, one does not want to minimize the number of mistakes made, but rather limit the expected costs of the decision. Let $\{w_1, \ldots, w_c\}$ be a finite set C of possible states and $\{a_1, \ldots, a_a\}$ a finite set A of possible actions. $L(a_i|w_j)$ shall be the cost, expressed as a real number, of the choice of action a_i if the state of the world is w_j.

The evidence is expressed as x. Assume the decision-maker choses action a_i. If the actual state of the world is w_j, the costs of the decision are $L(a_i|w_j)$. The conditional risk R of the choice of action a_i given the evidence x is therefore

$$R(a_i|x) = \sum_{j=i}^{c} L(a_i|w_j)\Pr(w_j|x)$$

The decision rule, also known as "Bayes decision rule", posits that the action with the smallest conditional risk should be chosen. (Table 7.2)[26]

When facing a choice between exactly two actions, a_1 and a_2, the decision maker should, conditional on the evidence x, chose according to the following rule:

$$\text{decide}\begin{cases} a_1 & \text{if } R(a_1|x) < R(a_2 \mid x) \\ a_2 & \text{else.} \end{cases}$$

[24] Kaye 1987, 55.

[25] Biemann 2009, 207.

[26] Bourmistrov-Jüttner 1987, 247.

Table 7.2 Decision matrix

	$Pr(w_1\|x)$	$Pr(w_2\|x)$	Expected costs
a_1	L_{11}	L_{12}	$Pr(w_1\|x)\,L_{11}+Pr(w_2\|x)\,L_{12}$
a_2	L_{21}	L_{22}	$Pr(w_1\|x)\,L_{21}+Pr(w_2\|x)\,L_{22}$

To simplify the notation in Table 7.2 and in the following, $(a_i|w_j)$ is written as L_{ij}. Table 7.2 shows that

$$R(a_1|x) = Pr(w_1|x)L_{11} + Pr(w_2|x)L_{12}$$

$$R(a_2|x) = Pr(w_1|x)L_{21} + Pr(w_2|x)L_{22}$$

Therefore the decision maker should chose action a_1 if

$$Pr(w_1|x)L_{21} + Pr(w_2|x)L_{22} > Pr(w_1|x)L_{11} + Pr(w_2|x)L_{12}$$

This can be re-written as

$$\frac{Pr(w_1|x)}{Pr(w_2|x)} > \frac{(L_{12} - L_{22})}{(L_{21} - L_{11})}$$

Since $Pr(w_2|x) = 1 - Pr(w_1|x)$ the following holds[27]

$$Pr(w_1|x) > \frac{(L_{12} - L_{22})}{(L_{21} - L_{11}) + (L_{12} - L_{22})} = \frac{1}{1 + \left(\dfrac{L_{21} - L_{11}}{L_{12} - L_{22}}\right)}.$$

The decision maker should, in other words, decide for a_1 when his subjective posterior probability of w_1 exceeds the right hand side of the above inequality. Since it is traditionally assumed in the legal literature that correct decisions have no costs associated with them—it would be better to say that their cost is, for normative reasons, not to be considered—the above inequality can be simplified to the following, which is the form as it was originally used by Kaplan in his seminal 1968 paper:[28]

$$Pr(w_1|x) > \frac{L_{12}}{L_{21} + L_{12}} = \frac{1}{1 + \left(\dfrac{L_{21}}{L_{12}}\right)}.$$

[27] Cullison 1969, 564 et seqq.; DeKay 1996, 111.

[28] Kaplan 1968, 1072.

The decision theoretic framework seems to provide an elegant explanation of the Common Law's two different standards for criminal and civil matters.[29] Common Law employs the (high) standard of "proof beyond any reasonable doubt" in criminal cases, and the (lower) standard of "preponderance of the evidence" ("balance of probabilities" in English law) in civil cases.[30] To reach a guilty verdict in a criminal case, the jury must be convinced beyond any reasonable doubt that the facts alleged by the prosecution are true. A "reasonable" doubt is one that is based upon reason and not purely on speculation, a merely possible doubt does not prevent a finding against the defendant.[31]

In a civil case, on the other hand, it is sufficient if the evidence adduced by the party bearing the burden of proof "when considered and compared with that opposed to it, has more convincing force, and produces in your [sc. the jurors'] minds belief that what is sought to be proved is more likely true than not true."[32] If the fact finder is inclined to believe the plaintiff more than the defendant, even to the slightest degree, then he or she must find for the plaintiff.[33] In other words, it is sufficient if the plaintiff's allegations are more probably true than not.[34]

According to normative decision theory this makes perfect sense, assuming different costs of errors in criminal and civil matters: since wrongly convicting an innocent person is widely considered to be a graver mistake than erroneously acquitting a guilty person, the expected error costs are minimized if the standard of proof in criminal cases is well above 50% (whether it can be quantified at all is highly controversial,[35] but nobody would dispute that a civil jury may find for the plaintiff under circumstances that would not permit a criminal jury to convict the

[29] In US law, a further intermediate standard of proof known as "clear and convincing evidence", which is applicable in certain civil cases (e.g., civil fraud), is well-established, see, e.g., *Addington vs. Texas,* 441 U.S. 418 (1979), 422, 423, while it is a matter of controversy whether English law recognizes such an intermediate standard of proof, Anderson et al. 2006, 243; McBride 2009, 325 et seq.

[30] See *Addington vs. Texas,* 441 U.S. 418 (1979), 422, 423; for English law *In Re H & Others* (minors) UKHL 16, AC 563 (1995), sect. 76; Wright 2009, 80.

[31] Jury instructions according to the Ninth Circuit Model Criminal Jury Instructions, 2003 edition, § 3.5 – Reasonable Doubt—Defined. Sheppard 2003 shows the development from "moral certainty" to "reasonable doubt" to "articulate doubt", which, according to him, explains the current practice in criminal law better.

[32] O'Malley et al. 2001, § 166.51.

[33] *Livanovitch v. Livanovitch,* 131 A. 799, 800 (Vt. 1926) ("If [...] you are more inclined to believe from the evidence that he did so deliver the bonds to the defendant, even though your belief is only the slightest degree greater than that he did not, your verdict should be for the plaintiff" (quoting the jury instructions); Pennsylvania Suggested Standard Civil Jury Instructions, 3rd ed. 2005, § 1.42; for English law Redmayne 1999, 172.

[34] Illinois Supreme Court Committee on Pattern Jury Instructions in Civil Cases (eds.), Illinois Pattern Jury Instructions: Civil, § 21.01 ("more probably true than not true"), available from www.state.il.us/court/CircuitCourt/CivilJuryInstructions/21.00.pdf (last visited 1 August 2012); Sand et al. 2007, Vol. 4, § 73.01, Instruction 73–2 ("by a preponderance of the evidence" means "more likely true than not true").

[35] See the references cited in Tillers and Gottfried 2007.

accused). On the other hand, it is a commonly held assumption that, in civil cases, the disutility of erroneously finding for or against the plaintiff is similar,[36] which means the error-cost minimizing decision threshold is $\geq 50\,\%$. As one commentator put it, "civil cases are the paradigm for symmetrical error costs."[37]

7.4 A Visceral Reaction to the Proposal of a "Balance of Probabilities" Standard in German Doctrine

Given Common Law's longstanding tradition of using a lower standard of proof for civil matters and the convincing explanation of the different standards by normative decision theory, Common Law scholars have been "puzzled" by the Continental European Civil Law's lack of clear distinction between standards of proof for civil and criminal matters.[38] Few would dispute that the degree of conviction required for finding for the plaintiff in Civil Law is much higher than that required by the Common Law's "preponderance of the evidence" or "balance of probabilities" standard.[39]

This becomes particularly obvious when one considers the reception the idea of a general standard of proof of a "balance of probabilities" received in Germany in the 1970s. Starting with the doctoral thesis of *Maassen*[40] in 1975, a number of authors have suggested a lower decision threshold in German civil procedure.[41] The idea met with visceral rejection and the authors were accused of all sorts of doctrinal errors. The ferocity of some of the responses is surprising given the usually quaint discourse in German civil procedural law. *Gerhard Walter*, who would later become professor for civil procedural law at the University of Berne, wrote in his post-doctoral thesis with regards to the new-fangled idea of a lower standard of proof for in civil matters:[42]

---

[36] *In re Winship* 397 U.S. 358, 371 (1970) (Harlan J. Concurring); Ball 1960, 817; Kaye 1987, 72; Lee 1997, 25; Posner 1999, 1504; Redmayne 1999, 171; Clermont and Sherwin 2002, 268; Stein 2005, 148; Zamir and Ritov 2012, 189; but see Tyree 1982, 93 et seq.

[37] Lee 1997, 25.

[38] In a strongly worded article, *Kevin M. Clermont and Emily Sherwin* "rudely wonder how civilians can be so wrong", Clermont and Sherwin 2002, 244. For an equally strongly worded rebuttal see Taruffo 2003.

[39] But see Gottwald 2000, 175; Brinkmann 2005, 3, who argue against any difference in principle between the German and the Common Law's standard of proof in civil cases.

[40] Maassen 1975.

[41] Motsch 1978, 335 et seq.; Nell 1983, 211. A precursor, not yet relying on a decision theoretic framework, was Kegel 1967, 335.

[42] Walter 1979, 182. In the German original: "Eine Demontage des "Überzeugungserfordernisses" würde also weithin zu einer Korrumpierung der Rechtsmoral in der Bevölkerung führen – wenn schon eine überwiegende Wahrscheinlichkeit genügt, um "einen Prozess zu gewinnen"! Man muss […] will man die Übereinstimmung eines Volkes mit seiner Justiz, den "Konsens" nicht verlieren, auf gewachsene und verankerte Traditionen Rücksicht nehmen."

> The removal of the requirement of inner conviction would lead to a corruption of the population's morale—if a preponderance of probabilities was enough to "win in court"! If one does not want to lose the accord, the consensus, of the people with their justice system, one has to respect grown and rooted traditions.

Others claimed that the "acceptance of jurisprudence" would depend on a high standard of proof.[43] For *Habscheid*, another influential civil proceduralist, the introduction of a standard of proof of a "balance of probabilities" touches the very root of the rule of law.[44]

The defenders of the traditional view resoundingly won the debate of the 1970s/1980s. Since the 1990s, hardly any German[45] author has questioned the high standard of proof in civil matters (notwithstanding the many exceptions to the rule developed primarily by the courts).[46] In 2010, *Prütting* stated that "such extreme notions [sc. of a general standard of proof of a balance of probabilities] have not caught on at any time in German jurisprudence and are not mentioned any more in any commentary on the Civil Procedure Act."[47]

The interesting question is why a standard of proof that has been traditionally applied by Common Law, and which can be intuitively explained by normative decision theory, has met with such resistance in Germany. *Clermont* and *Sherwin* conclude that the Civil Law countries weigh the perceived legitimacy of the justice system higher than the avoidance of error.[48] But that only begs the question as to why errors in favour of the plaintiff are apparently so much more detrimental to the perceived legitimacy of the justice system than errors in favour of the defendant. Why is it that lawyers in Civil Law countries seem to readily accept that many injured parties that are, under the applicable substantive law, entitled to compensation, do not receive compensation (which is the effect of a high standard of proof), while it appears to be unacceptable to the very same lawyers that a party that is not obliged to pay damages according to substantive law is ordered to pay damages? A behavioural analysis can shed some light on this question.

---

[43] Berger-Steiner 2008, Rz. 5.131. See also Hohl 1991, 155: "Le degré de vraisemblance à exiger du juge doit être suffisament élevé pour être acceptable sur les plans moral et éthique et légitimer la coercition judiciaire."

[44] Habscheid 1990, 118. In the German original: "Es ist für mich auch fraglich, ob der Gesetzgeber eine solche Regelung einführen kann, ohne an die Wurzeln des Rechtsstaats zu rühren."

[45] In Switzerland, the traditional view has never been under attack in the first place. This is about to change with the publication of my Habilitationsschrift "Beweismaß und Beweiswürdigung. Rationalität und Intuition" Tübingen 2015 (forthcoming).

[46] But see Wagner 2009, 172 et seq.

[47] Prütting 2010, 142. In the German original: "Es ist nicht zuletzt den klaren und beharrlichen Darlegungen Karl Heinz Schwabs zu danken, dass solche extremen Auffassungen zu keinem Zeitpunkt in der deutschen Rechtswissenschaft Fuß fassen konnten und in keinem Kommentar zur ZPO mehr Erwähnung finden."

[48] Clermont and Sherwin 2002, 269 ff.

7.5 The Behavioural Toolbox and its Application to the Civil Standard of Proof

7.5.1 Loss Aversion

Reference point-dependent valuations are a well-established finding from behavioural economics.[49] The reference point—whether something is considered a gain or a loss from a given reference point—influences people's acceptance of risk.[50] *Kahneman* and *Tversky*, who are at the root of the development of the theory of reference-dependent valuation, observed something else as well: losses loom larger than gains. "The aggravation that one experiences in losing a sum of money appears to be greater than the pleasure associated with gaining the same amount."[51] Most people find symmetric bets of the form (x,.50; -x,.50) unattractive. The averseness of symmetric bets generally increases with the size of the stake.[52] The ratio of G[ain]/L[oss] which makes an even chance to gain G or to lose L just acceptable lies between about 2 and 2.5 for both risky and riskless choice involving monetary outcomes and consumption goods.[53] This means that people experience about twice the disutility for a loss than they experience utility for a corresponding gain.[54]

Civil litigation provides a natural "frame" for outcomes.[55] Generally, the plaintiff frames the outcome of the litigation as a gain compared to the *status quo ante* trial. Conversely, the defendant sees the outcome as a loss.[56] While occasionally the parties' roles may be interchangeable, depending on who initiates the proceedings,[57] it is safe to say that in an overwhelming majority of cases, it is the plaintiff who asks the court to impose a change of the *status quo*, e.g., making the defendant pay, turning over possession of a good or stop behaving in a certain way. In all of these cases, the losing defendant will conceive compliance with the judgment as a loss.

If one uses the empirically observed median ratio G/L of about 2.25 and uses normative decision theory to compute the decision threshold which minimizes the expected error costs of the decision for or against the plaintiff, one arrives at a subjective posterior probability of about 70 %. That is still a long way from the "above 90 %" suggested in the German and Swiss literature, but also well above the 50 %

---

[49] Tversky and Kahneman 1991.

[50] Tversky and Kahneman 1992, 306.

[51] Kahneman and Tversky 1979, 279.

[52] Kahneman and Tversky 1979, 279.

[53] Tversky and Kahneman 1991, 154. Tversky and Kahneman 1992, 59, report a median value of about 2.25.

[54] Tversky and Kahneman 1992, 59, suggest that the median of the empirically observed values for the difference in weight of gains and losses is about 2.25.

[55] Rachlinski 1996, 118.

[56] Korobkin and Guthrie 1994,133 et seq; Babcock et al. 1995, 296 et seq.; Rachlinski 1996, 130 et seq.

[57] Clermont and Sherwin 2002, 268.

of the "balance of probabilities" of English law. *Zamir* and *Ritov* report just such a decision threshold from an experiment with Israeli lawyers and law students, who work and study in a legal system that uses the Common Law's "preponderance of the evidence" standard for civil cases.[58]

While on average the G/L ratio for which subjects are indifferent between symmetric bets is somewhat over 2, there are considerable inter-individual differences in loss aversion.[59] If loss aversion influenced the decision threshold, then judges with a higher loss aversion, as measured by the G/L ratio, should have a higher decision threshold.[60] A study with a sample of Swiss members of court (judicial clerks and judges) shows that this is indeed the case—judges with higher loss aversion need to be convinced to a higher degree that the plaintiff's allegations are true before they decide in favour of the plaintiff in a civil action.[61]

These results indicate that loss aversion, at least partially, explains the intuitive appeal of a decision threshold that is considerably higher than the 50 % posterior subjective probability of the Common Law's standard in civil cases ("more likely true than not"), although loss aversion alone cannot account for the intuitive appeal of a very high decision threshold such as the "almost certainty" required by Civil Law.

7.5.2 Omission Bias

The so called "omission bias" and its close relative, the "status quo bias", may further explain why errors of the type I (granting an unjustified claim) are considered so much more severe than errors of the type II (denying a justified claim). "Omission bias" refers to the tendency to feel more responsible for the negative consequences of acts than those of deliberate omissions. Consequently, regret is higher when an act has negative consequences than when an omission has negative consequences.[62] Correspondingly, actions of third parties that lead to negative outcomes are judged as morally more reprehensible than deliberate omissions with the same consequences.[63] While omission bias is stronger when decision makers anticipate learning the outcome of their decision, it is also present when they are blind to the

---

[58] Zamir and Ritov 2012, 180.

[59] Fehr and Goette 2007, 300; Gächter et al. 2010, 4.

[60] This requires the further assumption that the judge – who does not himself or herself gain or lose anything from his or her decision – vicariously experiences the gain or loss of the parties. This assumption is plausible, however, based on research that shows that judges are indeed influenced by the party's perspective despite having nothing at stake themselves, see Guthrie et al. 2001, 777.

[61] Schweizer 2013, 20.

[62] Kahneman and Tversky 1982, 173; Ritov and Baron 1990, 274; Gilovich and Medvec 1995, 380; Prentice and Koehler 2002, 610.

[63] Sugarman 1986, 70; Spranca et al. 1991, 82; Kordes-de Vaal 1996, 165; Prentice and Koehler 2002, 593.

outcome.[64] The latter is the situation a judge in a civil law suit is in, as the ground truth generally will not be learnt after the final judgment.

It has been suggested that the distinction between actions and deliberate omissions is due to a "moral overgeneralization."[65] Acts are usually deliberate and their foreseeable consequences intended, while omissions often occur unknowingly and their consequences are therefore unintended, too. However, when an omission is deliberate, there is not an ethically justified distinction between act and omission from the point of view of a consequentialist ethic.[66] Most people seem to apply a generally useful rule—acts are deliberate, omissions negligent if at all—to situations in which it is not applicable.[67]

If granting a civil action that leads to a change in the *status quo ante* filing is perceived as an act, while denying it is seen as an omission, then this could also explain why errors of the type I are considered graver than errors of type II. Note that this is rather arbitrary—in a sense, both are acts; the judge (or jury) cannot refuse to do something and abstain from a decision, he is forced to choose between granting and denying the claim. But it is very comparable to the situation in classic studies of regret and the action/inaction distinction. In one often cited example, an investor sells stock A and buys stock B, while another investor *decides against* selling stock B. Both own stock B when its share price tanks and incur a loss. An overwhelming majority believes the first investor will feel more regret,[68] although technically, "deciding against" is also an act—but one that does not change the status quo.

Zamir and *Ritov* report that Israeli law students anticipate that the more a judge is afraid of making a mistake, the more likely she will deny the claim, and that judges who erroneously[69] granted a claim will feel more regret than judges who erroneously denied a claim.[70] This is in line with the expectations based on the studies on the omission bias.

Using an online-questionnaire, I asked a sample of 156 Swiss members of court (judicial clerks and judges from the Cantons of Bern and Zurich) to decide whether they would grant or deny a request for repayment of a loan. The defendant disputed ever having received the loan, and the evidence in favour of the plaintiff was solid, but not decisive.[71] After having decided, each participant was told that newly discovered incontrovertible evidence proved their decision wrong, and asked to express their regret about the mistaken decision on a scale from 0 to 100. The average

---

[64] Ritov and Baron 1995, 124.

[65] Kordes-de Vaal 1996, 165; Sunstein 2005, 540.

[66] Sunstein 2004, 1582; Birnbacher 1995, 127, but see 209.

[67] Kordes-de Vaal 1996, 165.

[68] Kahneman and Tversky 1982, 173.

[69] Erroneously here, as throughout this article, means that the claim was granted although it did not exist under the applicable substantive law. It does not mean that the judge made any procedural errors.

[70] Zamir and Ritov 2012, 182.

[71] This is the same sample as the one for the study on the influence of loss aversion on the decision threshold. The results will be reported more fully in my forthcoming Habilitationsschrift.

regret of those granting the claim (N=65) was at 55.2 significantly higher than the average regret of those denying the claim (N=91) at 39.4.[72] This shows that Swiss judges feel similar to the Israeli students anticipating how Israeli judges would feel and demonstrates that the regret when making a type I error is indeed larger than when making a type II error. If judges strive to minimize their anticipated regret, they should lean towards denying uncertain claims. Again, behavioural insights can show why the intuition is to have a standard of proof that minimizes type I errors at the price of accepting more type II errors.

7.5.3 Status Quo Bias

Status quo bias describes the phenomenon that, *ceteris paribus*, a state of the world is preferred for no other reason than that it is the current state.[73] Changes of the *status quo* need more justification than maintaining the status quo.[74] On the other hand, maintaining the status quo seems justified *per se*. A particularly bitter example for the latter is reported by *Crandall et al* who show that the use of torture in questioning prisoners enjoys greater support if it is described as a long-standing practice rather than something to be newly introduced.[75]

In most cases of civil litigation, it is the plaintiff who requests a change of the *status quo ante* filing. There are exceptions to this rule[76]—negative declaratory actions come to mind—but even then, while the plaintiff does not request a change in status quo in these rare cases, neither does the defendant. In the overwhelming majority of cases, it is the plaintiff that requests a change of the *status quo*, while the defendant wants the *status quo* to be maintained. Deciding in favour of the plaintiff therefore requires more justification than deciding in favour of the defendant, which, translated into standards of proof, means that the standard must be well above 50 % to justify deciding for the plaintiff.

The reasons given for the assignment of the burden of proof to the plaintiff (in most cases) provides anecdotal evidence for the role status quo bias plays in the justification of a high standard of proof in civil cases. The assignment of the burden of proof is obviously the more important, the higher the standard of proof is.[77] In legal systems such as the German and Swiss one, the assignment of the burden of proof is often decisive for the outcome of the litigation, at least when the dispute is about facts that are not easily proven by documentary evidence.[78] Influential voices in the

---

[72] $t(154)=3.17, p<0{,}01$.

[73] Samuelson and Zeckhauser 1988, 8; Kahneman et al. 1991, 197; Schweitzer 1994, 470; Prentice and Koehler 2002, 597; Eidelman and Crandall 2009, 85.

[74] Connolly and Zeelenberg 2002, 213.

[75] Crandall et al. 2009.

[76] Clermont and Sherwin 2002, 268.

[77] Rüßmann 1987, n. 21.

[78] Stölzel 1913, XXXI.

German doctrine argue that it is fair to assign the burden of proof to the attacker (literally "*Angreifer*").[79] In other words, the mere fact that someone wants to change the *status quo* appears to justify making matters difficult for them—because these authors give no reasons as to why the "attacker" should bear the burden of proof, it seems to be self-evident.

7.6 Normative Implications of the Behavioural Insights for the Civil Standard of Proof

The section above has shown how insights from behavioural analysis of human decision-making can explain the ferocious defence of a high standard of proof in civil cases in Germany and Switzerland. But can behavioural insights justify the high standard on normative grounds? In the following, I argue that they cannot.

If the decision threshold should not only minimize "the total expected number of dollars coming from the wrong pockets"[80], but minimize the disutility of the parties, then taking into account loss aversion seems to be normatively justified at first sight.[81] As mentioned above, while taking into account loss aversion cannot justify a decision threshold of "above 90 %", it appears to justify one that is well above 50 %.

But while loss aversion may explain the intuitive appeal behind a higher decision threshold, it cannot justify it. The main problem is not even that reference points are malleable.[82] In many real world cases, the perceptions of plaintiffs and defendants of the trial's outcome can hardly be manipulated.[83] The basic problem is that there are no convincing reasons for the *status quo ante filing of the suit* to be the relevant reference point.[84] Why should the *status quo ante* the act (or omission) that supports the legal claim not be the relevant reference point? Suppose the act or omission in question may lead to liability. For example, the (future) plaintiff's car has been damaged by the (future) defendant, and the defendant is liable if he has been negligent. The plaintiff may well experience the award of damages by the court as a gain, because by that time—usually years after the accident—the *status quo* is the

[79] Leipold 1966, 48 et seq.; Prütting 1983, 263 et seq. These days, the consensus view is that it is impossible to reduce the assignment of the burden of proof to a single unifying principle, Ahrens 2008, 29 et seq.; Prütting 2009, n. 42.

[80] Kaye 1982, 497.

[81] Zamir 2012, 887 et seq.; Zamir and Ritov 2012, 172. Zamir and Ritov caution, however, against any premature normative conclusions, Zamir and Ritov 2012, 195 et seq.

[82] Korobkin and Guthrie 1994, 120 et seq.; Zamir and Ritov 2010, 262 et seq., 269 (on the malleability of reference points).

[83] Zamir 2012, 889 et seq.

[84] Redmayne 1999, 174.

damaged car,[85] and the compensation is an improvement. The defendant experiences the award as a loss since his current wealth is diminished.[86] But the plaintiff has certainly experienced the damage to his car as a loss from the then relevant baseline "intact car". If erroneously no damages are awarded, the plaintiff is stuck with his initial loss. While he may not experience the loss at the time of judgment, it seems arbitrary to take into account the defendant's loss aversion from the reference point "before filing", but not the plaintiff's loss aversion "before accident".

Now, one can argue that when damages are awarded erroneously, it is *the court* who inflicts a loss on the defendant, while the initial loss to the plaintiff has been inflicted by a private party. If a decision granting the claim is perceived as an act and one denying it as an omission, and the grant of the claim (generally) inflicts an unjustified loss on the defendant, then the perceived fairness of the court will be lower when erroneously granting a claim than when erroneously denying it. But while this may explain the intuitive appeal of a higher standard of proof in civil matters, it hardly provides a normative justification. If substantive law gives the plaintiff a claim and the claim would be granted if the facts supporting it were known to the court, why should the plaintiff bear the consequences of the uncertainty necessarily involved in fact finding? Everybody agrees that the standard of proof cannot be absolute certainty,[87] as then the enforcement of substantive law would be seriously imperilled. But once it is accepted that the administration of justice will never be error free, we must justify the distribution of these errors. Omission bias may provide an intuitive explanation, but hardly a rational basis, to burden the plaintiff with most of the errors.

As to the fear that a standard of proof of a "balance of probabilities" may undermine the perceived legitimacy of the court system and drive a wedge between the populace and its administrators of justice, empirical data does not confirm the concern. The World Values Survey seeks to investigate political and sociocultural change with a standardized survey that is carried out in over 50 countries.[88] In the last wave that is currently fully published (2005–2007), one question asks the respondents—representative samples for the population of each participating country—how much confidence they have in various institutions, among them the courts, police and civil service.[89] Possible answers range from "a great deal", "quite a lot" "not very much" and "none at all". Figure 7.1 summarizes the results for

[85] The fact that in most cases, the car will have been repaired by now makes the argument even stronger.

[86] Note that technically, this is not true. If the defendant were a company, it would have to make provisions for the liability at the time of the accident, because the liability exists irrespective of its enforcement by court order.

[87] Instead of many after him Mittermaier 1843, 74.

[88] See www.worldvaluessurvey.org (last visited 1 February 2014).

[89] "I am going to name a number of organizations. For each one, could you tell me how much confidence you have in them: is it a great deal of confidence, quite a lot of confidence, not very much confidence or none at all?", see WVS 2005 OECD questionnaire, A-Ballot, available from www.worldvaluessurvey.org (last visited 1 February 2014).

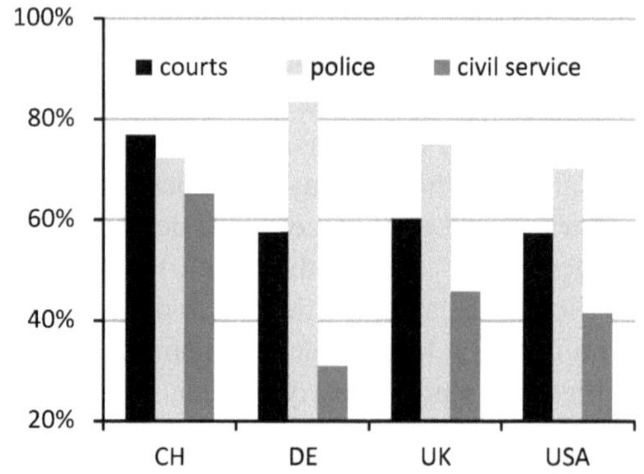

Fig. 7.1 Percentages of respondents having "a great deal" or "quite a lot" of confidence in the respective organizations. (from World Value Survey 2005)

Switzerland (CH), Germany (DE), the United Kingdom (UK) and the USA, giving the percentages of respondents answering with "a great deal" and "quite a lot".

Confidence in the courts and civil service is highest in Switzerland. There is, however, no systematic difference between the two countries in the sample with a standard of proof of "preponderance of the evidence" in civil matters (UK and USA) and those with the higher standard of "full conviction" (Germany and Switzerland). In fact, the US courts score higher than Germany, while the UK and Germany are essentially the same.[90] While the public confidence in the court system may be driven primarily by the criminal justice system—the survey does not differentiate between civil and criminal courts—if the standard of proof in civil cases really undermined the legitimacy of the court system, one would expect to see lower confidence in the UK and the USA versus Germany and Switzerland.

7.7 Conclusion

Behavioural insights can explain the intuitive appeal of a higher standard of proof in civil matters, but they cannot provide a normative justification for it. The visceral rejection any suggestion of a "balance of probabilities" standard of proof in civil matters has received in Civil Law countries such as Germany may be the result of loss aversion, omission bias and status quo bias, which all act together to make a higher standard of proof seem appealing.

Whether the Civil Law's higher standard of proof can be justified on normative grounds at all in the face of the decision theoretic critique is another question. Loss aversion, omission bias or status quo bias do not provide normative bases for a higher standard, primarily because it is not evident why the *status quo ante* judgment should deserve greater protection than the *status quo ante* breach of substantive law. If one considers the primary goal of the administration of civil justice being

[90] The figures for the courts are: CH 76.90 %; DE 57.50 %; UK 60.20 %; USA 57.40 %.

the enforcement of substantive law, it is hard to see how a standard of proof above 50 % posterior subjective probability could optimally serve this goal. The picture gets more complicated, however, if one takes into account the incentives provided by different standards of proofs.[91]

Bibliography

Ahrens, Hans-Jürgen. 2008. Die Verteilung der Beweislast. In *Karlsruher* Forum 2008*: Beweislast*, ed. Egon Lorenz, 7–53. Karlsruhe: Verlag Versicherungswirtschaft.

Anderson, Terence, David A. Schum, and William L. Twining. 2006. *Analysis of evidence, 2nd edn. Law in context*. Cambridge: Cambridge University Press.

Babcock, Linda, Henry S. Farber, Cynthia Fobian, and Eldar Shafir. 1995. Forming beliefs about adjudicated outcomes: Perceptions of risk and reservation values. *International Review of Law and Economics* 15:289–303.

Ball, V. C. 1960. The moment of truth: Probability theory and standards of proof. *Vanderbilt Law Review* 14:807–830.

Baumgärtel, Gottfried. 1996. *Beweislastpraxis im Privatrecht. Die Schwierigkeiten der Beweislastverteilung und die Möglichkeiten ihrer Überwindung*. Köln: Heymann.

Bender, Rolf. 1981. Das Beweismaß. In *Festschrift für Fritz Baur*, ed. Wolfgang Grunsky, Rolf Stürner, Gerhard Walter, and Manfred Wolf, 247–271. Tübingen: Mohr Siebeck.

Berger-Steiner, Isabelle. 2008. *Das Beweismass im Privatrecht. Eine dogmatische Untersuchung mit Erkenntniswert für die Praxis und die Rechtsfigur der Wahrscheinlichkeitshaftung*. Bern: Stämpfli.

Biemann, Torsten. 2009. Logik und Kritik des Hypothesentestens. In *Methodik der empirischen Forschung*, ed. Sönke Albers, Daniel Klapper, Udo Konradt, Achim Walter, and Joachim Wolf, 205–220. 3rd edn. Wiesbaden: Gabler.

Birnbacher, Dieter. 1995. *Tun und Unterlassen*. Stuttgart: Reclam.

Bourmistrov-Jüttner, Elena. 1987. *Subjektive Wahrscheinlichkeitstheorie und rationale Entscheidungstheorie in Anwendung auf die Rechtspraxis*. Ludwigs-Maximilian University: Munich.

Brinkmann, Moritz. 2005. *Das Beweismaß im Zivilprozess aus rechtsvergleichender Sicht*. Köln: Heymann.

Bühler, Alfred. 2010. Beweismass und Beweiswürdigung bei Gerichtsgutachten—unter Berücksichtigung der jüngsten Lehre und Rechtsprechung. Jusletter.

Clermont, Kevin M., and Emily Sherwin. 2002. A comparative view of standards of proof. *American Journal of Comparative Law* 50:243–276.

Connolly, Terry, and Marcel Zeelenberg. 2002. Regret in decision making. *Current Directions in Psychological Science* 11:212–216. doi:10.2307/20182815.

Crandall, Christian S., Scott Eidelman, Linda J. Skitka, and G. Scott Morgan. 2009. Status quo framing increases support for torture. *Social Influence* 4:1–10. doi:10.1080/15534510802124397.

Cullison, Alan D. 1969. Probability analysis of judicial fact-finding: A preliminary outline of the subjective approach. *University of Toledo Law Review* 1:538–598.

DeKay, Michael L. 1996. The difference between blackstone-like error ratios and probabilistic standards of proof. *Law & Social Inquiry* 21:95–132. doi:10.1111/j.1747-4469.1996.tb00013.x.

Demougin, Dominique, and Claude Fluet. 2006. Preponderance of evidence. *European Economic Review* 50:963–976. doi:10.1016/j.euroecorev.2004.11.002.

Deppenkemper, Gunter. 2004. *Beweiswürdigung als Mittel prozessualer Wahrheitserkenntnis. Eine dogmengeschichtliche Studie zu Freiheit, Grenzen und revisionsgerichtlicher Kontrolle tatrichterlicher Überzeugungsbildung (§ 261 StPO, § 286 ZPO)*. Göttingen: V & R Unipress.

[91] See Demougin and Fluet 2006; Fluet 2010; Kaplow 2012, 756 et seq.

Eidelman, Scott, and Christian S. Crandall. 2009. A psychological advantage for the status quo. In *Social and psychological bases of ideology and system justification*, ed. John T. Jost, Aaron C. Kay, and Hulda Thorisdottir, 85–106. Oxford: Oxford University Press.
Engel, Christoph. 2009. Preponderance of the evidence versus intime conviction: A behavioral perspective on a conflict between american and continental european law. *Vermont Law Review* 33:435–467.
Fehr, Ernst, and Lorenz Goette. 2007. Do workers work more if wages are high? evidence from a randomized field experiment. *American Economic Review* 97:298–317. doi:10.2307/30034396.
Finkelstein, Michael O., and William B. Fairley. 1970. A bayesian approach to identification evidence. *Harvard Law Review* 83:489–517.
Fluet, Claude. 2010. Liability rules under evidentiary uncertainty. *International Review of Law and Economics* 30:1–9. doi:10.1016/j.irle.2009.08.001.
Fuchs, Bianca. 2005. *Das Beweismaß im Arzthaftungsprozess*. Frankfurt a. M.: Peter Lang.
Gächter, Simon, Eric J. Johnson, and Andreas Herrmann. 2010. Individual-level loss aversion in riskless and risky choices. CeDEX discussion paper series.
Gilovich, Thomas, and Victoria Husted Medvec. 1995. The experience of regret: What, when, and why. *Psychological Review* 102:379–395. doi:10.1037/0033-295X.102.2.379.
Gottwald, Peter. 2000. Das flexible Beweismaß im englischen und deutschen Zivilprozess. In *Festschrift für Dieter Henrich zum 70. Geburtstag, 1. Dezember 2000*, ed. Peter Gottwald, Erik Jayme, and Dieter Schwab, 165–176. Bielefeld: Gieseking.
Gräns, Minna. 2002. *Das Risiko materiell fehlerhafter Urteile. (Diss. Uppsala 1995)*. Berlin: Duncker & Humblot.
Greger, Reinhard. 1978. *Beweis und Wahrscheinlichkeit. Das Beweiskriterium im Allgemeinen und bei den sogenannten Beweiserleichterungen*. Köln: Heymann.
Guthrie, Chris, Jeffrey J. Rachlinski, and Andrew J. Wistrich. 2001. Inside the Judicial Mind. *Cornell Law Review* 86:777–830.
Habscheid, Walther. 1990. Beweislast und Beweismass, ein kontinentaleuropäisch-angelsächsischer Rechtsvergleich. In *Festschrift für Gottfried Baumgärtel zum 70. Geburtstag*, ed. Hanns Prütting, 105–119. Köln: Carl Heymanns Verlag KG.
Hohl, Fabienne. 1991. Le degré de la preuve. In *Beiträge zum schweizerischen und internationalen Zivilprozeßrecht: Festschrift für Oscar Vogel*, ed. Ivo Schwander and Walter Stoffel, 125–159. Freiburg: Univ.-Verl.
Hoyer, Andreas. 1993. Der Konflikt zwischen richterlicher Beweiswürdigungsfreiheit und dem Prinzip "in dubio pro reo". *Zeitschrift für die gesamte Strafrechtswissenschaft* 105:523–556.
Kadner Graziano, Thomas. 2011. "Alles oder nichts" oder anteilige Haftung bei Verursachungszweifeln?: Zur Haftung für perte d'unce chance/loss of chance und eine Alternative. *Zeitschrift für Europäisches Recht* 19:171–200.
Kahneman, Daniel, and Amos Tversky. 1979. Prospect theory: An analysis of decision under risk. *Econometrica* 47:263–292.
Kahneman, Daniel, and Amos Tversky. 1982. The psychology of preferences. *Scientific American* 236:160–173.
Kahneman, Daniel, Jack L. Knetsch, and Richard H. Thaler. 1991. Anomalies: The endowment effect, loss aversion, and status quo bias. *Journal of Economic Perspectives* 5:193–206.
Kaplan, John. 1968. Decision theory and the factfinding process. *Stanford Law Review* 20:1065–1092.
Kaplow, Louis. 2012. Burden of proof. *Yale Law Journal* 121:738–859.
Kaye, David H. 1982. The limits of the preponderance of the evidence standard: Justifiable naked statistical evidence and multiple causation. *Law & Social Inquiry* 1982:487–516.
Kaye, David H. 1987. Apples and oranges: Confidence coefficients and the burden of persuasion. *Cornell Law Review* 73:4–77.
Kaye, David H. 2000. Bayes, burdens and base rates. *International Journal of Evidence and Proof* 4:260–267.
Kaye, David H. 2002. The error of equal error rates. *Law, Probability & Risk* 1:3–8. doi:10.1093/lpr/1.1.3.

Kegel, Gerhard. 1967. Der Individualanscheinsbeweis und die Verteilung der Beweislast nach überwiegender Wahrscheinlichkeit. In *Das Unternehmen in der Rechtsordnung: Festgabe für Heinrich Kronstein aus Anlass seines 70. Geburtstages am 12. September 1967,* ed. Kurt H. Biedenkopf, Helmut Coing, and Ernst-Joachim Mestmäcker, 321–344. Karlsruhe: C.F. Müller.

Kokott, Juliane. 1998. *The burden of proof in comparative and international human rights law. Civil and common law approaches with special reference to the American and German legal systems*. The Hague: Kluwer Law International.

Kordes-de Vaal, Johanna H. 1996. Intention and the omission bias: Omissions perceived as nondecisions. *Acta Psychologica* 93:161–172. doi:10.1016/0001–6918(96)00027-3.

Korobkin, Russell, and Chris Guthrie. 1994. Psychological barriers to litigation settlement: An experimental approach. *Michigan Law Review* 93:107–192.

Lee, Thomas R. 1997. Pleading and proof: The economics of legal burdens. *Brigham Young University Law Review*:1–34.

Leipold, Dieter. 1966. *Beweislastregeln und gesetzliche Vermutungen insbesondere bei Verweisungen zwischen verschiedenen Rechtsgebieten.* Schriften zum Prozessrecht, vol. 4. Berlin: Duncker & Humblot.

Lempert, Richard O. 1977. Modeling relevance. *Michigan Law Review* 75:1021–1057.

Lillquist, Erik. 2002. Recasting reasonable doubt: Decision theory and the virtues of variability. *U.C. Davis Law Review* 36:85–197.

Maassen, Bernhard M. 1975. *Beweismaßprobleme im Schadenersatzprozess.* Köln: Carl Heymanns Verlag KG.

McBride, Ennis. 2009. Is the civil 'higher standard of proof' a coherent concept? *Law, Probability & Risk* 8:323–351. doi:10.1093/lpr/mgp011.

Mittermaier, Carl Joseph Anton. 1843. Die Lehre vom Beweise. Im Deutschen Strafprozesse nach der Fortbildung durch Gerichtsgebrauch und deutsche Gesetzbücher. Johan Wilhelm Heyer's Verlagshandlung: Darmstadt.

Motsch, Richard. 1978. Vom Prozess als Beweis zum Überwiegensprinzip. In *Gesetzgebungstheorie, juristische Logik, Zivil- und Prozessrecht: Gedächtnisschrift für Jürgen Rödig,* ed. Ulrich Klug, Thilo Ramm, Fritz Rittner, and Burkhard Schmiedel, 334–348. Berlin: Springer.

Motsch, Richard. 1983. Vom rechtsgenügenden Beweis. Zur Entscheidung von Zivilsachen nach Wahrscheinlichkeit unter besonderer Berücksichtigung der Abstammungsfeststellung. Duncker & Humblot: Berlin.

Motsch, Richard. 2009. Comparative and analytical remarks on judicial fact-finding. In *Festschrift für Gerhard Käfer,* ed. Helmut Rüßmann, 241–271. Saarbrücken: Juris GmbH.

Musielak, Hans-Joachim. 1975. *Die Grundlagen der Beweislast im Zivilprozess.* Berlin: de Gruyter.

Nagel, Stuart, David Lamm, and Marian Neef. 1981. Decision theory and juror decision making. In *The trial process (Perspectives in law and psychology,* vol. 2, ed. Bruce Dennis Sales, 353–386. New York: Plenum Press.

Nell, Ernst Ludwig. 1983. *Wahrscheinlichkeitsurteile in juristischen Entscheidungen.* Berlin: Duncker & Humblot.

O'Malley, Kevin F., Jay E. Grenig, and William C. Lee, eds. 2001. *Federal jury practice and instructions.* Eagan: Westlaw.

Park, Roger C., Peter Tillers, Frederick C. Moss, D. Michael Risinger, David H. Kaye, Ronald J. Allen, Samuel R. Gross, Bruce L. Hay, Michael S. Pardo, and Paul F. Kirgis. 2010. Bayes wars redivivus: an exchange. *International Commentary on Evidence* 8:1–38. doi:10.2202/1554–4567.1115.

Paulus, Christoph G. 1997. Beweismaß und materielles Recht. In *Festschrift für Hans Friedhelm Gaul zum 70. Geburtstag*, ed. Eberhard Schilken, Ekkehard Becker-Eberhard, and Walter Gerhardt, 747–760. Bielefeld: Gieseking.

Posner, Richard A. 1999. An economic approach to the law of evidence. *Stanford Law Review* 51:1477–1546.

Posner, Richard A. 2007. *Economic analysis of law*, 7th edn. Austin: Wolters Kluwer Law & Business.

Prentice, Robert A., and Jonathan J. Koehler. 2002. A normality bias in legal decision making. *Cornell Law Review* 88:583–650.
Prütting, Hanns. 1983. *Gegenwartsprobleme der Beweislast. Eine Untersuchung moderner Beweislasttheorien und ihrer Anwendung insbesondere im Arbeitsrecht*. München: Beck.
Prütting, Hanns. 2009. Die non-liquet Situation und die Normentheorie. In *Handbuch der Beweislast: Grundlagen*, ed. Gottfried Baumgärtel, Hans-Willi Laumen, and Hanns Prütting, 135–158, 2nd edn. Köln: Carl Heymanns Verlag KG.
Prütting, Hanns. 2010. Beweislast und Beweismaß: Der Einfluss Leo Rosenbergs und Karl Heinz Schwabs auf die Entwicklung eines modernen Beweisrechts. *Zeitschrift für Zivilprozess* 123:135–145.
Rachlinski, Jeffrey J. 1996. Gains, losses and the psychology of litigation. *Southern California Law Review* 70(1):113–185.
Redmayne, Mike. 1999. Standards of proof in civil litigation. *Modern Law Review* 62:167–195.
Ritov, Ilana, and Jonathan Baron. 1990. Reluctance to vaccinate: Omission bias and ambiguity. *Journal of Behavioral Decision Making* 3:263–277. doi:10.1002/bdm.3960030404.
Ritov, Ilana, and Jonathan Baron. 1995. Outcome knowledge, regret, and omission bias. *Organizational Behavior and Human Decision Processes* 64:119–127. doi:10.1006/obhd.1995.1094.
Rosenberg, Leo. 1965. *Die Beweislast auf der Grundlage des bürgerlichen Gesetzbuchs und der Zivilprozessordnung*, 5th edn. München: Beck.
Rüßmann, Helmut. 1987. vor § 284. In Alternativkommentar zur ZPO, ed. Rudolf Wassermann. Hermann Luchterhand Verlag: Neuwied.
Samuelson, William, and Richard Zeckhauser. 1988. Status quo bias in decision making. *Journal of Risk and Uncertainty* 1:7–59. doi:10.1007/BF00055564.
Sand, Leonard B., Jed S. Rakoff, Steven A. Reiss, Walter P. Loughlin, Steven W. Allen, and John S. Siffert, eds. 2007. *Modern federal jury instructions—civil volumes*. Los Angeles: LexisNexis.
Schweitzer, Maurice. 1994. Disentangling status quo and omission effects: An experimental analysis. *Organizational Behavior and Human Decision Processes* 58:457–476. doi:10.1006/obhd.1994.1046.
Schweizer, Mark. 2013. The civil standard of proof—what is it, actually? Preprints of the Max Planck Institute for Research on Collective Goods, Bonn 2013/12
Sheppard, Steve. 2003. The metamorphoses of reasonable doubt: How changes in the burden of proof have weakened the presumption of innocence. *Notre Dame Law Review* 78:1165–1250.
Spranca, Mark, Elisa Minsk, and Jonathan Baron. 1991. Omission and commission in judgment and choice. *Journal of Experimental Social Psychology* 27:76–105. doi:10.1016/0022-1031(91)90011-T.
Stein, Alex. 2005. *Foundations of evidence law*. Oxford: Oxford University Press.
Stölzel, Adolf. 1913. *Schulung für die zivilistische Praxis*. 9th edn. Berlin: Vahlen.
Sugarman, David B. 1986. Active versus passive euthanasia: An attributional analysis1. *Journal of Applied Social Psychology* 16:60–76. doi:10.1111/j.1559-1816.1986.tb02278.x.
Summermatter, Daniel, and Claudia Jacober. 2012. Zum Beweismass beim Kausal- und Motivationszusammenhang: Versuch einer begrifflichen Klärung anhand der jüngeren Rechtsprechung im Zivil-, Straf- und Sozialversicherungsrecht. *HAVE*:136–149.
Sunstein, Cass R. 2004. Moral herustics and moral framing. *Minnesota Law Review* 88:1556–1597.
Sunstein, Cass R. 2005. Moral heuristics. *Behavioral and Brain Sciences* 28:531–541.
Taruffo, Michele. 2003. Rethinking the standards of proof. *American Journal of Comparative Law* 51:659–677.
Tillers, Peter, ed. 1988. Probability and inference in the law of evidence. The uses and limits of Bayesianism. Boston studies in the philosophy of science, vol. 109. Dordrecht: Reidel.
Tillers, Peter. 2011. Trial by mathematics—reconsidered. *Law, Probability & Risk* 10:167–173. doi:10.1093/lpr/mgr011.
Tillers, Peter, and Jonathan Gottfried. 2007. Case comment–United States v. Copeland, 369 F. Supp. 2d 275 (E.D.N.Y. 2005): A collateral attack on the legal maxim that proof beyond a reasonable doubt is unquantifiable? *Law, Probability & Risk* 5:135–157. doi:10.1093/lpr/mgl015.

Tribe, Laurence H. 1971. Trial by mathematics: Precision and ritual in the legal process. *Harvard Law Review* 84:1329–1393.
Tversky, Amos, and Daniel Kahneman. 1991. Loss aversion in riskless choice: A reference-dependent model. *Quarterly Journal of Economics* 106:1039–1061.
Tversky, Amos, and Daniel Kahneman. 1992. Advances in prospect theory: Cumulative representation of uncertainty. *Journal of Risk and Uncertainty* 5:297–323.
Tyree, Alan L. 1982. Proof and probability in the Anglo-American legal system. *Jurimetrics* 23:89–100.
Wagner, Gerhard. 2009. Ökonomische Analyse der Rechtsmittel. In *Ökonomische Analyse des Verfahrensrechts: Beiträge zum XI. Travemünder Symposium zur Ökonomischen Analyse des Rechts (26. bis 29. März 2008)*, ed. Reinhard Bork, Thomas Eger, and Hans-Bernd Schäfer, 156–193. Tübingen: Mohr Siebeck.
Walter, Gerhard. 1979. *Freie Beweiswürdigung*. Tübingen: Mohr Siebeck.
Walter, Hans Peter. 2009. Beweis und Beweislast im Haftpflichtprozess. Haftpflichtprozess, 47–68.
Wright, Richard W. 2009. Proving facts: Belief versus probability. In *Tort and insurance law*, ed. Helmut Koziol and Barbara C. Steininger, 79–105. Vienna: Springer Vienna.
Zamir, Eyal. 2012. Loss aversion and the law. *Vanderbilt Law Review* 65:829–894.
Zamir, Eyal, and Ilana Ritov. 2010. Revisiting the debate over attorneys' contingent fees: A behavioral analysis. *Journal of Legal Studies* 39:245–288. doi:10.1086/605510.
Zamir, Eyal, and Ilana Ritov. 2012. Loss aversion, omission bias, and the burden of proof in civil litigation. *Journal of Legal Studies* 41:165–207. doi:10.1086/664911.

PD Dr. Mark Schweizer Zurich. Lecturer (Privatdozent) for legal sociology, legal theory and civil procedural law at the University of St. Gallen; Senior Research Fellow with the Max Planck Institute for Collective Goods, Bonn; Part-time Judge at the Swiss Federal Patent Court, St. Gallen. CH-8006 Zurich, Huttenstrasse 40. mark.schweizer@gmail.com. Fields of Interest: Civil Procedure (Evidence), Intellectual Property (Patents), Legal Sociology, Behavioural Law and Economics, Bayesian Epistemology (Bayes Nets).

Chapter 8
How Role and Framing Influence Litigants' Perception of Civil Procedure

Edgar Klinger and Günter Bierbrauer

Abstract The interdisciplinary research between psychology and civil law is relatively new. In this article we discuss the issue of why parties in a civil trial choose litigation rather than informal settlement and analyse the different perceptions of plaintiffs and defendants which may have an influence on their procedural choices. Civil court statistics in Germany and other countries show a remarkable asymmetry in terms of winning or losing a case. Defendants lose approximately three times more often than plaintiffs. Proponents of framing theory argue that this asymmetry cannot only be explained on the legal merits of a case alone. On the one hand, defendants adopt a loss frame, because they are accused of some wrongdoing, which they are expected to compensate for. Plaintiffs, on the other hand, adopt a gain frame, because they expect some positive returns. This suggests that litigants may differ in their assessment of procedure, because different aspects of the same situation may be salient to them. In the context of a study involving participants who chose legal mediation rather than adjudication to settle their disputes, "plaintiffs" and "defendants" were asked to evaluate their experiences in retrospect on procedural outcome and procedural fairness. Our analyses show that defendants and plaintiffs differ in their assessments of fairness and outcome significantly. Disputants are sensitive to different procedural factors when they assess outcome and procedural fairness. The divergent perceptions based on the respective position in a trial may in part explain the asymmetry of civil outcome and require further research.

E. Klinger (✉)
Berufsakademie Ost-Friesland, Friedhofstrasse 36, 49536 Lienen, Germany
e-mail: edgarklinger@aol.com

G. Bierbrauer
University of Lucerne, Adolfstrasse 50, 49078 Lucerne, Switzerland
e-mail: g.bierbrauer@yahoo.de

K. Mathis (ed.), *European Perspectives on Behavioural Law and Economics*,
Economic Analysis of Law in European Legal Scholarship 2,
DOI 10.1007/978-3-319-11635-8_8

8.1 Introduction

Civil procedure is the body of law governing how litigants resolve disputes in the civil justice system. Our understanding of the psychology of dispute resolution from the disputants' perception is quite rudimentary and some authors question the ability of litigants to identify the most favourable procedure for them.[1] In a typical civil trial, the plaintiff demands some kind of compensation from the defendant because of some wrong done to him. Therefore, the plaintiff expects some gain, whereas the defendant expects some losses. Disputants' perceptions and evaluation of their options are critical, because such perceptions may guide their procedural choice, for example, whether to accept a settlement suggested by a judge, to mediate or to reject settlement and pursue a trial.

For legal experts, the outcome of a trial depends on its legal merits alone. A look at the court statistics in Germany and other countries where such data are available shows, however, a remarkable asymmetry in terms of winning and losing a case. Defendants loose approximately three times more often than plaintiffs (Table 8.1). A similar pattern applies to former years. The numbers are based on the decision on which party must bear the litigation costs according to the German rule "losers pay all". Most legal scholars are not aware of this fact or are not even interested in this apparent asymmetry. What are the reasons for this asymmetry? From a legal standpoint, one can argue that a plaintiff's legal basis for a claim is more substantiated than that of a defendant. Therefore, the chances of winning the trial are better for plaintiffs than defendants. However, recent research on the mere position in a trial shed new light on this phenomenon.

In a civil trial, litigants must choose whether to settle for a certain outcome typically proposed by the judge, or to pursue a more attractive but uncertain outcome. All choices involve different degrees of risk. As argued by Rachlinski[2], plaintiffs typically choose between accepting a sure gain by settling a case, and accepting an uncertain but potentially more rewarding outcome by litigating further. In contrast, defendants chose between a sure loss by settling, and accepting an uncertain but

Table 8.1 Outcomes of civil proceedings at German courts

	Plaintiff bears the costs of the proceeding completely	Defendant bears the costs of the proceeding completely
Lower regional courts (*Amtsgerichte*)	123,237	539,300
District courts (*Landgerichte*)	62,951	94,167

[1] Shestowsky and Brett 2008.

[2] Rachlinski 1996.

potentially worse outcome by litigating further. Thus, the strategies chosen by the litigants and the risks involved may to some degree determine the outcome of a trial. The same offer of settlement may be more attractive when perceived as a potential gain (from the plaintiff's point of view) than when it is perceived as a potential loss (as perceived from the defendant's point of view).

Traditionally, rational choice or economic models of decision-making prevailed in early research efforts to explain litigants' choices of procedure. The underlying logic of expected utility models of litigation behaviour assumes that litigants make choices according to rules, which maximize economic utility. However, research in cognitive psychology has shown that, under certain conditions, people make decisions that are suboptimal from the perspective of a rational model.[3] Economic utility models fail to take into account the nature of cognitive processes that intervene in decision-making and, consequently, the support for economic models of litigant behaviour has been decreasing, whereas evidence for cognitive models has been growing.[4] As a result, the main interest of this study is to focus on these intervening cognitive processes. Moreover, research in the context of expected utility models and framing has been conducted mainly in laboratory settings using mostly undergraduate participants rather than in the context of real legal disputes. There is a need for more field research in order to test generalizability, effect sizes, and situational influences. Before we deal with our main theoretical focus, i.e. the cognitive perspective of procedural choice, we will briefly review two other theoretical traditions of procedural justice that have been used to explain whether disputes will be settled prior to engagement in formal litigation.

8.2 The Psychology of Procedural Preferences

8.2.1 The Instrumental Perspective

The first wave of research directly relevant for explaining whether disputes will be settled prior to engaging in formal litigation is procedural justice theory, because it deals with satisfaction of procedural fairness and outcome fairness. The two components may be of direct or indirect relevance for whether or not disputants seek settlement.[5] Researchers began to assess procedural preferences experimentally in the 1970s. Thibaut and Walker[6] were originally interested in whether people preferred to use either the adversarial or the non-adversarial trial procedures in their disputes. As defined by the researchers, the adversarial procedure assigns responsibility for the presentation of evidence to the disputants and it is the essential characteristic

[3] E.g. Kahneman et al. 1982.

[4] Rachlinski 1996; Shestowsky 2004.

[5] Lind and Tyler 1988; Tyler 1987.

[6] Thibaut and Walker 1975.

of trials in the US civil justice system. In contrast, in the non-adversarial model, evidence is controlled by the decision maker or by the judge. This model dominates in the legal system of central Europe. Thibaut and Walker[7], as well as several other researchers, found that if individuals view procedures as fair (e.g. perception of due process), then outcomes will be viewed as just, even if the outcome is not favourable. Therefore, the consistent finding in these studies was a preference for an adversarial procedure[8]. In addition, Thibaut and Walker's theory of procedural justice also specified which procedural detail was important for the perception of fairness. The preference of disputants for the adversarial procedure was motivated by their desire to obtain maximum process control ("to tell their story") and decision or outcome control ("to influence decision-making"), because this might enable them to influence the final decision. This line of reasoning has been referred to as the "instrumental perspective" and "suggests that assessments of procedural fairness are based on the favourability of the outcomes received: where people feel that they have control over decisions, they believe that the procedure is fair; where they feel that they lack control, they believe it is unfair"[9].

8.2.2 The Non-Instrumental or Normative Perspective

A later wave of influential research on procedural justice was conducted by Tyler and his colleagues[10]. As an alternative, he proposes a "normative perspective (which) leads to a focus on people's internalized norms of justice and obligations".[11] Consequently, he argues that people are more concerned about how they are treated, rather than about the result they obtain. Tyler summarized the four elements of procedure that contribute to the judgment of fairness: "opportunities for participation (voice), the neutrality of the forum, the trustworthiness of the authorities, and the degree to which people receive treatment with dignity and respect".[12] This leads to the observation that people's perception of how fair a procedure is, tend to depend more on process characteristics than on whether the outcome favoured them, regardless of whether the outcome is positive or negative. As Tyler and others[13] have repeatedly shown, procedural fairness is important in almost all situations. It can be hypothesized that it is perhaps even more important for defendants, because the stakes are higher for them.

[7] Thibaut and Walker 1975.

[8] Walker et al. 1974.

[9] Tyler 1990, p. 7.

[10] Tyler 1990; Tyler 2000; Lind and Tyler 1988.

[11] Tyler 1990, p. 4.

[12] Tyler 2000, p. 121.

[13] Tyler 1990; Lind and Tyler 1988.

8.2.3 The Cognitive Perspective

A plethora of studies have demonstrated that human decision-making in many situations does not conform to the prediction of economic models[14]. In a civil trial, litigants must choose whether to settle or to pursue what is perhaps a more favourable but risky outcome decided by the judge. Due to the different risks involved for plaintiffs and defendants, it makes sense to analyse their choices from a social-psychological perspective, and more specifically, from the particular role they play in a trial. Research in the context of framing theory developed by Kahneman and Tversky[15] has demonstrated that when people choose among gains, they tend to make risk-averse choices, preferring sure gains to larger but riskier gains. Conversely, when people choose among losses, they tend to make risk-seeking choices, preferring riskier outcomes to smaller but certain losses. Kahneman and Tversky[16] relied on empirical evidence and their approach is a "behavioural decision theory" that focuses on how individuals actually make decisions, and not on how they make "rational decisions". Therefore, in the context of the economic utility framework, plaintiffs and defendants will evaluate their decisions identically, as they are indifferent between settlement and trial.

However, Rachlinski[17] argues that litigants' risk preferences will vary systematically, depending upon whether they are in the role of a plaintiff or a defendant. In a simulation study he had law students role-play either a plaintiff or a defendant. Consistent with framing theory, he found that the majority of the plaintiff-subjects (77 %) preferred settlement, i.e. the risk averse option, while the majority of the defendant–subjects (69 %) preferred trial, i.e. the risk-seeking option.

As defendants choose the risk-seeking option of a trial, we can assume that they are more likely to lose their case than plaintiffs who are more conservative and settle. This may explain in part the asymmetry in the court statistics. However, there is no direct evidence for this hypothesis and this study cannot answer this question directly. If, however, we assume that role has a major impact on the cognitions of the parties, we suggest that plaintiffs and defendants will focus their attention on different aspects of the procedure, which in turn influences their procedural choices.

8.3 Cognitions Involved in Framing and Loss Aversion

Although a wealth of studies have meanwhile been published in the context of framing theory, to the best of our knowledge none of them deal directly with the cognitions underlying the processes that lead to loss aversion or risk-seeking behaviour.

---

[14] Shestowsky 2004; Kahneman and Tversky 1979; Guthrie 2003.

[15] Kahneman and Tversky 1984.

[16] Kahneman and Tversky 1984.

[17] Rachlinski 1996.

In the foregoing discussion, we argue that disputants' procedural choices depend in part on the role they assume in the trial. In the context of framing theory, plaintiffs are likely to favour risk-averse choices and settle, whereas defendants tend to make risky choices and prefer trial. A central feature of framing theory is the "principle of loss aversion". This is illustrated in the famous non-symmetric S-shaped curve "which represents diminishing sensitivity for both gains and losses…(where) the response to losses is stronger than the response to corresponding gains. This is loss aversion"[18]. Furthermore, "Framing effects were attributed to the fact that alternative formulations of the same situation make different aspects of it accessible"[19].

If people show different degrees of sensitivity when they are faced with either gains or losses, one could expect corresponding changes in their cognitions that cause or mediate their perceptions. When defendants are assumed to experience loss, then we can conclude that they attend more strongly to procedural features, such as respectful treatment by the judge or mediator, the amount of voice and the perceived competence of the judge or mediator. When, on the other hand, defendants experience potential gains, they are less concerned about losses and will therefore attend more to procedural features, such as the degree to which the judge or mediator managed to broaden the issue or neutrality of the mediator.

8.4 Overview of the Study

The data for our study are based on a rather complex survey involving participants who voluntarily decided to have their dispute settled in a program of in-court mediation offered in the jurisdiction of the State of Mecklenburg-Vorpommern, Germany[20]. The study was conducted in five different courts involving one Higher District Court (OLG), two District Courts (LG), one Administrative Court (VG), and a Social Security Court (SG). The majority of cases documented came from the two District Courts (LG) and most of the conflicts dealt with issues related to building and construction disputes, sales contracts and tenancy disputes. The mediations were conducted by judges who had been trained as mediators, with most of them having several years of mediation experience. At the end of their sessions, participants were asked to respond to various questions relating to the procedure, the judges' behaviour and some general questions regarding their satisfaction with the programme. For this analysis, however, we focus only on their evaluation of procedure. The settlement rate across the various courts ranged from 62 to 88 %. Note that this is a post-hoc analysis of survey data and can be viewed as incomplete with regard to the topic of our study. Based on procedural justice theory, two dimensions are most important for actors in general and for our participants: How do they evaluate their (1) outcome fairness and (2) the procedural fairness of a trial.

[18] Kahneman 2011, pp. 282–283.

[19] Kahneman 2003, p. 716.

[20] Bierbrauer and Klinger 2010.

It should be noted that the data for this analysis came from a survey that was not designed to test the hypotheses for the present study, namely which cognitive variables intervene in disputants' choices. Instead, this study depends on a post-hoc analysis of data, which were available and suitable from a larger survey involving litigants who took part in a program of in-court mediation. Therefore, the variables employed in this analysis may be deficient from the perspective of a complete design. This shortcoming must be taken into account when interpreting and discussing the results. Furthermore, the study will not directly answer the question of why defendants lose more often in a civil trial than plaintiffs. Instead, its focus is on the different cognitions of plaintiffs and defendants, which in turn may influence their procedural choices. In another context, there is some evidence in support of our arguments. If we assume that defendants not only worry more about the outcome, they should also feel more deprived of their autonomy needs. In a study by Van Prooijen[21] participants who were deprived of autonomy were particularly more sensitive or attended more to the fairness of decision-making procedures than participants who were not deprived. Combining these arguments leads to our prediction that defendants are more sensitive to fairness outcome factors than plaintiffs.

8.4.1 Participants

Our analysis is based on 214 completed questionnaires; 111 questionnaires came from former "plaintiffs" and 103 from former "defendants". Their mean age was 49 years and ranged from 18 to 80 years; 70 % were males and approximately 63 % had an academic background.

8.4.2 Survey Instruments

As mentioned above, the data of this analysis are part of a larger study related to in-court mediation. Altogether 22 items dealt with procedural facets. For instance, "The mediator's questions were appropriate to explore all relevant facts of the dispute." (competence of the mediator), "I never experienced the mediator as biased or unfair." (neutrality of the mediator), "Sometimes I felt offended during the mediation." (face-saving). Likert-type response scales with scores ranging from 1 (completely agree) to 4 (completely disagree) were employed. Some of the scales were reverse-scored. Procedural fairness and outcome fairness were assessed by the following two items: "Taken together, how satisfied are you with the way this mediation was conducted?" and "How satisfied are you with the outcome of this mediation?" Again, four-point Likert-type scales were employed with scores ranging from "highly satisfied" (4) to "not at all satisfied" (1).

[21] Van Prooijen 2009.

8.5 Results

Given the nature of our data set, we cannot infer the relative importance for outcome and procedural fairness as perceived by plaintiffs and defendants, because our respondents were not asked to indicate their perceived overall fairness. Instead, we estimated the amount of variance for plaintiffs' and defendants' evaluations of outcome and procedural fairness explained by the procedural facets.

In order to reduce the complexity of our 22 procedural facets, a principle component exploratory factor analysis was conducted. It revealed six factors with eigenvalues > 1, which explain 58.4 % of the total variance. The Kaiser-Meyer-Olkin-criterion of sampling adequacy is high (.824), indicating that all items could be included in the factor analysis. Table 8.2 shows the labels, the eigenvalues and the percentages of the total variance explained by the six factors.

Perceived procedural and outcome fairness of plaintiffs and defendants are relatively high and do not differ significantly. Both plaintiffs ($M=3.42$, $\sigma=0.63$) and defendants ($M=3.43$, $\sigma=0.71$) report high perceived procedural fairness, $t(212)=0.04$, n.s. Outcome fairness is somewhat lower for both plaintiffs ($M=2.96$, $\sigma=0.60$) and defendants ($M=3.04$, $\sigma=0.74$), $t(152.013)=0.77$, n.s. Procedural and outcome fairness are significantly correlated for plaintiffs ($r=.39$, $p<0.0001$) and for defendants ($r=0.60$, $p<0.0001$).

For defendants approximately one third of the variance of outcome fairness (corrected $R^2=0.29$) is predicted by three procedural factors: (1) broadening of issue ($\beta=0.47$), (b) perceived competence of the mediator ($\beta=0.22$), and (3) face-saving ($\beta=0.20$). For plaintiffs, however, outcome fairness is not predicted by the perceptual factors (corrected $R^2=0.07$) (Table 8.3).

A different pattern emerges with regard to the determinants of procedural fairness (Table 8.4). Both defendants (corrected $R^2=0.50$) and plaintiffs (corrected $R^2=0.41$) attend to procedural factors, but give different weights to these factors. For defendants, the perceived competence of the mediator is the most important factor ($ß=0.40$), whereas this factor is relatively unimportant for plaintiffs ($ß=0.27$). For plaintiffs, neutrality of the mediator is the most important factor ($ß=0.43$). Interestingly, face-saving is important only for defendants ($ß=0.17$), but not for plaintiffs. A similar pattern was observed for outcome fairness, where face-saving was only important for defendants ($ß=0.20$).

Table 8.2 Procedural factors of perceptions

Nr.	Factor label	Eigenvalue	Percentage of total variance explained by the factor (%)
1	Competence of the mediator	5.69	25.9
2	Broadening of issue	1.91	8.7
3	Neutrality of the mediator	1.64	7.5
4	Identification of interests	1.35	6.1
5	Communication	1.24	5.6
6	Face-saving	1.01	4.6

Table 8.3 Determinants of perceived outcome fairness

Plaintiffs			Defendants		
Factor	β	t	Factor	β	t
Neutrality of the mediator	0.27	2.43**	Broadening of issue	0.47	4.38*****
Broadening of issue	0.19	1.77*	Competence of mediator	0.22	2.07**
			Face-saving	0.20	1.83*
Corrected $R^2=0.07$			Corrected $R^2=0.29$		
$F\ (6, 78)=2.01$, n.s.			$F\ (6, 60)=5.55, p<.0001$		

*$p<0.10$; **$p<0.05$; *****$p<0.0001$

Table 8.4 Determinants of perceived procedural fairness

Plaintiffs			Defendants		
Factor	β	t	Factor	β	t
Neutrality of mediator	0.43	5.42*****	Competence of mediator	0.40	5.16*****
Broadening of issue	0.39	4.94*****	Neutrality of mediator	0.35	4.29*****
Competence of mediator	0.27	3.45****	Broadening of issue	0.30	3.87*****
Communication	0.15	1.80*	Communication	0.30	3.76*****
			Face-saving	0.17	2.11**
Corrected $R^2=0.41$			Corrected $R^2=0.50$		
$F\ (6, 89)=12.24, p<0.0001$			$F\ (6, 79)=14.98, p<0.0001$		

*$p<0.10$; **$p<0.05$; ****$p<0.001$; *****$p<0.0001$

8.6 Discussion

One of the primary goals of our study was to examine how disputants evaluate the various facets of fairness in the framework of procedural justice research. According to framing theory, actors who perceive prospective losses, namely defendants, should worry more about the possible negative outcomes of a dispute. Framing theory postulates that defendants tend to be risk seeking, because they try to avoid as much of a loss as possible. But why should they accept a particular outcome? Our results show that when defendants evaluate the outcome of a dispute settlement process, they are also sensitive to procedural facets of the settlement process, namely efforts to broaden the issue, their perceptions of the mediator's competence and the support of all parties to keep the defendant's face saved.

On the other hand, as plaintiffs expect gains, they are less concerned about procedural aspects. Instead, their outcome evaluations may depend on other aspects, e.g. their outcome expectations.

As expected, unlike outcome fairness, procedural fairness is predicted to a higher degree by procedural factors. However, disputants assign different importance to these factors. Whereas plaintiffs are more sensitive to the impartiality (neutrality) of the mediator, for defendants the perceived competence of the mediator and efforts to broaden the issue are more important.

Interestingly, face-saving is only important for defendants with regard to both outcome and procedural fairness. This is in line with Rachlinski's prediction that "Defendants…may have a greater interest in personal vindication of their good name than their adversaries"[22], which supports our argument that procedural factors are more important for defendants than for plaintiffs. As a result, the divergent perceptions based on the position in a trial may in part explain the asymmetry of civil outcome. This phenomenon requires further research.

8.7 Conclusions

The present research may have practical and theoretical implications. Disputants who file claims in a civil court can settle via negotiation, mediation, trial or other supplementary procedures. Lawyers and judges need to understand their case not only from a legal perspective, but also from the dynamics of the trial in order to advise disputants on how the various procedures might best satisfy their needs and to teach them about their risks involved. Furthermore, they should educate their clients about their dispute resolution options and teach them to anticipate how their procedural choices are in part influenced by their position in the trial. Our study is an attempt to supplement the research conducted largely in laboratory settings. As mentioned above, because of the history of the study we could not answer the ambitious questions raised in the introduction. However, we were able to shed some light on the different cognitions of the disputants involved in evaluating mediation results.

Nevertheless, several key questions remain unanswered. We were not able to demonstrate that there is a direct link between position, procedural choice and why defendants lose more often. Furthermore, we did not ask our respondents about their outcome expectations ex ante, i.e. before dispute settlements started. For instance, Shestowsky and Brett[23] have shown that ex ante and ex post evaluations of disputants' perceptions differ. In particular, in post-experience evaluations, process matters more than outcomes. Further studies need to control a larger variety of perceptions directly relevant to framing and loss.

Bibliography

Bierbrauer, Günter, and Edgar Klinger. 2010. Gerichtliche Mediation in Mecklenburg-Vorpommern. *Neue Juristische Wochenschrift* 45:14–16.

Guthrie, Chris. 2003. Prospect theory, risk preferences, and the law. *Northwestern University Law Review* 97:1115–1163.

[22] Rachlinski 1996, p. 129.

[23] Shestowsky and Brett 2008.

Kahneman, Daniel. 2003. A perspective on judgment and choice. *American Psychologist* 58:697–720.
Kahneman, Daniel. 2011. *Thinking fast and slow*. London: Penguin Books.
Kahneman, Daniel, and Amos Tversky. 1979. Prospect theory: An analysis of decisions under risk. *Econometrica* 47:263–291.
Kahneman, Daniel, Paul Slovic, and Amos Tversky. 1982. *Judgment under uncertainty: Heuristics and biases*. New York: Cambridge University Press.
LaTour, Stephen, Pauline Houlden, Laurens Walker, and John Thibaut. 1976. Some determinants of preference for modes of conflict resolution. *Journal of Conflict Resolution* 20:319–356.
Lind, E. Allan, and Tom Tyler. 1988. *The social psychology of procedural justice*. New York: Plenum Press.
Rachlinski, Jeffrey. 1996. Gains, losses, and the psychology of litigation. *Southern California Law Review* 70:113–185.
Schweizer, Mark. 2005. Kognitive Täuschungen vor Gericht: eine empirische Studie. Diss., Zürich.
Shestowsky, Donna. 2004. Procedural preferences in alternative dispute resolution: A closer, modern look at an old idea. *Psychology, Public Policy, and Law* 10:211–249.
Shestowsky, Donna, and Jeanne Brett. 2008. Disputants' perceptions of dispute resolution procedures: An ex ante and ex post longitudinal empirical study. *Connecticut Law Review* 41:63–107.
Thibaut, John, and Laurens Walker. 1975. *Procedural justice*. Hillsdale: Erlbaum.
Tyler, Tom. 1987. The psychology of dispute resolution concerns in mediation: Implications for the mediation of disputes by third parties. *Negotiation Journal* 3:367–374.
Tyler, Tom. 1990. *Why people obey the law*. New Haven: Yale University Press.
Tyler, Tom. 2000. Social justice: Outcome and procedure. *International Journal of Psychology* 35:117–125.
Van Prooijen, Jan-Willem. 2009. Procedural justice as autonomy regulation. *Journal of Personality and Social Psychology* 96:1166–1180.
Walker, Laurens, Stephen LaTour, E. Allan Lind, and John Thibaut. 1974. Reactions of participants and observers to modes of adjudication. *Journal of Applied Social Psychology* 4:295–310.

Edgar Klinger Lecturer at the Welfenakademie, Braunschweig, Germany, and at the BAO, Leer, Germany. D-49536 Lienen, Germany, Friedhofstrasse 36, Tel. 0049 5483 8708, Fax. 0049 5483 7219951. edgarklinger@aol.com. Fields of Interest: Legal Psychology, Conflict Management, Social and Cross-Cultural Psychology, International Management.

Prof. Günter Bierbrauer, Ph. D. Professor of Legal Psychology at the University of Lucerne. D-49078 Osnabrueck, Germany, Adolfstrasse 50, Tel. 0049 541 45945, Fax. 0049 541 38099440. g.bierbrauer@yahoo.de. Fields of Interest: Legal Psychology, Conflict Management, Social and Cross-Cultural Psychology.

Chapter 9
Investment Suitability Requirements in the Light of Behavioural Findings

Challenges for a Legal Framework Coping with Ambiguous Risk Perceptions

Rainer Baisch and Rolf H. Weber

The illusion that we understand the past fosters overconfidence in our ability to predict the future
Daniel Kahneman (Thinking, fast and slow, 2011, p. 218)

Abstract The findings of behavioural finance research. Have undoubtedly influenced the traditional understanding of the processes and patterns that allow the financial markets to function.[1] Perceptions, which used to be based on the assumptions of rational behaviour gradually allow for human flaws.[2] Not only the structural information asymmetries between the various financial market participants interfere with the efficient allocation of capital; moreover, there is also a need to address other factors that may substantially influence markets, such as emotions, reference

[1] A good collection of early key papers is Kahneman et al., Judgment under uncertainty: Heuristics and biases, 1982; see also Kahneman and Tversky, Choices, values, and frames, 2000; legal implications stemming from behavioural findings are described by Korobkin and Ulen, Calif Law Rev 88:1051–1144. See also Moloney, How to protect investors: lessons from the EC and the UK, pp. 67–74, 2010 regarding the irrational and uninformed investor

[2] Cunningham, Wash. Lee Law Rev 59:836, 2002 resumes that behavioural finance is "a marriage of cognitive psychology and the financial economics of market inefficiency".

R. Baisch (✉) · R. H. Weber
Rechtswissenschaftliche Fakultät, University of Zurich, Rämistrasse 74/38, 8001, Zurich, Switzerland
e-mail: rainer.baisch@rwi.uzh.ch

R. H. Weber
e-mail: rolf.weber@rwi.uzh.ch

K. Mathis (ed.), *European Perspectives on Behavioural Law and Economics,*
Economic Analysis of Law in European Legal Scholarship 2,
DOI 10.1007/978-3-319-11635-8_9

biases, overconfidence and inertia impair rational choice.[3] Since such insights from the field of behavioural economics are often not in line with the common legislative model developed on the basis of the rational investor concept, the question arises which possible reactions of the law (especially of financial market law) to the insights provided by other disciplines might be valuable.[4] Today's approach towards the point-of-sale (POS) regulations for investment advisory and portfolio management services includes a mandatory assessment regarding the individual appropriateness and suitability of financial investments.[5] The following analysis of presently debated regulatory code-of-conduct requirements fostering investor protection is based on behavioural findings.

9.1 Introduction

One of the elementary topics regarding financial market regulation culminates in the question as to which degree of paternalistic emphasis would be inevitable.[6] Is there just the necessity of having criminal law against fraud in place? What kind of private law design is best suited for settlement and compensation? Are people entitled to make their own choices despite the fact that they err and, thus, will influence general welfare in a negative way?

This contribution assesses the effectiveness of a regulatory approach in financial markets in light of behavioural law findings, envisaging the enforcement of a *Code of Conduct* developed for financial intermediaries, while assuming that a biased behaviour is shown by retail investors, particularly by focusing on the following objectives:

- Perform a mandatory suitability test prior to any investment advice as well as an on-going assessment of the suitability of the recommended financial instruments embracing loss-aversion and attitude towards risk,

[3] However, the role of psychology in economics was already discussed by Keynes, The general theory of employment, interest, and money, p. 315, 1936 referring to animal spirits (162) and unrealistic optimism or pessimism as causes for booms and busts.

[4] An interesting exemplification showing the reaction of law in response to biased decision-making processes is the justification of the business judgment rule as a yardstick which can be seen as a limitation of the hindsight bias that otherwise would affect the judges; see Rachlinski, University of Chic Law Rev 65:574, 1998: "For example, in corporate law, the business judgment rule protects corporate officers and directors from liability for negligent business decisions because, in part, of the tendency for adverse outcomes to seem inevitable" and p. 625: "The business judgment rule and subsequent remedial measures rules, for example, make a great deal of sense as a response to hindsight bias".

[5] Already Rapp, Ohio North University Law Rev 24:189, 1998 stated in relation to financial industry standards of conduct that none is "more frequently cited, and least objectively applied, than the 'suitability' requirement".

[6] Libertarians prefer the freedom of choice, while condemning paternalism; see e.g. Boaz 1997; on the other side, paternalists mistrust freedom of choice and argue against some occurrences of libertarianism; see e.g. Goodin 1991.

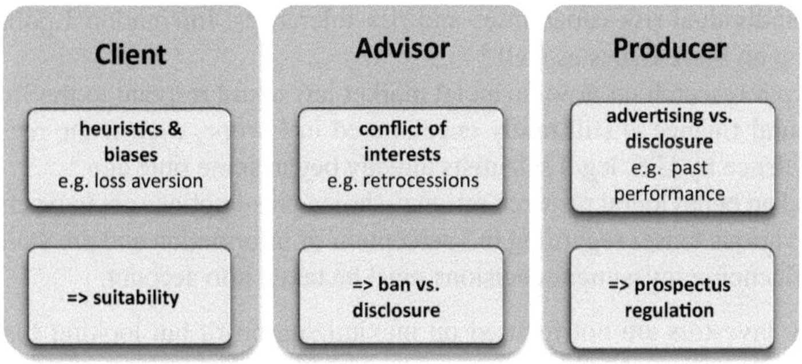

Fig. 9.1 Potential areas of POS-regulation

- Counteract conflicts of interest and
- Optimize the documentation for financial products sold to retail investors.

Figure 9.1 allocates potential causes and areas of misconduct within the scope of POS-regulation, each with an example and a reference to the regulatory segment:

The traditional *disclosure-paradigm* is based on the assumption that transparent and effectively processed information will enable the investor to make well-founded investment decisions. Having a type of *homo oeconomicus* in mind, financial market laws used to be designed for responsible and knowledgeable actors. Following the financial crisis culminating in the collapse of *Lehman Brothers* and widespread losses in portfolios of small retail clients, regulators are still strengthening the respective rules and their surveillance.

While for products traded at stock exchanges information asymmetry might be partly reduced, such effect cannot be presupposed for *structured products*. Therefore, the investor faces limitations to evaluate the price. In consequence, the regulator is challenged to act in order to secure the product's quality and pricing. However, it can be criticized that the design of legal measures for transparency does not sufficiently take into consideration, whether an investor is capable and (under the behavioural aspects) willing to assimilate the information made available to him. Therefore, it must be assumed that the provision of information alone is not sufficient, since the capacity and willingness to handle information might be limited.

The European regulatory approach within *MiFID*[7] provides for a suitability test, which, however, did not prevent private European investors from losing money with *Lehman* certificates. Assessing investment suitability requires the right set of questions to cope with diverging experience, personal investment objectives as well

[7] MiFID stands for Market in Financial Instruments Directive, 2004/39/EC of the European Parliament and of the Council of 21 April 2004 on markets in financial instruments, *30.4.2004*, OJ L 145/1-44.

as with individual risk-capabilities and risk-tolerances. International politics have picked up on these issues as well.[8]

In-depth research on how financial market law could respond to the findings of behavioural finance is still rarely encountered in Europe, even if the reception of such evidence by U.S. legal scientists already began some time ago.[9]

Based on behavioural research rational-choice presumptions are to be challenged and the various biases regarding the perception of information and the validating of facts influencing investment decisions must be taken into account:

- Many investors are not focused on maximizing profit but looking for security and conservation of value;
- Decisions are influenced by emotions, often based on overconfidence and impaired by further biases;
- The past performance orientated marketing instruments are leading to immoderate expectations.

Therefore, can enhanced prevention based on higher information requirements be effective? Will a stricter *Code of Conduct* at the point of sale really lead to better investor protection? How should the risk tolerance be assessed to allow for a comprehensive suitability test?

In general: Is it possible to de-bias detrimental human shortcomings through law while avoiding distending paternalism?[10]

In addition, looking at the necessary enforcement strategy, the question could be asked as to whether the market participants need *the carrot or the stick* approach to implement processes to cope with potential new requirements.

Building on the dichotomy between a rational choice assumption and the results of hindsight observation this contribution begins with a recap of some typical biases. Consecutively the occurrence of POS-regulation, especially independence

---

[8] In the OECD G20 High-Level Principles on Financial Consumer Protection, published in October 2011, <http://www.oecd.org/regreform/liberalisationandcompetitioninterventioninregulatedsectors/48892010.pdf>) the principle *Disclosure and Transparency* is stressed in sect. 4; the following formulation exemplifies that this principle is clearly understood in a comprehensive manner: "Financial services providers and authorised agents should provide consumers with key information that informs the consumer of the fundamental benefits, risks and terms of the product. They should also provide information on conflicts of interest associated with the authorised agent through which the product is sold." Addressing risks it is stated: "The provision of advice should be as objective as possible and should in general be based on the consumer's profile considering the complexity of the product, the risks associated with it as well as the customer's financial objectives, knowledge, capabilities and experience. Consumers should be made aware of the importance of providing financial services providers with relevant, accurate and available information."

[9] See e.g., Camerer et al. 2003; Sunstein and Thaler 2003. In German language see e.g. Schmies 2007.

[10] The first question is whether it is possible to overcome undesirable biases. Depending on adequate measures this seems to be at least partially possible. The subsequent questions are whether it is advisable to do so and whether law could be an appropriate corrective; see Cunningham 2002, p. 787, with further references. Cognitive biases, e.g. overconfidence, can have valuable positive effects, but they should not be ignored by the market actors and regulators.

provisions and the suitability concept are described, followed by the respective approaches in the US and EU jurisdiction with Swiss law.[11] Subsequently the ways of assessing a risk profile adjusted to someone's individual risk tolerance are explained. Finally, deduced conclusions look at a legal framing in lieu of the findings.

9.2 Rational Choice vs. Behavioural Findings

9.2.1 Recap: Rational Behaviour of a Homo Oeconomicus

It would go beyond the scope of this contribution to guide through the developments in philosophical and economic research encompassing Bernoulli's expected utility hypothesis, Bayes's theorem, Smith's invisible hand and von Neumann-Morgenstern's utility theorem, or Fama's efficient market hypothesis (EMH), Markowitz's portfolio selection theory and Sharpe's capital asset pricing model (CAPM). However, to basically understand the starting point of Simon's bounded rationality as well as Tversky and Kahneman's approach to the decision-making theory under uncertainty and their prospect theory, some foundations must be laid. Thus, the fundamentals and outcomes of the rational choice approach are important for the understanding of Thaler's[12] and Shiller's [13] research and the latest bestseller from Kahneman or the nudges from Thaler and Sunstein.[14]

The fundamental armamentarium of an economist is still based on the assumption of full rationality.[15] But what is covered by this premise? The following ingredients should be known:

- Individuals are supposed to have explicitly defined preferences;
- Any taken decision aims at maximising these statically fixed preferences;
- These preferences are based on the real costs and benefits, while all available options are known;
- The uncertainties at hand are expressed in probabilities and the resulting percentages are one-to-one used to weight the expected value.

Just a small example: These axioms give a clear indication that an individual would prefer an 11 % gamble chance to win ten millions (=1,100,000) instead of taking 1,000,000 for sure. However, depending on income and wealth not very many

[11] See for a god overview also the World Bank working paper from Boskovic et al. 2010.

[12] E.g. Thaler 1991 and 2002.

[13] E.g. Shiller 2000.

[14] Kahneman 2011 ; Sunstein and Thaler 2008.

[15] Camerer et al. 2003.

individuals would choose accordingly. Violating Bayes' rule[16] can be based on stereotypes and the disregard of prior probabilities; alternatively, the people are failing to process and classify information correctly. But in the face of studies, which show a wide spread blithely ignored mathematical incompetence, it is unrealistic to expect people to ponder and evaluate probabilities correctly.[17]

Based on the assumption that the vast majority of transactions and the predominant share of assets are associated with professional market participants it could be argued that the irrational activity of Jane Bloggs will not influence the market and the EMH stays valid. However, the behaviour of institutional investors based on a kind of rational herding impeaches the EMH-credibility. Even sceptic actors are tempted to run with the bulk because their performance is evaluated against market indices. Therefore, it might be riskier to swim against the stream than to swim with it despite the potential of asset overvaluation and bubbles.[18]

9.2.2 Rational Choice Challenges Based on Behavioural Research

Sunstein and Thaler summarize research by psychologists and economists over the past three decades, contesting the rationality of judgments and decisions by individuals:[19]

- Individual predictions are not in line with Bayes' rule,[20]
- Heuristics systematically lead to errors,[21]
- Preferences may reverse,[22]

---

[16] In principle, Bayes's theorem in says that the probability of a hypothesis (the posterior probability) is a function of new evidence (the likelihood) and previous knowledge (prior probability).

[17] Ben-Shahar and Schneider 2010, p. 42, are summing up some relevant studies: "A standard test of numeracy asks people how often a flipped coin comes up heads in 1000 tries, what 1 % of 1000 is, and to turn a proportion (1 in 1000) into a percentage. 30 % of women of above-average literacy 'had 0 correct answers, 28 % had 1 correct answer, 26 % had 2 correct answers, and 16 % had 3 correct answers' (Schwartz et al. 1997). Most of the people in another study had at least some college education, but 40 % 'could not solve a basic probability problem or convert a percentage to a proportion' (Lipkus et al. 2001). No wonder that 'after receiving quantitative risk reduction data about the benefit of mammography, most women did not apply this information correctly when asked to estimate their risk for death from breast cancer with and without mammography'; (accuracy ranged from 7–33 %; Schwartz et al. 1997)."

[18] Avgouleas 2009, p. 453–454; Shiller 2005, p. 154; see also FSA 2009, The Turner Review, A Regulatory Response to the Global Banking Crisis, pp. 40–41, where this phenomenon is described.

[19] Sunstein and Thaler 2003. Some of the findings might be criticised while based on laboratory experiments, but the real-world performance seems in average not to be any better. Only some learning effects can improve the decision-making process; see on anchoring and overconfidence: De Bondt and Thaler 1990; Shiller 2000, pp. 136–147.

[20] Grether 1980.

[21] Tversky and Kahneman 1973; Tversky and Kahneman 1974; Kahneman and Frederick 2002.

[22] This means preferring A to B as well as B to A. In the legal context, see Sunstein et al. 2002 .

- Personal harming emerges due to a lack of self-control,[23] and
- The choice varies even depending on the wording of a problem.[24]

Camerer et al. 2003[25] identified two lines of research:

- Line 1 based on experimental work by cognitive psychologists identifying (i) decision-making anomalies (patterns of judgment and choice, inconsistent with utility maximisation and/or Bayesian updating) and (ii) the arguably underlying heuristics (cognitive shortcuts).[26]
- Line 2 governed by economists extending the rational choice paradigm to cope for normal bounds on rationality.[27]

Behavioural economics identified various anomalous phenomena but the results were not much more than a "laundry list of departures from rational choice" in the beginning.[28] Then a more scientific approach led to economic functions: by adding parameters to standard rational theory anomalies like loss-aversion,[29] loss aversion in combination with the endowment effect[30] and inconsistency of decisions in relation to people's own experiences of gains and losses was studied.[31] Social preferences beyond materialistic utility maximisation were also taken into account.[32] Additionally, self-control problems causing or delaying action, which would be in the best interest, suggested themselves.[33]

However, the importance of simplified models in economics assuming for e.g. perfect competition, perfect information, and—of course—perfect rationality is beyond dispute. By lifting tight restrictions, innovative research results are to be achieved, as it was done with models including information costs.[34] Camerer et. al.

---

[23] Frederick et al. 2002.

[24] Camerer 2000, pp. 294–95; Johnson et al. 1993, p. 48.

[25] Camerer et al. 2003, p. 1215.

[26] Tversky and Kahneman 1974, p. 1124 , stated, that relying on the representativeness heuristic to judge probabilities "leads to serious errors, because similarity, or representativeness, is not influenced by several factors that should affect judgments of probability." Individuals tend to disregard familiar common facts codetermining probabilities under uncertainty while focusing only on facts before their face.

[27] Simon 1955, pp. 103–110.

[28] Camerer et al. 2003, p. 1216; see also Camerer and Loewenstein 2004.

[29] Camerer 2000, tbl.16.1 shows ten examples of patterns; for the basics: Kahneman and Tversky 1979; Tversky and Kahneman 1991.

[30] Kahneman et al. 1991 .

[31] Tversky and Kahneman 1991, pp. 1047–48 ; Strahilevitz and Loewenstein 1998, p. 285.

[32] Charness and Rabin 2002, pp. 849–51 found that individuals are concerned with increasing social welfare; Fehr and Schmidt 1999, pp. 855–56 looked at an economic environment determining whether fair or selfish types dominate; Loewenstein et al. 1989, pp. 438–39 worked on social utility functions that could be used to predict individual behaviour in situations where decisions had personal as well as consequences for another party; Rabin 1993, pp. 1281–82 looked at a "fairness equilibrium" in which people like to help those helping them and hurt those who are hurting them.

[33] See Laibson 1997, pp. 444–45; O'Donoghue and Rabin 1999, pp. 118–120.

[34] See Shefrin and Meir Statman introducing BAPM, *behavioral asset pricing model*, 1994 and *behavioral portfolio theory*; in that theory, investors divide their money into mental account layers of a portfolio pyramid corresponding to goals 2000.

2003 saw in "relaxing the assumptions of perfect rationality … a logical next step in this productive progression".

Paternalism is widely accepted to protect lives (mandatory use of seat belt) or minors (sale of alcohol). A latent phobia can be observed amongst market liberals who are afraid of too much paternalism with respect to the outcomes of behavioural research. In fact, an important cognition based on behavioural research is a widening of the category of idiots requiring protection. To avoid paternalism, good regulation will impose minimal restrictions on those who behave rationally, but will guide the others.[35]

Less known fact is that the early roots of behavioural economics go way back to Adam Smith, who published The Theory of Moral Sentiments in 1759.[36] Smith's statement that we suffer more falling back from better to worse than enjoying a rise vice versa expresses the nature of loss aversion.[37] The behavioural approach does not reject the neoclassical approach; the neoclassical theoretical foundation is based on the fact that one or more assumptions are modified or challenged, simplified or relaxed.

9.2.3 Limitations of Rational Choice

While the efficient market hypothesis proclaims that prices in financial markets reflect the fundamental value balancing any new information, behavioural finance describes anomalies that are inconsistent with this thesis and assumes that the influence of arbitrage is limited Fig. 9.2.[38]

Based on emotions humans do not like to regret a former decision, while reference biases and the manner how information is framed and anchored have a major impact on the way they are processed. Overconfidence influences the assessment of probabilities and due to inertia decisions are refused. Next, some basic anomalies (or better departures from rational choice) are to be looked at in more detail.

Fig. 9.2 Limitation of rational choice

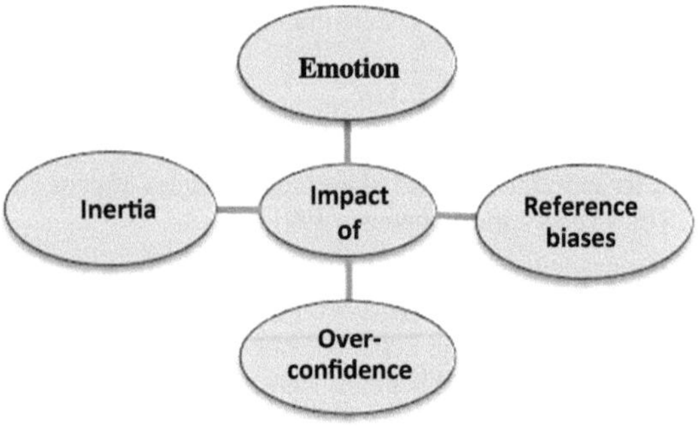

[35] Camereret al. 2003, p. 1218.

[36] Smith1892, originally 1759, p. 311 .

[37] Camerer and Loewenstein 2004, p. 5.

[38] Langevoort 1992; Avgouleas 2012, p. 57 et seq.

9.3 Relevant Biases and Heuristics

9.3.1 Some Preliminary Remarks Regarding Biases and Heuristics

Wikipedia lists more than one hundred biases;[39] some are better known than others—not only through recent bestsellers from Akerlof & Shiller,[40] Thaler & Sunstein or Kahneman. This sub-chapter refers to some relevant and remarkable biases, which financial market participants and regulators should be aware of. Therefore, heuristics are (often unconscious) methods while biases are predictions and affinities; in principle, heuristics are causing biases, but this differentiation is not really important because many are interfering with each other and affecting others.[41] Loss aversion contributes to the endowment effect and probability misjudgement is partially accounting for loss aversion.

Systematic biases can be categorized into those with cognitive provenance and those with emotional backgrounds. Additionally heuristics can be classified along the process chain of information from perception over processing and validation to decision. Figure 9.3 shows the classification of some better known examples:

	perception →	**processing & validation** →	**decision**
cognitive	probability misjudgement selective perception	anchoring mental accounting overconfidence	self-attribution hindsight bias
emotional	herding	reflection effect	endowment effect optimism bias

Fig. 9.3 Behavioural findings along the information process chain

A lot of research is and will be done on these phenomena. Some literature deals with heuristics and biases explaining behaviour that is not in line with rational choice, like mental shortcuts, under conditions of uncertainty. The papers on prospect theory are more specific, looking at utility functions under conditions of risk. For the jurisprudence and the regulators (as well as for this contribution) it is most important to accept the lack of rational choice, unclear preferences and susceptible individuals and assume the according behaviour.

---

[39] See <http://en.wikipedia.org/wiki/List_of_cognitive_biases>. For a good overview regarding investor biases see Pompian 2012.

[40] Akerlof and Shiller 2010.

[41] "Cognitive biases are heuristic strategies operating at a subconscious level [...]"; Cunningham 2002, p. 787.

On the one hand, swamping disclosure requirements misjudge the abilities of retail investors, while on the other hand, slack regulation was common in the problematic field of inducements, which are causing conflicting interests; the effect of utility maximisation—thereby motivating bankers to create and sell products which are not in the best interest of their clients—was misjudged. Certainly, areas exist, where rational choice assumption must be relaxed, and other areas, where they must be kept in mind intensively.

9.3.2 *Prospect Theory and Loss Aversion*

Kahneman and Tversky presented their "prospect theory" which challenges the expected utility theory formulated by von Neumann and Morgenstern based on monitored deviating decisions.[42] Thaler made a "very brief summary of prospect theory"[43] which is recounted here in an even shorter version: Analysing the results of a series of survey questions designed to highlight discrepancies between behaviour and expected utility theory, Kahneman & Tversky generalized the results of their questionnaires, clearly indicating that gains are treated differently than losses; risk seeking was observed for losses but risk-aversion for gains.

Additionally, outcomes received with certainty outweigh relative to uncertain outcomes. A theory based on that can predict individual choices, even in the cases in which expected utility theory is violated, by replacing the objective probabilities through subjective decision weights and the utility function through a value function, defined by changes in wealth rather than in final asset positions.

The acknowledgement that unpleasant feelings about losses are dominating long-term considerations is important for any kind of risk assessment. Accepting suboptimal utility preferences by an average investor will lead to a too risk-averse risk categorisation which than will result in an amendable performance of this portfolio. Looking at the process of financial decision-making it is obvious that everyone's individual degree of loss aversion should have an important impact. Thereby, it must also be considered that investors tend to incorporate sunk cost in their decision-making process, which veils the present facts.[44]

9.3.3 *Endowment and Disposition Effect*

Jolls tagged the debate over the Coase theorem and the endowment effect as "central point of contact" between law and economics and behavioural economics.[45]

[42] Kahneman and Tversky 1979 . Neumann and Morgenstern 1944. A prospect is a gamble (x, p, y, q) that pays x with probability p and y with probability q.

[43] Thaler 1980, pp. 41–43.

[44] This is especially true when we hold on to assets based on the former purchasing price and are not willing to accept that only the current price and the future potential should be assessed.

[45] Jolls 2006, p. 4. The Coase theorem is a centerpiece of law and economics; basically it states that allocating legal rights to one party or another will not affect outcomes if transaction costs are sufficiently low; see Coase 1960.

Thaler described this effect (which is a corollary effect of loss aversion[46]) as the tendency of people to refuse to give up entitlements they hold even though they would not have bought those entitlements initially.[47] This pattern—to prefer holding on to someone's belongings and neither selling nor buying—is related to the status quo bias.[48] The chicken or egg problem, whether the preference to stick to the status quo results from or triggers loss aversion is not really relevant. There is also a close interrelation to inertia[49] and the regret aversion bias.[50]

Based on rational choice assumptions opportunity costs are equivalent to out-of-pocket costs. But in real life out-of-pocket costs are perceived like a loss, which based on loss aversion leads to a corresponding weighting, while opportunity costs appear similar to foregone gains. The result is that goods (or investments) that are already in someone's possession (Thaler worded it "included in the individual's endowment") are valued higher than those for which money would have to be spent; this is intensified by a certain degree of ubiquitous inertia. Vice versa, giving away a good compared to the alternatively possible gain of money intensifies the effect. Thaler called this underweighting of opportunity costs the *endowment effect*, thereby contradicting the Coase theorem.[51]

What kind of impact does the endowment effect have in the field of investment decisions? Selling a share or another investment is influenced by the so-called disposition effect: investors tend "to sell winners too early and ride losers too long".[52] Shefrin and Statman also based their assumption on the work of *Thaler*'s mental accounting[53] and regret aversion.[54] As a result it can be stated that based on the principle of loss aversion various effects lead investors to suboptimal decisions.

---

46 Jolls et al. 1998, p. 1550.

47 Thaler 1980, pp. 43–47.

48 Samuelson and Zeckhauser 1988.

49 Gal 2006.

50 Regret aversion bias is the tendency to avoid making a decision due to the fear of the later probability to experience the pain of regret; in consequence, people will avoid taking decisive actions because they fear that, in hindsight, whatever action they may select could prove less than optimal.

51 Kahneman 1990 were working with chocolate bars and mugs; different from an experiment with tokens subjects who initially were given mugs rarely sold them, while those not initially given mugs seldom bought them. Shogren et al. 1994 criticised the situation of artificial scarcity in this experiment and found by using the same goods little evidence of the endowment effect. However, the experiment by Carmon and Ariely 2000 using basketball tickets confirmed the endowment effect.

52 Shefrin and Statman 1985.

53 Thaler 1984.

54 Regret aversion has been discussed by Thaler 1980; Kahneman and Tversky 1982. Regret results from the ex-post perception, that with the ex-post knowledge a different decision would have been more favourable.

9.3.4 Overconfidence

> Psychological studies show that most people are overconfident about their own relative abilities [...] assessing their position in a distribution of peers on almost any positive trait—like driving ability [...]—a vast majority of people say they are above the average, although of course, only half can be.[55]

Overconfidence can have many positive effects. Looking at retirement savings the expectation to live longer than average should lead to higher savings. But while choosing investment strategies this trait induces suboptimal portfolios (prediction overconfidence). There are various other forms of overconfidence, which can influence decisions.[56]

The very common expectation to be smarter than the market, which often results in a higher trading frequency, is also based on overconfidence. Barber and Odean showed that portfolios with a low trading activity performed better; as a result overconfidence will get people a lower return on average.[57] The other common example, the fact that it is impossible to find an assembly, in which half of the group assesses themselves as below-average drivers,[58] gives a clear indication of a latent omnipresent overestimation of one's own capabilities.

According to Kahneman the pervasive optimistic bias, which "may well be the most significant of the cognitive biases", generates the illusion, that we have substantial control of a planned project or our lives.[59] The planning fallacy, the tendency to overestimate benefits and underestimate costs, leads to risky projects. The same can be true in regard of investment decisions. Because people do not take into account the real complexity of the world and instead focus on their narrow understanding, the basis of the assessment is just a reduced and perhaps not representative set of facts. Kahneman introduces the concept he labels *What You See Is All There Is (WYSIATI)*:[60] The mind deals primarily with Known Knowns, rarely considers Known Unknowns and disregards the possibility of Unknown Unknowns.[61]

One might think overconfidence and loss aversion are dragging in different directions, because the first might lead to a risky decision and the second might prevent from deciding that way. However, overconfidence tends to foster a misdirected judgment, while loss aversion hinders later correcting a wrong decision. That implies, buying a certain share people relate back to their information horizon and

---

[55] Camerer and Lovallo 1999, p. 306.

[56] Barber and Odean 2001.

[57] Barber and Odean 2001.

[58] Svenson 1981.

[59] Kahneman 2011, p. 255.

[60] Kahneman 2011, p. 85 et seq .

[61] "There are known knowns; there are things we know that we know. There are known unknowns; that is to say, there are things that we now know we don't know. But there are also unknown unknowns—there are things we do not know we don't know." Donald Rumsfeld, February 2002; <http://www.defense.gov/transcripts/transcript.aspx?transcriptid=2636>. Additionally their might be unknown (unconscious) knowns.

would not do so, when having the expectation of losses. Loss aversion might make its appearance only, if there are alternatives available, or later, when a decision to sell shares would be reasonable. Therefore, POS-regulation has to avoid potential abuses of those human limitations.

9.3.5 Findings for the Regulator

Looking at retail investors the regulator must abandon the idea of decision-making based on rational choice assumptions. Therefore, disclosure is necessary but will alone not lead to optimal investment allocation. Accompanied by herding, bubble-building and wrongly incentivized staff at the POS, rules for a code of conduct must accept these findings from behavioural research.

Keeping in mind that the professionals from the financial industry are also aware of these effects, it cannot be ignored, that those biases might be capitalized. Looking at product flyers with attractive recent return curves or highlighted assurance that the capital is protected, it is not farfetched to assume that at least some behavioural weaknesses are exploited. Starting from this apprehension, a closer look at the POS-regulation is inevitable.

However, the introduction of subdivisions to further classify retail investors or independent agencies to scrutinize financial products does not seem to be preferable.[62] Clients are too disparate to be pigeonholed and the national financial authority should be capable enough to act against hazardous financial products that should not pass the suitability test to begin with.[63] Therefore, the regulator must focus on conflict of interest issues and proper suitability tests with simultaneous consideration of ways to optimize disclosure and appropriate actions to avoid unfair advertising practices.

9.4 POS-Regulation

9.4.1 Mitigation of Conflicts of Interest

All kinds of inducements and incentives like trailer fees, retrocessions and other commissions are common as means of sales promotion in the banking and fund industry. Conflicts of interest are to be monitored to the extent that such payments may influence investment advisory services. Long-term considerations will lead to recommendations triggered by the hope for satisfied customers, while short-term temptations might result in preferring a good salary and high bonuses.

[62] Avgouleas 2009 makes those two proposals for reform.

[63] However, the grey capital market, closed-end funds and investment companies will remain a challenge.

What is true for an individual advisor himself at the POS is also true for banks and other financial intermediaries as a whole or for a certain division. Especially MiFID II is going to strengthen the independence of investment advice and portfolio management services.[64] The days are gone when undisclosed fees were helping to line one's pockets. However, looking at international regulatory activities huge differences exist; some aim to eliminate such kind of payment flows at all for independent advice, others just demand a full disclosure approach. While for many investment products like shares or bonds an efficient formation of prices—liquid markets presumed—is at least not impossible based on Modern Finance Theory, in contrast, many of the structured products do not facilitate a clear price evaluation.[65]

In the face of information overload and the widespread unwillingness of investors to take note of information, EU regulators are introducing KI(I)D's and PRIP's.[66] The scepticism remains: will a retail investor really process that information? And based on the behavioural findings: May things go wrong anyway?

The intention of this contribution is to advocate for a clear disclosure of any kind of administrative cost in connection with the purchase of an investment product.[67] Especially in the case of structured products, investors need clear information which amount of money is invested and how much is deducted immediately or later for any kind of fees in order to rationally evaluate the product. In section 6, a positive aspect of some structured products will be discussed: there are structured products in the markets, which can help to meet the risk preferences of investors.

9.4.2 *Appropriateness and Suitability*

The other major topics regarding POS-regulation are the so-called suitability and appropriateness tests. While suitability contains a link to present as well as future aspects, *appropriateness* just reflects the past. Based on detailed conduct of

[64] MiFID II proposal Art. 24 (5); European Commission proposal for a Directive of the European Parliament and of the Council on markets in financial instruments repealing Directive 2004/39/EC of the European parliament and of the Council, Brussels, 20.10.2011; <http://ec.europa.eu/internal_market/securities/docs/isd/mifid/COM_2011_652_en.pdf>.

[65] According to Hens and Rieger 2008, p. 27 most of the common structured products do not "follow rational guideline, but instead use behavioral factors, like loss-aversion or probability misjudgment to be attractive in the eyes of potential investors".

[66] KI(I)D (Key Investor (information) Document) and PRIP (Packaged Retail Investment Product); see Commission Regulation (EU) No 583/2010, OJ L 176, 1.7.2010, 1–15; Commissions Proposal for a regulation on key information documents for investment products, COM (2012) 352, 3.7.2012, <ec.europa.eu/internal_market/finservices-retail/docs/investment_products/20120703-proposal_en.pdf>.

[67] See Article 33 of the level 2 MiFID-ID (MiFID Implementing Directive, Commission Directive 2006/73/EC of 10 August 2006 implementing Directive 2004/39/EC of the European Parliament and of the Council as regards organisational requirements and operating conditions for investment firms and defined terms for the purposes of that Directive, *2.9.2006, OJ L 241/26–58*) regarding the obligation to inform clients about costs.

business rules for investment firms in combination with the just discussed transparency requirements these tests implement the general obligation to act fairly, honestly and professionally and in accordance with the best interests of the client—previously known as fiduciary duty.[68]

The assessment of suitability shall determine on an individual basis not only whether the customers have the necessary expertise to trade in the specific financial instrument, but also whether they understand and can take the associated risks—and all of that in line with the individual financial status and investment objectives Fig. 9.4.

> Investor education rather than investor regulation is probably the best way to respond to the increasing recognition of the substantial role that cognitive biases play in investor behaviour. Nevertheless, the insights from finance do suggest a couple of areas where existing legal rules should change.[69]

This statement from 2002 reflects behavioural findings; however, it also exemplifies the traditional approach preferring education—often named investor empowerment—instead of protection; but the need for some rules to be adjusted was already recognized with reference to NASD 2310.[70] Cunningham stated: "[…], reformers should give consideration to broadening the concepts underlying the fair dealing and suitable requirements to include a psychological component."[71]

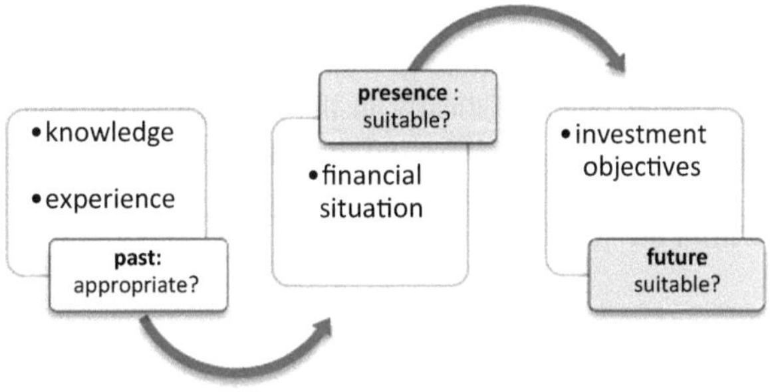

Fig. 9.4 Temporal classification of appropriateness and suitability

[68] According to Rapp 1998, p. 212, "the most common characterization offered is that suitability is an amorphous concept, with no accepted definition, and bereft of case law guidance".

[69] Cunningham 2002, p. 797. At 788: "It also means that such investor education must include not only tutelage in the principles of finance and insights from behavioral finance, but also explanation of how these axioms may collide."

[70] See below 5.1. NASD (National Association of Securities Dealers) is the former name of the American self-regulatory organization for broker-dealers, which is now consolidated with the member regulation, enforcement and arbitration functions of the New York Stock Exchange FINRA (Financial Industry Regulatory Authority). Founded and registered with the SEC in 1939 the NASD was based on the 1938 Maloney Act amendments to the Securities Exchange Act of 1934. NASD as the one and only "Registered Securities Association" supervised the conduct of its members under the oversight of the SEC. Section 15A of the Securities Exchange Act of 1934 was enacted in 1938 to extend regulatory authority under the federal securities laws to the over-the-counter securities markets. NASD created a system of cooperative regulation of broker-dealers and was responsible for the adoption and enforcement of the rules to protect investors and the public interest.

[71] Cunningham 2002, p. 798.

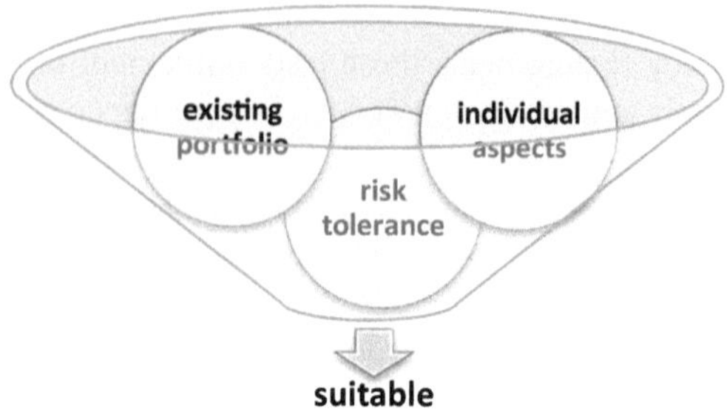

Fig. 9.5 Elements of suitability

Another ten years earlier, practical and legal issues of suitability were reviewed in detail for the first time, acknowledging that suitability "concerns the type of investment vehicles that an investor will utilize to attain investment goals that may range from rampant speculation to simply maintaining the real value of a pool of funds".[72] Shortcomings in the suitability assessment regarding "the information-gathering techniques currently employed by brokers" as well as problems due to "the resultant communication failures between the broker and the customer concerning the latter's investment goals" were identified Fig. 9.5.[73]

In Europe the introduction of suitability requirements in 2004 with MiFID changed the retail investor protection regime significantly, setting a new "high-water mark of the extent to which the new regulatory strategy for the retail markets intervenes paternalistically in the investor's decision".[74] But obviously the financial crises tsunami surpassed that high-water mark and the dam is now fortified by strengthening the requirements regarding the investor's individual risk-tolerance within the suitability assessment.

9.5 Comparison of Current Legal Frameworks

9.5.1 USA: FINRA Rules

The U.S. suitability assessment has a long tradition coined by the strict differentiation between execution and advisory services. For the U.S. Securities and Exchange Commission (SEC) the compliance with suitability requirements used to be a commitment for securities dealers, based on the *Shingle Theory*: The SEC's shingle theory has an ancient lineage, but is still viable and holds that when a broker hangs out its shingle to do business it impliedly represents that it will deal fairly with his customers and in accordance with industry standards, particularly if making

[72] Anderson and Winslow 1992, p. 105.

[73] Anderson and Winslow 1992, p. 118.

[74] Moloney 2008, p. 614.

suggestions regarding securities. This *fiduciary duty* and the respective suitability doctrines were used to ensure the protection of investors from unscrupulous broker-dealers.[75]

In contrast to investment advisers, broker-dealers used to be seen as salesmen; therefore, significant differences were made between the obligations and limitations imposed on broker-dealers under the shingle theory and those imposed on investment advisers under fiduciary law especially regarding disclosure of conflicts of interest and the nature and extent of advice that is provided. In principle, based on this doctrine a broker-dealer should recommend an investment only if there are reasonable grounds to believe that a recommendation with respect to the financial situation and the investment objectives was suitable for the customer; this assessment did not imply that an investment had to be in the best interest of the investor. The suitability regime applies whenever a client relies on the broker-dealer, however, the situation, where he serves solely as an order clerk to an unknown client is exempted.[76]

However, investment advisers are seen as fiduciaries. Based on *SEC vs. Capital Gains Research, Inc.*,[77] the U.S. Supreme Court officially recognized that investment advisers serve as fiduciaries to their clients and held that they must therefore at least expose all conflicts of interest. But the basic approach of this theory is directed against excessive pricing and non-disclosure. Therefore, partially fraudulent sales practices, which take advantage of potential ignorance were addressed and not product suitability.

With the standards set by the industry suitability were established and since 2012, the FINRA Rule 2111[78] replaces NASD *Suitability* Rule 2310 (also FINRA Rule 2090 *Know Your Customer* the NYSE Rule 405):[79]

---

[75] The theory applying in principle the concept of fair pricing and full disclosure had its origins in early SEC administrative cases like re Duker & Duker, 6 SEC 386, 388 (1939) and Charles Hughes & Co. v. SEC, 139 F.2d 434 (2d Cir. 1943). In Hughes a broker-dealer lost his license because he charged 40 % more than the market price and did not disclose true market prices to investors; he petitioned to overturn the revocation, but the Court of Appeals found (446) that someone who "actively solicits customers and then sells them securities at prices far above the market as were those which petitioner charged here must be deemed to commit fraud". Emphasising the (i) financial literacy of the investors ("…customers were almost entirely single women or widows who knew little or nothing about securities…."), (ii) information asymmetry ("expert knowledge and proffered advice") of the broker-dealer; and (iii) the reliance of investors ("confidence… instill[ed] in the customers") a theory of fiduciary responsibility resulted, see Ormsten, Franklin D. 1998, Securities Arbitration Commentator, Vol. X, No. 8, available at<http://www.sacarbitration.com/shingle.htm>.

[76] Mundheim 1965, p. 450.

[77] Laby 2011; not originally mentioned in the Investment Advisers Act from 1940 fiduciary duties are assumed since that decision from 1963.

[78] See <http://finra.complinet.com/en/display/display_viewall.html?rbid=2403&element_id=9859&print=1>.

[79] Rule 2310 is the former (since 1939) Article III, § 2 of the NASD Rules of Fair Practice.

> A member or an associated person must have a reasonable basis to believe that a recommended transaction or investment strategy involving a security or securities is suitable for the customer, based on the information obtained through the reasonable diligence of the member or associated person to ascertain the customer's investment profile. A customer's investment profile includes, but is not limited to, the customer's age, other investments, financial situation and needs, tax status, investment objectives, investment experience, investment time horizon, liquidity needs, risk tolerance, and any other information the customer may disclose to the member or associated person in connection with such recommendation.

Supplementary to rule 2111 it is clarified that the suitability assessment is threefold: (i) reasonable basis (general perspective), (ii) customer-specific and (iii) quantitative (churning). It is also relevant that the customer must have the financial ability to meet the commitments emerging from any order.

It is noteworthy that the US regulation does not differentiate between retail and professional clients.

9.5.2 EU: MiFID

Deviating from the US, the EU implemented two different regimes for retail clients[80,81]: (i) the suitability test in case of providing a service or transaction that entails an element of recommendation (investment advice or portfolio management) and (ii) the appropriateness test in case of providing non-advised services involving 'complex' products or approaching customers regarding non-advised transactions in 'non-complex' products.[82] Another major divergence to the US regime can be seen in the categorisation of clients combined with the opting-in/-out-provisions.[83]

---

[80] Business with the other categories eligible counterparties and professional investors and the opting-in/out provision are not relevant here.

[81] MiFID Article 19 (4) and (5).

[82] The current MiFID suitability requirements are set out in Art. 19 (4) of MiFID and Art. 35 of the MiFID-ID; the current MiFID appropriateness requirements are set out in Art. 19 (5) and (6) and Art. 36–38 of the MiFID-ID. MiFID Article 19 (6) (together with Article 38 of the MiFID-ID) allows to skip the appropriateness test for certain types of 'execution-only' business, if all of the following criteria are met: (i) execution only of orders involving shares admitted to trading on a regulated market, UCITS and other non-complex financial instruments; (ii) the service is provided at the initiative of the client; (iii) the client is informed that there is no suitability assessment; (iv) compliance with Art. 18 of MiFID (conflicts of interest).

[83] While *eligible counterparties* are more or less exempted from the conduct of business regime it applies in principle to the other two categories *retail* and *professional investors*. There are different ways to qualify as a professional: (i) There are specified professionals like financial institutions or pension funds; (ii) investors who meet specific turnover, balance-sheet and capital criteria; (iii) public bodies with specific financial tasks; (iv) other institutional investors. All of them may request non-professional status. On the other hand it is possible to opt in to be classified as professional on request providing that competence and asset-based fitness tests are met. See Moloney 2008, pp. 595–597.

Test	Business	Information	Text
Appropriateness Art. 19 (5) MiFID	Execution-only business in unlisted shares and complex financial instruments	knowledge and experience	*«... ask the client or potential client to provide information regarding his knowledge and experience in the investment field relevant to the specific type of product or service offered or demanded so as to enable the investment firm to assess whether the investment service or product envisaged is* ***appropriate*** *for the client.»*
Suitability Art. 19 (4) MiFID	Portfolio management & investment advice	knowledge and experience + financial situation + investment objectives + other relevant circumstances	*«... the investment firm shall obtain the necessary information regarding the client's or potential client's knowledge and experience in the investment field relevant to the specific type of product or service, his financial situation and his investment objectives so as to enable the firm to recommend to the client or potential client the investment services and financial instruments that are* ***suitable*** *for him.»*

Fig. 9.6 MiFID's approach to appropriateness and suitability

The regulatory intensity-level depends on the advice; the suitability regime "assumes a need for intervention in the firm/investor relationship beyond disclosure".[84] Looking at the MiFID-ID there are clear indications what kind of information must be obtained to assess suitability. Figure 9.6 summarises the requirements based on the criteria set out in Art. 35 (1) of the MiFID-ID Fig. 9.7.

However, ESMA found shortcomings in the implementation of the MiFID suitability requirements; especially, (i) the failure to ask clients the right questions; (ii) the failure to collect the necessary and relevant information; (iii) the failure to interpret correctly the information provided by the client; and (iv) even where the right information is collected, the failure to recommend a suitable investment.[85] Therefore, *Guidelines on certain aspects of the MiFID suitability requirements*[86] were published in July 2012 stating inter alia:[87]

> General guideline 8 (rec. 57):
> In order to match clients with suitable investments, investment firms should establish policies and procedures to ensure that they consistently take into account:
> (a) all available information about the client that is likely to be relevant in assessing whether an investment is suitable, including the client's current portfolio of investments (and asset allocation within that portfolio);
> (b) all material characteristics of the investments considered in the suitability assessment, including all relevant risks and any direct or indirect costs to the client."

[84] Moloney 2008, p. 599.

[85] See <www.esma.europa.eu/news/ESMA-publishes-MiFID-guidelines-enhance-investor-protection?t=322&o=page%2FNews-investors> for details.

[86] Available at <http://www.esma.europa.eu/system/files/2012-387.pdf>.

[87] The guidelines are based on the relevant legislation: for this example additional on Art. 13(2) of MiFID and Art. 5 of the MiFID-ID.

Information 35 (1)		Text	Key elements
(a) investment objectives	Art. 35 (4) MiFID-ID	*«The information regarding the investment objectives of the client or potential client shall include, where relevant, information on the length of time for which the client wishes to hold the investment, his preferences regarding risk taking, his risk profile, and the purposes of the investment.»*	- investment period - risk preferences - risk profile - investment purpose
(b) risk absorbing capacity	Art. 35 (3) Mi FID-ID	*«The information regarding the financial situation of the client or potential client shall include, where relevant, information on the source and extent of his regular income, his assets, including liquid assets, investments and real property, and his regular financial commitments.»*	- source and extent of income - liquid assets, investments - real property - financial commitments
(c) experience and knowledge	Art. 37 (1) MiFID-ID	*«(a) the types of service, transaction and financial instrument with which the client is familiar; (b) the nature, volume, and frequency of the client's transactions in financial instruments and the period over which they have been carried out; (c) the level of education, and profession or relevant former profession of the client or potential client.»*	- product experience - transaction experience - education - profession

Fig. 9.7 Required information for a suitability test according to MiFID

And supplemental as a supporting guideline (rec. 60):
A firm should establish policies and procedures which enable it to ensure inter alia that:

(a) the advice and portfolio management services provided to the client take account of an appropriate degree of risk diversification;
(b) the client has an adequate understanding of the relationship between risk and return, i.e. of the necessarily low remuneration of risk free assets, of the incidence of time horizon on this relationship and of the impact of costs on his investments;
(c) the financial situation of the client can finance the investments and the client can bear any possible losses resulting from the investments;
(d) any personal recommendation or transaction entered into in the course of providing an investment advice or portfolio management service, where an illiquid product is involved, takes into account the length of time for which the client is prepared to hold the investment; and
(e) any conflicts of interest are prevented from adversely affecting the quality of the suitability assessment.

With those additional guidelines important missing and neglected elements like portfolio suitability[88], risk diversification and risk assessment are stressed by the

[88] See Rapp 1998, 193, who already 15 years ago stated, that "guided by principles of Modern Portfolio Theory (MPT), the offending recommendation may take on a markedly different

EU authorities. The upcoming MiFID II Directive is not relying on a process-based model anymore, with 'systems and controls' and its proper application by investment firms and their management oversight, but embodies "a move back to 'command and control' intervention".[89]

Instead of the "responsibilisation" of household "investors" through the regulatory system and related empowerment models imposing obligations on them as self-responsible "financial citizens" those investors are now "consumerized".[90] Overreliance on disclosure and financial literacy strategies combined with a weak approach towards behavioural realities and conflicts of interest are going to be replaced by a policy based on active intervention and product regulation. This increasingly interventionist and precautionary approach to household investments replaces empowerment through literacy by empowerment through enforcement.

Instead of weak industry-run mediation-based ombuds systems, arbitrage-oriented alternative dispute resolution models are now on the rise. It is apparent that ESMA accepts the need to address behavioural biases with appropriate regulation.[91] The MIFID itself is not addressing this in a very demonstrative way; but having this approach in the ESMA Guidelines will certainly have an impact on the further development.

9.5.3 Comparison: EU—US

The understanding of 'suitability' in the US used to be closely linked to the 'know-your-customer' obligation, accentuating that

> Brokers are expected to tailor investment recommendations to the particular objectives and circumstances of individual investors and to have both a reasonable basis for and belief in the merit of a particular recommendation based upon objective factors and known information.[92]

In Europe 'know-your-customer' is looked at more as an answer to money laundering and recently tax fraud and alike, while the meaning of 'suitability' is seen closely linked to a product.

FINRA 2011 went slightly further than the basic MiFID level 1 regime, both in terms of the current status and of the perspective including risk tolerance. However, looking at the ESMA Guidelines on certain aspects of the MiFID suitability requirements published in 2012, the client's attitude to risk and tolerance for losses is now a significant part of the suitability requirements.

character. Indeed, instead of being an "unsuitable" investment, the risky security may be seen as a wise investment that is consistent with, if not in fact compelled by, a responsible portfolio investment objective that is well-suited to the customer".

[89] Moloney 2012, p. 179.

[90] Moloney 2012, p. 177.

[91] Opening statement of Steven Maijoor, Chair of ESMA, at the ESMA Investor Day, 12 December 2012, Paris; <http://www.esma.europa.eu/system/files/2012-_818.pdf>.

[92] Rapp 1998, p. 189.

Obviously, the spectrum of what aspects are to be observed under the suitability test was remarkably extended in recent years. Especially the risk dimension of suitability has clearly influenced the regulation. In the past, the aspect of portfolio suitability was neglected in the regulatory approach on both sides of the Atlantic. An example: A hedging derivative may generally appear as rather unsuitable for retail clients, even more so in the case of an individual investor in retirement. However, within a risk-absorbing hedging strategy such a product may perfectly suit. Therefore, the portfolio suitability is very important.

The following figure compares the main regulatory elements and also highlights recent developments towards a more comprehensive understanding of the suitability assessment Fig. 9.8:

	MiFID	**ESMA**	**NASD 2310**	**FINRA 2011**
PAST	knowledge and experience	knowledge and experience (proportionality approach)		investment experience
PRESENCE	financial situation	financial situation: - income and total assets - financial commitments - marital status and children - employment status and age	financial status tax status	financial situation and needs other investments tax status age
FUTURE	investment objectives	investment objectives time horizon liquidity needs hedge a risk	investment objectives	investment objectives time horizon liquidity needs
RISK	MiFID-ID Art. 35(4): risk preferences, risk profile	**client's attitude to risk and tolerance for losses**		**risk tolerance**
			other information used or considered to be reasonable	any other information the customer may disclose

Fig. 9.8 Comparison of the US and EU approach

9.5.4 Switzerland: Emergence of the Financial Services Act (FSA)

The underlying consideration in the field of investment advice and portfolio management services, that an optimal advice can only be provided when the individual status of the customer, his portfolio and investment objectives are known, is also broadly accepted in Switzerland. However, investment decisions taken after an advice free of charge are likely to be classified as execution only without any suitability requirements. The Swiss contract law is not specific in this regard, but the case law clearly demonstrates that the courts assume underlying fiduciary duties as well as a duty of care when it comes to investment advice or portfolio management. However, clients found themselves in a legal limbo after having followed the advice to invest in Lehman certificates. The Federal Court held that a requirement for a suitability test (Article 19, paragraph 4 MiFID) cannot be deduced from Article 11 *Stock Exchange and Securities Trading Act* (SESTA).[93] Therefore, it must be concluded, that the suitability approach is not yet properly established for regulatory purposes in Swiss law.

But things are on their way. In the Distribution Report, which refers to the findings in the Madoff and Lehman cases (published in March 2010 by the Swiss Financial Market Supervisory Authority, FINMA[94]), a disharmony was diagnosed regarding the risk profiles of financial products in relation to the purchasers.[95] From today's perspective it is quite unlikely that the legislator is not going to introduce clear provisions regarding the suitability and risk assessment in the upcoming Financial Services Act (FSA, the German acronym is FIDLEG).

The FINMA signals the revision of the Circular 2009/1, Guidelines on asset management, Guidelines for the recognition of self-regulation in asset management as minimum standard,[96] thus adapting Swiss financial market law. The new version of this Circular refers to recent decisions of the Federal Court[97] and must be understood as a minimum standard against which FINMA assesses the rules of conduct of self-regulatory organisations in the financial industry. The adaption stipulates a

[93] Decision 4A_525/2012, 3 February 2012, E. 3.3; see also BGE 133 III 97 E. 5.4.

[94] FINMA report, *Madoff-Betrug und Vertrieb von Lehman Produkten: Auswirkungen auf das Anlage beratungs- und Vermögensverwaltungsgeschäft,* 2. March 2010, <http://www.finma.ch/d/finma/publikationen/documents/bericht-lehman-madoff-20100302-d.pdf>.

[95] See FINMA Distribution report, 2; the report especially noted that the risk awareness and risk appetite of customers was insufficiently clarified and the offered products were not sufficiently tailored to their personal risk capacity.

[96] The revision of FINMA-Circ. 2009/1, Guidelines on asset management, sets out the duties of asset managers when dealing with clients. The revised circular entered into force on 1 July 2013 and the end of 2013 rules of conduct are to be adjusted; <http://www.finma.ch/e/regulierung/Documents/finma-rs-09-01-e.pdf>.

[97] Although the Federal Court ruled in its decision, 4A_140/2011, 27. June 2011, in favour of the bank because of the clients' experience, in E. 2.1 (clients' risk profile) and in E. 3.1 (inquiring of clients' readiness to assume risk) the risk element within the suitability assessment was accentuated.

duty to investigate the risk profile of a client and information requirements regarding risk disclosure.[98]

In addition, it is worth to note, that another important aspect, namely concerning conflicts of interest, was clearly decided in favour of the complaining investor; recent decisions from the Federal Court in the area of conflicting interests obliged a bank to return retrocession fees received in combination with the portfolio management.[99] The just mentioned FINMA *Circular 2009/1, Guidelines on asset management*, also addresses this aspect with a rephrasing of the respective margins 27–31.

9.6 Risk assessment

9.6.1 Ways to Embrace Risk preferences

Risk taking behaviour shown in the process of decision-making regarding investment in financial products depends on subjective as well as objective aspects; the subjective risk attitude can be analysed and combined with objective data describing investment alternatives and the client's profile.[100] The advisory process should be affected by all elements shown in Fig. 9.9.

While the way investment alternatives are presented in combination with biases and heuristics strongly effects the risk perception, those aspects are to be considered to avoid undue conduct in the advisory process.[101] Therefore, a proper and regulation-compliant advice is based on the risk preferences and the return expectations as well as prior experience and loss-absorbing capacity.[102] However, a customer may not follow this advice and decide differently; this is then to be documented in a lean manner.

---

[98] Newly inserted were margins 7.1: "Taking the clients' experience and knowledge into consideration, a risk profile should be drawn up, outlining the clients' risk tolerance and risk capacity." and 7.2: "The investment strategy is to be defined with clients based on their risk profile, financial situation and investment restrictions." Accordingly, margin 17 was also extended. Asset managers used to be obligated to review the investment strategies employed on a periodical basis; now it is to be assessed "whether the clients' risk profile is in line with their current financial circumstances. If this is not the case, clients are to be made aware of this and it must be written down".

[99] BGE 138 III 755; BGE 132 III 460.

[100] See the analysis from Nosić and Weber 2010 regarding determinants of risk taking behaviour, finding that risk taking behaviour is affected by subjective risk attitudes, risk perception and return expectations. They argue (29–30) that "objective measures of risk, such as historical volatility and return, are not able to determine risk taking behavior nearly as well as subjective measures, i.e. subjective risk and return perceptions".

[101] See Vrecko et al. 2009.

[102] Nosić and Weber 2010 (30 of the SSRN-version) state that behavioural biases such as overconfidence and excessive optimism significantly affect risk behavior and suggest that the advisory process could try to incorporate some of these findings to correct "investors' erroneous beliefs". Therefore, enhancing the financial literacy of customers and explaining that some investments are more risky than initially perceived.

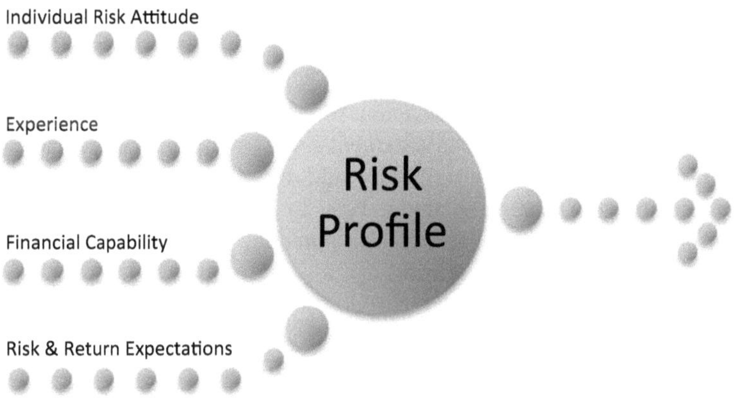

Fig. 9.9 Elements of a risk profile

In principle, clients can be grouped into standardised segments or assessed individually. The standardisation can be primarily based on available assets and income giving a reference point regarding the loss-absorbing capability. In addition, the level of investment experience, the family status, retirement plans and education are potential criteria. Furthermore, investment motives, expected returns and the individual attitude towards losses can be determined by standardised questionnaires.

This exemplifies that a basic risk assessment is possible by efficient categorisation methods. However, based on the behavioural findings, the reliability that the result from clients ticking boxes does reflect the actual mindset of the customers is doubtful. It has to be taken into account that even if those factors are probably captured in the beginning, most of them may change in the future. It is also probably impossible to detect the own attitude towards losses just by simple questionnaires. Therefore, some "training" and education prior to the risk assessment might help based on real questions like the following example:[103]

> In addition to whatever you own, you have been given 1,000.
> Which option you would prefer
> A: 50 % chance of getting 1,000 or B: 500 for sure
> and
> In addition to whatever you own, you have been given 2,000.Which option you would prefer
> C: 50 % chance of losing 1,000 or D: loosing 500 for sure

The typical outcome of such kind of test reflects risk-aversion for positive prospects and risk seeking for negative ones. Based on real values of an individual client questions like the following could be asked:

> The actual volume of your bankable assets is 200,000.
> Which option you would prefer
> A: 20 % chance of getting 20,000 or B: 4,000 for sure

[103] Kahnemann and Tversky 1979, p. 273, reported that the majority of subjects chose B in the first problem and C in the second.

and
Which option you would prefer
C: 40 % chance of loosing 20,000 or D: loosing 8,000 for sure

After a short discussion about the decisions of the customer, the investment strategy can be analysed including a clear statement on the potentially acceptable overall losses.[104] High quality advisory services would repeat a risk analysis based on risk/return expectations at least on an annual basis to cope with changing circumstances.[105] Of course also non-bankable assets, potential inheritance amounts and the future cash flows are to be considered.

9.6.2 *ESMA's Approach to Risk Assessment*

In Europe the discussion on the ESMA papers exemplifies that the industry is quite reluctant to implement risk preferences in the suitability process. An interesting comment regarding the ESMA Guidelines is the following one:[106]

> With respect to the "suitability" assessment, the Group believes that the Guidance places too much emphasis on "relevant risks". The concept of risk is very abstract and is, too often, subject to underestimation by investors and investment firms alike. The capacity of an investor to bear a permanent loss should instead be used (or at least to a similar extent) by investment firms. The loss-sustaining capacity of the investor should be considered carefully, and in a practical manner.

Two things are to be distinguished, namely (i) the potential to absorb losses based on sufficient resources and (ii) the clear decision or the specific temper to bear losses as part of a risky strategy. Therefore, an investment advisor or a portfolio manager has to gain "a very «clear understanding» and an «in-depth knowledge» of the profile of the client, of his psychology and of his investment strategy. Excellent

[104] Within that discussion key cognitive biases should be addressed: "(1) reference-point-related issues (including conservatism, excessive loss aversion, and frame dependence); (2) probabilistic analysis issues (including representativeness and overconfidence); and (3) mental errors (the brain functioning outside of one's awareness—namely, anchoring, regret and addiction)." See Cunningham 2002, p. 792.

[105] Weber et al. 2012 analysed differences in self-reported risk attitude during the interesting time slot from September 8 to June 9 under online brokerage investors and reported substantial changes in risk taking over that period of time. They find (p. 31 of the SSRN-version) regarding the subjective judgments of risk and return expectation "that it is the more emotion-based components of these judgments that drive changes in risk taking". Not the risk attitude itself changed but the personal awareness towards it—after the experience of losses.

[106] SMSG (Securities and Markets Stakeholder Group), Advice to ESMA, 15 February 2012, 2; <http://www.esma.europa.eu/content/Advice-Guidelines-certain-aspects-MiFID-suitability-requirements>. The SMSG is composed of 30 individuals who represent financial market participants, their employees' representatives, and consumers, users of financial services, including ten from financial institutions and five academics.

understanding by the investment firm of the client is the key to making suitable investments." [107]

Looking at the General Guideline 8 cited above, there is no clear recapitulation to assess individual risk preferences of the client. It seems that the focus is more on his available funds instead of his personal expectations and attitudes towards risks. One of the respective Supporting Guidelines stipulates that policies and procedures should be established to ensure that, inter alia, "the financial situation of the client can finance the investments and the client can bear any possible losses resulting from the investments".

The SMSG-advice requires that much more weight be put on this criterion and clarifies the concern in a quit palpable way:[108]

> The loss sustaining capacity of an investor should be considered carefully, and in a practical manner. It should not be considered in an abstract way as currently mentioned in the "Supporting Guidelines". Potential losses should be understood through concrete examples, in proportion to the amount to be invested. For example: such as "How would you cope permanently with losing 10,000 euros on your 50,000 euros investments?". In addition, rather than mentioning "possible losses", the Guidelines could refer to "permanent losses" or at least "long term losses" in order to highlight the reality of loss bearing. Otherwise, an investor might simply anticipate that she will recoup her losses quickly. Long term losses could possibly be described by mentioning a five year period or by reference to a given time frame provided by the client regarding the duration of his investment.

This statement is in line with the scope of General Guideline 5 regarding the collection of information about the client. In one of the respective Supporting Guidelines it is stressed that self-assessment should be counterbalanced by objective criteria and that it should not be asked whether a client feels comfortable with taking risk, but "what level of loss over a given time period the client would be willing to accept, either on the individual investment or on the overall portfolio".[109]

9.6.3 Method for Risk Assessment

Due to the biases the client is exposed to, the investment firm should establish methods to guide the decision-making process. One task is to recognise rational from irrational aspects.[110] First of all it must be clarified, that there cannot be *an* optimal portfolio, because of the individual needs, risk attitudes, status and life cycle. Based on a long-term strategy, which incorporates behavioural aspects and

---

[107] SMSG-Advice to ESMA (supra note 107), p. 6.

[108] SMSG-Advice to ESMA (supra note 107), p. 8.

[109] ESMA Guidelines (supra note 87), p. 33.

[110] Hens and Bachmann (2008), p. 105.

individual preferences like loss aversion[111], the individual asset allocation must be determined.[112]

It is vital to have a common understanding of risk between the advisor and the client. Most clients might perceive risk in a negative way, instead of embracing risk because it can be used in a positive way to optimise the portfolio structure. In investment analysis risk is evaluated mathematically on the basis of past volatility and standard deviations to evaluate possible returns. While uncertainty and variability characterise the estimation of expected returns, the analysis of the past is based on facts; however, the past performance is not a secure indicator for the future. Customers' unsuitability complaints against advisors often criticise, in hindsight, the degree of risk exposure, which was entailed in the recommended investment.[113] *Modern Portfolio Theory* assumes rational, wealth-seeking investors who are risk-averse.[114] While a risk-free investment shows no variability in the expected rate of return, in combination with risky assets, risk-taking is compensated within a portfolio by higher expected returns aiming at reaching the maximum theoretical return associated with the level of risk being taken. Thereby, two kinds of risks are to be distinguished: non-systematic investment-specific and systematic market risk. The non-systematic risk includes the counterparty risk and the risk of a particular investment that can be reduced by means of diversification, while the systematic risk is not diversifiable. [115]

Assuming this approach to risks, and with the aid of a questionnaire, an interview or computer-aided risk profiler, the individual awareness of risk and the respective expectations regarding the return can be fathomed. However, emphasis should not only be put on the use of any kind of questionnaire; especially, a physical meeting with a specifically trained representative of the investment firm should be considered as very valuable to get to *know* the customer. A questionnaire being an essential tool to evaluate his profile should not be more than a tool. In view of the potential disadvantages, like being too long as well as very complex, it is not unlikely that a combination of lacking knowledge, biases at work and flippancy due to information overload will lead to poor and wrong results. Especially, the existence of inexperienced

[111] See Cunningham 2002, p. 799, who also emphasizes the significance of loss aversion: "Of all the biases and factors that one could possibly ask about, however, one's degree of loss aversion is striking for its relevance, reliability, and accessability. Loss aversion relates directly to problems of regret (a universal characteristic of claimants in nonsuitability cases); it is a good indicator of the sorts of securities that would or would not make the investor comfortable, and it is relatively easy to elicit through conversion and observation."

[112] Hens and Bachmann 2008, p. 106.

[113] See Rapp 1998, pp. 243–244.

[114] The *Modern Portfolio Theory* is widely used in practice in the financial industry, but the basic assumptions are challenged by the findings of behavioural economics. See Markowitz 1952.

[115] Systematic risk is defined as the covariance between an individual security or mix of assets in a portfolio and the market in general. A high volatility of a security or a portfolio in relation to the market volatility implies a greater systematic risk, which is expressed numerically as the beta coefficient based on regression analysis of historical data.

investors or clients confronted with unfamiliar topics together with in-built flaws or the potential of guidance in a certain direction on purpose sound a note of caution.

9.6.4 *Restrictions and limitations*

A risk profile must combine the subjective component of risk, which is the individual attitude towards risk, with the objective risk absorbing capacity. The problem is that any kind of traditional financial risk tolerance questionnaire is based on self-evaluation, which includes automatically the negative outcome of many biases. In combination with a preceding introduction or under supervision those effects could be de-biased. However, it is ineluctable that real life financial decisions will always be subject to irrational influences.[116]

Costs are a further key factor; what might be practicable in the area of private banking could be ineffective by way of a cost-benefit analysis in normal retail banking. Therefore, the regulator is also asked to provide advice for the financial intermediaries, how they can comply with the requirements based on somehow standardised assessments. In fact, computers can check questionnaires, analyse inconsistencies and suspicious discrepancies as well as examine portfolio structures and diversification on a regular basis.

9.7 Conclusion

9.7.1 *Behavioural Findings are Inescapable for Financial Market Regulation*

The regulatory approach embraces behavioural findings especially in the area of risk profiles. However, as discussed above, it is not easy to get hold of reliable data when keeping an acceptable cost-benefit ratio in mind.

Part of the complexity of effective retail market regulatory intervention is to identify the *typical* retail investor and to look at the approach to investment decisions; this classification is exacerbated by the fundamental divergences in the economic theory as demonstrated above. Neo-classical economic theory advocates investor protection only if market failures—primarily based on information asymmetries—occur; however, (i) the various behavioural biases that influence the financial decisions of individuals as well as (ii) the disability to manage information properly and (iii) its overload are calling for another regulatory facet. Not discussed here is that (iv) financial intermediaries might be tempted to use common biases to sell products which are not in the best interest of the client.

[116] Lucarelli and Brighetti 2011 provide detailed analysis relating risk with focus on Italy.

Behavioural finance makes it obvious that biases cannot be prevented through disclosure. "Disclosure has considerable attractions as a retail market tool, but the challenge for regulators is to resist the temptation to make disclosure the panacea for investor protection."[117] What is the target of regulation, the empowered investor or the irrational and uninformed investor? This contribution emphasises the fact that even experienced investors are prone to irrational decisions. Therefore, the approach to risk assessment must be based on the latter model.

9.7.2 *Outlook on the Swiss FSA*

Investors are looking for predictable returns and they dislike losses. Therefore, the downside potential should be clarified during the conduct with the customer. Most investors will be more than happy to surrender part of the upside potential when this can be combined with a cap of any potential losses. This is also true for Switzerland.

Some key issues for the (upcoming) Swiss FSA:[118]

1. The responsibility for any part of the suitability assessment remains with the financial intermediary; any form which shifts some part on to customers, e.g. through questionnaires, is not in line with the regulatory requirements.
2. The customers risk attitude matters; therefore, the focus is not on risk absorbing capacity.
3. Any kind of abuse of behavioural biases and heuristics for example in brochures or during any kind of personal contact should be prohibited.
4. Mitigation of conflicts of interest should be solved through sound disclosure and (to the extent unavoidable) by prohibition in the context of independent advice.
5. Smart enforcement mechanisms in line with the European developments will foster the customer's confidence in the reliability of the Swiss financial market.

A potential barrier to obtaining acceptance with the chosen approach to suitability is the rejection of paternalistic regulation. Therefore, any kind of outcome has to be avoided which overrides people's ability to make choices too paternalistically. On the one hand, human limitations should be recognized, especially regarding the complexity of financial decision-making; on the other hand, removing choices and investment opportunities from the customers must be avoided to.[119] There is also some truth behind the critique that suitability requirements are problematic in terms of supervision and enforcement.[120] The tendency, at least of the reputable market participant, to behave accurately and in line with the requirements should bolster the confidence that costumers will be advised on a new level. The quality

---

[117] Opening statement of Steven Maijoor, Chair of ESMA, at the ESMA Investor Day, 12 December 2012, Paris; <http://www.esma.europa.eu/system/files/2012-_818.pdf>.

[118] In 2014 the Federal Council will launch the consultation on FSA (FIDLEG). This contribution was finished before this process was started.

[119] See Jolls 2006, pp. 39–40.

[120] Moloney 2010, pp. 243, advocates mystery shopping.

of advisory and portfolio management services in Switzerland could be pivotal in the global competition, attracting new and satisfying the—therewith even better known—established customers.

Acknowledgement This contribution was written within the University Research Priority Program *Regulation of Financial Markets* from the University of Zurich.

Bibliography

Akerlof, George A., and Robert J. Shiller. 2010. *Animal spirits: How human psychology drives the economy, and why it matters for global capitalism*. Princeton: Princeton University Press.

Anderson, Seth C., and Donald A. Winslow. 1992. Defining suitability. *Kentucky Law Journal* 81:105–122.

Avgouleas, Emilios. 2009. The global financial crises and the disclosure paradigm. *EFCR* 4:440–475.

Avgouleas, Emilios. 2012. *Governance of global financial markets*. Cambridge: Cambridge University Press.

Barber, Brad M., and Terrance Odean. 2001. Boys will be boys: Gender, overconfidence, and common stock investment. *Quarterly Journal of Economics* 116:261–292.

Ben-Shahar, Omri, and Carl E. Schneider. 2010. The failure of mandated disclosure. University of Chicago Law & Economics, Olin Working Paper No. 516.

Boaz, David. 1997. *Libertarianism: A primer*. New York: The Free Press.

Boskovic, Tanja, Caroline Cerruti, and Michel Noel. 2010. Comparing European and U.S. securities regulations: MiFID versus corresponding U.S. regulations. World Bank working paper; no. 184. Washington, D.C.

Camerer, Colin. 2000. Prospect theory in the wild: Evidence from the field. In *Choices, values, and frames*, ed. D. Kahneman and A. Tversky, 288–300. New York: Russell Sage Foundation.

Camerer, Colin, and George Loewenstein. 2004. Behavioral economics: Past, present and future. In *Advances in behavioral economics*, ed. C. F. Camerer, G. Loewenstein, and M. Rabin, 3–51. New York: Russell Sage Foundation.

Camerer, Colin, and Dan Lovallo. 1999. Overconfidence and excess entry: An experimental approach. *American Economic Review* 89:306–318.

Camerer, Colin F., Samuel Issacharoff, George F. Loewenstein, Ted O'Donoghue, and Matthew Rabin. 2003. Regulation for conservatives: Behavioral economics and the case for 'Asymmetric Paternalism'. *University of Pennsylvania Law Review* 151:1211–1254.

Carmon, Ziv, and Dan Ariely. 2000. Focusing on the forgone: How value can appear so different to buyers and sellers. *Journal of Consumer Research* 27:360–370.

Charness, Gary, and Matthew Rabin. 2002. Understanding social preferences with simple tests. *Quarterly Journal of Economics* 117:817–869.

Coase, Runacy H. 1960. The problem of social cost. *Journal of Law and Economics* 3, 1–44.

Cunningham, Lawrence A. 2002. Behavioral finance and investor governance. *Washington and Lee Law Review* 59:767–837.

De Bondt, Werner F. M., and Richard H. Thaler. 1990. Stock market volatility—Do security analysts overreact? *American Economic Review* 80:52–57.

Fehr, Ernest, and Klaus M. Schmidt. 1999. A theory of fairness, competition, and cooperation. *Quarterly Journal of Economics* 114:817–868.

Frederick, Shane, George Loewenstein, and Ted O'Donoghue. 2002. Time discounting and time preference: A critical review. *Journal of Economic Literature* 40:351–401.

Gal, David. 2006. A psychological law of inertia and the illusion of loss aversion. *Judgment and Decision Making* 1:23–32.

Goodin, Robert. (1991). Permissible paternalism: In defense of the Nanny state. *The Responsive Community* 1:42–51.
Grether, David. 1980. 'Bayes' rule as a descriptive model: The representativeness heuristic. *Quarterly Journal of Economics* 95:537–557.
Hens, Thorsten, and Kremena Bachmann. 2008. *Behavioural finance for private banking*. Chichester: Wiley.
Hens, Thorsten, and Marc Oliver Rieger. 2008. The dark side of the moon: Structured products from the customer's perspective. Working Paper No. 459.
Johnson, Eric J., John C. Hershey, Jacqueline Meszaros, and Howard C. Kunreuther. 1993. Framing, probability distortions, and insurance decisions. *Journal of Risk and Uncertainty* 7:36–51.
Jolls, Christine. 2006. Behavioral law and economics. Yale Law School, Public Law Working Paper No. 13.
Jolls, Christine, Cass R. Sunstein, and Richard Thaler. 1998. A behavioral approach to law and economics. *Stanford Law Review* 50:1471–1550.
Kahneman, Daniel. 2011. *Thinking, fast and slow*. New York: Farrar, Straus and Giroux.
Kahneman, Daniel, and Shane Frederick. 2002. Representativeness revisited: Attribute substitution in intuitive judgment. In *Heuristics and biases—The psychology of intuitive judgment*, ed. T. Gilovich, D. Griffin, and D. Kahneman, 49–81. Cambridge: Cambridge University Press.
Kahneman, Daniel, and Amos Tversky. 1979. Prospect theory: An analysis of decision under risk. *Econometrica* 47:263–291.
Kahneman, Daniel, and Amos Tversky. 1982. The psychology of preferences. *Scientific American* 246:160–173.
Kahneman, Daniel, and Amos Tversky, eds. 2000. *Choices, values, and frames*. New York: Russell Sage Foundation.
Kahneman, Daniel, Paul Slovic, and Amos Tversky. 1982. *Judgment under uncertainty: Heuristics and biases*. Cambridge: Cambridge University Press.
Kahneman, Daniel, Jack L. Knetsch, and Richard H. Thaler. 1990. Experimental test of the endowment effect and the Coase theorem. *Journal of Political Economy* 98:1325–1348.
Kahneman, Daniel, Jack L. Knetsch, and Richard H. Thaler. 1991. Anomalies: The endowment effect, loss aversion, and status quo bias. *Journal of Economic Perspectives* 5:193–206.
Keynes, John M. 1936. *The general theory of employment, interest, and money*. London: Macmillan.
Korobkin, Russell B., and Thomas S. Ulen. 2000. Law and behavioral science: Removing the rationality assumption from law and economics. *California Law Review* 88:1051–1144.
Laby, Arthur B. 2011. Current issues in fiduciary law, SEC v. Capital gains research bureau and the investment advisers act of 1940. *Boston University Law Review* 91:1051–1104.
Laibson, David. 1997. Golden eggs and hyperbolic discounting. *Quarterly Journal of Economics* 112:443–478.
Langevoort, Donald C. 1992. Theories, assumptions, and securities regulation: Market efficiency revisited. *University of Pennsylvania Law Review* 140:851–920.
Lipkus, Isaac M., Greg Samsa, and Barbara K. Rimer. 2001. General performance on a numeracy scale among highly educated samples. *Medical Decision Making* 21:37–44.
Loewenstein, George F., Leigh Thompson, and Max H. Bazerman. 1989. Social utility and decision making in interpersonal contexts. *Journal of Personality and Social Psychology* 57:426–441.
Lucarelli, Caterina, and Gianni Brighetti, eds. 2011. *Risk tolerance in financial decision making*. Basingstoke: Palgrave Macmillan.
Markowitz, Harry. 1952. Portfolio selection. *Journal of Finance* 7:77–91.
Moloney, Niamh. 2008. *EC securities regulation*. Oxford: Oxford University Press.
Moloney, Niamh. 2010. *How to protect investors: Lessons from the EC and the UK*. Cambridge: Cambridge University Press.
Moloney, Niamh. 2012. The investor model underlying the EU's investor protection regime: Consumers or investors? *European Business Organization Law Review* 13:169–193.
Mundheim, Robert H. 1965. Professional responsibilities of broker-dealers: The suitability doctrine. *Duke Law Journal* 1965:445–480.

Von Neumann, John, and Oskar Morgenstern. 1944. *Theory of games and economic behavior*. New York: Wiley.
Nosić, Alen, and Martin Weber. 2010. How risky do I invest: The role of risk attitudes, risk perceptions, and overconfidence. *Decision Analysis* 7:282–301.
O'Donoghue, Ted, and Matthew Rabin. 1999. Doing it now or later. *American Economic Review* 89:103–124.
Pompian, Michael M. 2012. *Behavioral finance and wealth management*. 2nd ed. Hoboken: Wiley.
Rabin, Matthew. 1993. Incorporating fairness into game theory and economics. *American Economic Review* 83:1281–1302.
Rachlinski, Jeffrey. 1998. A positive psychological theory of judging in hindsight. *University of Chicago Law Review* 65:571–625.
Rapp, Robert N. 1998. Rethinking risky investments for that little old lady: A realistic role for modern portfolio theory in assessing suitability obligations of stockbrokers. *Ohio Northern University Law Review* 24:189–279.
Samuelson, William, and Richard J. Zeckhauser. 1988. Status quo bias in decision making. *Journal of Risk and Uncertainty* 1:7–59.
Schmies, Christian. 2007. Behavioral Finance und Finanzmarktregulierung. In *Recht und Verhalten,* Hrsg. C. Engel, et al., 165–188. Tübingen: Mohr Siebeck.
Schwartz, Lisa M., Steven Woloshin, William C. Black, and Welch H. Gilbert. 1997. The role of numeracy in understanding the benefit of screening mammography. *Annals of Internal Medicine* 127:966–972.
Shefrin, Hersh, and Meir Statman. 1985. The disposition to sell winners too early and ride losers too long: Theory and evidence. *Journal of Finance* 40:777–790.
Shefrin, Hersh and Meir Statman. 1994. Behavioral capital asset pricing theory. *Journal of Financial and Quantitative Analysis* 29:323–349.
Shefrin, Hersh and Meir Statman. 2000. Behavioral portfolio theory. *Journal of Financial and Quantitative Analysis* 35:127–151.
Shiller, Robert J. 2000. *Irrational Exuberance*. (Second edition 2005). Princeton: Princeton University Press.
Shogren, Jason F., Seung Y. Shin, Dermot J. Hayes, and James B. Kliebenstein. 1994. Resolving differences in willingness to pay and willingness to accept. *American Economic Review* 84:255–270.
Simon, Herbert A. 1955. A behavioral model of rational choice. *Quarterly Journal of Economics* 69:99–118.
Smith, Adam. 1892. Originally 1759. *The theory of moral sentiments*. London.
Strahilevitz, Michal A., and George Loewenstein. 1998. The effect of ownership history on the valuation of objects. *Journal of Consumer Research* 25:276–289.
Sunstein, Cass R., and Richard H. Thaler. 2003. Libertarian paternalism is not an oxymoron. *University of Chicago Law Review* 70:1159–1202.
Sunstein, Cass R., Daniel Kahneman, David Schkade, and Ilana Ritov. (2002). Predictably incoherent judgments. *Stanford Law Review* 54:1153–1215.
Svenson, Ola. 1981. Are we less risky and more skillful than our fellow drivers? *Acta Psychologica* 47:143–148.
Thaler, Richard H. 1980. Toward a positive theory of consumer choice. *Journal of Economic Behavior and Organization* 1:39–60.
Thaler, Richard. 1984. Using mental accounting in a theory of consumer behavior. Working Paper, Cornell University.
Thaler, Richard H. 1991. *Quasi-Rational economics*. New York: Russell Sage Foundation.
Thaler, Richard H. 2002. *The winner's curse: Paradoxes and anomalies of economic life*. New York: The Free Press.
Thaler, Richard H., and Cass R. Sunstein. 2008. *Nudge: Improving decisions about health, wealth and happiness*. New Haven: Yale University Press.
Tversky, Amos, and Daniel Kahneman. 1973. Availability: A heuristic for judging frequency and probability. *Cognitive Psychology* 5:207–232.

Tversky, Amos, and Daniel Kahneman. 1974. Judgment under uncertainty: Heuristics and biases. *Science* 185:1124–1131.
Tversky, Amos, and Daniel Kahneman. 1991. Loss aversion in riskless choice: A reference-dependent model. *Quarterly Journal of Economics* 106:1039–1061.
Vrecko, Dennis, Alexander Klos, and Thomas Langer. 2009. Impact of presentation format and self-reported risk aversion on revealed skewness preferences. *Decision Analysis* 6:57–74.
Weber, Martin, and Elke U. Weber, and Alen Nosić. 2012. Who takes risks when and why: Determinants of changes in investor risk taking. Review of Finance 17:847–883. (Columbia Business School Research Paper No. 12/29).

Rainer Baisch Zurich. Scientific Assistant. CH-8001 Zurich, Rämistrasse 74/38, Tel. +41 (0)44 634 48 84. rainer.baisch@rwi.uzh.ch. Fields of Interest: Financial Market Law, Commercial and Corporate Law, Insolvency and Reorganization Law.

Prof. Dr. Rolf H. Weber Zurich. Professor of International Business Law at the University of Zurich. Visiting Professor at Hong Kong University and Attorney-at-law in Zurich, CH-8001 Zurich, Rämistrasse 74/38, Tel. +41 (0)44 634 48 84. rolf.weber@rwi.uzh.ch. Fields of Interest: International Finance and Economic Law, Internet Law and Governance, Antitrust Law.

Chapter 10
Retail Investors and Disclosure Requirements

Geneviève Helleringer

Abstract Disclosures are among the most common techniques introduced. The purpose of such regulation is to correct, for the benefit of the potential retail investor, information asymmetries relating to the characteristics of the financial products and the motivations of the intermediary advisor. The devil is in the detail, however, and it has become apparent that disclosing without assessing "how" to disclose may create unexpected and harmful side-effects. For this reason, there is a need for a research agenda centred around the limits deriving from motivation in the use of financial information and in good decision-making. This research design would disentangle connections between financial law and emotions and, in particular, financial law and happiness as well as financial law and altruism.

10.1 Introduction

Consumers make predictable costly mistakes. This is also true in the context of retail purchase on the financial market. On the financial market, consumers, i.e. retail investors, make predictable mistakes that are excessively costly.[1] They buy high and sell low, invest in attractively presented instruments they do not understand and pay

[1] Chater et al. 2010.

G. Helleringer (✉)
Law Department, Essec Business School,
Avenue B. Hirsch, 95 000 Cergy-Pontoise, France
e-mail: helleringer@gmail.com

Institute of European and Comparative Law, Oxford University,
St Cross Road, Oxford OX1 3UL, United Kingdom

K. Mathis (ed.), *European Perspectives on Behavioural Law and Economics*,
Economic Analysis of Law in European Legal Scholarship 2,
DOI 10.1007/978-3-319-11635-8_10

excessive fees.[2] This outcome appears all the more disappointing since the financial market may provide opportunities: finance is a tool that has the potential to improve the well-being of modest investors.[3]

However, consumers are often ill-prepared to make sound decisions about increasingly complex retail financial products. They are more generally unable to benefit fully from this market because of their limited financial literacy, as shown by evidence on the American[4] and the European financial markets.[5] Investors do not understand basic concepts such as diversification, investment costs, inflation and compound interest. In addition, retail investors also suffer from an asymmetry in information and are victims of the fact that intermediaries, on the financial market, often have incentives and interests that are not aligned with those of the investors. Less informed consumers interact with better informed sellers; incentives of the investors and advisors are at least arguably misaligned in a market on which advice is ubiquitous. Under such circumstances, a market failure can be observed. Market forces are insufficient to protect retail investors from making poor investment decisions.

In every jurisdiction, regulatory responses have been designed to protect investors. Disclosures are among the most common technique introduced. The purpose of this regulation is to correct the information asymmetry provided to the potential retail investor, relating to the characteristics of the financial products and the motivations of the intermediary advisor. The devil is in the detail, however, and it has become apparent that disclosing without assessing "how" to disclose may create unexpected and harmful side-effects.[6]

In this chapter, I will first explain how mandatory disclosure requirements have been largely promoted in the retail finance market (1). I will then analyse why results of such disclosure policy have turned out to be disappointing (2). Finally, I will outline suggestions which take into account perceptual and motivational cognitive limitations to provide more efficient disclosures (3).

10.2 The Rise of Mandatory Disclosure Requirements

Regulatory effort for consumer protection was first imposed to provide retail investors with extensive information on financial products. Rather than regulating the financial products design, transparency was meant to address the financial market failure.

Standard economic theory offers several explanations why the provision of information occurring 'naturally', as a function of market forces, only encourages

[2] See e.g., Barber 2005: past performance and the amount spent on marketing are the two main factors that account for the level of retail investment. The cost of management fees does not have an impact. See, however, the critical observations of Coates and Hubbard 2007.

[3] Schiller 2012.

[4] In a 2012 study, the American financial authority stressed that "American investors lack basic financial literacy", see SEC 2012 report.

[5] Chater et al. 2010.

[6] See already Loewenstein et al. 2013.

a suboptimal disclosure level. Information provided in financial investments (e.g. product risk warnings, financial disclosures) can be analysed as quasi-public goods. Such goods are associated with what economists call the free-rider problem: even if a large number of retail investors will benefit from clearer information being posted on a particular financial product, it is unlikely to be worth the time or money of any one retail investor to devote much effort to seeking disclosure of further clearer information.

Providing information has a cost,[7] in particular the cost of information seeking as well as the cost of enforcing disclosure regulations. Consequently, the choice to make disclosure mandatory imposes a cost on subjects. This may however, be justified on the basis of an efficiency argument[8] whereby, as soon as societal gains are to be obtained they become superior to the societal costs.[9]

Whereas bans on financial products design, marketing and sale to individuals remained very limited, regulations have, more recently, imposed two new types of mandatory disclosure requirements. Some are directed at reducing asymmetry in information around the risks products create. In parallel, certain bans on financial products design, marketing and sale to individuals have also been introduced. Others, more original, pertain to the mechanic of the market itself and, in particular, to market trends (e.g. past profits cannot be used to predict future profits) and incentives enjoyed by intermediaries (e.g. potential conflict of interest created by the remuneration structure). For example, the Credit Card Accountability Responsibility and Disclosure Act of 2009, the Affordable Care Act and the Dodd-Frank Wall Street Reform and Consumer Protection Act. All these examples are packed with disclosure requirements. The same is also true of the Sarbanes-Oxley Act. This act was implemented in the aftermath of the highly publicised accounting irregularities following the failures of companies such as Enron and WorldCom. Interestingly the act does not ban or require certain corporate or auditor practices, but instead mandates disclosure. [10] For example, it does not require corporations to include financial experts on their boards of directors, but requires firms to disclose this, and if not, to explain why not.[11]

"Targeted-transparency"[12] through mandatory disclosure of information is promoted as an attractive alternative to so-called 'hard' forms[13] of regulation and an effective tool to improve consumer welfare.

[7] Jovanovic 1982.

[8] Coffee 1984.

[9] A comprehensive accounting of costs, moreover, should include the time that people need to process the information, the opportunity costs of distracting attention from existing information, and even, in some cases, the hedonic cost of dealing with the information.

[10] Ripken 2006.

[11] Similarly, it does not require corporations to adopt a code of ethics for senior financial officers but, if no ethics code is adopted, requires corporations to disclose why they failed to do so.

[12] Archong et al. 2013.

[13] Beales et al. 1981: "[i]nformation remedies are most likely to be the most effective solution to information problems. They deal with the cause of the problem, rather than its symptoms, and leave the market maximum flexibility."

Pursuant to a neo-classic analysis, disclosure advances consumers' knowledge, about the price and various other features of the considered products. As a consequence, transaction costs are reduced. Disclosure is compatible with the game of market forces as they favour: revelation of information by sellers about their product; competition between prices; and the lifting of the veil on inadequacies of competitors' products.[14]

10.3 Disappointing Results Yielded by Mandatory Disclosure

The European Scoreboard analyses, every year, the performance of various sectors of the market in Europe. The 2013 edition showed, as did the previous one, that the market for investments, pensions and securities ranks worst out of fifty consumer markets for overall market performance. In particular, the financial market ranks worst for ease of comparing products and services sold by different suppliers; worst in trust that suppliers will respect consumer protection rules; worst for overall satisfaction; and fourth worst in experiencing problems.

Disclosure appears more effective in books than in real life. Indeed, it has failed to remedy market inadequacies in the financial sector. Two main reasons may be put forward for this: financial literacy and attention limits. Both reveal a misconception of retail investors as *homo oeconomicus*

10.3.1 A Misconceived Consumer as Homo Economicus

For a long time, the regulatory system misconceived retail investors as *homo oeconomicus*. First generation disclosure requirements were coloured by this misconception and as a result merely aimed at addressing the standard economic market failure which derived from insufficient information and misaligned interests.[15] They gave retail investors a significant role in facilitating the circulation of information, envisioning rational and vigilant consumers, who read uninviting small prints; self-assess their preferences; made their decisions with cool blood; engage with complexity rather than relying on rules of thumb; and did not fall into the trap of overconfidence.[16]

[14] Durkin and Elliehausen 2002, 109 et seq.

[15] Durkin and Elliehausen 2002, 109 et seq.

[16] It been understood that professional investors do fall into such traps see: Thaler Richard, Sunstein Cass. R. 2014, p. 124; Huang 2005, p. 501; Langevoort 1996; Hirshleifer and Shumway 2003, p. 1009.

Such regulatory design reflects the fundamental assumption that consumers know their preferences best[17] and are thus able to determine the best investment of themselves at the lowest costs.[18]

Whereas standard economics assumes that people are "selfish calculating machine",[19] social sciences such as sociology psychology or neuroscience tend to shape a different image of the consumers.[20] They focus on the complexities of actors, taken individually and collectively, and how emotions and bias interact with decision-making.[21] Consequently, in addition to economic market failure and externalities thereby created, additional market failures are "behavioural".[22] They represent "internalities", *i.e.,* costs that will be borne by individuals, imposed by themselves and that are not internalized at the time of decision.[23] Disclosures are likely to address such internalities only if they are such that they succeed in protecting consumers against themselves. Issues relating to financial literacy as well as attention limits demonstrate the complexity of achieving this.

10.3.2 Financial Literacy

The Promises of Consumer Financial Education The level of education in financial matter represents a factor in suboptimal choice making.[24] "Financial education can be compared to a road map to the American Dream. I believe that we need to teach all Americans the necessary tools to read that map, so that they can reach the Dream."[25] Financial illiteracy is an important contributor to suboptimal choices, in terms of investors lacking the ability to make investment choices that are welfare-enhancing. There is a broad consensus about the need for high financial literacy, across the political spectrum: "Liberals envision an empowered consumer, confidently

---

[17] "All human behavior can be viewed as involving participants who maximize their utility from a stable set of preferences and accumulate an optimal amount of information and other inputs in a variety of markets." Becker 1976.

[18] For a similar (mis)conception in the context of credit reporting, see, Staten and Cate 2004. Does the Fair Credit Reporting Act Promote Accurate Credit Reporting? Building Assets, Building Credit: A Symposium on Improving Financial Services in Low- Income Communities. See also Osovsky 2014.

[19] Bowles and Gintis 2000, p. 1413.

[20] "...Orthodox economic model of consumer behavior is, in essence, a model of robot-like experts. As such, it does a poor job of predicting the behavior of the average consumer. This is not because the average consumer is dumb, but rather that he does not spend all of his time thinking about how to make decisions." Thaler 2000, p. 269 and 287.

[21] See namely Oren 2008; Wright 2007; Camerer and Loewenstein 2004.

[22] Sunstein 2011.

[23] Hernstein et al. 1993, p. 149–185.

[24] Fox et al. 2005, p. 197.

[25] Secretary of the Treasury Paul O'Neill 2002. The State of Financial Literacy and Education in *America: Hearing Before the S. Comm. on Banking, Housing, and Urban Affairs*, 107th Cong. (testimony of Paul O'Neill, Secretary of the U.S. Department of the Treasury).

navigating the marketplace. Conservatives divine a responsible consumer, who understands her decisions and therefore can be held accountable for them. Free-marketers see flourishing innovation and abundant choices".[26]

There is a broad ambition for providing better training to retail investors in financial skills. It is envisioned training could turn consumers into active market players, who make strategic decisions about their own credit, insurance and savings, by comparing different products, understanding financial terms, avoiding abusive offers, etc.[27] However, the US National Strategy for Financial Literacy has stressed that "Personal financial management is an extremely complex matter that requires significant resources and commitment by consumers to understand and evaluate the multitude of products available in the broad financial services market... [T]he marketplace is constantly changing, with new products, services, and providers emerging to meet consumer demand. As a result, the range of topics and issues that consumers must evaluate is vast and ever-growing."[28]

Behavioural Limits on the Efficacy of Consumer Financial Education Various aspects account for the limited results that financial education of consumers yields.

There is, first, a selection effect as investors who decide to attend personal-finance classes tend to be better informed and more cautious investors.[29] Second, concerns have been raise in connection with the assessment of the effects of financial-literacy education. In particular, participant's self-assessments of improvements in their knowledge, confidence, and behaviours are common[30] but also unreliable. People are classically biased to overestimate how much they have learned and how much they will change their behaviour in the future.[31] Tough experimental data show that test scores may well remain unchanged.[32] Finally, the long term effect of financial training appears to remain limited.[33] Such trainings focus on consumer' confidence and aim at reinforcing it. A side effect, however, is that this can encourage consumer over-optimism which in turn causes a bias which plagues their financial decisions.[34]

[26] Willis 2008, p. 284.

[27] See Willis 2008, p. 201.

[28] US fin. Literacy & educ. Comm'n, taking ownership of the future: the national strategy for financial literacy at vii (2006).

[29] Willis 2008, p. 207. Consumers with more education, more financial knowledge, and lower financial discount rates were found more likely to accept an offer of a brief, free credit-counseling session. See Meier and Sprenger 2007.

[30] See Willis 2008, p. 205.

[31] Willis 2008, p. 205.

[32] Hershey et al. 1998, p. 467. See also Choi et al. 2006, p. 335–337. Employees who reported at the end of a retirement-investing seminar that they would increase their savings generally failed to do so.

[33] See Anthes and Most 2000; Todd 2002.

[34] Benartzi et al. 2007, p. 81.

10.3.3 Attention Limits

Information Overload The amount of information that retail investors can process is an important question. When excessive information is available, this may lead to "information overload".[35] In such circumstances, under pressure, investors may opt for a default choice, which appears to them a relief.[36] Less, may therefore, be more, as has been advocated.[37]

Motivation Limits More often than not, the language of financial disclosures fails to be engaging.[38] Even when engagement is high, empirical evidence suggests that consumers are unlikely to read the boilerplate. The following anecdote is particularly illustrative of this failure to read all information provided.

PCpitstop.com, a computer software maker, put a clause in an end-user license agreement promising $1000 to consumers who responded. After four months and 3000 downloads, only one consumer responded to claim the $1000.[39]

Biases and Bounded Rationality Besides lack of time and impatience, various biases, such as the status quo bias, and over-optimism, discourage investors from taking disclosures into account. Retail investors, therefore, show the same behavioural traits, which drive consumers towards choices that are inconsistent with their long-term preferences.

For the last decade, behaviour scholars have reiterated that regulatory measures are largely aimed at the wrong target: regulations are not enough informed by a clear and complete understanding of why investors make mistakes or have misconceptions. It is this lack of understanding which justifies the importance of behavioural research in the field of consumer finance and its growing interest for regulators as well as academics.[40]

In law and behavioural studies, research focuses on the limits on consumers' attention and how this can lead them to make suboptimal choices. Here attention encompasses exogenous and endogenous forms of attention, as well as orientating, selective, sustained, executive attention.

Attentional Processes and its Limits Attention has developed as a particularly complex area of research for psychologists. It is safe to note that attention processes

---

[35] For an overview of the literature of disclosure regulations and proposals see Marotta-Wurgler 2010.

[36] See Iyengar and Lepper 2000, p. 996. ("[A]s both the number of options and the information about options increases, people tend to consider fewer choices and to process a smaller fraction of the overall information available regarding their choices…") Agnew and Szykman 2005, p. 64–66. See also Issacharoff 2010.

[37] Howells 2005, p. 363.

[38] Hochhauser, Mark. Lost in the Fine Print: Readability of Financial Privacy Notices, at http://www.privacyrights.org/ar/GLB-Reading.htm.

[39] Ben-Shahar and Schneider 2010.

[40] Shiller 2003, p. 83–104. In addition, disclosure to regulators assist in their task of maintaining systemic stability.

are a multiform phenomenon affecting performance. Neurological models of attention, such as those proposed by Posner and Petersen in 1990, have differentiated separate subcomponents of attention, such as sustained attention and selective attention, which can be defined functionally and, to some extent, anatomically. More psychological models of attention have explored the neuropsychological processes involved in attentional control.[41] In particular, "executive processes" or "higher-order cognitive capabilities" are seen to overlap with attention and are called upon in order to formulate new plans of action and to select, schedule and monitor appropriate sequences of action.

In the regulatory field, the bulk of research focuses on higher cognition and on the limits affecting its processes. In particular, it tackles cognition-limits in connection with information delivered to investors and conclusions drawn. The idea here is that, though in theory, consumers are likely to make rational choices, they also suffer from defects in their attention capacity that lead them to make decisions that are ultimately detrimental. What accounts for such defects and the bounded responsibility that comes with them, are the limitations on the amount of information to which people can attend at any point in time. This has largely been commented on in discussions around the "bottle neck theory" which is based on a discovery made by psychologists (e.g. Broadent) in Oxford in the 1960s.

These limits explain why the human brain relies so readily on short-cuts or heuristics. They also lead to cognitive biases that accompany heuristics. Until recently, these cognitive biases have long been over looked.[42] However, they have become increasingly familiar to lawyers interested in the actual behaviour of consumers. In particular, the focus here has been on framing[43] availability heuristics;[44] probability neglect;[45] confirmation bias;[46] overconfidence in personal beliefs; loss aversion;[47] sunk-cost fallacy;[48] status quo bias; optimism bias;[49] and omission bias.[50]

---

41 For a review, see Spinnler 1991.

42 See namely, Gilovich et al. 2002; Kahneman 2011; Sunstein 2011, p. 1349.

43 Decision makers tend to be influenced by the way in which information is presented, e.g., test participants are more likely to opt for surgery if they are told that the 'survival' rate is 90 %, than they would if they are told that the mortality rate is 10 %.

44 Events coming immediately to mind (e.g., a recent financial market crash) are rated as more probable than events that are less mentally available.

45 A propensity to ignore probability all together when a decision is made under uncertainty.

46 A propensity to interpret information (or search for information) in a manner that confirms one's preconceptions or hypothesis.

47 A preference for avoiding losses over making gains: e.g., test participants prefer to receive a sure EUR46 than have a 50 % chance of making EUR100 (whereas a logical rational agent would take the bet).

48 A propensity to avoid feelings of regret: money and time is invested in a project with dubious results rather than admitting mistake.

49 The tendency to overestimate pleasing outcomes.

50 The inclination to judge harmful actions as worse than equally harmful inactions.

10.4 Insights Towards More Efficient Disclosures

As a consequence of the above, suggestions to improve regulation have been on oriented towards the salience of information, clearer language and simplified disclosures.[51] It needs to acknowledge that there are some positive results, although some new limits have become more apparent, which are encouraging a renewed reliance on psychological insights in order to inform legal regulations.

10.4.1 Perceptual Limitations

The impact of disclosures might not be as dramatic as one might have hoped. However they are not insignificant, despite Mercer Palmiter and Taha titling their 2010 article "Worthless warnings".[52] Their title should not be taken literally, in their experiment they test the effectiveness of disclaimers in mutual fund advertisements, in particular the "past returns do not guarantee future returns" disclaimer. They suggest that we need to be cautious, their findings is *not* that disclaimers never work but that the specific wording negotiated by the industry with the SEC is ineffective. However, they also show that a stronger disclaimer—one that would inform investors in a more straightforward manner, e.g. "high fund returns generally do not persist" would be quite effective. Beyond simplification, making disclosures works requires attention to be pay towards the salience of information—capital letters and trigger words such as "WARNINGS" are useful tool.

These measures respond to identified limits in cognition, i.e. limits on the amount of information people are able to attend to at a certain point in time. Interestingly, the possibility of training and increasing cognition processes is a route that has been considered. There is some empirical evidence relating to the efficacy of training in order to improve attention and executive control performance. Strict conditions are however required to achieve improvement which includes quite intensive training. It is had been found that training achieves better results with younger subjects. Unfortunately, there is little evidence that benefits translate beyond the trained function itself. This represents a serious limit on financial literacy training.

10.4.2 Motivational Limitations

Observations and experimental research also show that solving the perceptual threshold problems does not fully eradicate costly mistakes on behalf of consumers.[53] It is not enough to enable consumers to make good decisions that are in line

[51] Beshears et al. 2009.

[52] Mercer et al. 2010.

[53] Mercer et al. 2010.

with their long term objectives. Even when subjects have the perceptual capacity to attend to the information provided by a disclosure, they do not always do so. This observation leads us to give further attention to the notion of "decision-making".

Rational decision-making does not necessarily mean purely logical decisions, e.g., "logical" under the prism of behavioural economists. The behavioural economists' paradigm is heavily centred on high level cognition, understood as a top down mechanism.[54] Psychologists invite us to adopt a broader spectrum for decision-making,[55] and to refer to more qualitative dimensions, including whether tasks at hand are "cold" or rather "hot", i.e., they are affectively loaded.

Bounded Motivation Standard economic theory analyses attention as resource. Because it is a scarce resource, people need to decide how to allocate it but attend to this issue by make rational decisions. Even if it only takes a split second, top-down executive control is at play. However, psychologists have suggested an alternative way of viewing attention. They have suggested that people may not always "decide" how to allocate their attention. Attention might be captured by certain items. Other items may fail to elicit attention even if they are intrinsically important and would rationally require focus to be given to them. In the vocabulary of psychology, what is at stake is "motivation". Motivators may be extrinsic or internal. There are few extrinsic motivators in paying attention to a disclosure in the absence of direct penalty for not doing so. Motivators are therefore more internal and more attuned to long term benefits. There is however little feedback about the comparative consequences of taking into account disclosures or not taking them into account. As a consequence, subjects cannot build a prediction model that would enable them to compute the mismatch between what they expected and what happened and how disclosures could have altered what was decided. As a consequence, it is difficult to amend future conduct and the motivator remains very moderate.

Bounded motivation renders many disclosures useless because consumers ignore them. Two researchers from the University of Zürich, Hüsser and Wirth have opened the way however, in meeting this challenge. Last year they reproduced an experimental design[56] that had been used by Beshears, Choi, Liabson and Madrian in 2010 on past performances.[57] Beshears et alii had tested cognition limits but not motivation limits. Hüsser and Wirth modified the design so that they could concentrate on motivation limits. They found that disclaimers, warning investors that past performance does not guarantee future results, are ineffective when consumer investors have limited attentional motivation.

Having a broader perspective on decision-making enables the recognition that "motivation" limits may also explain why investors do not make good decisions. Motivations have to do with emotions.

[54] It is modelled as an arousal biased competition for neuronal capacity: the BCM model.

[55] Hertwig and Ortmann 2001.

[56] Hüsser and Wirth 2013.

[57] Beshears et al. 2009.

Individual and Social Motivational Limits How can limits to motivation be explained? Psychological studies point in two directions: one is individual and the second social.

Individual Limits First, the lack of motivation may be individual. Typically, information is available, understandable, ready to use, but investors will disregard it. A hypothesis put forward by psychological theory is that such lack in attention is a result of fear. What is to be done with the information is unclear for the investor, it seems too difficult or time consuming for them. For various reasons the mind prefers an easier option: ignoring information.

In other words, when information is unpleasant to deal with, it often disappears in the background. People do not attend to it. An experiment exploring the use of information by investors when able to look up online, their portfolio has shown two attitudes of investors.[58] Firstly, investors will log in more and look up the value of their portfolio, after a rise in the market. On the contrary investors 'put their head in the sand' after the market declines.[59]

The most obvious implication of motivated attention for mandatory disclosure policies is that disturbing messages might well be ignored or downplayed.

Emotional health warnings are referred to as 'fear appeals'. Research shows that such scary warnings unaccompanied by immediate options for remediating action can backfire. The psychological mechanism may be that people are deterred by fear from thinking about the risks. As a consequence, they become less likely to respond to warnings.[60]

In a similar manner, people have been shown to suffer from unrealistic optimism, especially with respect to personal risks.[61] Such unrealistic optimism could well weaken the effects of disclosure.

The described biases impact the effectiveness of any disclosure policies that aim at mitigating selective provision of information by firms. Even if companies do not engage in selective withholding of information (whether voluntarily or due to disclosure regulations), consumers may, in effect, take up the slack by only paying attention to information that supports their decisions and ignoring or downplaying that which does not. If financial intermediaries would prefer not to post information, but are forced to do so by regulations, consumers interested in buying specific products advertised, may take over the 'editing' role that regulations prevent intermediaries from implementing. They will ignore information that, if attended to, would reduce their pleasure in imagining how their life would be changed in the unlikely event that the investments perform at the highest possible level.

Fish and Willkinson-Ryan's (2013) experiment on mutual fund fees corroborates this hypothesis. Without explaining at length the details of the experimental design,

[58] See Fischer and Wilkinson-Ryan 2014, p. 605.

[59] Karlsson et al. 2009, p. 95–115. See also Sicherman et al. 2012. *To Look or Not to Look: Financial Attention and Online Account Logins*. Available at http://www8.gsb.columbia.edu/sites/financialstudies/files/files/financialattn.pdf.

[60] Leventhal 1971, p. 1208–1224; Rogers 1975; Loeber et al. 2011, p. 292–298.

[61] Sharot 2011.

their experiment involved recorded the information that participants chose to look at. Interestingly, they observed that the absence of time pressure made no significant difference in the amount of information consulted.

It therefore, may be more plausible that splitting up into small parts, delimited step, the decision agenda for investors may be a possible means of reducing fear. Fundamental research in the field of attention control and decision-making is a focus of one of the experiment psychology labs at Cambridge University, which is providing encouraging insights in this direction.

Social Limits From a social perspective, motivation may derive from a specific cultural background which has to do with trust. There can be seen to be a general ambient mistrust towards institutions and this mistrust can be expressed as mistrust of financial advisors.[62] Collective representations regarding the behaviour of others or the motivations of others are powerful guide in behaviour and decision-making.

"Insinuation anxiety effects" are a typical example illustrating how disclosure of misaligned incentives may backfire. Disclosing that an advisor has a conflict of interest does have the intended consequence of decreasing advisee trust. Perversely, due to psychological mechanisms, disclosing that an advisor has no conflict of interest, on the other hand, may also decrease trust under certain circumstances.[63] It has however been hypothesised that this latter effect characterises a culture in which there is a high level of distrust.[64] Although, in more cooperative culture the potential backfire is less likely.

Chater & alii's[65] experiment on the misalignment of interests of investors and of their advisors confirms this hypothesis: an instruction asking participants to give some thought about the personal interest of the advisor and how aligned it is with their own creates a knee-jerk effect. Participants will not listen to the advice of the advisor, even if in the specific situation the fee of the advisor is proportional to the gains made by the participant. In other words, they will not listen even if in the situation at hand, there is no conflict of interest and not reason to distrust the advisor.

The mere fact that the question of how trustworthy the advisor is raised triggers influences. The nature of such influences varies with the level of trust, which in turn differs among cultures. It also varies among investors as a consequence of individual differences.

Another unexpected effect of disclosure of a conflict of interest relating to trust is "insinuation anxiety". The advisee may fear that rejecting advice once he has learnt of a conflict of interest will send a negative signal to the advisor, i.e. that the advisee believes the advice is biased and the advisor is corrupt. The way insinuation

[62] Aghion, Philippe. La société de la défiance; Peyrefitte Alain 1995: the author describes how men tend to be "obsessed" with welfare when they perceive it is at risk (see spec. p. 401–402). By contrast the ethos of trust ("*confiance*") enables men to build a more satisfactory society; trust cannot be imposed but is a result at the intersection of individual and social factors (self-confidence, confidence in others and in men as well as in God).

[63] Experimental data collected by the author, forthcoming.

[64] See Algan et al. 2012.

[65] Yann et al. 2013.

anxiety bias works is that the investment advisor discloses that he/she will receive a financial benefit if the investor buys into the new fund he/she recommends. Without disclosure, the investor might not want to invest due to risk-aversion or satisfaction with current investments, but customers may fear, on disclosure, that their failure to follow the advisor's recommendation to do so is likely to be interpreted as a signal of distrust towards the advisor and their ability to transcend the conflict.

Experiments have been conducted in which conflicted advisors interacted with advisees who either were or were not informed of the conflict:[66] data showed conflicting effects at play. Disclosure increased distrust in advice but it also increased advisees' feelings of pressure to comply with it, which might be explained by the "panhandler effect", also called "insinuation anxiety".[67] Which of the two influences is stronger seems to depend on the local culture, and whether emphasis is put on the holistic cohesiveness of society or whether behaviours are more individualistic.[68]

Yet another unexpected effect of disclosure of a conflict of interest, relating to trust, is the pressure to comply with the distrusted advice it might create. The demand effect, results from the fact that once a conflict has been disclosed, the advisor's interests become common knowledge, and, in some situations, advisees may feel pressured to help advisors obtain their personal interests.[69] For example, once a financial advisor discloses that he or she earns a large commission fee if their customer purchases a specific financial product, the retail investor may implicitly feel that he or she is being asked to "help" the financial advisor get the fee.

Training Trust In the same way that we asked whether we can train attentional processes, we may ask whether the level of trust can be raised. In order to examine whether trust can be built up effectively, we need to consider what the components of the construct designed as "trust" are. Interesting insights are found in psychological literature, which conceptualises often two different dimensions in trust: "cognitive trust", on the one hand, and "affective trust", on the other.

Affective Trust "Affective trust" is the confidence a customer places in a service provider on the basis of feelings generated by the level of care and concern the service provider demonstrates.[70] It is characterised by feelings of security and perceived strength of the relationship. Personal experiences are important, because they are based on emotions. Customers are not merely on the receiving end of services but are co-makers of expressed emotions.[71] Can this dimension of trust be improved? Manipulation only has a modest impact effective.[72]

---

66 Sah et al. 2012, 2013.

67 Sah et al. 2012, 2013.

68 In several of the experiments, advisees ended up being more likely to comply with the advice, even though they trusted it less.

69 Sah et al. 2012, 2013.

70 Rempel et al. 1985.

71 Locked 1996.

72 Johnson et al. 2005.

Could it be further tested? If yes, the research question would be: Is it possible to rebuild trust? No experiment has addressed this question for now, though we can imagine a paradigm. An advisor is paid with a fee proportional to what is invested or a flat fee—a condition where interests are not aligned—and lets the participant know that there is an amendment and that from now on fee will be proportional to the gains made. It would be interesting to test whether the willingness to follow the advice given by the professional advisor increases.

Cognitive Trust Cognitive trust is a customer's confidence and willingness to rely on a service provider's competency and reliability. Knowledge is accumulated from observations of the service provider behaviour and from reported reputation. An example may be useful: although cognitive trust is knowledge-driven the need for trust presumes a state of incomplete knowledge (other there is not need for this risky step called "trust"). Can cognitive trust be improved? More competent advisor would help. The cognitive trust experienced by unsophisticated recipients of advice is all the stronger now that savvy can help recipients make sense of the information. Instead of attempting to provide information directly to consumers, disclosure requirements could make information available in standardised formats. It would then be the role of intermediaries to process this information, understand it and provide it to end users in a form that is meaningful for them.[73] Such service could be for a fee.[74]

10.5 Conclusion

There is a need for a research agenda designed to centre around the limits derived from motivation in the use of financial information and in good decision-making. It would disentangle connections between financial law and emotions and, in particular, financial law and happiness as well as financial law and altruism.[75]

Bibliography

Agnew, Julie R, and Lisa R Szykman. 2005. Asset allocation and information overload: The influence of information display, asset choice, and investor experience. *The journal of Behavioral Finance* 6 (57): 64–66.

Algan, Yann, Pierre Cahuc, and André Zylberberg. 2012. *La fabrique de la défiance*. Paris: Albin Michel.

Anthes, William L., and Bruce W Most. 2000. Frozen in the headlights: The dynamics of women and money. *Journal of Financial Planning* 13 (9): 130.

[73] Non-profit organizations, such as the Consumer's Checkbook (http://www.checkbook.org/) perform functions along this line.

[74] Loewenstein et al. 2014.

[75] Research conducted with the support of the Leverhulme Trust Fund.

Barber, Brad M., Terrance Odean, and Lu Zheng. 2005. Out of sight, out of mind: The effects of expenses on mutual funds flows. *Journal of Business* 78:2095.

Beales, Howard, et al. 1981. Information remedies for consumer protection. *American Economic Review* 71 (2): 410

Becker Gary, S. 1976. The economic approach to human behavior.

Ben-Shahar, Omri, and Carl E. Schneider. 2010. The failure of mandated disclosure, University of Chicago, The Law School John M. Olin Law & Economics Research Paper no. 516.

Benartzi, Shlomo, and Richard H. Thaler. 2007. Heuristics and biases in retirement savings behavior. *Journal of Economic Perspectives* 21 (3): 81.

Beshears, John, James Choi, David Laibson, and Brigitte Madrian. 2009. How does simplified disclosure affect individual's mutual fund choices? *NBER* working paper no. 14859.

Bowles, Samuel, and Herbert Gintis. 2000. Walrasian economics in retrospect. *Quaterly Journal of Economics* 115:1411–1413.

Camerer, Colin F., and George Loewenstein. 2004. Behavioral economics: Past, present, future. In *Advances in behavioral economics,* ed. Colin F. Camerer et al. Princeton University Press and Russell Sage Foundation.

Chater, Nick, Steffen Huck, and Roman Inderst. 2010. Consumer decision-making in retail investment services. a behavioural economics perspective. EU Report. http://ec.europa.eu/consumers/archive/strategy/docs/final_report_en.pdf. Accessed April 2014.

Choi, James J, et al. 2006. Saving for retirement on the path of least resistance. In *Behavorial Public Finance* 304:335–37. ed. Edward J. McCaffrey and Joel Slemrod. Russell Sage Foundation.

Coates, John, and Glenn Hubbard. 2007. Competition in the mutual fund industry: Evidence and implications for policy. *Harvard Law and Economics Discussion Paper* no. 592.

Coffee, John C. Jr. 1984. Market failure and the economic case for a mandatory disclosure system. *Virginia Law Review*. 70 (4): 717–753.

Durkin, Thomas, and Gregory Elliehausen. 2002. Disclosure as a consumer protection. In *The impact of public policy on consumer credit,* eds. Thomas A. Durkin and Michael E. Staten. Springer Science & Business Media (109, 110).

Fischer, Jill E., and Tess Willkinson-Ryan. 2014. Why do retail investors make costly mistakes? An experiment on mutual fund choice. *University of Pennsylvania Law Review* 162:605.

Fox, Jonathan et al. 2005. Building the case for financial education. *Journal of Consumer Affairs* 39 (1): 195–197.

Fung, Archong, Mary Graham, and David Weil. 2013. Targeting transparency. *Science* 340 (6139): 1410–1411.

Gilovich, Thomas, Dale Griffin, and Daniel Kahneman, eds. 2002. *Heuristics and biases: The psychology of intuitive judgment*. Cambridge: Cambridge University Press.

Hernstein, Richard, George Loewenstein, Drazen Prelec, and William Vaughan. 1993. Utility maximization and melioration: Internalities in individual choice. *Journal of Behavior Decision Making* 6:149–185.

Hershey, Douglas A., et al. 1998. Challenges of training pre-retirees to make sound financial planning decisions. *Educational Gerontology* 24:447–467.

Hertwig, Ralph, and Andreas Ortmann. 2001. Experimental practices in economics: A methodological challenge for psychologists? *Behavioral and Brain Sciences* 24:383–451.

Hirshleifer, David A., and Tyler Shumway. 2003. Good day sunshine: Stock returns and the weather. *Journal of Finance* 58:1009.

Howells, Geraint. 2005. The potential and limits of consumer empowerment by information. *Journal of Law and Society* 32 (3): 349–363.

Huang, Peter H. 2005. Regulating irrational exuberance and anxiety in securities markets. In *The law and economics of irrational behaviour,* ed. Francesco Parisi and Vernon L. Smith, 501. San Francisco: Stanford Economics and Finance.

Hüsser, Andreas, and Werner Wirth. 2013. Gravitation toward prior performance in mutual fund advertisings: Do consumer investors' processing abilities account for biased information processing? *The Journal of Consumer Affairs* 47 (Summer 2013): 219–242.

Issacharoff, Samuel. 2010. *Disclosure, Agents and Consumer Protection*, New York University Law and Economics Working Papers, Paper 228.

Iyengar, Sheena S., and Mark R. Lepper. 2000. When choice is demotivating: Can one desire too much of a good thing? *Journal of Personality and Social Psychology* 79:995–996.
Johnson, Devon, and Kent Grayson. 2005. Cognitive and affective trust in service relationships. *Journal of Business Research* 58:500–507.
Jovanovic, Boyan. 1982. Truthful disclosure of information. *The Bell Journal of Economics* 13 (1): 36–44.
Kahneman, Daniel. 2011. *Thinking, fast and slow*. Cambridge University Press.
Karlsson, Niklas, George Loewenstein, and Duane Seppi. 2009. The ostrich effect: Selective avoidance of information. *Journal of Risk and Uncertainty* 38 (2): 95–115.
Langevoort, Donald C. 1996. Selling hope, selling risk: Some lessons for law from behavioral economics about stockbrokers and sophisticated customers. *California Law Review* 84 (627): 682–685.
Leventhal, Howard. 1971. Fear, appeals and persuasion: The differentiation of a motivational construct. *American Journal of Public. Health* 61:1208–1224.
Locked, Karen. 1996. A funny thing happened! The management of consumer emotions in service encounters. *Organization Science* 7 (1): 40–59.
Loeber, Sabine, Sabine Vollstadt-Klein, Sophia Wilden, Sven Schneider, and Christine Rockenbach. 2011. The effect of pictorial warnings on cigarette packages on attentional bias of smokers. *Pharmacology Biochemistry and Behavior* 98 (2): 292–98.
Loewestein, George, Cass. R. Sunstein, and Robert Golman. 2013. Disclosure: Psychology changes everything. *Annual Review of Economics* 6:391–419.
Marotta-Wurgler, Florencia. 2010. Does disclosure matter? *NYU Center for Law, Economics and Organization*, Working Paper No. 10–54.
Meier, Stephan, and Charles Sprenger. 2007. Selection into financial literacy programs: Evidence from a field study 10–13 (*Fed. Reserve Bank of Boston*, Public Policy Discussion Paper No. 07–5).
Mercer, Molly, Alan Palmiter, and Ahmed Taha. 2010. Worthless warnings? Testing the effectiveness of disclaimers in mutual fund advertisements. *Journal of Empirical Legal Studies* 7 (3): 429–459.
Oren, Bar-Gill. 2008. The behavioral economics of consumer contracts. *Minnesota Law Review* 92:749.
Osovsky, Adi. 2014. The misconception of the consumer as *homo economicus*: A behavioral economic approach to consumer protection in the credit reporting system (working paper available on SSRN).
Peyrefitte, Alain. 1995. *La société de confiance*. Paris: Odile Jacob.
Rempel, John K., John G. Holmes, and Mark P. Zanna. 1985. Trust in close relationships. *Journal of Personality and Social Psychology* 49 (1): 95–112.
Ripken, Susanna. 2006. The dangers and drawbacks of the disclosure antidote: Toward a more substantive approach to securities regulation. *Baylor Law Review* 58 (1): 139–204.
Rogers, Ronald W. 1975. A protection motivation theory of fear appeals and attitude change. *Journal of Psychology* 91 (1): 93–114.
Sah, Sunita, George Loewenstein, and Daylian Cain. 2012. The burden of disclosure: Increased compliance with distrusted advice. *Journal of Personality and social Psychology: Interpersonal Rel. and Group Processes* 104 (2): 289–304.
Sah, Sunita, George Loewenstein, and Daylian Cain. 2013. Insinuation anxiety: increased pressure to follow less trusted advice after disclosure of a conflict of interest. http://papers.ssrn.com/sol3/papers.cfm?abstract_id=1970961. Accessed April 2014.
Schiller, Robert. 2012. *Finance and the good society*. Princeton: Princeton University Press.
Secretary of the Treasury Paul O'Neill. 2002. The State of Financial Literacy and Education in *America: Hearing Before the S. Comm. on Banking, Housing, and Urban Affairs*, 107th Cong. (testimony of Paul O'Neill, Secretary of the U.S. Department of the Treasury).
Sharot, Tara. 2011. *The optimistic bias*. Pantheon.
Shiller, Robert. 2003. From efficient markets to behavioral finance. *Journal of Economic Perspectives* 17 (1): 83–104.

Sicherman, Nachum, George Loewenstein, Duane Seppi, and Stephen Utkus. 2012. To Look or Not to Look: Financial Attention and Online Account Logins. http://www8.gsb.columbia.edu/sites/financialstudies/files/files/financialattn.pdf. Accessed April 2014.

Staten Michael E., and Fred H. Cate. 2004. Does the fair credit reporting act promote accurate credit reporting? Building assets, building credit: A symposium on improving financial services in low-income communities.

Sunstein, Cass. 2011. Empirically informed regulation *University of Chicago Law Review* 78:1349.

Sunstein, Cass. 2014. *Nanny statecraft*. Yale: Yale University Press.

Thaler, Richard H. 2000. Toward a positive theory of consumer choice. In *Choices, values, and frames*, ed. Daniel Kahneman and Amos Tversky, 269–287. Yale: Cambride University Press.

Thaler, Richard, and Cass R Sunstein. 2008. *Nudge: Improving decisions about health, wealth, and happiness*. Princeton: Yale University Press, at 124.

Todd, Richard M. 2002. Financial literacy education: A potential tool for reducing predatory lending? *The Region* (Federal Reserve Bank of Minneapolis) 16:6.

Willis, Lauren E. 2008. Against financial literacy education, *Iowa Law Review* 94:197, 22§-27, at 284.

Wright, Joshua D. 2007. Behavioral law and economics, paternalism, and consumer contracts: An empirical perspective. *NYU Journal of Law and Liberty* 2:470.

Prof. Geneviève Helleringer Paris and Oxford. Associate professor at Essec Business School, Avenue B. Hirsch, 95 000 Cergy-Pontoise, France. helleringer@essec.fr. Fellow of the Institute of European and Comparative Law (IECL), St Cross Building, St Cross Road, Oxford OX1 3UL. genevieve.helleringer@law.ox.ac.uk. Fields of Interest: Contract, corporate and financial law, alternative dispute resolution, conflicts of interest, drawing on insights from economics, sociology, psychology as well as comparative law.

Chapter 11
Behavioural Antitrust

A "More Realistic Approach" to Competition Law

Andreas Heinemann

Abstract The paper explores the potential of behavioural economics for competition law. After a summary of the most important behavioural findings from a competition law perspective, several applications are presented. Behavioural economics does not only influence basic concepts like the definition of relevant markets but also affects the competition law analysis of specific conduct like vertical agreements, practices on aftermarkets, tying and bundling, conditional rebates, predatory pricing and merger control. Moreover, the behavioural insights have an impact on the shaping of remedies and sanctions. In spite of these consequences, it seems more appropriate to describe this development as a "behavioural turn" than a "behavioural revolution" since traditional analysis is not replaced but complemented. Therefore, the new insights can be integrated into the existing system without major frictions. Although the behavioural approach more often makes a case for enforcement than against it, it cannot be blamed for greater interventionism. The goal of the "more realistic approach" is, no more and no less, to base competition law on a more reliable foundation.

11.1 Introduction

In the field of competition law, the most important change of the last decades has been the revolution brought about by the Chicago School of Antitrust Analysis in the 1970s. The Chicago School placed efficiency at the core of competition law and attacked traditional concepts protecting the competitive process as such or allowing for goals of competition law other than efficiency.[1] As a consequence, the

[1] Bork 1993 (first edition 1978); Posner 1976, 1979. For a discussion of the different and possibly conflicting goals of competition law see Stucke 2013, p. 34 et seq.; Zimmer 2012.

A. Heinemann (✉)
Commercial, Economic and European Law, University of Zurich,
Rämistrasse 74/40, Zurich 8001, Switzerland
e-mail: andreas.heinemann@rwi.uzh.ch

K. Mathis (ed.), *European Perspectives on Behavioural Law and Economics*,
Economic Analysis of Law in European Legal Scholarship 2,
DOI 10.1007/978-3-319-11635-8_11

form-based approach focusing on certain types of restrictions was replaced by an effects-based approach, calculating the effects of the behaviour in question on efficiency in every single case. In Europe, the transition to an effects-based perspective has been called the "more economic approach".[2] The new approach is modelled on the basic assumption that market participants act perfectly rational and maximise their own profit or utility. In practice, the effects-based approach has led to a more lenient competition policy, especially in the field of vertical restraints and the abuse of dominant positions. There is hardly a jurisdiction in the world which has not been affected by the Chicago revolution.

The great achievement of the Chicago School is the fact that competition policy has been brought in line with the insights of the economic mainstream. Thus, consistency between legal and economic sciences has been created. However, the main weakness of the Chicago approach is its focus on theoretical models which are often far away from the reality of markets. A "more realistic approach" is urgently needed.[3] In this respect, behavioural economics in general and behavioural law and economics in particular seem promising. Model assumptions are replaced by empirically backed descriptions of human behaviour. Thus, consistency could be created not only between competition law and the model assumptions of industrial organization but also between antitrust and behavioural sciences.

The reception of behavioural economics in competition law began later than in other branches of law. The seminal article creating explicitly the relationship between behavioural economics and competition law dates from 2002.[4] In spite of its growing importance,[5] behavioural antitrust cannot yet be qualified as an established sub-discipline, let alone a recognized tool of analysis in legal practice.[6] Despite these uncertainties, the tension between the traditional assumption of the rational, selfish and utility-maximising person and the insights of the empirical behavioural studies are palpable. The goal of this paper is to revise conventional competition analysis from the perspective of behavioural economics. To this end, stock has to be taken of its main findings. In a second step, these results will be applied to selected competition law problems before some general conclusions are drawn.

---

[2] For a discussion whether efficiency or the "freedom to compete" should be the goal of competition policy see for example Schweitzer 2009; Vanberg 2011; Zäch and Künzler 2009.

[3] See Tor 2013 (passim, for example at 16) who underlines the empirical character of behavioural economics as opposed to the theoretical alignment of the rationality hypothesis.

[4] Tor 2002, in particular 548 et seq. For a history of behavioural antitrust see Huffman 2012, 120 et seq.

[5] See for example Arnaudo 2013; Bennett et al. 2010; Engel 2011 (with focus on the experimental foundations); Haucap 2011; Morell 2011, p. 187 et seq.; Reeves and Stucke 2011; Salinger 2010; Stucke 2007, 2013; Tor 2003, 2004, 2013; Tor and Rinner 2011; Van den Bergh 2013.

[6] See Tor 2013, p. 88: "behavioral antitrust clearly can advance the law by offering a better understanding of the behavior of antitrust actors, though the approach still is nascent".

11.2 Behavioural Economics from a Competition Law Perspective

11.2.1 General Context

Behavioural economics is a branch of economics that underpins neoclassical economics with insights from psychology, and in turn, contributes to behavioural sciences by its economic perspective and the abundant experimental practice it has developed.[7] The branch has developed since the 1960's and has acquired universal notoriety since the Nobel Memorial Prize in Economics for Daniel Kahneman in 2002 at least.[8] In substance though, the behavioural approach in economics reaches back much further. Already Adam Smith, the father of classical economics, had a strong affinity to behavioural thinking by underlining the social and altruistic qualities of man which are at the basis of every political and economic organization. In his first book, the Theory of Moral Sentiments, he explained:

> How selfish soever man may be supposed, there are evidently some principles in his nature, which interest him in the fortune of others, and render their happiness necessary to him, though he derives nothing from it, except the pleasure of seeing it.[9]

Subsequently, the behavioural and institutional roots of economics passed into oblivion,[10] before being resuscitated by informational, institutional and behavioural economics. This development did not pass unnoticed by legal sciences.[11] The application of behavioural economics to law led to the new branch of behavioural law and economics providing the economic analysis of law with a more precise picture of human decision-making.[12] The ambition of the new approach is to replace mere assumptions on human behaviour (for example the rationality assumption of traditional

[7] For introductions into behavioural economics see e.g. Angner 2012; Wilkinson and Klaes 2012.

[8] One of the best introductions to the field is his revised Nobel lecture, see Kahneman 2003a.

[9] Smith 1997 (first edition 1759), 1. See Ashraf, et.al. 2005, 142, who underline that "Adam Smith's world is not inhabited by dispassionate rational purely self-interested agents, but rather by multidimensional and realistic human beings".

[10] This statement has to be taken with a big grain of salt. There have always been efforts to combine behavioural sciences and economics. One example is cultural anthropology as applied to the economic sphere; see for example Kottak 2012, chapter on economic systems.

[11] Legal sciences do not have the same degree of methodological unification compared to economics. Therefore, the relationship of law with psychology and the behavioural sciences never has been cut. Only one example is the work of the *Gruter Institute for Law and Behavioral Research* (founded in 1981), see for example Gruter 1991.

[12] See the apt characterization by Tor 2008, at I.: "the behavioral approach thus provides an empirically-based middle ground between the theoretical abstractions of the rational-actor model and the implicit, intuitive, and unstructured view of human behavior of traditional legal scholarship." For general outlines of behavioural law and economics see Engel, Englerth, et al. 2007; Englerth 2010; Fleischer and Zimmer 2011; Jolls, et al. 1998; Korobkin and Ulen 2000; Loacker 2012; Sunstein 2000.

economics[13]) with empirical behavioural findings.[14] From a systematic perspective, "behavioural antitrust" is a subfield of behavioural law and economics, i.e. the application of behavioural law & economics to the field of competition law.

11.2.2 *Behaviour of Consumers and Firms*

Often, the findings of behavioural economics are restricted to the behaviour of consumers, thus creating an asymmetry between consumers and firms. Firms are considered to act as rational profit maximizers because they transact incessantly which is why errors can be constantly corrected. Firms which are not able to control cognitive biases are driven out of the market since they cannot keep up with competitors acting more professionally.[15]

This starting point has been criticized, however.[16] Empirical evidence shows that firms, too, are subject to cognitive biases.[17] This seems plausible as firms are no black boxes but complex organisations based on individual behaviour of managers and other employees.[18] Group pressure and the fear of ostracism by peers may influence the behaviour of individuals. It has been shown that friendship between managers enables and stabilizes cartels,[19] and that internal sanctions against cartel members (which are not necessarily self-serving but in the general interest of the cartel) are an effective means to maintain collusion even between greater numbers of firms.[20] In the same vein, information exchange between competitors may strengthen trust and thus facilitate collusion even if the information exchanged is unobjectionable under conventional standards.[21]

Moreover, firms are exposed to complex situations, too, in which they may recur to rules of thumb triggering biases comparable to those of consumers.[22] The

---

[13] For a nuanced description of the development of the law and economics movement including the assumption of rationality see Elkin-Koren and Salzberger 2013, 14 et seq. with the conclusion at 31: "The insistence of most scholars to continue the Chicago path in this realm too, therefore, makes their work of little contribution to the real world of law".

[14] Tor 2013, p. 32.

[15] Posner 1998; for a similarly sceptical view regarding the application of behavioural law and economics to firms and their decision-makers see R. Fleischer 2013, 222–223. But see Morell 2011, 216, who discusses the applicability of the behavioural approach to small retailers.

[16] See for example Tor 2013, p. 52 et seq.

[17] See Armstrong and Huck 2010.

[18] See Reeves and Stucke 2011, p. 1540: "the assumption that bounded rational consumers magically transform themselves individually or collectively into rational, far-sighted, strategic maximizers with perfect willpower upon entering the workplace is empirically suspect"; Tor 2013, p. 54 et seq.

[19] Ingram and Roberts 2000.

[20] Roux and Thöni 2013.

[21] Bennett, et al. 2010, p. 124.

[22] The effects of these biases are ambivalent and depend highly on the circumstances of the specific case.

result is not necessarily a restriction of competition or the use of market power, but sometimes the contrary: It has been suggested that firms sometimes renounce on fully using their market power but content themselves with a "fair" remuneration.[23] Generally, the question may be asked if not only consumers but also firms have a tendency to "satisficing"[24] instead of maximizing.[25]

A priori no assumptions should be attributed to firms, but their real conduct should count no matter if it is compatible with traditional assumptions or not.[26] Such a "realistic" approach is at the very heart of behavioural economics.

11.2.3 Restrictions of Rationality Particularly Relevant for Competition Law

Behavioural economics has established that real human beings do not necessarily have a stable, context-free and consistent system of preferences and that they do not always maximize their own utility but will bear cost in order to intervene against unfair behaviour. Moreover, they lack willpower, have only restricted computational capacity and they do not act perfectly rational since human behaviour is subject to heuristic fallacies. Therefore, even if there were a consistent system of preferences, choices do not necessarily reveal them.[27] The number of biases identified by behavioural economics is impressive.[28] The following summary is restricted to deviations from the rationality assumption of special relevance to competition law.[29]

Prospect Theory According to prospect theory, developed by Daniel Kahneman and Amos Tversky,[30] gains and losses—contrary to conventional economics—are not attributed the same value: A loss is perceived stronger than a gain of the same amount of money.[31] This has an impact on choice: People tend to renounce an option for action if a risk of loss is involved. Even if the expected value of that option exceeds the value of the (sure) alternative, many people will refrain from acting.

Loss and risk-aversion is at the heart of many heuristic fallacies: As real life decisions constantly imply uncertainty, a preference for the status quo can be

[23] See Tor 2013, pp. 23–24 with further references.

[24] Simon 1956.

[25] Armstrong and Huck 2010, p. 22 et seq.

[26] See Tor 2013, p. 32 et seq., underlining the occurrence of bounded rationality in all classes of actors and emphasizing the limited constancy and uniformity of this phenomenon.

[27] The revealed preference theory was coined by Samuelson 1938.

[28] For an overview see for example Kahneman 2011, p. 107 et seq.

[29] And thus deviates from the frequently used categories of bounded rationality, bounded willpower and bounded self-interest, see Jolls et al. 1998, p. 1476.

[30] Kahneman and Tversky 1979.

[31] See Kahneman, et al. 1991, p. 194: The "disutility of giving up an object is greater than [in the original article: "that"] the utility associated with acquiring it".

observed. A form of this status quo bias is the default bias which makes people stick to pre-settings. Moreover, the endowment effect describes the phenomenon revealed in experiments that man values objects more after they have been acquired than before. Obviously, loss aversion is behind this finding that is incompatible with basic assumptions of the standard model of consumer behaviour.

Truncated Reasoning Other fallacies may be classified into biases where people take no account, or too little account of relevant information (so-called "truncated reasoning") or where they, in the contrary, take into consideration information which is irrelevant (so-called "overreaching reasoning", see *infra*). Examples of truncated reasoning follow.

According to the short-term bias, people seem to emphasize short-term outcomes thus neglecting the development over the full period. To a certain extent, preference for the present may be explained by discounting, i.e. the division of payments in the future by one plus the discount rate for each period of time in question. However, according to the findings of behavioural economics, the preference for the present is stronger than can be explained by usual discounting. Hyperbolic discounting leads to inconsistency over time.[32] Choices which are made under the overwhelming influence of immediate payoffs reveal economic myopia which has a huge impact on transactions that extend over more than one period of time. The short-term bias may drive consumers in economic decisions which are negative for them in the long run thus raising the question whether competition law should counteract.

Another example of behavioural shortcomings is the treatment of opportunity costs. Behavioural economics underlines that opportunity costs are often underweighted relative to out-of-pocket costs. Although opportunity costs are highly relevant for the assessment of different options, their significance is often too abstract for consumers. This may be explained by loss aversion and the endowment effect. Opportunity costs are rather seen as foregone gains than as actual losses.[33] Similarly, anchoring may be classified as "truncated": If agents rely in a particular way on the first piece of information they get, other information necessarily does not get the same degree of attention.

Overreaching Reasoning The preceding examples concern situations in which agents do not take into consideration all relevant factors. However, a negative impact on the quality of decisions may also be caused by the opposite mechanism, i.e. by relying on factors which are not objectively relevant but which are relied on heavily by the acting subject. One example is sunk costs. Costs which have already been incurred and which cannot be influenced anymore should not influence decisions according to the recommendations of traditional economics. Behavioural economics has produced abundant evidence that this recommendation is often disregarded in reality. Due to the sunk cost fallacy, not only the consequences of a decision in

---

[32] For hyperbolic discounting see Rubinstein 2003; Wilkinson and Klaes 2012, p. 293 et seq., with discussion and further references.

[33] Cf. Jolls, et al. 1998, p. 1482.

the future are taken into consideration, but also the expenses which have been made in the past even though they cannot be reversed.

Another example is the availability heuristic. Frequency or probability is estimated by "the ease with which instances come to mind".[34] Information which is easily available because it is salient or recent will be given excessive weight. This phenomenon leads to suboptimal decisions.

Framing The afore mentioned biases, along with other cognitive prejudices may be used to influence decisions. If for example a certain option is described as a forgone opportunity, and the alternative as an actual loss, decision makers may be induced to choose the former rather than the latter, since a forgone opportunity is given lower weight than an actual loss of the same objective value. The impact of framing on decision-making is an important component of behavioural economics.[35] Of special importance in this context is the concept of "reference point". In order to assess if there is a loss or "only" a forgone opportunity, the zero point of the value scale has to be defined. This may be, but is not necessarily the status quo. Framing the reference point in different ways has a considerable influence on decision-making.[36]

Default biases may be understood as a form of framing. As people tend to consider the default as the normal setting they do not see a particular reason why to deviate from it and therefore stick to the default. Thus, defaults have a huge impact on human behaviour.

11.2.4 Bounded Rationality as a New Form of Market Failure

The heuristics and distortions mentioned are highly relevant for competition policy. To the extent that loss averseness, truncated or overreaching reasoning and framing create consumer inertia, they increase switching costs thus facilitating market foreclosure.[37] On the other hand, although cognitive biases have a big influence on the market process, they do not undermine the system as a whole. Decision biases should rather be considered as another form of market failure.[38] It is recognized that in the case of natural monopolies, public goods, external effects and information asymmetry, state action may be indicated if the benefits from public intervention exceed the costs due to market failure (and government failure[39]).

[34] Kahneman 2011, p. 129.

[35] Cf. Tversky and Kahneman 1981.

[36] See Wilkinson and Klaes 2012, p. 164 et seq.

[37] Bennett, et al. 2010, p. 121.

[38] Bar-Gill 2004, p. 1428 et seq.; Bennett et al.2010, p. 113 and 115.

[39] The positive theory of regulation has complemented the normative approach by pointing to the costs caused by wrong intervention or by rent-seeking behaviour; see the seminal contributions by Tullock 1967 and Krueger 1974.

A similar conclusion may be drawn for cognitive biases. Insofar as no rational utility maximizing takes place, it may be necessary for the state to intervene in order to achieve the best results for the economy as a whole. Many forms of regulation come into consideration, such as consumer protection law.[40] In this article, the implications of the behavioural approach for competition policy shall be considered.[41] Through various examples, it will become apparent at which point of the analysis behavioural arguments are relevant.

11.3 Applications

The pertinence of behavioural economics for competition law will be examined through the examples of vertical agreements, aftermarkets, tying and bundling, conditional rebates, predatory pricing, merger control, remedies and sanctions. At the beginning, however, stands the question, fundamental for competition law analysis, if behavioural economics influences the way relevant markets are defined.

11.3.1 Definition of Relevant Markets

According to the European Commission, a "relevant product market comprises all those products and/or services which are regarded as interchangeable or substitutable by the consumer, by reason of the products' characteristics, their prices and their intended use".[42] This definition refers to real consumer behaviour, not to behaviour how it should be under the assumptions of traditional economics. If consumers are subject to biases which reduce the ability or willingness to access information, to assess offers and to act accordingly, relevant markets may be narrower then with fully informed consumers free of prejudice. This is the case, for example, with brand loyalty: If consumers stick to a certain brand, and if the SSNIP test reveals inflexibility in spite of a "small but significant, non-transitory increase in price", the relevant market may be restricted to that brand.[43] All kinds of consumer

---

[40] For the political relevance of behavioural economics for consumer protection law see for example the reflections of the European Commission, Directorate-General SANCO (Health and Consumers) (accessed 11 February 2014); see generally Thaler and Sunstein 2009.

[41] For a behavioural link between consumer protection and competition law see for example Metha 2013.

[42] European Commission, Notice on the Definition of Relevant Market for the Purposes of Community Competition Law, OJ 1997, C 372/5, n. 7.

[43] Desai and Waller 2010, p. 1475: "If one takes the notion of brands and branding seriously, however, there will be instances where a single brand of a product or service *is* the relevant market, even if there are physically identical or similar alternatives" (emphasis in the original). See also Rose 2010, p. 107, who discusses the question if a tee shirt with the logo of a certain music group sold at £ 18 belongs to a different market than a plain tee shirt sold at £ 3, adding: "But in fact what

markets are concerned by this phenomenon, for example fashion, cars, luxury goods and electronic products.[44]

The example shows that the field of market definition is based on actual preferences even if these tastes were to be qualified as boundedly rational. Thus, market definition appears as a gate which has always been wide open to considerations which today are labelled behavioural.[45] Moreover, behavioural analysis might have an influence on methodological awareness when practicing the SSNIP test: Consumers might react stronger to an increase in price for the relevant product than to a decrease in price for alternative ones. Framing may therefore lead to a stronger willingness to switch thus defining markets larger and underestimating market power of the manufacturer of the relevant product. A more lenient treatment of conduct practiced on that broadly defined market would be the consequence. It is therefore important to take framing effects into consideration when shaping consumer surveys.[46]

11.3.2 Vertical Agreements

The field of US antitrust law in which Chicago School-inspired thinking has led to the most spectacular overrulings is that of vertical agreements. In *Sylvania*, the U.S. Supreme Court withdrew the *per se* interdiction for certain territorial restrictions in distribution systems.[47] In *State Oil Co. v. Khan*, the Supreme Court made the fixing of maximum prices subject to the rule of reason.[48] And finally, in *Leegin*, the Supreme Court repealed the *per se* interdiction for resale price maintenance (RPM) with respect to the vertical fixing of minimum prices.[49] The changes in case law were explicitly based on new economic insights, according to which restrictions of intrabrand competition in a context of sufficient interbrand competition are regularly considered not dangerous but rather efficiency-enhancing. One standard argument for the more lenient treatment of RPM is that distributors will invest more in service and promotion if intrabrand price competition is excluded. Free-riding on these activities by other distributors is prevented if RPM applies to all of them.

courts have been doing all along may be closer to behavioral economics than to more conventional economic theories of rational behavior" (108).

[44] For the phenomenon of herding in this context see Stucke 2012, p. 552.

[45] See Petit and Neyrinck 2010, at I. A: "In the present state of EU competition law, the practice of market definition seems to already incorporate—at least in part—the findings of behavioral economics".

[46] Tor 2013, p. 77.

[47] U.S. Supreme Court—*Continental T.V., Inc. v. GTE Sylvania Incorporated*, 433 U.S. 36 (1977) overruled U.S. Supreme Court—*United States v. Arnold, Schwinn and Co.*, 388 U.S. 365 (1967).

[48] U.S. Supreme Court—*State Oil Co. v. Khan*, 522 U.S. 3 (1997) overruled U.S. Supreme Court—*Albrecht v. Herald Co.*, 390 U.S. 145 (1968).

[49] U.S. Supreme Court—*Leegin Creative Leather Products, Inc. v. PSKS, Inc.*, 551 U.S. 877 (2007) overruled the centenary U.S. Supreme Court—*Dr. Miles Medical Co. v. John D. Park and Sons Co.*, 220 U.S. 373 (1911).

Equivalently, an increase in interbrand competition is expected because RPM allows new manufacturers to penetrate the market via motivated distributors which are not impeded by free riders. Certainly, RPM may facilitate horizontal agreements between manufacturers or between retailers because it may serve as an instrument to detect price-cutting manufacturers or to organize collusion between distributors. But this would fall under the *per se* interdiction for hardcore cartels. For the remainder, the US Supreme Court prefers the flexibility of the rule of reason.

This leaves space for taking into account the less positive sides of RPM. The argument—often put forward—that RPM avoids double marginalization[50] can only justify price ceilings, i.e. maximum prices, not minimum RPM. The goal of avoiding free-riding may be relevant in certain cases. But this depends on the circumstances of the single case, in particular on the nature of the product in question (for example in case of experience or complex products[51]). Often, a selective distribution system may be a less intrusive means than RPM. In our context, the behavioural aspects of the problem are to be explored. If brand loyalty is strong (for whatever reason or bias), market power of the trademark owner will be considerable so that interbrand competition is reduced. In that scenario, the linkage between restrictions of intrabrand competition and strong interbrand competition is less convincing. Apart from that, behavioural research has shown that manufacturers use RPM much more often than explicable in terms of efficiency: Different mental shortcuts, like for example anchoring, make them exaggerate the disadvantages stemming from retailer price-cutting. Dealers or media reports dramatizing occasional price-cutting lead to availability and representative biases. Due to loss aversion and fairness-driven behaviour (in particular the rejection of free-riding), the harm of price-cutting is overestimated.[52] Often, RPM is even detrimental for those who practice it, in the sense that the manufacturer's profits could be higher without vertical price fixing.[53] Anticompetitive effects occur mainly if RPM is practiced industry-wide, if concentration and barriers to entry are high, or if the manufacturer has significant market power.[54] Behavioural explanations have also been given for the much-debated question why retailers respect non-binding vertical price recommendations. This might be due to loss aversion of their clients: If the recommended price creates a reference point, higher prices will be interpreted as losses by consumers.[55] However, this only

---

[50] Cf. for example Motta 2004, p. 307 et seq.

[51] See European Commission, Guidelines on Vertical Restraints [hereinafter 2010 Vertical Guidelines], OJ 2010, C 130/1, n. 225.

[52] See the detailed analysis by Tor and Rinner 2011 with an impressive table enumerating all biases involved in RPM, 821–822.

[53] Tor and Rinner 2011, p. 839 et seq., analysing empirical data from the US where—due to the repeal of legislative acts allowing diverging state law in 1975—the effects of RPM could precisely be studied. The authors use the behavioural approach also in order to explain the tardiness of learning effects.

[54] Tor and Rinner 2011, p. 854 et seq. and 861.

[55] Puppe and Rosenkranz 2011. But see Buehler and Gärtner 2013, who explain RPM as a communication device in a self-enforcing relational contract serving to transfer information from manufacturer to retailer for maximizing joint surplus.

explains why retailers do not increase prices above the recommended price. It does not explain the frequently observed fact that retailers do not undercut the recommended price either.[56]

The starting point in European competition law is different from US antitrust since the concept of *per se* interdiction is unknown: At least in theory, any restrictive agreement may be justified under Art. 101(3) TFEU with the burden of proof on the defendant.[57] Although shifts have taken place in European competition law, too, as regards the assessment of vertical restraints, the legal categories had not to be altered therefore. The new economic insights have been integrated by fine-tuning of the relevant block exemption regulations and the accompanying guidelines.[58] Even though a more positive assessment of vertical restraints has taken place, RPM is still black-listed,[59] which means that it is not block exempted. As regards the direct application of the efficiency defence (Art. 101(3) TFEU), it is not sufficient to point in a general way to the advantages of RPM. These efficiencies have to be specified and proven in the single case. Moreover, the other requirements of Art. 101(3) TFEU have to be proven, e.g. the indispensability of RPM for attaining the efficiency goals.[60] As a result, European competition law still is rather hostile to RPM but does not bar the resort to the efficiency defence.[61] As regards behavioural influences, there are some allusions in the vertical guidelines. For example, brand loyalty is taken into account,[62] and vertical restraints with respect to branded products are assessed more strictly.[63] But this is remote from a systematic reception of behavioural analysis.

However, the categories of European competition law appear sufficiently broad to integrate the behavioural approach. Behavioural analysis could turn out to justify the rules on vertical restraints in European competition law or, at least, give an additional argument for the stricter treatment prevalent in the EU.

---

[56] Cf. Puppe and Rosenkranz 2011, p. 326.

[57] In this context, a distinction has to be drawn between the burden of production and the burden of proof. The administrative procedure before the European Commission follows the inquisitorial system (as opposed to the adversary system) meaning that the public authority has to investigate the facts, including those in favour of the accused party (though with duties of the parties to cooperate). The rules on burden of proof become only relevant if the inquiry does not lead to a clear result (case of *non liquet*).

[58] The current texts are: Commission Regulation (EU) No 330/2010 on the application of Article 101(3) of the Treaty on the Functioning of the European Union to categories of vertical agreements and concerted practices, OJ 2010, L 102/1; 2010 Vertical Guidelines.

[59] See Art. 4(a) Regulation 330/2010.

[60] The proposal of Tor and Rinner 2011, p. 858 et seq., of a structured rule of reason analysis under US antitrust law taking into consideration the boundedly rational aspects of RPM contains similar, though not identical elements.

[61] For details, see 2010 Vertical Guidelines, n. 223 et seq.

[62] 2010 Vertical Guidelines, n. 117.

[63] See 2010 Vertical Guidelines, n. 104: "Vertical restraints agreed for non-branded goods and services are in general less harmful than restraints affecting the distribution of branded goods and services. Branding tends to increase product differentiation and reduce substitutability of the product, leading to a reduced elasticity of demand and an increased possibility to raise price".

11.3.3 Aftermarkets

A classical problem of competition law is the status of aftermarkets, i.e. markets for accessories, spare parts or services for a main product. To what extent does the assessment of aftermarkets depend on the competitive situation in the primary market? The Chicago School argued that restrictions on aftermarkets are harmless if there is effective competition in the primary market. Clients who are not satisfied with the conditions on the secondary market can choose a competing product on the primary market. Thus, sufficient competitive pressure is guaranteed.[64] According to this view, it is not the competition between manufacturers of accessories and spare parts or between providers of services for a certain product which counts but the overall competition between entire "systems" of main products including the aftermarkets.

The opposing view finds that there is no general systems market but separate markets for primary and secondary products. The US Supreme Court decided in the *Kodak* case that secondary markets deserve a separate analysis. If a firm has market power in such a secondary market, the application of antitrust law may be justified even if there is effective competition on the primary market. Everything depends on the circumstances of the specific case.[65] This corresponds to the situation in European competition law. Primary and secondary markets are considered separate relevant markets.[66] It depends on the circumstances of the specific case though, if a dominant position exists and if this position has been abused.[67] Part of the analysis is the question to what extent customers are informed about prices on secondary markets and if they really take into account this information for their purchase decision on the primary market.

This leads over to the contribution of behavioural economics. In the context of aftermarkets, e.g. the razor and blades business model, two underestimation biases may be observed: First, consumers systematically underestimate how often they will need secondary products in the future. And second, they are subject to a misperception of price in that they underestimate the price level for those secondary products.[68] Empirical observations show that consumers very often do not use consistent discount rates when assessing the advantages and disadvantages of different payment options between the price for the primary product and the payments for secondary products distributed over a longer period of time.[69]

The decisive question is if restraints of competition on secondary markets should be tolerated if there is sufficient competition on primary markets. In this context, the relevance of behavioural insights for the competitive assessment on these secondary

---

64 See for example Bork 1993, p. 436 et seq.

65 US Supreme Court—Eastman Kodak Co. v. Image Technical Services, Inc, 504 U.S. 451 (1992).

66 See for example ECJ, 31.5.1979, Case 22/78 *Hugin/Commission*, ECR 1979, 1869, n. 8.

67 See for example European Commission, XXVth Report on Competition Policy 1995, n. 87.

68 See Gabaix and Laibson 2006.

69 See the analysis by Bechtold 2007, p. 38 et seq.; Van den Bergh 2013, p. 224 et seq.

markets has to be determined. Is a firm, active on a primary market, allowed to exclude competition on secondary markets by unilateral conduct (for example by the refusal to deliver spare parts or information essential for repair or maintenance services) or by contract (for example tying of primary and secondary products)? The existence of the underestimation biases mentioned does not, in itself, justify the application of competition law since the clients might learn over time.[70] If, however, a market analysis shows that competitive pressure stemming from adaptive clients capable of learning is insufficient, behavioural analysis gives an additional argument in favour of the application of competition law even in cases of effective competition in the primary markets.[71]

The important message in our context is that behavioural economics does not give answers *a priori* but requests an analysis of how markets really are. The example of aftermarkets impressively underlines the advantages of an approach close to reality.

11.3.4 Tying and Bundling

By tying or bundling, customers are required to buy an additional product or functionality with the good they basically want to purchase. The main problem linked to tying and bundling in competition law is the danger of foreclosure. Competitors may be driven out of the market if market power is used to impose goods on customers which then will not resort to competitors of the tying firm any longer. Another concern of tying and bundling underlined in European competition law is exploitation: If the customer prefers to buy the main product separately, she may be placed at a disadvantage if she is compelled to acquire an additional product at the same time.

The Chicago School attacked this line of reasoning on the basis of the single monopoly profit theory: There is only one monopoly profit to be earned. Higher payments for the tied product actually are part of the price of the tying product. If the monopoly is lawful, nothing can be said against the distribution of the monopoly rent to both products. If, by contrast, the monopoly is anticompetitive, antitrust law should directly attack this monopoly, but not ban tying since tying often enhances efficiency or, at least, does not cause any damage.[72] Later, game theory showed that the traditional scepticism of antitrust law against tying may well be justified although a *per se* interdiction is not justified.[73]

In European competition law, tying is explicitly mentioned as a putative restrictive agreement in Art. 101(1) lit. e TFEU and as a possible abuse of a dominant position

---

[70] Their knowledge could also be improved by consumer protection law, e.g. by information obligations imposed on the manufacturer and the dealers in order to specify the consequences of purchase decisions on future expenses for accessories.

[71] Bennett, et al. 2010, p. 122.

[72] Bork 1993, p. 365 et seq.

[73] See Motta 2004, p. 464 et seq. with further references.

in Art. 102(2) lit. d TFEU. However, tying is justified by the Block Exemption Regulation on Vertical Agreements[74] if market shares do not exceed 30 per cent. The Vertical Guidelines explain that no anti-competitive effects can be expected if buyers have sufficient alternatives to buy the tying product or its substitutes without the tied product. This is the case if there are sufficient competitors in the market for the tying product and if they do not practice tying themselves.[75]

Behavioural aspects have been touched upon in the European *Microsoft* case. One issue of the case is the question if the intervention of competition law against bundling is indicated although customers could easily switch to competitors' products, and if there is no exploitation since the tied product is given for free. The European Commission answered in the affirmative. The Commission held that the tying of the operating system Windows and the Windows Media Player (WMP) was an abuse because the ubiquitous presence of *Microsoft*'s media player prevented Original Equipment Manufacturers (OEMs) from shipping third party streaming media players, thus harming competition on the market for streaming media players.[76] The fact that customers do not pay an extra-price for the media player or that they are not forced to use the WMP does not change this fact. The Commission did not consider the possibility to download competing media players as a satisfying alternative since consumers did not have sufficient incentives to do so. In fact, only few users did so in the relevant period of time. Moreover, indirect network effects increased the attractiveness of the WMP.[77]

Even if software downloads were not as easy and fast in the period of time scrutinized by the European Commission (1999–2004) as they are today, one could have argued[78] that nothing prevented users from downloading competing media players, so that neither exploitation nor exclusion took place. There were no exclusivity clauses between *Microsoft* and OEMs or software developers either.[79] If consumers kept using the WMP of their own accord, their choice was—in this view—due to advantages of the *Microsoft* product compared to competing media players.[80]

The European Commission, however, did not rely on rational, but on actual behaviour of consumers. Its line of argumentation can best be explained by

[74] Commission Regulation (EU) No 330/2010 on the application of Article 101(3) of the Treaty on the Functioning of the European Union to categories of vertical agreements and concerted practices, OJ 2010, L 102/1; 2010 Vertical Guidelines.

[75] 2010 Vertical Guidelines, n. 214 et seq., in particular n. 220.

[76] European Commission, 24.5.2004, COMP/C-3/37.792—Microsoft, OJ 2007 L 32/23 (short version).

[77] As a consequence of the ubiquitous distribution of the Windows Media Player, developers had strong incentives to produce complementary content and applications rather for this platform than for competing media players.

[78] And *Microsoft* did so in the European proceedings, see e.g. General Court, 17.9.2007, T-201/04—*Microsoft/Commission*, ECR 2007, II-3601, n. 996.

[79] And *Microsoft* did so in the European proceedings, see e.g. General Court, 17.9.2007, T-201/04—*Microsoft/Commission*, ECR 2007, II-3601, n. 994–995.

[80] See Stucke 2012, p. 560: "Through the lens of neoclassical economic theory, such behavior, rather than exploitive, appears benign".

behavioural economics, for example by the influence of default settings on human behaviour.[81] Due to the status quo bias, people tend to stick with the default even if it would be cheap or nearly costless to switch to another option.[82] In the *Microsoft* case, the European Commission made a clear statement in this sense:

> A supply-side aspect to consider is that, while downloading is in itself a technically inexpensive way of distributing media players, vendors must expend resources to overcome end-users' inertia and persuade them to ignore the pre-installation of WMP.[83]

Hence, default settings influence the outcome even if transactions costs are low.[84] On the other hand, consumers' preference for integrated products may also serve as an argument against the application of competition law: If consumers have only a limited capacity to decide by themselves on the choice of different components, it may be efficient to offer them a bundled product.[85] We will come back to this point when the influence of behavioural economics on the design of remedies is studied.[86]

11.3.5 Conditional Rebates

In general, rebates are part of normal price competition: The seller contents himself with less money for the good in question than normally required. If rebates are based on the quantity sold, they may serve to pass efficiency gains (either completely or partially) on to the customer. However, rebates may also serve to foreclose markets to the detriment of competitors. This is the case with certain conditional rebates practiced by dominant firms and having the same effect as exclusive purchasing agreements. If customers are reliant on a certain amount of goods of the dominant firm (for example must stock items), the dominant firm may use this non-contestable quantity as leverage to conquer the contestable part of the demand. The instrument is quantity rebates with retroactive effect: Purchases beyond a certain threshold trigger rebates which are not only applied to quantities beyond the threshold but to the entirety of purchases. This creates a strong incentive to reach the threshold and therefore not to buy goods from the dominant firm's competitors.

---

[81] See the analysis of Stucke 2012, p. 562 et seq.; Stucke 2013, p. 2 et seq.

[82] See Chap. 11.2.3. The relevant behaviour can also be interpreted as risk averseness: if the product works, it would be risky to switch to a competing product whose user-friendliness cannot be assessed before trying.

[83] European Commission, 24.3.2004, COMP/C-3/37.792—Microsoft (full text, available at accessed 11 February 2014), n. 870.

[84] Bennett, et al. 2010, p. 121.

[85] Bennett, et al. 2010, pp. 121–122.

[86] See Chap. 11.3.8.

All this is standard industrial economics.[87] In addition, the foreclosure effects of conditional rebates may be based on behavioural economics.[88] Starting point is the uncertainty inherent to conditional rebate schemes. This is not only the case with rebate schemes lacking transparency. Even if the conditions for the rebate are clear,[89] the uncertainty of the customer about reaching the threshold until the relevant point in time (for example until the end of the year) will have an impact on her behaviour. Moreover, the (irrational) relevance of sunk costs and loss aversion may lead to a lock-in of customers who do not want to lose the rebate they have reckoned on. This may make them stick with a certain supplier even if the expected value of renouncing on the rebate and buying somewhere else is higher than the completion of the rebate scheme.[90] The huge success of frequent flyer programs illustrates the impact of rebates on loyalty.

11.3.6 Predatory Pricing

The practice on predatory pricing is ambiguous in our context. In US antitrust law, not only must it be shown that the price in question is below an appropriate measure of cost but also that short term losses due to price undercutting are to be recouped in the medium and long term.[91] Under European competition law, there is no such requirement of proving the prospect of recouping the losses.[92] The recoupment test can already be criticized under traditional assumptions: If no advantages in the future were to be expected, a rational firm would not engage in below-cost activities.[93]

---

[87] See the analysis in European Commission, Guidance on the Commission's Enforcement Priorities in Applying Article 82 of the EC Treaty [now: Art. 102 TFEU] to Abusive Exclusionary Conduct by Dominant Undertakings, OJ 2009, C 45/7, n. 37 et seq.

[88] See the analysis by Morell 2011, p. 216 et seq.

[89] This was not the case in ECJ, 9.11.1983, Case 322/81—*Michelin/Commission*, ECR 1983, 3461, n. 83: "Furthermore, the lack of transparency of Michelin NV's entire discount system, whose rules moreover changed on several occasions during the relevant period, together with the fact that neither the scale of discounts nor the sales targets or discounts relating to them were communicated in writing to dealers meant that they were left in uncertainty and on the whole could not predict with any confidence the effect of attaining their targets or failing to do so".

[90] Morell 2011, p. 222 et seq., who points at the same time to the fact that there is not (yet) sufficient empirical data to underpin the behavioural basis of the effect of rebates on foreclosure (at 241).

[91] See for example U.S. Supreme Court—*Brooke Group Ltd. v. Brown and Williamson Tobacco Corp.*, 509 U.S. 209 (1993). But see Supreme Court Justice Stevens' dissenting opinion in this case (which is closer to the legal assessment in Europe): "When a predator deliberately engages in below-cost pricing targeted at a particular competitor over a sustained period of time, then price-cutting raises a credible inference that harm to competition is likely to ensue".

[92] ECJ, 2.4.2009, Case C-202/07 P—*France Télécom/Commission*, ECR 2009, I-2369, n. 29 et seq., 110, 113.

[93] The practice of US antitrust law seems to work the opposite way: If the plaintiff cannot show a rational prospect of recoupment, there cannot be an antitrust violation so that summary judgment is granted for the defendant.

Hence, already on the basis of the rational choice approach, a recoupment test does not seem necessary.[94]

Behavioural economics comes in as an additional argument insofar as it supports the insight that voluntary short term losses are only incurred if advantages in the future will compensate for it.[95] If there were any biases involved, such as hyperbolic discounting, the gains in the future must even be very high. According to the Chicago School, predatory pricing should be a rather rare phenomenon since it will be difficult to recoup losses in the real world, because prices above marginal cost will spur market access.[96] However, this finding is based on the assumption that actors behave rationally and calculate by the expected value of the different options. If, by contrast, actors are subject to an overconfidence bias and if they are risk seeking because losses are beyond the reference point, they may well engage in predatory practices even if the expected value is negative.[97] Besides, it might sometimes be the case that firms do not maximize profits but market shares. Depending on the cultural context, they may also be driven by non-monetary goals like patriotism for example.[98] Moreover, predatory pricing may develop a stronger deterrence than explicable by conventional economics if—due to the availability bias—competitors overestimate the sustainability of low-cost campaigns because they were under the influence of particularly aggressive strategies in the (recent) past.[99] Predatory pricing strategies may be successful precisely because competitors know that the relevant actor is boundedly rational and will continue his low-cost strategy even if he loses money.[100]

These are strong arguments against a too generous assessment of below-cost practices. In light of the few predation cases in Europe, the lower requirements for the establishment of predation in European competition law do not seem to have caused over-enforcement, let alone false positives. Rather, rejecting the recoupment test makes sure that a concept recognized in theory is actually applied in practice.[101]

---

[94] See Reeves and Stucke 2011, pp. 1151–1152.

[95] For an early contribution from a psychological perspective see Gerla 1985.

[96] In this sense U.S. Supreme Court—*Matsushita Elec. Indus. Co. v. Zenith Radio Corp.*, 475 U.S. 574, 589 (1986): "there is a consensus among commentators that predatory pricing schemes are rarely tried, and even more rarely successful".

[97] See the ground-breaking analysis of Tor 2003, for example 54: "Because loss aversion generates risk seeking for losses, market participants will tend to take high-risk opportunities, such as predatory pricing strategies, against the odds, in the hope of winning a negative expected value gamble and eliminating a painful loss".

[98] Leslie 2010, pp. 293–295.

[99] Tor 2003, p. 56.

[100] Leslie 2010, p. 297 et seq.

[101] See also Van den Bergh 2013, p. 223: "Under current law, the abuse system of the European Union is more hospitable to behavioral insights than the U.S. prohibition" (with respect to the assessment of predatory pricing); Petit and Neyrinck 2010, at II.A: "On close examination, EU predatory pricing law seems even behavioralist in essence".

11.3.7 Merger Control

Barriers to entry are highly relevant in merger control. When market access is easy, the threat to competition is low.[102] The theory of contestable markets went so far as to saying that—in absence of barriers to entry—even a monopoly may be a competitive market since raising prices above the competitive level will undoubtedly attract new competitors.[103] With this insight, the analysis of market entry barriers has become an important part of competition law practice. However, potential competition is not put on the same level with actual competition because, in reality, many barriers to entry exist. There may be legal obstacles, imperfect information, difficult access to the relevant technology, strategic behaviour by the incumbent, and, above all, sunk costs. For practical purposes therefore, the degree of contestability has to be determined.

It has been discussed if behavioural insights may be used in the context of merger control.[104] To a certain extent, authorities already follow a behavioural angle. In the Horizontal Merger Guidelines of the European Commission, consumer loyalty to a certain brand and reputation are specified as examples for barriers to entry. Therefore, real consumer behaviour may be relied upon in order to underline negative effects of a merger. In the literature, it has been suggested that overconfident managers may systematically overestimate efficiencies due to a merger, and that therefore—against conventional wisdom—most mergers cannot be presumed procompetitive.[105]

On the other hand, the overconfidence bias, if applied to firms, may work in the direction of stronger contestability. If potential competitors systematically overestimate their prospects of success, there may be more market entrants than explicable by the extent of barriers to entry.[106]

Against this backdrop, the impact of behavioural economics on merger analysis is ambivalent. Authorities are well-advised to explore the opposed effects as far as possible. In this context, behavioural insights are particularly valuable for merger control.[107]

[102] See European Commission, Guidelines on the Assessment of Horizontal Mergers under the Council Regulation on the Control of Concentrations between Undertakings, OJ 2004, C 31/5, n. 68: "When entering a market is sufficiently easy, a merger is unlikely to pose any significant anti-competitive risk. Therefore, entry analysis constitutes an important element of the overall competitive assessment".

[103] Baumol, et al. 1982.

[104] See for example Oldale 2010; Werden, et al. 2011.

[105] Reeves and Stucke 2011, p. 1560 et seq.

[106] For a comprehensive analysis of this phenomenon and the conclusions to be drawn from it see Tor 2002.

[107] Reeves and Stucke 2011, p. 1580: "More generally, it may be the case that behavioral economics finds its best fit in merger review [...]. At times, neoclassical theory cannot explain the evidence of the merging parties' behavior, intent, motives, or post-merger plans".

11.3.8 Remedies

The insights of behavioural economics may be used to reach a better design of remedies. Good examples are the European *Microsoft* cases. In its 2004 decision, the European Commission obliged *Microsoft* to offer—in addition to the integrated version containing the Windows Media Player (WMP)—a Windows version without WMP.[108] However, as *Microsoft* kept the right to sell the full Windows program for the same price as the version without WMP, this remedy was useless: The Windows version without the media player was not accepted by the market.[109]

The lessons from this failure were later drawn in the European browser case. In 2009, the European Commission accused *Microsoft* of abusing its dominant position by tying again, this time with respect to the Internet Explorer and its integration into the Windows operating system. The case was solved through the commitment by *Microsoft* to make a choice screen available asking users to download the browser of their choice in addition to, or instead of, the Internet Explorer.[110] From a behavioural perspective, this approach is by far preferable: The ballot screen prompts users to make an active choice thus breaking the power of defaults and minimizing the impact of market dominance while maintaining and strengthening the autonomy of consumers.[111]

However, it is important in this context not to create a counter-productive "choice overload".[112] Behavioural economics has pointed to the restricted computational capacity of man. Choice therefore should stay manageable. This path is followed in the European *Google* investigation. The European Commission has accused *Google* of the abuse of a dominant position by—*inter alia*—giving favourable treatment to its own specialized web search services over those of competitors.[113] The procedure will probably end with the adoption of a commitments decision.[114] The commitment

---

[108] This is one of the differences between the European and the American *Microsoft* case. In the US, *Microsoft* undertook to renounce on exclusive dealing contracts and to allow OEM's as well as end-users to remove the visibility of the WMP by putting it on the "Add/Remove" list. However, the American authorities did not interfere with product design by imposing an obligation to sell "modular" Windows, see Court of Appeals for the D.C. Circuit, 30.6.2004 (accessed 11 February 2014), 15: "the district court, by remedying the anticompetitive effect of commingling, went to the heart of the problem Microsoft had created, and it did so without intruding itself into the design and engineering of the Windows operating system. We say, Well done!".

[109] See Heinemann 2005, p. 79 (with the proposal to prefer a must carry approach over a software removal remedy at 80–81).

[110] European Commission, 16.12.2009– *Microsoft (Tying)*, OJ 2010, C 36/7. *Microsoft* did not respect the commitment, though, and was fined for non-compliance with its browser choice commitments, see European Commission, 6.3.2013—*Microsoft (Tying)*, OJ 2013, C 120/15.

[111] For a behavioural perspective on the commitments in the European browser case see Bennett, et al. 2010, p. 130.

[112] Stucke 2012, p. 570 et seq.

[113] See for example European Commission, Press Release IP/13/371 of 25.4.2013.

[114] Under Art. 9 Regulation 1/2003 on the Implementation of the Rules on Competition Laid Down in Articles 81 and 82 of the Treaty, OJ 2003, L 1/1. As regards "search neutrality", the European case will be stricter than the US case: The Federal Trade Commission (FTC) closed the

on the vertical search topic will oblige *Google* to display three rival services whenever it displays its own specialized search services. The presentation of the rivals' services has to be as visible and as attractive as *Google's* own services.[115] The restriction to three competitors (which will have to be chosen on the basis of objective criteria, for example the results in *Google's* organic search results) can well be explained by the goal of avoiding information overload on the part of consumers.

Hence, even if not expressly referred to, behavioural economics plays an important role when it comes to the elaboration of competition law remedies.

11.3.9 Sanctions

Behavioural insights have been reflected in the context of sanctions, too. According to the theory of optimal deterrence, fines should equal the cartel rent divided by the probability of detection.[116] This concept is based on the assumption that decision makers act rationally and that they will calculate costs and benefits on the basis of said formula. However, this calculus will not yield the optimal result if decision makers have a different perception of probabilities. If they are overconfident and assess the risk of detection lower than objectively founded, the fine will be too weak for deterrence.[117] Hubris may well explain the fact that cartels are still being practiced in spite of the important increase in fines over the last decades.

In European competition law, the level of fines has risen constantly in recent times. Instead of further increasing fines, it seems preferable to think about criminal sanctions against the responsible managers. In this respect, US law could serve as a model.[118] In the US, criminal enforcement including imprisonment is considered an important reason for the decrease in domestic cartel activity.[119] From a behavioural angle, loss aversion plays an even more important role if the risk is not a fine but jail, especially if the profile of the typical offender is taken into consideration.[120] Generally, the availability bias could be used for deterrence by increasing even more public awareness of prosecution activities and sanctions.

investigation with respect to the allegations of "search bias" since it saw the practices in question justified as innovations, see FTC, News Release of 3 January 2013 (accessed 11 February 2014).

115 Almunia 2014.

116 See the seminal paper by Landes 1983. However, behavioural economics casts doubt on the idea that people actually think in terms of optimal deterrence, see Sunstein, et al. 2000.

117 Reeves and Stucke 2011, p. 1569.

118 See Baer and Hosko 2013, p. 2. In 2013, US courts imposed 28 prison terms for antitrust violations with an average sentence of more than two years per defendant.

119 See Wils 2008, p. 183 et seq. with further references.

120 Most illustrative Liman 1977, pp. 630–631: "For the purse snatcher, a term in the penitentiary may be little more unsettling than basic training in the army. To the businessman, however, prison is the inferno, and conventional risk-reward analysis breaks down when the risk is jail. The threat of imprisonment, therefore, remains the most meaningful deterrent to antitrust violations".

11.4 The Impact of Behavioural Economics on Competition Law

The examples outlined above have shown that behavioural economics is highly relevant for competition law in many respects. This does not only apply to substantive competition law, but also to analytical tools like market definition and to the design of smart remedies and sanctions. Not taking into account the new insights would lead to flawed results. In the following section, the extent of the behavioural impact on competition law shall be evaluated. From the perspective of European competition law, it shall be analysed if reforms are indicated or if the new insights can be taken into account within the existing system. Moreover, it will be determined what impact behavioural economics has on the activities of competition authorities.

11.4.1 A "Behavioural Turn" or a "Behavioural Revolution" in Competition Law?

Traditionally, competition is defined as a situation in which firms strive to establish business contacts with buyers (or suppliers) by proposing better products or more advantageous conditions in terms of price or service than other firms selling (or buying) substitutable products. Clients (or furnishers) are supposed to deal with the firm submitting the most attractive proposal.

Behavioural economics does not fundamentally question this mechanism but eliminates the fiction of perfect rationality with respect to the mechanism's actors. It complements traditional analysis with human behaviour beyond the *homo oeconomicus* hypothesis.[121] For the design of competition law, this means that rules should be avoided which are exclusively based on the rationality assumption. It is equally true that rules should not be based on constantly irrational behaviour either, since the *homo sapiens* is complex and multi-faceted. For this reason, Herbert Simon's term of "bounded rationality" has widely been adopted.[122] While boundedly rational conduct is variable and heterogeneous, there are nevertheless behavioural regularities.[123] As a consequence, competition law should be sufficiently flexible to react to the diversity of human behaviour. On the other hand, the goal of legal certainty requires a sufficient degree of predictability. In US law, a structured rule of reason analysis responds to this goal.[124] In European competition law, such a structure is provided for by the law, since a distinction is made between a general prohibition (in Art. 101(1) TFEU) and its exceptions (in Art. 101(3) TFEU).

---

[121] For a general discussion of this concept see Kirchgässner 2013.

[122] Simon 1957; see also Kahneman 2003b.

[123] Tor 2013, p. 84. The title of Dan Ariely's bestselling book is "Predictably Irrational", see Ariely 2009.

[124] See Tor 2013, p. 80 et seq.

Generally, behavioural economics seems to be used as a corrective against exaggerations of economic modelling. The behavioural approach creates a new legitimacy to refer to real behaviour of market actors. In this sense, it is not primarily the details of behavioural sciences which are important since they may be perfectible. Rather, a counterweight is created against an approach which is at risk of losing or having lost touch with reality.[125] In any event, the point is that empirical evidence must not be disregarded with the argument that it is not compatible with economic theory.[126] To the contrary, economic theory and the application of competition law has to be adapted strictly to the empirical evidence found. This is the best guarantee for avoiding enforcement errors.

In this sense, behavioural antitrust aims at providing competition law with a more realistic view on the conduct of market actors. The central issue is how to provide a more reliable basis for the application of competition law. If rational choice cannot fully explain the conduct of individuals and firms, the standard model has to be enriched by more realistic components.[127] Behavioural economics is highly useful in this context insofar as its findings are sufficiently robust. This means that behavioural economics is not supposed to replace traditional analysis but to complement it, and only to the extent that its insights have proven their value. Thus, predictability is not put at risk.

In view of the complementary character of behavioural analysis, it appears more appropriate to speak of a "behavioural turn" of competition law than of a "behavioural revolution".

11.4.2 Need for Reforms or Reception within the Existing System?

Even though it is more a turn than a revolution, the legal rules currently in force have to be checked as to their permeability for the behavioural insights. European competition law appears to be in need of receptiveness rather than of reform in order to achieve this aim.

Recognition Within the Existing System It is possible to take behavioural economics into account within competition law under two conditions. The first one sounds self-evident: Law must allow its application to real world behaviour. This condition is not fulfilled if the legal rules blind out practices which are not in

[125] Cf. Reeves and Stucke 2011, p. 1581: "Behavioral economics thus can fill in the analysis and explain the real-world evidence when neoclassical economic theory cannot". See also Tor 2013, p. 73 et seq., who underlines the importance of case-specific evidence from the perspective of behavioural antitrust.

[126] See Christian Morgenstern's poem "The Impossible Fact": "For, he reasons pointedly/That which must not, cannot be" (in the German original: "Weil so schliesst er messerscharf/nicht sein kann, was nicht sein darf").

[127] Therefore, courts should not grant summary judgment to the defendant with the argument that the conduct in question cannot be explained rationally; see the criticism by Tor 2013, p. 74.

accordance with the rationality assumption. If, for example, in the field of predatory pricing, it is *a priori* said that no anticompetitive behaviour can be found if a reasonable prospect of recouping losses cannot be proven, there is no possibility to find predation on the basis of less rational behaviour.[128] Therefore, openness to facts and real behaviour is needed.

The second condition requires sufficient flexibility of legal rules in order to integrate the lessons of behavioural economics. In US antitrust law, the broadly formulated codes seem sufficiently open, but the existing case law with its precedents establishes a narrower framework. It is the task of scholars and courts to develop this framework further in order to take into account the new insights.[129] European competition law seems, already in its current state, open to a behavioural turn. Starting point is the distinction in Art. 101 TFEU between prohibition (section 1) and justification (section 3). This dualism allows taking into account real behaviour in its diversity on the level of the prohibition. For Art. 101(1) TFEU, it is sufficient that an agreement has as its object, not necessarily effect, the restriction of competition. Efficiencies come in only on the next level, that of justification. In spite of the more economic approach,[130] European competition law has never given efficiency an absolute status. The ECJ, for example, has repeatedly underlined the structural aspects of European competition law and the goal of protecting "competition as such".[131] Therefore, on the level of the prohibition, it is not necessary to find a welfare loss in a narrow sense.[132] Although Art. 102 TFEU does not have the same structure as Art. 101 TFEU, it is interpreted in the same two-tiered sense, i.e. in categories of prohibition and justification.[133]

Against this backdrop, the concepts of anticompetitive object (Art. 101(1) TFEU) and of abuse (Art. 102 TFEU) appear sufficiently broad to encompass distortions of competition due to boundedly rational behaviour. Various gateways have been described in the survey on selected anticompetitive practices.[134] The leeway for incorporating behavioural analysis may be illustrated by the example of customer foreclosure which is relevant both for restrictive agreements and the abuse of a dominant position. According to traditional analysis, in order to prove foreclosure, it is necessary to show that competitors do not have access to customers due to the strategy in question. Exclusivity agreements and fidelity rebates, for example, are

---

[128] See Chap. 11.3.6.

[129] Tor 2013, p. 80 et seq.

[130] Schweitzer 2009; Vanberg 2011; Zäch and Künzler 2009.

[131] ECJ, 6.10.2009, Joined Cases C-501/06 P et al.—*GlaxoSmithKline Services and others/Commission and others*, ECR 2009, I-9291, n. 63.

[132] ECJ, 6.10.2009, Joined Cases C-501/06 P et al.—*GlaxoSmithKline Services and others/Commission and others*, ECR 2009, I-9291, n. 63.: Ibid.: "Consequently, for a finding that an agreement has an anti-competitive object, it is not necessary that final consumers be deprived of the advantages of effective competition in terms of supply or price".

[133] See the priority paper of the European Commission, Guidance on the Commission's Enforcement Priorities in Applying Article 82 of the EC Treaty [now: Art. 102 TFEU] to Abusive Exclusionary Conduct by Dominant Undertakings, OJ 2009, C 45/7, n. 37 et seq. supra note 87.

[134] See Chap. 11.3.

relevant in this context since they may bar competitors from continuing or establishing commercial contacts with the clients concerned. While an exclusivity agreement blocks competitors on the basis of legal commitments, fidelity rebates raise barriers because the non-contestable part of the demand may be used as a leverage to lower the price for the contestable portion to the point that competitors cannot keep up anymore.[135]

Behavioural economics goes one step further. Exclusionary conduct may occur, even if competitors are not foreclosed legally or economically, but simply factually, due to actual and not necessarily reasonable behaviour of customers. An example is the bundling part of the European *Microsoft* case.[136] As media players (at least in their basic versions) have been distributed for free, and since no technical obstacles existed, users had the possibility of downloading competing media players so that—on the basis of traditional legal and economic analysis—it would have been possible to deny foreclosure. However, since consumers rely to a great extent on default settings and renounce on choosing third party software in spite of the better quality of the competing product and in absence of any noteworthy switching costs, it was correct to find foreclosure. The result cannot be explained by traditional economics, but requires referral to behavioural insights. The outcome of the European *Microsoft* case shows that the rules in force are sufficiently flexible to meet this requirement.

Debiasing? The focus of this paper is on the impact of bounded rationality on competition law. It has been demonstrated that competition law follows—or at least should follow—a factual approach. Markets are analysed as they really are, not as they should be. If a certain conduct is anticompetitive, competition law should step in, no matter if the behaviour in question is due to bounded rationality of the actor or if it makes use of the bounded rationality of other market participants.

From a policy perspective, the question may be asked if—in cases of bounded rationality—the problem should not be tackled at the roots. If it is possible to fix behavioural market failure by appropriate rules, the application of competition law may no longer be required. Thus, "Debiasing through Law"[137] may render the intervention by competition law unnecessary. An example is the razor and blade-problem.[138] If legal provisions established transparency regarding follow-up costs of durable goods and total costs over the economic lifetime of a product and if this influenced consumer behaviour, underestimation biases would disappear and effective competition would be strengthened with respect to primary and secondary markets in their entirety. There would be less need for the application of competition law, at least from the angle of cognitive biases. Hence, taking into account bounded

[135] European Commission, Guidance on the Commission's Enforcement Priorities in Applying Article 82 of the EC Treaty [now: Art. 102 TFEU] to Abusive Exclusionary Conduct by Dominant Undertakings, OJ 2009, C 45/7, n. 39.

[136] European Commission, 24.3.2004, COMP/C-3/37.792—Microsoft (full text, available at accessed 11 February 2014), n. 870.

[137] See the seminal paper by Jolls and Sunstein 2006.

[138] See Chap. 11.3.3.

rationality in other fields of law, like consumer protection, may affect competition law.

However, there is also the opposite mechanism, in the sense that competition renders debiasing less necessary. The market mechanism and learning effects may reduce biases or at least their extent so that there is less reason for intervention.[139] The effects of markets on judgment and choice are not that clear-cut, though.[140] In particular, biases may be exploited systematically. Expectations to the corrective forces of the market mechanism must therefore not be exaggerated.[141] They have to be shown in the specific context.

11.4.3 Behavioural Antitrust and the Role of Competition Authorities

Although behavioural antitrust has only just begun, it has already been confronted with several reproaches including short-termism, paternalism and exaggerated interventionism.

Short Term Bias of Competition Authorities? The preceding analysis deals with bounded rationality of consumers and businesses. It has been suggested to apply behavioural economics to the activities of public authorities and their servants themselves.[142] This proposal is in line with public choice theory which applies economic tools to public actors. The combination of behavioural economics and public choice could be called "Behavioural Public Choice".[143] In our context, it has to be asked if competition authorities themselves run the risk of driving under the influence of different biases. A criticism often advanced against competition authorities, especially in the context of innovative industries, is that they prefer short term static efficiency over long term dynamic thinking.[144] However, a closer look at the relevant cases shows that this reproach is unfounded. There is no disagreement about the necessity of long term thinking as such but about the way in which future—which means uncertain—developments are to be integrated into antitrust analysis. According to Frank Easterbrook's error cost approach, the sum of the costs of false

---

[139] Bennett, et al. 2010, pp. 125–126: "It will be unnecessary to intervene, and could indeed have negative unintended consequences, where the problems in the market would otherwise be self-correcting. This will be true, for example, where there are market solutions, where consumers may learn, or where firms can self-regulate".

[140] See the detailed analysis of Tor 2013, p. 43 et seq.; see also Tor 2002, 563, against the frequently advanced argument that irrational decisions cancel each other out in the aggregate.

[141] Garcés 2010, p. 151.

[142] See generally Jolls and Sunstein 2006, pp. 233–234. For a special focus on competition authorities see Bennett, et al. 2010, p. 129; Kovacic and Cooper 2012.

[143] This term is used by Frey and Stutzer 2012, p. 663.

[144] For a summary see Heinemann 2009, pp. 625–626; see also Kovacic and Cooper 2012, p. 782, who explain activism of competition authorities with hyperbolic discounting of long-term costs.

positives, of false negatives and of the system itself has to be minimized.[145] To simplify, authorities should abstain from intervention when the costs of over-enforcement exceed the costs of under-enforcement. As the losses in long-term dynamic efficiency due to antitrust intervention may be high, "errors on the side of excusing questionable practices are preferable" because—*inter alia*—"the economic system corrects monopoly more readily than it corrects judicial errors", and "in many cases the costs of monopoly wrongly permitted are small, while the costs of competition wrongly condemned are large".[146]

This position amounts to a presumption against the application of competition law. As the long-term impact on innovation is unclear, but possibly high, interference is advised against. The problem of this argument however, is that the long-term impact of competition law abstinence on innovation is likewise unclear, but possibly even higher, in particular if the conduct in question aims precisely at preventing competitors from developing innovative products in the future. Such strategies do not only reduce dynamic efficiency with respect to competitors but also with respect to the incumbent himself: His own incentives to innovate are diminished if competition by substitution is impeded by his exclusionary conduct.[147] More generally, behavioural antitrust underlines the risk of under-enforcement in cases in which the rationality assumption pleads against the application of competition law, but where the actors' real behaviour requires enforcement.[148]

In sum, the application of competition law in innovative markets cannot be reduced to thinking in terms of static efficiency. Competition authorities regularly analyse the effects not only of the relevant conduct but also of the authority's intervention on the incentives to innovate of all market actors including the incumbent. Therefore, the reproach of a short term bias has to be rejected.[149] Of course, other biases cannot be excluded. However, if competition authorities are independent, biases due to political influence or lobby groups can be eliminated or at least be reduced to a minimum.[150]

---

[145] Easterbrook 1984.

[146] Easterbrook 1984, p. 15.

[147] See the European Commission's *Microsoft* decision, n. 783. See also Petit and Neyrinck 2010, at II.C, calling into question effects on the incentives to innovate because competition law intervention against dominant firms is rare and managers do not take into account events of very low probability.

[148] Tor 2013, p. 75; see also Reeves and Stucke 2011, p. 1543: "It [scil. Behavioural Antitrust] calls into question our preoccupation with the cost of false positives (which has taken prominence over the last 30 years) while not attending to the cost of false negatives".

[149] Biases can rather be attributed to the opposite position. Easterbrook himself uses the term when saying: "Yet precision is unobtainable, and the bias in favor of business practices is appropriate" (Easterbrook 1984, p. 40).

[150] The scepticism of Kovacic and Cooper 2012 against increased competition law activity is based on the premise of strong political influence on competition authorities with political overseers having "a relative preference for policies that maximize outputs or otherwise convey the appearance of action" (at 782).

Paternalism? Findings of behavioural economics may be controversial in detail, but the existence of boundedly rational behaviour is beyond doubt. The normative question is how politics and law should respond to this fact. According to the most famous concept, people should be given a nudge in order to make better decisions.[151] To this end, the power of defaults has to be used. If people regularly choose the path of least resistance, defaults should be set where the outcome will be the best for everyone or for society as a whole. While people do not have to stick to the default, they have to make an effort in order to change it. The authors of *Nudge* themselves have endorsed the label "Libertarian Paternalism" for their concept of choice architecture.[152]

The proposal has been met with severe criticism from some commentators discerning a threat to liberty and individual autonomy.[153] This attack has been specifically directed at behavioural antitrust.[154] These concerns cannot be confirmed in our context. The central goal of behavioural antitrust is to provide a more solid basis for the application of competition law. Of course, whoever considers these general rules too interventionist, will not find comfort in the behavioural turn. But this is due to the general rules and to their application to specific cases and not to the improvement of the factual basis. An example is the European *Microsoft* browser case.[155] The remedy was (implicitly) based on behavioural arguments, i.e. consumer inertia, but it promoted active choice and thus autonomy. The European rules on tying and bundling may be discussed, but it is not the behavioural basis of the remedy that is the proper target for the paternalism verdict.

Does Behavioural Antitrust Lead to More Intervention? Closely linked to the reflections on paternalism is the question if behavioural antitrust necessarily leads to more frequent or more intense interventions by competition law. In this respect, a distinction has to be drawn between the methodological rationale behind the behavioural approach and its application to specific competition law problems. As regards the former, behavioural analysis leads to a more reliable basis for decision-making, yet not necessarily to a modification of the rules. Therefore, as a methodological tool, it is neutral with respect to the outcome. In principle, behavioural antitrust works in either direction.[156]

[151] Thaler and Sunstein 2009.

[152] Thaler and Sunstein 2009, pp. 5–6 and 15.

[153] See for example Wright and Ginsburg 2012. For a more balanced discussion see Kirchgässner 2013, p. 269 et seq.

[154] Wright and Stone 2012. According to the authors' "irrelevance theorem", there is no difference between behavioural antitrust and rational-choice models if all firms are subject to the same biases. Detailed analysis of Tor 2013, p. 43 et seq.; see also Tor 2002, p. 563, against the frequently advanced argument that irrational decisions cancel each other out in the aggregate.

[155] European Commission, 16.12.2009—*Microsoft (Tying)*, OJ 2010, C 36/7. *Microsoft* did not respect the commitment, though, and was fined for non-compliance with its browser choice commitments, see European Commission, 6.3.2013—*Microsoft (Tying)*, OJ 2013, C 120/15.

[156] See Reeves and Stucke 2011, p. 1543: "Behavioral economics does not necessarily call for less or more antitrust regulation"; Bennett, et al. 2010, p. 129: "In summary, we cannot assume that behavioral economics implies more intervention". For a future perspective see Tor 2013, p. 71,

As regards the application of the behavioural approach to specific competition problems, our survey has shown heterogeneous results.[157] However, overall, there are more constellations in which the behavioural approach leads to the application of competition law than to abandonment.[158] This is due to the fact that its insights may plead for the application of competition law even though traditional economic analysis would suggest reservation. Taking for example vertical restraints, aftermarkets, tying and predatory pricing, the application of competition law in some constellations is backed by behavioural insights whereas the assumption of rational choice would indicate otherwise. However, the examples show at the same time that the rationality assumption oversimplifies and does not fully grasp the economic phenomena. The application of competition law in these cases is not due to a tightening of the substantive rules but instead to a more exhaustive appreciation of the facts. Moreover, the impact of behavioural analysis has to be determined separately for every single problem.

11.5 Outlook

In real life, economic actors do not always behave as rationally as implied by the standard model. The consequences for competition law are ambivalent: There are situations in which the application of competition law may be indicated although a conventional analysis based on the rationality assumption would advise abstention. The opposite constellation is equally conceivable, though, i.e. no need for intervention precisely because of the real behaviour of market participants. Competition law is therefore well advised to follow the insights of behavioural economics closely and to pay attention to them when applying the law to specific cases. Competition law rules must be able to embrace the real behaviour of market actors in contrast to fictional conduct underlying abstract models. Prudence should therefore be exercised with respect to rules of *per se* legality. For example, the popular message according to which restrictions of intrabrand competition are benign if there is sufficient interbrand competition does not stand close examination since cognitive biases may outweigh pressure stemming from interbrand competition. Hence, behavioural law and economics provides (additional) arguments for flexible rules on vertical restrictions excluding black and white thinking inspired by the *homo oeconomicus* assumption.

Since the mid-1990ies, European competition law has been under the influence of the "more economic approach" giving central weight to an effects-based and efficiency-oriented analysis under the assumption of rational choice. At the same

who underlines the analytical potential of behavioural antitrust for antitrust scholars of any policy predisposition once certain wide-spread errors will have been removed.

[157] See Chap. 11.3 of this paper.

[158] This may in part explain assessments establishing a one-sided link between the behavioural approach and intervention; see for example Huffman 2012, p. 106: "Until very recently, all of the writing advocating Behavioral Antitrust favored increased antitrust enforcement".

time, the European Court of Justice has upheld more traditional concepts such as the protection of the competitive process in itself. The Court thus pursues the objective to defend legal certainty against a too radical case-by-case approach. A stronger orientation towards behavioural insights may help to reconcile economic analysis and the need for clear and general rules. The "behavioural turn" should be used to transform the "more economic approach" into a "more realistic approach". Behavioural antitrust has the potential to overcome the ideological confrontations between the classical antitrust schools and to help solving specific problems. Thus, the behavioural approach is particularly promising for the field of competition law.

Bibliography

Almunia, Joaquín. 2014. Statement on the Google investigation. SPEECH/14/93 of 5.2.2014.

Angner, Erik. 2012. *A course in behavioral economics*. Houndmills: Palgrave Macmillan.

Ariely, Dan. 2009. *Predictably irrational: The hidden forces that shape our decisions*. New York: Harper.

Armstrong, Mark, and Steffen Huck. 2010. Behavioral economics as applied to firms: A primer. *Competition Policy International* 6 (1): 3–45.

Arnaudo, Luca. 2013. The quest for behavioral antitrust: Beyond the label battle, towards a cognitive approach. *The Dovenschmidt Quarterly* 2:77–88.

Ashraf, Nava, Colin F. Camerer, and George Loewenstein. 2005. Adam Smith, behavioral economist. *Journal of Economic Perspective* 19:131–145.

Baer, William J., and Ronald T. Hosko. 2013. Cartel prosecution: Stopping price fixers and protecting consumers. Statement of 14.11.2013.

Bar-Gill, Oren. 2004. Seduction by plastic. *Northwestern University Law Review* 98 (4): 1373–1434.

Baumol, William J., John C. Panzar, and Robert D. Willig. 1982. *Contestable markets and the theory of industry structure*. San Diego: Harcourt Brace Jovanovich.

Bechtold, Stefan. 2007. *Die Kontrolle von Sekundärmärkten-Eine juristische und ökonomische Untersuchung im Kartell- und Immaterialgüterrecht*. Baden-Baden: Nomos.

Bennett, Matthew, John Fingleton, Amelia Fletcher, Liz Hurley, and David Ruck. 2010. What does behavioral economics mean for competition policy? *Competition Policy International* 6 (1): 111–137.

Bork, Robert. 1993 (1978). *The antitrust paradox-a policy at war with itself*. 2nd ed. (1st ed.) New York: The Free Press.

Buehler, Stefan, and Dennis L. Gärtner. 2013. Making sense of nonbinding retail-price recommendations. *American Economic Review* 103 (1): 335–359.

Desai, Deven R., and Spencer Waller. 2010. Brands, competition, and the law. *Brigham Young University Law Review* 2010 (5): 1425–1499.

Easterbrook, Frank H. 1984. The limits of antitrust. *Texas Law Review* 63 (1): 1–40.

Elkin-Koren, Niva, and Eli M. Salzberger. 2013. *The law and economics of intellectual property in the digital age: The limits of analysis*. Milton Park: Routledge.

Engel, Christoph. 2011. Die Bedeutung der Verhaltensökonomie für das Kartellrecht. In *Beitrag der Verhaltensökonomie (Behavioral Economics) zum Handels- und Wirtschaftsrecht*, eds. Holger Fleischer and Daniel Zimmer. 100–121. Frankfurt a. M.: Verlag Recht und Wirtschaft.

Engel, Christoph, Markus Englerth, Jörn Lüdemann and Indra Spiecker genannt Döhmann, eds. 2007. *Recht und Verhalten: Beiträge zu Behavioral Law and Economics*. Tübingen: Mohr Siebeck.

Englerth, Markus. 2010. Verhaltensökonomie. In *Ökonomische Methoden im Recht*, ed. Emanuel V. Towfigh and Niels Petersen, 165–199. Tübingen: Mohr Siebeck.

Fleischer, Romy Nicole. 2013. *Die Dynamik des Wettbewerbsschutzes im US-amerikanischen, europäischen und australischen Kartellrecht-Eine rechtsvergleichende Untersuchung zu Sec. 2 Sherman Act, Art. 102 AEUV und Sec. 46 CCA 2010*. Cologne: Carl Heymanns Verlag.
Fleischer, Holger, and Daniel Zimmer, eds. 2011. *Beitrag der Verhaltensökonomie (Behavioral Economics) zum Handels- und Wirtschaftsrecht*. Frankfurt a. M.: Verlag Recht und Wirtschaft.
Frey, Bruno S., and Alois Stutzer. 2012. The use of happiness research for public policy. *Social Choice and Welfare* 38:659–674.
Gabaix, Xavier, and David, Laibson. 2006. Shrouded attributes, consumer myopia, and information suppression in competitive markets. *Quarterly Journal of Economics* 121:505–540.
Garcés, Eliana. 2010. The impact of behavioral economics on consumer and competition policies. *Competition Policy International* 6 (1): 145–152.
Gerla, Harry S. 1985. The psychology of predatory pricing: Why predatory pricing pays. *Southwestern Law Journal* 39:755–780.
Gruter, Margaret. 1991. *Law and the mind: Biological origins of human behavior*. Newbury Park: Sage Publications.
Haucap, Justus. 2011. Bounded rationality and competition policy. In *Competition policy and the economic approach: Foundations and limitations,* eds. Josef Drexl, Wolfgang Kerber, and Rupprecht Podszun, 217–229. Cheltenham: Edward Elgar.
Heinemann, Andreas. 2005. Compulsory licences and product integration in european competition law: Assessment of the european commission's microsoft decision. *International Review of Intellectual Property and Competition Law* 36:63–82.
Heinemann, Andreas. 2009. Intellectual property rights and merger control: How to secure incentives to innovate in the long run. In *Technology and competition: Contributions in honour of Hanns Ullrich,* eds. Josef Drexl, Reto M.Hilty, Laurence Boy, Christine Godt, and Bernard Remiche, 601–626. Brussels: Larcier.
Huffman, Max. 2012. Marrying neo-Chicago with behavioral antitrust. *Antitrust Law Journal* 78 (1): 105–145.
Ingram, Paul, and Peter W. Roberts. 2000. Friendships among competitors in the sydney hotel industry. *American Journal of Sociology* 106:387–423.
Jolls, Christine, and Cass, R. Sunstein. 2006. Debiasing through law. *Journal of Legal Studies* 35 (1): 199–241.
Jolls, Christine, Cass R. Sunstein, and Richard Thaler. 1998. A behavioral approach to law and economics. *Stanford Law Review* 50:1471–1550.
Kahneman, Daniel. 2003a. Maps of bounded rationality: Psychology for behavioral economics. *American Economic Review* 93:1449–1475.
Kahneman, Daniel. 2003b. A perspective on judgment and choice: Mapping bounded rationality. American Psychologist 58:697–720.
Kahneman, Daniel. 2011. *Thinking, fast and slow*. London: Allen Lane.
Kahneman, Daniel, and Amos Tversky. 1979. Prospect theory: An analysis of decision under risk. *Econometrica* 47:263–291.
Kahneman, Daniel, Jack L. Knetsch, and Richard H. Thaler. 1991. The endowment effect, loss aversion, and status quo bias. *Journal of Economic Perspectives* 5 (1): 193–206.
Kirchgässner, Gebhard. 2013. *Homo Oeconomicus*. 4th ed. Tübingen: Mohr Siebeck.
Korobkin, Russell B., and Thomas S. Ulen. 2000. Law and behavioral science: Removing the rationality assumption from law and economics. *California Law Review* 88 (4): 1051–1144.
Kottak, Conrad Phillip. 2012. *Cultural anthropology*. 15th ed. New York: McGraw-Hill.
Kovacic, William E., and James C. Cooper. 2012. Behavioral economics and its meaning for antitrust agency decision making. *Journal of Law, Economics & Policy* 8 (4): 779–800.
Krueger, Anne. 1974. The political economy of the rent-seeking society. *American Economic Review* 64 (3): 291–303.
Landes, William M. 1983. Optimal sanctions for antitrust violations. *University of Chicago Law Review* 50:652–678.
Leslie, Christopher R. 2010. Rationality analysis in antitrust. *University of Pennsylvania Law Review* 158 (2): 261–353.

Liman, Arthur L. 1977. The paper label sentences: Critique. *The Yale Law Journal* 86 (4): 630–635.
Loacker, Leander D. 2012. Verhaltensökonomik als Erkenntnisquelle für die Rechtsetzung. In *Interdisciplinary studies of comparative and private international law,* ed. Bea Verschraegen, 45–97. Vienna: Jan Sramek Verlag.
Metha, Judith, ed. 2013. *Behavioural economics in competition and consumer policy*. Norwich: ESRC Centre for Competition Policy.
Morell, Alexander. 2011. *(Behavioral) Law and Economics im europäischen Wettbewerbsrecht-Missbrauchsaufsicht über Zielrabatte*. Baden-Baden: Nomos.
Motta, Massimo. 2004. *Competition policy. Theory and practice*. Cambridge: Cambridge University Press.
Oldale, Alison. 2010. Behavioral economics and merger analysis. *Competition Policy International* 6 (1): 139–143.
Petit, Nicolas, and Norman Neyrinck. 2010. Behavioral economics and abuse of dominance: A fresh look at the article 102 TFEU case-law. *Austrian Competition Journal* 203–209.
Posner, Richard A. 1976. *Antitrust law: An economic Perspective*. Chicago: University of Chicago Press.
Posner, Richard A. 1979. The Chicago school of antitrust analysis. *University of Pennsylvania Law Review* 127 (4): 925–948.
Posner, Richard A. 1998. Rational choice, behavioral economics, and the law. *Stanford Law Review* 50:1551–1575.
Puppe, Clemens, and Stephanie Rosenkranz. 2011. Why suggest non-binding retail prices? *Economica* 78:317–329.
Reeves, Amanda P., and Maurice E. Stucke. 2011. Behavioral antitrust. *Indiana Law Journal* 86:1527–1586.
Rose, Vivien. 2010. The role of behavioral economics in competition law: A judicial perspective. *Competition Policy International* 6 (1): 103–109.
Roux, Catherine, and Christian Thöni. 2013. Collusion among many firms: The disciplinary power of targeted punishment. Accessed 11 Feb 2014.
Rubinstein, Ariel. 2003. "Economics and psychology"? The case of hyperbolic discounting. *International Economic Review* 44 (4): 1207–1216.
Salinger, Michael A. 2010. Behavioral economics, consumer protection, and antitrust. *Competition Policy International* 6 (1): 65–86.
Samuelson, Paul A. 1938. A note on the pure theory of consumer's behaviour. *Economica* 5 (17): 61–71.
Schweitzer, Heike. 2009. The role of consumer welfare in EU competition law. In *Technology and competition: Contributions in honour of Hanns Ullrich,* eds. Josef Drexl, Reto M. Hilty, Laurence Boy, Christine Godt, and Bernard Remiche, 511–539. Brussels: Larcier.
Simon, Herbert A. 1956. Rational choice and the structure of the environment. *Psychological Review* 63 (2): 129–138.
Simon, Herbert A. 1957. *Models of man-social and rational*. New York: Wiley.
Smith, Adam. 1997 (first edition 1759). *The theory of moral sentiments*. Washington: Regnery Publishing.
Stucke, Maurice E. 2007. Behavioral economists at the gate: Antitrust in the twenty-first century. *Loyola University Chicago Law Journal* 38:513–591.
Stucke, Maurice E. 2012. Behavioral antitrust and monopolization. *Journal of Competition Law & Economics* 8:545–574.
Stucke, Maurice E. 2013. The implications of behavioral antitrust. *The University of Tennessee: College of Law Faculty Scholarship*.
Sunstein, Cass R., ed. 2000. *Behavioral law & economics*. Cambridge: Cambridge University Press.
Sunstein, Cass R., David Schkade, and Daniel Kahneman. 2000. Do people want optimal deterrence? *The Journal of Legal Studies* 29 (1): 237–253.
Thaler, Richard H., and Cass R. Sunstein. 2009. *Nudge: Improving decisions about health, wealth and happiness*. London: Penguin Books.

Tor, Avishalom. 2002. The fable of entry: Bounded rationality, market discipline, and legal policy. *Michigan Law Review* 101 (2): 482–568.
Tor, Avishalom. 2003. Illustrating a behaviorally informed approach to antitrust law: The case of predatory pricing. *Antitrust* 18 (1): 52–59.
Tor, Avishalom. 2004. A behavioural approach to antitrust law and economics. *Consumer Policy Review* 14 (1): 2–5.
Tor, Avishalom. 2008. The methodology of the behavioral analysis of law. *Haifa Law Review* 4:237–327.
Tor, Avishalom. 2013. Understanding behavioral antitrust. Texas Law Review 92(forthcoming).
Tor, Avishalom, and William J. Rinner. 2011. Behavioral antitrust: A new approach to the rule of reason *Leegin*. *University of Illinois Law Review* 2011:805–864.
Tullock, Gordon. 1967. The welfare costs of tariffs, monopolies, and theft. *Western Economic Journal* 5 (3): 224–232.
Tversky, Amos, and Daniel Kahneman. 1981. The framing of decisions and the psychology of choice. *Science* 211:453–458.
Van den Bergh, Roger. 2013. Behavioral antitrust: Not ready for the main stage. *Journal of Competition Law & Economics* 9:203–229.
Vanberg, Viktor J. 2011. Consumer welfare, total welfare and economic freedom: On the normative foundations of competition policy. In *Competition policy and the economic approach: Foundations and limitations,* eds. Josef Drexl, Wolfgang Kerber, and Rupprecht Podszun, 44–71. Cheltenham: Edward Elgar.
Werden, Gregory J., Luke M. Froeb, and Mikhael Shor. 2011. Behavioral antitrust and merger control. *Journal of Institutional and Theoretical Economics* 167:126–142.
Wilkinson, Nick, and Matthias Klaes. 2012. *An Introduction to behavioral economics*. 2nd ed. Houndmills: Palgrave Macmillan.
Wils, Wouter P. J. 2008. *Efficiency and justice in European antitrust enforcement*. Oxford: Hart Publishing.
Wright, Joshua D., and Douglas H. Ginsburg. 2012. Behavioral law and economics: Its origins, fatal flaws, and implications for liberty. *Northwestern University Law Review* 106 (3): 1033–1088.
Wright, Joshua D., and Judd E. Stone II. 2012. Misbehavioral economics: The case against behavioral antitrust. *Cardozo Law Review* 33 (4): 1517–1553.
Zäch, Roger, and Adrian Künzler. 2009. Reining in the 'more economic approach': Some overriding constraints from constitutional law and economics. In *Technology and competition: Contributions in honour of Hanns Ullrich,* eds. Josef Drexl, Reto M. Hilty, Laurence Boy, Christine Godt, and Bernard Remiche, 541–555. Brussels: Larcier.
Zimmer, Daniel, ed. 2012. *The goals of competition law*. Cheltenham: Edward Elgar

Prof. Dr. Andreas Heinemann Zurich. Professor of Commercial, Economic and European Law at the University of Zurich. CH-8001 Zurich, Rämistrasse 74/40, Tel. +41 (0)44 634 15 52; Fax +41 (0)44 634 15 89. andreas.heinemann@rwi.uzh.ch. Fields of Interest: Swiss, European and International Economic Law with a special emphasis on Competition and Intellectual Property Law.

Chapter 12
New York Times v. Sullivan in European Context

The Optimal Liability for Libel from the Perspective of Behavioural Law and Economics

Mariusz J. Golecki

Abstract The evolution of tort liability for defamation seems to create one of the most puzzling phenomena within the area of economic analysis of tort law. Whereas generally tort law evolves from negligence towards strict liability, the US Supreme Court established the platform for the revival of negligence-based tort law in case of libel and defamation. In *Gertz* v. *Robert Welch* (1974) the court explicitly advised for the application of the negligence rule if the plaintiff was a "private person". The paper concentrates on these changes in two aspects: the relation between them and new British libel laws and the economic analysis of defamation within a context of European Convention on Human Rights (art. 10). Applying the standard rational choice theory various law and economics scholars proposed different alternatives based on the balance between public good (freedom of speech) and actual damage to the individual. The consideration having been already presented and discussed in law and economics literature concentrated on the internalization strategy, assuming full rationality and free access to information for agents (journalists, publishers) and adjudicators (courts and juries). I suggest that a more modern approach to judicial process requires the reference to cognitive limitations of adjudicators and systemic errors committed by judges. Generally the divergence between prediction and post diction may lead to a lower level of risk-aversion and a higher level of publication in case of standards such as in the *Reynolds* standard in English common law or the generally accepted balancing strategy applied by the ECHR in *Bladet Tromso and Stensas v. Norway* (1999).

M. J. Golecki (✉)
Department of Legal Theory and Philosophy of Law, Faculty of Law and Administration, University of Łódź, Kopcinskiego 8, 90-232 Łódź, Poland
e-mail: mjgolecki76@gmail.com

K. Mathis (ed.), *European Perspectives on Behavioural Law and Economics*,
Economic Analysis of Law in European Legal Scholarship 2,
DOI 10.1007/978-3-319-11635-8_12

12.1 Introduction

The ongoing debate on media regulation and freedom of speech in Europe reflects profound tension between different interests and values. On the one hand, freedom of expression seems to be an underpinning of any democratic state, whereas on the other, the protection of individual's privacy and reputation may confine its scope to a considerable extent. The degree to which freedom of speech and right to privacy may interact and possibly conflict seems to be reflected by the laws on defamation.

The consequential reasoning presented in New York Times v. Sullivan 376 U.S. 254 (1964) effectively led to ban for the application of the common law strict liability in defamation cases on grounds of its unconstitutionality.

The main reason for this radical change of liability standard was the argument in favour of freedom of speech as protected by the 1st Amendment of the U.S. Constitution. In *Gertz* v. *Robert Welch* 418 U.S. 323 (1974) the Court explicitly advised for the application of the negligence rule if the plaintiff was a "private person". However the States remained free to "define for themselves the appropriate standard of liability". This left open floor for speculation concerning the optimal standard of liability.

The paper focuses on two issues. Firstly, on the influence of hindsight bias upon the assessment of risk in case of libel and on finding potential precautions and recommendations how to minimize its effect and potential administrative cost.

Secondly on the relationship between rules and standards as producing different attitude towards risk will be discussed in context of various regulatory instruments. Generally, as it has already been indicated (cf. Rothbart and Snyder 1970; Kahneman and Tversky 1982; Guttel and Harel 2008), the divergence between prediction and postdiction may lead to lower level of risk-aversion and higher level of publication in case of standards such as in the case of e.g. *Reynolds* standard in English common law or the generally accepted balancing strategy applied by the ECHR (Art. 10 of the European Convention on Human Rights as applied in e.g. *Bladet Tromso and Stensas v. Norway* (1999).[1]

The paper will thus concentrate on the evaluation of these changes in two aspects: the relation between the new British libel laws and other legal systems, namely the American and European regulations, and the economic analysis of libel law.

The Leveson Reports' (Part J, Chap. 3) recommendations and recently enacted the UK Defamation Act 2013 sec. 2–4, which supplements prediction inducing *Reynolds* standard with post-diction inducing statutory defence (Defamation Act 2013 sec. 2–4) will be scrutinized from this perspective. Some recommendations will be offered in the last part of the paper.

The first, descriptive part will concentrate on the evaluation of these changes in two aspects: the relation between a new British libel laws and the other legal systems, namely the American and European regulations, and the economic analysis of the libel law within a context of European Convention on Human Rights (art. 10). Both topics seem relevant and strongly connected.

[1] Cf. Rothbart and Snyder 1970; Kahneman and Tversky 1982; Guttel and Harel 2008.

12.2 *New York Times v. Sullivan* and the Constitutionalisation of Defamation

In principle in the common law reputation was protected by a set of remarkably strict rules. The author of a defamatory statement was held strictly liable for any injury inflicted upon the person defamed. A defamatory statement was one which injured the reputation of another. Traditionally there are two forms of defamation torts: libel and slander. Whereas slander refers to oral expressions, insulting mimes or gestures, libel is to be made in a permanent form, including writing, printing, making pictures, broadcasting by radio or television. In the common law the tort of libel was generally actionable *per se*. This means that the plaintiff did not have to prove any harm suffered due to defamatory statement. The plaintiff only had to prove that the statement was defamatory, that it referred to him, and that it was communicated to a third party. The plaintiff in a libel action was not in any case required to prove negligence. The defendant could defend only by proving that the defamatory statement came within one of the three recognized defences: justification, privilege (absolute or qualified) and fair comment. The defence of justification served as a complete defence based on the assumption that the statement was true. The privilege was based on the assumption that dissemination of the information outweighs the protection of reputation when information is generally in public interest. Traditional common law privilege comprised both the absolute and qualified form. The absolute privilege applied in particular, formalized situations such as parliamentary debates, judicial proceedings and official communications by state officials, whereas qualified privilege pertained to communication of information where there was not only an interest but also a duty to disclose information on the ground of public interest[2]. The third common law defence, namely the so called "Fair comment" was of slightly different character as it allowed non-malicious statements of opinion or comments on facts that were reasonably believed to be in the public interest. Thus the traditional common law liability for libel was based on strict liability. Moreover the action for libel was exceptional one since the defamed person-the plaintiff did not have to prove actual harm. These or similar rules operated in the United States at the level of state common law till 1964, when in *New York Times Co.* v. *Sullivan* the United States Supreme Court put forward a revolutionary change in liability for libel, departing from previously accepted common law regulations.

The Court found strict liability for libel unconstitutional due to the fact that it remained in contradiction with the constitutional protection of freedom of speech as

[2] The defence has been extended by Lord Nicholls' proposition in *Reynolds v. Times Newspapers Ltd* [2001] 2 AC 127, where the House of Lords acknowledged that the mass media could have been entitled to the qualified privilege, provided certain conditions were met, including the following: (1) The seriousness of the allegation (2) The public nature of the information (3) The source of the information (4) The steps taken to verify the information (5) The status of the information (6) The urgency of the matter; (7) Whether comment was sought from the plaintiff; (8) Whether the plaintiff's side of the story was covered (9) The tone of the article (10) The circumstances of the publication including the timing. (*Ibidem* at 205). This doctrine was confirmed in *Loutchansky v. Times Newspapers Ltd* [2002] 1 All ER 652.

envisaged by the 1st Amendment to the American Constitution. The U.S. Supreme Court explicitly referred to instrumental reasons, emphasizing that strict liability may result with suppressing or limiting freedom of speech, especially in those cases, where the plaintiff was public official or public figure. The Court clearly stated that strict liability enhances potential cost of fact finding and risk of cost bearing, leading thus to the so called "chilling effect", resulting with too cautious approach of journalists and publishers alike. This reasoning was based on the assumption that:

> A rule compelling the critic of official conduct to guarantee the truth of all his factual assertions—and to do so on pain of libel judgments virtually unlimited in amount—leads to a comparable "self-censorship." Allowance of the defense of truth, with the burden of proving it on the defendant, does not mean that only false speech will be deterred. [...] Under such a rule, would-be critics of official conduct may be deterred from voicing their criticism, even though it is believed to be true and even though it is in fact true, because of doubt whether it can be proved in court or fear of the expense of having to do so. They tend to make only statements which "steer far wider of the unlawful zone". The rule thus dampens the vigor and limits the variety of public debate. It is inconsistent with the First and Fourteenth Amendments. The constitutional guarantees require, we think, a federal rule that prohibits a public official from recovering damages for a defamatory falsehood relating to his official conduct unless he proves that the statement was made with "actual malice"—that is, with knowledge that it was false or with reckless disregard of whether it was false or not.[3]

The U.S. Supreme Court required a defamed public official to prove "actual malice" in order to recover damages. In *Gertz* v. *Robert Welch, Inc.* (1974), the initial position of the Court was slightly changed. The Court distinguished between public and private figures, stating that the later did not have to prove actual malice. Thus the Court in fact established two different rules and two different standards of liability: actual malice in case of defamed officials and negligence in case of private persons. Explaining the relevance of the distinction between private and public persons the Court held that:

> [...] so long as they do not impose liability without fault, the States may define for themselves the appropriate standard of liability for a publisher or broadcaster of defamatory falsehood injurious to a private individual. This approach provides a more equitable boundary between the competing concerns involved here. It recognizes the strength of the legitimate state interest in compensating private individuals for wrongful injury to reputation, yet shields the press and broadcast media from the rigors of strict liability for defamation.[4]

Strikingly enough both decisions of the U.S. Supreme Court created an abyss between the two shores of the Atlantic Ocean in terms of the difference between the rules adopted and evolving in the American and English legal systems. It should be mentioned that English defamation law puts the burden of proof on the defendant, rather than the plaintiff, and has been considered an impediment to free speech in much of the developed world. In many cases of libel tourism, plaintiffs sued in England to censor critical works when their home countries would reject the case outright. In the United States, the 2010 Speech Act finally made foreign libel judgements unenforceable in the American courts if they don't comply with the US free speech law, largely in response to the English laws.

---

[3] *New York Times Co.* v. *Sullivan*, 376 U.S. 254 (1964), 279–280.

[4] *Gertz v. Robert Welch, Inc.*, 418 U.S. 323 (1974), 347–348.

The present British debate on media regulation reflects profound tensions between different interest and values. On the one hand, freedom of speech seems to be an underpinning of any democratic state, whereas on the other, the protection of individual's privacy and reputation may confine its scope to a considerable extent. The extent to which freedom of speech and right to privacy may interact and possibly conflict seems to be reflected by the laws on libel, supported by *The Leveson Report*, which finally (Part J, ch. 3) contained some recommendations concerning the change of the procedure. *The Leveson Report* (Part J, ch. 3) recommended a change of procedure and the establishment of the quasi compulsory arbitration procedure. The common law doctrine of libel, albeit often criticised for being too crude, "irrational and remarkably strict", remained untouched by the Report. Nevertheless the substantial changes have been introduced with the enactment of the Defamation Act 2013. Two issues require particular attention. Firstly, the optimisation of the liability rule for libel by introduction of the requirement of serious harm. Section 1 of Defamation Act 2013 states that:

1. A statement is not defamatory unless its publication has caused or is likely to cause serious harm to the reputation of the claimant.
2. For the purposes of this section, harm to the reputation of a body that trades for profit is not "serious harm" unless it has caused or is likely to cause the body serious financial loss.

The result of this amendment seems to be essential since *prima facie* libel ceases to be a tort actionable *per se*. Nevertheless tort liability for libel remained strict liability, departing from the solution adopted in the United States. Secondly, the objective character of tort of libel seems to be conditional upon the availability of newly constructed defences specified in Sec. 2–4. In general, Defamation Act 2013 Sec. 2–4 replaced all existing common law defences. Since 2013, defences are limited to the following four categories: Firstly, the defence of truth defined as a defence for defamation if the allegation is substantially true. Secondly, the defence of honest opinion consisting of a demonstration that the statement complained of was a statement of opinion that an honest person could have held on any facts which existed when the statement was published. The defence could only be defeated if the plaintiff shows that the defendant did not in fact hold the opinion. Thirdly, the defence of public interest has been defined as a defence based on the assumption that the statement complained of was, or formed part of a matter of public interest, and a publication was reasonably believed to be in the public interest. The defence may be relied upon irrespective of whether it is a statement of fact or a statement of opinion. Fourthly, the defence of peer-reviewed statement in scientific or academic journal has been introduced on the assumption that the publication of a statement in a scientific or academic journal is privileged if the statement relates to a scientific or academic matter. However a publication is not privileged if it is proven to be made with malice.

Given the fact that the United Kingdom is not only a party to the European Convention on Human Rights, but also incorporated the essential part of Convention to is legal system through the enactment of the Human Rights Act 1998, the question arises about the relationship between English tort of Libel and the protection of the freedom of expression in the Convention. Article 10 of the European Convention on Human Rights, on Freedom of Expression, reads as follows:

1. Everyone has the right to freedom of expression. This right shall include freedom to hold opinions and to receive and impart information and ideas without interference by public authority and regardless of frontiers. This article shall not prevent States from requiring the licensing of broadcasting, television or cinema enterprises.
2. The exercise of these freedoms, since it carries with it duties and responsibilities, may be subject to such formalities, conditions, restrictions or penalties as are prescribed by law and are necessary in a democratic society, in the interests of national security, territorial integrity or public safety, for the prevention of disorder or crime, for the protection of health or morals, for the protection of the reputation or rights of others, for preventing the disclosure of information received in confidence, or for maintaining the authority and impartiality of the judiciary.

Given the fact that the European Court of Human Rights became a *quasi*-constitutional court in Europe, one must inquire as to the similarities and differences between the protection of freedom of expression under the 1st Amendment to the U.S. Constitution as established in the *Sullivan* and *Gertz* judgements and the doctrine applied by the European Court of Human Rights. It seems that although the adopted standard of liability for defamation may seem alike, the legal techniques adopted by the ECHR as well as the burden of proof in the U.S. and under the ECHR are essentially different.

The liability for defamation under the ECHR seems to be based on the requirement of good faith on the defaming person, be it private or public. The protection of the freedom of expression is thus conditioned upon the assumption that the person acts in good faith on accurate facts, provided with the information which is precise and verified accordingly with the requirements of "ethics of journalism"[5]. This standard of liability differs considerably from the Common Law strict liability rule and seems to be comparable to the American *negligence* based tort liability for libel in case where the harm concerns private individuals. This requirement is thus stricter than the American one and more indulgent than the English one. It seems that there exists one standard for the press informing on public issues and other potential defendants in defamation cases. However, as it has been illustrated in two Scandinavian cases, the way in which the standard of care is applied varies considerably from situation to situation. In *Bladet Tromso and Stensas v. Norway* (1999) the ECHR found that there was no negligence on behalf of the newspaper which had published a false defamatory statement concerning the behaviour of the crew of a seal-hunting ship, *The Harmoni*.[6] The Court admitted that the information was in fact defamatory and imprecise, but it refused to find defendant liable of

[5] Cf. *Schwabe v. Austria*, Judgment of 28 August 1992, par. 37, Series A No. 313.

[6] *Bladet Tromso and Stensas v. Norway*, Judgment of 20 May 1999, [GC] No. 21980/93, ECHR 1999-III.

reckless behaviour. The ECHR rested upon the assumption that it was sufficient for the newspaper to have relied on a public report produced for the government, even if the report has not been published by the Government who wanted to check the allegations. The knowledge about the later facts was not sufficient to create serious doubt concerning the allegations. Nonetheless, it appears that this decision was controversial, even within the Court, as three judges dissented.

On the other hand In *Pedersen and Baadsgaard v. Denmark* (2004), however, the Court decided that it was not sufficient to rely on information concerning the police chief, who had allegedly deliberately hidden vital evidence, and the journalists should have verified the piece of evidence by themselves, instead resting upon assumption that the evidence was supported by procedural failures in a trial.[7] This case raised many comments and controversies, especially in light of the fact that it has been decided by a 9–8 majority. Some critics suggested that the Court actually adopted strict liability rules instead of "good faith" and the negligence standard since there was no negligence on behalf of the press[8]. The two cases demonstrate to what extend the problem of standard of care remains controversial even among the very judges taking part in the process. Generally it could be suggested that the negligence prevails, however judges also take the proportion between the harm and the quality of investigation into account. Additionally the ECHR, in some other cases, emphasised that the public nature of the issue should also be taken into account. The same could be said about the principle of proportionality which allowed the Court to curb some extravagant judgements of the national courts.[9]

Comparing the standard liability for libel in ECHR, the U.S. law and the English Common Law after the most recent reform of 2013 some preliminary observations could be offered. Firstly, although *New York Times Co.* v. *Sullivan* led to essential alterations of the liability regime for defamation in American law, English law remained faithful to the objective strict liability rule, albeit with some exceptions. The rule, as presently interpreted and amended by the Defamation Act 2013, seems to be rather complex. Defamation is no longer actionable *per se* and the general defence of true information essentially modified the traditional Common Law tort of libel. As it now stands, the English rule is based on conditional strict liability—the defamatory (defendant) is liable provided the plaintiff proves the existence of harm (of financial, not purely psychological or emotional nature), there is a causal link between the defamatory statement and the harm and finally, the defendant is unable to prove that the defamatory statement is true. Actually defamation is thus regarded as a false defamatory statement.

---

[7] *Pedersen and Baadsgaard v. Denmark*, Judgement of 17 Decemner 2004, para 78, [GC], No. 49017/99.

[8] The other explanation may link this case to the criminal procedure and criminal liability for false allegation rather than simple civil liability for defamation.

[9] This pertains especially to English law, where defamation cases were till 2013 decided with the jury. Cf. *Tolstoy Miloslavsky v. United Kingdom*, Judgment of 13 July 1995, Series A No. 316-B. The plaintiff in this case was able to satisfy the ECHR that libel damages of £ 1.5 million awarded against him by the English jury was exuberant constituting a violation of his right to freedom of expression under Article 10 of the ECHR.

Secondly, unlike English law, the ECHR adopted negligence rules based on the assumption that there should be substantial link between harm suffered and the precautions taken by the author of defamatory statement. Actually it seems that the ECHR applies a variation of the Hand formula, assessing liability for false defamation within a light of both the quality of investigation and the public nature and social benefit resulting from the circulated defamatory information. Accordingly, with the decisions of the ECHR, defamation is regarded as a false statement leading to harm and negligently investigated. Additionally the vague notions such as "good faith", "public issue" or "proportionality" lead to the situation in which the Court modifies the standard or the application thereof. Liability for defamation under the ECHR seems to be based on the typical standard inducing *ex post* law-making, case-by case decisions rather than the application of ready and well *ex ante* established legal rules.

The divergence between these two strikingly different styles of adjudication adopted in Europe leads to the question on the economic difference between those solutions adopted by the ECHR and the English law. Since tort law plays an important role as the tool minimising aggregated social costs of harm, precautions and administering the system, the economic analysis of libel laws concentrates on the comparison of different liability regimes, adjusting the incentive structure with the expected output.

12.3 Economic Analysis of Libel

The difference between English law (after the enactment of the Defamation Act 2013) and the doctrine having been established around European Convention of Human Rights could be classified as the difference between strict liability and negligence based tort liability. The comparison of the two most popular liability standards in tort law constitutes one of the classic issues in law and economics of tort law. It seems however, that beginning with the pioneering article of J. P. Brown, who set stage and the economic framework for comparison of different liability regimes, there is no single answer to the question of economic superiority of either strict or negligence based liability regimes[10]. Generally negligence is found to internalise all relevant costs and to lead to the efficient outcome, i.e. efficient levels of precaution in paradigmatically, symmetrical cases, as having been analysed by J. P. Brown, who assumed that two subjects X and Y control the variables influencing the probability of an accident. In this model, it has been observed that the higher the precaution cost, the lower the probability of an accident. The problem however consists in the systemic tendency of decision makers, such as judges and jurors, to establish the expected legal standard on a level substantially higher than the optimal one. In other words, in reality, negligence based regime leads to over-deterrence and

[10] Brown 1973.

loss of social welfare due to the establishment of a too demanding and thus inefficient standard of care.[11]

Additionally it should be observed that libel does not constitute a typical symmetrical situation, since it is generally accepted that only one person, namely the defamatory individual has control upon the level of precautions. Assuming that libel is to be generally defined as an untrue statement which injures the reputation of another, the injuring defendant, be it press or private person, controls at least the level of care concerning the fact finding process. Thus the tort of defamation seems to be strictly linked with the probability of false allegations, and the perpetrator is supposed to act on the findings concerning proper facts. This is also important from yet another perspective. The defamatory statement about important public issues, as it has been highlighted in English, American and Convention based law, plays an important role in democratic society. From the economic point of view, the true information about some improper functions or behaviours of public officials enables public control and thus should be treated as a public good. This also means that freedom of speech is exposed to the chilling effect due to the imbalance between expected benefits of the perpetrator (private benefits) and potential costs of both investigation and possibly damages in cases where the investigation turns out to be insufficient. These instrumental considerations actually loom large in cases of economic analysis of libel. Theoretically in case of asymmetric torts, where only the perpetrator controls the level of precautions and thus the probability of harm, strict liability has been suggested as a proper liability regime since it leads to both optimal level of precautions and optimal level of activity at the same time. Although it has been held that libel creates an example of a "single activity accident", namely the actions of journalists/publishers potentially causing damage to an individual, the "potential chilling effect" means that the actors are not able to fully internalise private benefits, as it happens in case of public goods[12]. In other words, perfect internalization of potential harms due to strict liability rule leads to structural over deterrence, since the private costs of investigation and publication are not balanced with potential private benefit from publication of true, precise and relevant information, constituting public good. The main reason for this is relatively simple and consists of an inability of the potential journalist or investigator to discriminate or monopolise the dissemination of a given piece of information. The investigator does not acquire an exclusive right to publication. If the facts are meanwhile found by the competitor, the journalist remains with investment costs (assuming he conducted a proper investigation) and actually no gains from publication. Given the fact that single activity accidents should be optimally internalized by the strict liability rule in the absence of additional externalities, the *Sullivan rule* seems to be inefficient.[13] However the counterargument for the negligence rule presented in *Gertz* seems to be strong. The court referred to information as public good. This means that there are relevant positive externality effects and that the economic characteristics of libel

[11] Brown 1973; Shavell 1980.

[12] Lee 1981; Renas et al. 1983.

[13] Shavell 1987.

change, making the whole analysis assumptions a sensitive subject. Since the seminal works of R. Posner, S. Shavell or N. Garupa, there has been no agreement as to whether negligence or strict liability is more efficient in enhancing both the spread of public information and the protection against defamation.[14]

Various law and economics scholars proposed different alternatives based on the balance between public good (freedom of speech) and actual damage to the individual.[15] The considerations having been already presented and discussed in law and economics literature concentrated on the internalization strategy, assuming full rationality and free access to information both for agents (journalists, publishers) and adjudicators (courts and juries). A more modern approach to judicial process however, requires the reference to cognitive limitations of adjudicators and systemic errors committed by judges. It seems particularly important that in classical standard economic analysis, it is wrongly believed that there is no difference between *ex post* and *ex ante* assessment of probabilities. It seems however that the problem of the assessment of probabilities is the most important key factor in case of libel, since the attitude towards risk plays a crucial role in taking the decision on both verification of facts and publication of allegations, based on this verification. Therefore it is indispensable to analyse the potential insight of the behavioural approach to law and economics of libel. The concise presentation of pivotal findings of behavioural L&E serves two major purposes: firstly it is explanatory in a sense that it enables understanding of psychological and cognitive processes. Secondly, and probably more importantly it allows conjecture of the standard rational choice model adopted in law and economics. As we've observed already, systemic errors of decision makers lead to over deterrence and chilling effects in cases of negligence based liability regimes. On the other hand, strict liability leads to chilling effect and potentially suboptimal solution even without reference to cognitive limitations of agents. It appears however, that both negligence and strict liability regimes may induce different effects in terms of risk-aversion and incentive structure. Given the fact that information about the content of rules and standards is costly and that the agents have limited cognitive abilities, the difference between past events and future contingencies seems to play a crucial role in designing an optimal liability regime for libel. This however requires setting the standard rationality choice assumptions aside and concentrating on the systemic "errors" and other effects induced by the cognitive limitations of potential agents.

12.4 Rationality Assumption in Context of Libel

According to the standard model adopted in law and economics scholarship, individuals act as rational utility maximizers. The foundations of rational choice theory have been elaborated by J. von Neumann and O. Morgenstern in the 1944 book of

[14] Posner 2003; Shavell 1992; Garoupa 1999.

[15] Epstein 1986; Spier 1997.

Theory of Games and Rational Behaviour.[16] The key concept of rationality refers to the so-called instrumental rationality which can be adequately defined as the capability of the decision maker to choose optimal decision given the alternatives available to other agents. The notion of rationality of agents as players participating in a strictly defined interaction (game) means that both actors aim at maximizing their utility functions. Moreover, the concept of rationality refers to the theory of revealed preferences based on the subjective theory of values. Hence, moral norms are limited to hypothetical imperatives and should be linked to the actions of a player aiming to maximize their satisfaction. Therefore, the notion of rationality is a purely instrumental concept. It is connected to the effective realization of aims rather than to the autonomous choice of those aims. According to this theory a given subject has permanent (invariable), ordered and non-transferrable preferences with regards to all possible states of things or actions. Such a subject may be called *homo oeconomicus*. This notion is not connected to behaviour of particular individuals but rather is used as a convenient tool for predicting future actions. Therefore, the concept of *homo oeconomicus* is predicative rather than descriptive. The only criterion of rationality used within this notion is connected to the existence of a limited coherence of preferences. Nevertheless, the process of their formation is basically outside the scope of the research of law and economics. According to R. Posner, the concept of *homo oeconomicus* should not serve as a basis for explaining the mechanism of decision-making process, hence it is not a psychological theory but rather a model for predicting decisions which are to be made in the future. The primary aim of this notion is to introduce some order to existing relations rather than to describe or to explain them.

It is assumed that the decision-making process is deliberative, i.e. that it is a process of a conscious character, controlled, free, sequential and based on criteria and rules. Although this model could be regarded as the adequate reconstruction of adjudication and law making practice, nevertheless, it does not take into account the characteristic features of the cognitive apparatus. It has been stressed that a crucial influence upon the process of decision-making is being performed by unconscious, automatic processes, of associational character, that would be intuitive.

The role of intuition in the process of law application has been traditionally stressed by supporters of the American realism[17]. Nevertheless, it seems that the attempts that are formulated within those movements that aim to explain the indeterminacy of decisions of law application are unsatisfactory. The indeterminacy of decisions means that their content dependent not only on the legal rules or legal reasons but also on other elements of unconscious character: intuition, impulses, complexes. Those explanatory attempts failed firstly, because of their purely speculative character. They were not verified empirically or the proposed verification was incorrect and proved unsatisfactory within the light of later achievements in the field of cognitive psychology or cognitive sciences. It seems that the only exception to this state of affairs is behavioural economic analysis of law which is just a

[16] von Neumann and Morgenstern 1944.

[17] Hutcheson 1934; Frank 1949.

modification of a classical economics in order to take into consideration the limits of cognition (bounded rationality) and to examine the consequences of the so-called duality of cognitive processes (DPT).

The concept of bounded rationality has been introduced in cognitive psychology,[18] and later on successfully applied in economics[19] and legal theory.[20] The theory of bounded rationality, at least to some extent, supplements traditional rational choice theory. It takes into account the fallibility of human cognitive abilities are not unlimited and therefore human agents including judges and officials have limited computational skills and memory. This observation is generally shared even by some classical authors within mainstream analytical legal theory and jurisprudence. It seems that law and economics may respond to cognitive failures in the same way as classical economics responded to the problem of market failure, and later on to the problem of bounded rationality.[21] Firstly, following classical behavioural law and economics literature, it should be observed that agents often take their cognitive limitations into account, attempting to minimize the costs of the decision-making process and at the same time trying to diminish the rate of errors.[22] This state of affairs leads to wide usage of mental shortcuts and rules of thumb in some specific contexts. The problem remains however, given the assumption that in some cases because of these tools, human behaviour differs in systematic ways from that predicted by the standard economic model, namely the rational choice theory, and it should be emphasized, that this strategy may result in predictable mistakes.[23] The departures from the standard model are generally divided into two categories: judgment and decision-making. Both judgments and decisions demonstrate systematic departures from rational choice model. This finding refers both to legal and non-legal context. It has been observed that judges are prone to both types of departures from standard rational choice model.[24] This phenomenon is partly explained by the way in which economic actors apply the so called rules of thumb). In the context of applying law, those rules of thumb are very often based on the so called availability heuristics, where the frequency of some event is estimated by judges on basis how easy it is to recall other instances of this type.[25]

The proposed application of these findings to the optimization of tort liability for libel hypothesis is based on two crucial observations.

Firstly, the effects of the application of heuristic are predictable, which means, that the rate of error is potentially controllable, which gives potential space for regulatory, institutional and practice-oriented improvements. Those improvements

---

[18] Simon 1955.

[19] Kahneman et al. 1982.

[20] Sunstein 2005; Vermeule 2006.

[21] Sunstein 1996.

[22] Jolls et al. 1998.

[23] Rachlinski 1998, 2011.

[24] Vermeule 2006, 2009.

[25] Kahneman et al. 1982.

could be reflected in normative models of tort law, explaining suboptimal results of existing rules or suggesting the reform.

Secondly, it is assumed that in some context heuristics are useful and approximately provide with sound basis for decision. At the same time they lead to errors in particular situational contexts and circumstances. Certainly it means that legal theoreticians should pay much more attention to the nature of the interplay between intuition and deliberations, since those relations are of complex nature. It is possible however to discover some propensities of these processes and do distinguish between their respective application. Concurringly the identification of those situations, where agents typically make mistakes and refer to heuristics which turn out to be an inadequate tool for the solution of conceptual problem based on e.g. assessment of probability, seems to be not only feasible, but necessary for any sound model of applying law.

It does not necessarily mean, however, that legal theory should uncritically adopt the findings proposed by cognitive psychology or behavioural law and economics. It seems that the complexity of cognitive process requires a more independent approach, based on implementation of the results of empirical studies conducted also in strictly legal context, including some experiments design to verify the theoretical propositions applied to application of law understood as a specific type of decision-making process followed by particular justification produced within a process of legal discourse.

Thus some fundamental theoretical explanations of the characteristics, origin and the nature of cognitive process are to be applied as defeasible hypothesis. One such theory is associated with dual process model[26]. According to the dual process theory (DPT), intuitive processes in the form of heuristics and cognitive inclinations may be explained with the acceptance of a hypothesis of a complex character of cognitive process where alongside conscious (deliberative) activities there are also unconscious (intuitive) activities. The functional complexity is being analysed within DPT with regard to evolutionary psychology as well as experimental cognitive psychology. According to the second thesis the delimitation between the two systems: (intuitive PT1 and deliberative PT2), is of a purely functional character. Still it is claimed that their activities may correspond with an action of relevant parts of human brain.[27] Moreover, it is also stressed that intuitive processes are connected with emotions.[28] The DPT urges theoreticians to take the position of scepticism towards the commonly accepted assumptions concerning the deliberative character of decision-making process within the field of law application. According to some dual-process theories, a clear distinction between intuition and deliberation is possible. Intuitive processes, on the one hand, are described as unconscious, automatic, fast, parallel, effortless, and having a high capacity. Deliberate decisions on the

[26] Cf. Sloaman 2002.

[27] Kahneman 2003.

[28] Rachlinski 2007–2008, 2011.

other hand, are thought to be accessible to conscious awareness, slow, sequential, effortful, rule-governed and having a limited capacity.[29]

The strong separation thesis has been offered by S. Sloman, who claims that intuition and deliberation are completely distinct and separable processes, since they are: "two systems, two algorithms that are designed to achieve different computational goals".[30]

On the other hand, some theories proposed a very weak or even a "no separation" thesis. For example, the so called integrative model of automatic and deliberate decision-making is based on the assumption that every decision is based on an automatic process.[31]

Generally speaking, the role of intuition seems to be twofold: on the one side, it is a condition, if not a necessary condition, for initiating a decision-making process. The significance of intuition is increasing within the situation of information deficit, shortening of the time horizon and activities performed within uncertainty. Hence, one may accept, following R. Posner, that intuition is increasing the effectiveness of decision-making process also within the meaning of economics, allocative effectiveness which is connected to the economic costs of decision-making and law application.[32]

On the other hand one may observe several problems linked to the influence of intuition upon the process of law application. One of the problems concerns legal institutions which are understood as a set of formal and informal rules which successfully shape the motivation of decision-makers The question arises whether the negligent attitude towards intuition and its non-inclusion as a factor co-shaping the content of decision may lead to the introduction of regulations which would lead to sub-optimal allocation of resources due to unrealistic assumptions concerning the cognitive processes and concurringly decision-making process. Within this context one may imagine an increased number of legal conflicts, putting too high costs on the participants of legal proceedings or increasing the costs of functioning of judicial system or administration. In the American jurisprudence, especially within the behavioural economic analysis of law, is has been pointed out that many regulations which did not take into consideration the significance of intuition tend to lead to inefficient allocation of resources.[33]

In behavioural law and economics literature, it has been pointed out that heuristics and biases lead to systemic problems and inadequacies strongly influencing the application of law process. The notorious example of this phenomenon refers to the quality and capacity of jury members during tort law and criminal trials. Generally speaking jurors have to determine the probability of an event that occurred. Within the context of American tort law, this problem refers to the negligence standard, where these determinations are obscured and weaken by the so called hindsight

[29] Kahneman 2003.

[30] Sloman 2002.

[31] Glöckner and Ebert 2011.

[32] Posner 2003.

[33] Jolls et al. 1998.

bias, where jurors' determinations are likely to be afflicted by the inclination of decision makers to attach an excessively high probability to an event because it ended up occurring. Hindsight bias has been widely analysed. As a result plaintiffs are more prone to winning weak cases. It is believed that defendant over-optimism depends on the risk-aversion and is thus context dependant. Although hindsight bias seems to be treated in behavioural law and economics literature as quasi universal phenomenon independent from any legal culture, the above findings deal predominantly with the American law and at first glance they depend on many institutional and legal variables. Such a variable within a context of tort liability for libel seems to be the presence or absence of jury. This consideration has been contemplated quite recently within the context of the reform of English libel law. It is necessary to mention the fact that all defamation cases under the Senior Courts Act 1981 in the Queen's Bench Division, and the County Courts Act 1984, were generally "tried with a jury", unless the trial required prolonged examination of documents. Notorious cases where the probability of past events such as the knowledge of some possible contingences was overestimated led to over-deterrence in American courts, where negligence plays still crucial role in case of libel in private sphere. At the same time this effect could not have been observed in the U.K., where although jury played very important role and assisted in all processes concerning defamation, the regime of liability is based on strict liability rule rather than on negligence. On the other hand it is difficult to estimate how the presence of strict liability rule in case of libel influenced the journalists and investigators, who had to assess the probability of truth/false facts deciding on publication of defamatory statement. It seems that they might have been reluctant in calculating the subjective probability of past events. Additionally the effect consisting in increasing number of cases and limitation of freedom of speech has been attained in yet another way. English jurors used to set the level of damages in libel cases so high that the rulings attracted attention of ECHR as it happened in *Tolstoy Miloslavsky v. United Kingdom*, where the ECHR decided that the damages awarded by the jury were contradictory to the principle of proportionality and contradictory with art 10 of the European Convention of Human Rights. This tendency to awarding highly disproportionate amount of damages in English courts, resulting with chilling effect, finally found its institutional solution. According to Section 11 of Defamation Act 2013 all defamation cases previously having been assisted by jury will now be "tried without a jury" unless the court orders otherwise. Such cases will be referred through a Defamation Recognition Commission to an arbitrator, namely the Independent Regulatory Board. When deciding on costs the Courts will take into account, whether the party in a dispute has chosen not to use the arbitration service and successful party would be required to pay all of the proceedings costs, if unreasonably having refused to use the arbitration service. In other words the problem with excessive damages awarded by jury has been resolved institutionally.

Secondly, it seems that the ignorance about the complex character of the cognitive process by the organs dealing with the application of law leads to the adoption of too rigorous requirements. Such an attitude results in allocative ineffectiveness as the standards are based on the assumption of a purely deliberative and rational character of decision-making process. Moreover, within the prescribed conditions it is not possible to achieve an institutional point of equilibrium as the participants of a legal discourse still accept an unrealistic assumption concerning a uniquely deliberative character of those decisions that concern the application of law. This attitude is reflected in systemic flaws committed during the process of the application of law.[34] Within the context of tort liability for libel one may point out that too rigorous standards of diligence and systemic flaws resulting in adjudication concerning the evaluation of rationality of actions, based on delusion of hindsight bias may lead to systemic over-deterrence. The influence of intuitive processes on the application of law is visible within heuristics which are gradually recognized (discovered), classified and explained within the context of duration of cognitive processes (cognitive aspect) as well as in regard to the consequences of their effect on the process of law application (institutional and legal aspect). The processes of this type consist of heuristics: availability, representation, anchoring and adjusting.[35] Heuristics of availability is linked to the process of estimation of a given action as more probable in the context where this situation is more available as a hypothetical imagination than as a remembrance.[36] A particular type of availability involved in libel cases is delusion of hindsight bias which is connected to the process of ascription of greater probability to situations which are already known to have happened, still their original probability (*ex ante*) was minimal. Anchoring and adjusting heuristics are discernible within the process of non-reflexive acceptance of a given number and subsequent adjustment of the quantity according to the process of receiving of further, more detailed information. All this processes may to some extend influence not only judges and jurors but also journalists and investigators who inadequately respond to some data or simply commit errors. Two types of errors-positive and negative errors-may strongly influence the soundness of decision whether to publish information based on a verification process. It should be stressed that verification rarely leads to perfect knowledge. More often verification and fact finding process only increase the probability of truth finding. The question is how decision makers respond to uncertainty about past facts and how they try to predict future decisions of courts, depending on whether their behaviour is shaped by rules or standards

Heuristics of representation is visible within the process of categorization of objects with regard to their similarity to the prototype (exemplary, prototypical categorization). This type of categorization differs from theoretical categorization, based on rule where the object is categorized due to the description of its necessary features. The process of categorization attracted attention of many scholars in cognitive sciences, especially cognitive linguistics, neuropsychology and cognitive psychology. Two general views on the essential characteristics of this process have been presented so far. Some scholars claim that categorization has a unified structure and thus could be embraced in a single model.[37] The other view is based on the

[34] Rachlinski 1998; Sunstein 2005; Vermeule 2009.

[35] Rachlinski 2007–2008.

[36] Kahneman 2003.

[37] Nossofsky 1992.

opposite assumption, namely the belief that categorization is not only complex but also hybrid-in different situations subjects categorize objects according to different patterns explained by different categorization strategies.[38] The difference between the two approaches seems to be relevant for the understanding of the psychological characteristics of categorization, and it pertains to such areas of cognitive psychology as the theory of learning, processing or deciding. It seems that the distinction between the two approaches (monism vs. pluralism) is even more important for legal theory, and more precisely for the descriptive theory of legal interpretation and adjudication. The categorization process is being understood as a kind of decision-making process pertaining to the relationship between a given object (On) and a general category (Cn). Generally an item could be classified as belonging to the category or not. A review of the literature on concepts and categorization suggests four different models of categorization (categorization strategies)[39]. In deciding whether the object On belongs to a particular category Cn, the categorization may be based on following strategies:

1. Determination whether the test object matches with a rule which defines a given category. The rule on the category A sets out some conditions for category membership such as C1, C2, C3. Those conditions should be confronted with the characteristic of the objects. The process of identification thus concentrates on decoding procedure. Some basic characteristics of an object should be reviewed and checked for the presence of features F1, F2, F3, corresponding the conditions encoded in a given rule. Some of these features of the object and conditions contained in rule may by negative, some other positive. In case of a given positive condition if positive match is being detected, the correct decision should reflect the fact that "O" belongs to category A. This strategy is commonly described as a rule-based strategy. The agent who applies a rule-based categorization strategy in order to produce a categorization decision should engage in three step process, namely:
   - Selectively apprehending each feature (F1, F2, F3) of the object "O" (e.g. dimensions-F1, colour-F2, location F3) corresponding with the conditions embedded in a rule (C1, C2, C3).
   - Determining whether for each apprehended characteristic (feature) the perceptual information coincides with the value endorsed in rule and contained within its conditions (e.g. 'Is this item big enough?')
   - Blending and confronting the outcomes of the 2nd stage in order to determine the final categorization.[40]
2. Determination of the similarity of the test object "O" to a memorized exemplars E1, E2 of a given category Cat. A. In this case the categorization procedure is based on a serious of automatic computations of similarity between the object

[38] Allen and Brooks 1991; Smith et al. 1998.

[39] Smith et al. 1998, p. 169.

[40] Cf. Smith and Sloman 1994.

O1 and the exemplary representations of some objects (exemplars) E1, E2, E3 belonging to the category Cat. A. The exemplary based categorization strategy operates in a following manner, containing two step procedure:

- Retrieving stored exemplars similar to the tested object;
- Selecting the category whose retrieved exemplars are on some measure most similar to the test object.[41]

It is assumed that the exemplars are stored in long term memory (LTM) and the computations are performed with the engagement of working memory (WM). The categorization decision is thus based on a process of retrieving of the most similar exemplars belonging to the category, where it is assumed that the exemplars had been previously identified as belonging to the category. The whole process is thus based on the retrieval of memorized objects, the comparison of the objects and the identification of the most similar one.[42]

3. Determination of the similarity between a given object O and the prototype of a given category (Prot. A). In this case it is assumed that the categorization strategy is based on the comparison between the prototype and the object.[43] The correspondence between the prototype or the radial metaphor based on a given prototype and the object is especially discernible in some theories of categorization referred to law. Sometimes it is claimed that many legal concepts are just prototypes and the linguistic categorization in law is strongly connected to the way prototypes are shaped by both; language habits and legal discourse.
4. A very similar story may be offered in regard to the fourth categorization strategy, namely the theory based categorization. It has been claimed that the categorization strategy may well be based on determination on whether the features of the test object are best explained by the so called 'theory' that underlies the category.[44] This categorization strategy reminds the rule-based categorization at least in some respect. However there is an essential difference between the two. Whereas the content of the rule seems to be observable and determinable, the content of a given theory is not. The rule is so to speak 'publically accessible' whereas the category-shaping or supporting theory is not, being a merely 'private' explanation for the existence of a given category. Thus even if the concept of the theory based strategy of categorization seems intellectually attractive, the underlying theory seems to be underdeveloped.

The main differences between rule-based and exemplar similarity categorization strategies include five basic characteristics:[45]

[41] Estes 1994.

[42] Nosofsky 1986.

[43] Hampton 1995.

[44] Murphy and Medin 1985.

[45] Cf. Smith et al. 1998.

- Whereas rule application involves selective attention to and apprehension of the critical attributes (conditions with respect to the rule and features in respect to the test object), the exemplar-similarity procedure supporting the exemplar similarity categorization does not induce any of these processes, relying exclusively on the retrieval of the stored exemplars. Concurringly the rule application is always based on selection belonging to the analytic process, whereas exemplar-similarity is rather holistic, taking the whole object into account rather than selecting particular characteristics and discriminating against specific features—conditions contained within a category-creating rule.
- The rule application procedure involves attending to some special attributes indicated by the rule. Additionally this procedure attaches different weights to different attributes, whereas exemplar similarity strategy does not refer to any selective attention during the most important exemplar-retrieval stage. Thus the exemplar similarity procedure may give the same weight to all attributes.
- The conditions endorsed by the rule are more abstract than the representation of the test object. Hence the rule application strategy is based on the assumption that the categorizer determines whether the information in the tested object meets the conditions of the rule. In contrast, in many cases of exemplar similarity the representations of both exemplar and test objects are assumed to be at the same level of specificity.
- Working memory is usually more actively involved in rule application. This may result from two apparently different reasons. Firstly, the rule could be a new one or a complex one. In both cases the agent (the categorizer) needs to refer to the working memory in order to understand and to apply the rule, especially if the rule contains numerous conditions, both positive and negative ones. From the purely functional perspective both situations must lead to a considerable load on working memory, whereas the retrieval of exemplars from long-term memory usually induces a relatively small load on working memory.
- The distinction between exemplar similarity and rule-following concerns the absence or presence of some serial processing. It seems that serial processing seems linked rather to the rule application than to retrieval and selecting processes, since the rule refers to many potential conditions, which may require multiple acts of selective attention and serial operations which finally lead to strategic or controlled processing rather than automatic processing. According to rule based categorization strategy seems to be based on conscious and complex information processing, whereas the exemplary similarity potentially embraces intuitive and subconscious processing.

The experimental verification of the hybrid categorization process, which aimed at differentiation and separation of the two categorization processes, had been offered by Allen and Brooks.[46] In the experiment subjects' task was to categorize some fancy, imaginary animals into two categories; 'Builders' and 'Diggers'. The difference between the two consisted on some external features such as shape, the presence

[46] Allen and Brooks 1991.

of spots, or the length of legs. Subjects were asked to categorize according to the number of positive and negative matches referred to the rule containing some conditions. A number of negative matches was a proxy for exemplary categorization, whereas positive match expressed the effectiveness of the rule based categorization. There were two stages of the experiment: a training stage, when subjects learned to correctly categorize a set of ten animals, and a test stage, when subjects were tested on some novel animals as well as on some that they had learned. The training phase contained an additional element, namely, one group of subjects was taught an additional rule according to which they were able to distinguish the Builders from the Diggers: e.g. 'If an animal has at least two of the following three critical (attribute) values—long legs, angular body, spotted covering—it is a Builder; otherwise, it is a Digger'.

The same animals were displayed to the second group of subjects, the second group not being familiar with a given the rule. They were told to guess at first time whether the fancy animal was a Builder or a Digger. Later on it was but on subsequent trials they would be able to remember what it was. Thus, the first group was induced to use a rule strategy for categorizing the animals whereas the second group was induced to use a memory based exemplary similarity strategy. The differences observed between the 'Rule' and 'Memory' groups referred directly to the questions about differences between rule application and exemplar-similarity procedures.

12.5 Behavioural L&E of Libel or on the Difference Between Post Diction vs. Prediction

Addressing the problem of behavioural response to different types of risks and uncertainties, E. Guttel and A. Harel observed that: "The propensity to be more risk averse when faced with rule-based norms (as compared to standards-based norms) challenges the traditional legal preference for specified and precise regulation in the context of constitutional rights"[47]. They emphasize that not only standards cause uncertainty, even as it has been many times suggested by judges. Standards may certainly result with chilling effects, however so may complex rules. Unfortunately courts do not pay much attention to the potential chilling effects of rules. They often rely on the assumption that only standards produce uncertainty and can result with chilling effects. However this conclusion is seriously weakened given the fact that the investigation on prediction and post-diction inevitably leads to the conclusion according to which rules may create chilling effect as well. This happens as a result of the fact that the information about the content of the rule is costly and sometimes the application of rule may induce incumbent to lawful behaviour. Thus Guttel and Harell come to the conclusion that complex rules may produce more serious chilling effects than the chilling effects of the standards. As an example they refer to the U.S. Supreme Court decision in *Hill v. Colorado*, where the Court contemplated

[47] Guttel and Harel 2008, p. 483.

whether a given rule which limited the freedom of expression was vague and led to the chilling effect. The rule stated that the following action was unlawful:

> Within 100 feet of the entrance to any health care facility [...] for any person to "knowingly approach" within eight feet of another person, without that person's consent, "for the purpose of passing a leaflet or handbill to, displaying a sign to, or engaging in oral protest, education, or counselling with such other person."[48]

The court qualified the above rule as "bright-line prophylactic rule [...] offering clear guidance and avoiding subjectivity, to protect speech itself".[49] The question arises how the difference between post-diction and prediction shapes the outcome of application of different regimes of liability for libel. Given the fact that different tort liability regimes apply either standards or rules the impact of this finding may be helpful in context of specific problems concerning the nature of publication, the character of verification and the quality of decision concerning the publication. Comparing strict liability rule applied in current English law and the more flexible negligence standard applied by the ECHR seems to be interesting in this respect.

Taking into account that post-diction results with overestimation of risk and prediction generally induces more optimistic approach and underestimation of the same risk, two different regimes differ substantially in this respect. English law applies complex strict liability rule, referring to the estimation of facts of past events. Since strict liability imputes liability only if the defendant is unable to prove that the statement was based on true facts, the assessment of probability of those facts being true seems to be crucial for a given journalist or potential defendant. Thus the strict liability even if in fact very close to negligence, if taken as a whole, namely the rule and the defence, still defers substantially from negligence, because the good faith standard applied by the ECHR seems to be future oriented rather than past oriented. In other words whereas the English strict liability rule induces post-diction, the standard established by the ECHR induces prediction of the assessment of the verification—truth finding process rather than the probability of a given fact. Since actors tend to be optimistic the standard leads to greater volume of publication that is seems to be the case if the analogical rule is being applied. In other words the potential effect of over deterrence and hindsight bias on judges side seems to be balanced by the prediction and under deterrence on journalists side. It seems that to some extend the complexity of the standard, may overcome the problem with asymmetry between the public benefit from a given publication and the limited private profit discounted by the probability of damages awarded to the potential plaintiff. The journalist taking up decision whether to publish under the shadow of Art. 10 of the Convention may also be more focused on the optimization of verification procedure. The verification procedure serves rather as a shield against liability though.

Just to illustrate the problem, let us assume that a given jurisdiction adopts liability rule for libel. Let *SC* mean the aggregated social cost of tort of libel, *Cd* the cost of lost public information if it has not been disclosed, *Ci* the costs of detailed

[48] *Hill v. Colorado* 530 U.S. 703, 707 (2000).

[49] *Hill v. Colorado* 530 U.S. 703, 729 (2000).

analysis of facts (investigation and verification, which may be treated as an equivalent of typical costs of prevention), Ce the cost of a mistake and harm suffered by the defamed person.

The economic aim of tort law is to minimise aggregated social cost of accidents, preventive costs and loss of public good (information):

$$min\ SC = Cd + Ci + Ce.$$

When a journalist makes a mistake and takes the false information as a true one this may result (but not always should result) with the necessity of paying compensation in form of damages D. The amount of compensation will be dependent upon the regime of tort liability. The regime of tort liability is to be reflected by the γ parameter, where the value of the parameter varies between 0 and 1. In case of no liability rule $\gamma = 0$, which means that there is virtually no expected influence of the outcome of litigation and potential on the behaviour of the publisher. For the negligence rule $\gamma > 0$. Under $\gamma = 1$ I assume the full compensation under strict liability rule.

The starting point for the examination of economic results of liability regime and the application of rules vs. standards is modelling potential publisher's strategies.

A given publisher may potentially engage in three potential actions:

- Publishing without verification of facts, relying on probability of truthfulness
- Verifying the initial allegation
- Publishing without verifying the credibility of allegation

However, when the publisher produces a defamatory statement which turns out to be false, it results with a loss denominated as Ce. Under negligence standard $Ce = Cd$x $1/Ci$, whereas for strict liability $Ce = Cd$.

The acceptance of the second strategy (b) will result in the verification cost Ci, which is the cost of the proper investigation. I assume that a detailed examination may increase the probability of true finding. Nevertheless, the examination of a case according to any given standard of journalist ethics is an imperfect method. Let α be the probability that the proper decision on publication seems to be improper (negative error) the true article is not published. Let β be the probability that the examination reveals that the allegation is true while in fact it is false. According to the standard assumption of law and economics $\alpha < 0.5$ and $\beta < 0.5$ (an epistemic assumption). However given the fact that post-diction generates higher degree of risk-aversion, I assume $\alpha < 0.7$ and $\beta < 0.3$. Therefore the value of a given case is following:

1. When the publisher fails to publish without verification, then:

$$V1 = pv - Cd - Ci,$$

where $Cd = 0$, $Ci = 0$, $p = 1$, then $V1 = v - Cd$
The private benefit $V1 = 0$.

2. When the publisher publishes without verification, then:

$$V2 = pv - (1 - p)\gamma D$$

3. In cases where publisher engages in verification, then value of publication holds as follows:

$$V3 = p(1 - \alpha)v - \left[(1 - p)\beta\gamma D\right] - Ci \quad \text{(III)}$$

Given the fact that the risk neutrality assumption should be suspended it seems that the application of liability standard expands the 3rd strategy and will thus result with more verification and more publication based on this verification, whereas the strict liability leads to the underinvestment in verification followed with suboptimal production of public good. It seems that the application of negligence standard will at least to some extend overcome the chilling effect resulting from the asymmetry between public benefit and private benefit under the assumption that information is regarded as public good.

Acknowledgement This research was supported by the European Union and the State of Hungary, co-financed by the European Social Fund in the framework of TÁMOP-4.2.4.A/ 2-11/1-2012-0001 'National Excellence Program'.

Bibilography

Allen, Scott W., and Lee Brooks. 1991. Specializing the operation of an explicit rule. *Journal of Experimental Psychology: General* 120:3–19.
Brown, John Prather. 1973. Toward an economic theory of liability. *Journal of Legal Studies* 2:323–349.
Diamond, Peter. 1974. Single activity accidents. *Journal of Legal Studies* 3:107–162.
Epstein, Richard. 1986. Was New York Times v. Sullivan wrong? *University of Chicago Law Review* 53:782.
Estes, William Kaye. 1994. *Classification and cognition*. New York: Oxford University Press.
Evans, Jonathan. 2008. Dual-processing accounts of reasoning, judgment, and social cognition. *Annual Review of Psychology* 59:255–278.
Frank, Jerome. 1949. *Law and the modern mind*. London: Stevens.
Garoupa, Nuno. 1999. The economics of political dishonesty and defamation. *International Review of Law & Economics* 19:167–180.
Gigerenzer, Gerd. 2007. *Gut feelings: The intelligence of the unconscious*. New York: Oxford University Press.
Glöckner, Andreas, and I. Ebert. 2011. Legal intuition and expertise. In *Handbook of intuition research,* ed. M. Sinclair. Cheltenham: Edward Elgar.
Golecki, Mariusz. 2011. *Między pewnością a efektywnością. Marginalizm instytucjonalny wobec prawotwórczego stosowania prawa*. Warszawa: Wolters Kluwer Polska.
Guthrie, Chris, Jeffrey Rachlinski, and Andrew J. Wistrich. 2007. Blinking on the bench: How judges decide cases. *Cornell Law Review* 93:1–43.
Guttel, Ehud, and Alon Harel. 2008. Uncertainty revisited: Legal prediction and legal postdiction. *Michigan Law Review* 107:467.
Hampton, James A. 1995. Testing the prototype theory of concepts. *Journal of Memory and Language* 34:686–708.

Hutcheson, Joseph. 1934. The judgement intuitive: The unction of the 'Hunch' in judicial decision. In *Recueil d'Etudes sur le sources du droit de l'honneur de Francois Geny,* vol. 2. Paris: Cambridge University Press.
Jolls, Christine, R Sunstein Cass, and Richard Thaler. 1998. A behavioral approach to law and economics. *Stanford Law Review* 50:1471.
Just, Marcel Adam, and Patricia A. Carpenter. 1980. A theory of reading: From eye fixations to comprehension. *Psychological Review* 87:329.
Kahneman, Daniel. 2003. *A* perspective on judgment and choice. Mapping bounded rationality. *American Psychologist* 58:697–720.
Kahneman, Daniel, and Tversky, Amos. 1982. Variants of uncertainty. *Cognition* 11:143–157.
Kahneman, Daniel, Paul Slovic, and Amos Tversky. 1982. *Judgment under uncertainty: Heuristics and biases.* New York: Cambridge University Press.
Lee, Gary L. 1981. Strict liability versus negligence: An economic analysis of the law of libel. *Brigham Young University Law Review* 2:398–406.
Murphy, Gregory L, and Medin, Douglas L. 1985. The role of theories in conceptual coherence. *Psychological Review* 92 (3): 289–316.
von Neumann, John, and Oskar Morgenstern. 1944. *The theory of games and economic behavior.* Princeton: Princeton University Press.
Nosofsky, Robert M. 1986. Attention, similarity, and the identification-categorization relationship. *Journal of Experimental Psychology: General* 115:39–57.
Nosofsky, Robert M. 1992. Exemplars, prototypes, and similarity rules. In *From learning theory to connectionist theory: Essays in honor of William K. Estes,* ed. W. K. Estes. Hillsdale: Lawrence Erlbaum.
Pietrzykowski, Tomasz. 2012. *Intuicja prawnicza. W stronę zewnętrznej integracji teorii prawa.* Warszawa: Difin.
Posner Richard, A. 2003. *Economic analysis of law.* 6th ed. New York: Walters Kluwer.
Rachlinski, Jeffrey. 1998. A positive psychological theory of judging in hindsight. *University of Chicago Law Review* 65:571–625.
Rachlinski, Jeffrey J. 2009. Heuristics, biases and philosophy. *Tulsa Law Review* 43:865–883.
Rachlinski, Jeffrey J. 2011. Processing pleadings and the psychology of prejudgment. *DePaul Law Review* 60:413–429.
Rothbart Myron, and Snyder Mark. 1970. Confidence in the prediction and postdiction of an uncertain outcome. *Canadian Journal of Behavioral Science* 2(1):38–43.
Simon, Herbert A. 1955. Behavioral model of rational choice. *Quarterly Journal of Economics* 69 (1): 99–118.
Shavell, Steven. 1980. Strict liability versus negligence. *Journal of Legal Studies* 10:107–164.
Shavell, Steven. 1987. *Economic analysis of accident law.* Cambridge: Harvard University Press.
Shavell, Steven. 1992. Liability and the incentive to obtain information about risk. *Journal of Legal Studies* 21:259–270.
Shavell, Steven. 1995. The appeals process as a means of error correction. *Journal of Legal Studies* 24:379–426.
Sloman, Steven A. 2002. Two systems of reasoning. In *Heuristics and biases: The psychology of intuitive judgment,* eds. T. Gilovich, D. Griffin, and D. Kahneman. New York: Cambridge University Press.
Smith, Edward E., and Steven A. Sloman. 1994. Similarity—Versus rule-based categorization. *Memory and Cognition* 22:377–386.
Smith, Edward E., Andrea L. Patalano, and John Jonides. 1998. Alternative strategies of categorization. *Cognition* 65:167–196.
Spier, Kathryn E. 1997. A note on the divergence between the private and the social motive to settle under a negligence rule. Journal of Legal Studies 26:613–621.
Stephen M. Renas, Rishi Kumar, Charles J. Hartmann, and Donn G. Shankland. 1983. Toward an economic theory of defamation, liability, and the press. *Southern Economic Journal* 50:451–460.
Sunstein, Cass, ed. 1996. *Behavioral law and economics.* New York: Cambridge University Press.

Sunstein, Cass. 2005. Moral heuristics. *Behavioral and Brain Sciences* 28 (4): 531–542.
Vermeule, Adrian. 2006. *Judging under uncertainty. An institutional theory of legal interpretation.* London: Harvard University Press.
Vermeule, Adrian. 2009. *Law and the limits of reason*. Oxford: Oxford University Press.

Mariusz J. Golecki Łódź and Debrecen. Professor at the University of Łódź, Department of Legal Theory and Philosophy of Law, Faculty of Law and Administration, ul. Kopcinskiego 8/12 90-232 Łódź, Poland, and John von Neumann Senior Research Visiting Scholar and Visiting Professor, University of Debrecen, Faculty of Law H-4028 Debrecen Kassai ut. 26 Hungary. Tel. +48 42 635 46 24; Fax +48 42 665 59 92, mjgolecki76@gmail.com. Fields of Interest: Economic Analysis of Law, Legal Philosophy and Legal Theory, Theory of the EU law, Comparative Law.

Index

K. Mathis (ed.), *European Perspectives on Behavioural Law and Economics*,
Economic Analysis of Law in European Legal Scholarship 2,
DOI 10.1007/978-3-319-11635-8

MIX
Papier aus verantwortungsvollen Quellen
Paper from responsible sources
FSC® C105338

If you have any concerns about our products,
you can contact us on
ProductSafety@springernature.com

In case Publisher is established outside the EU,
the EU authorized representative is:
Springer Nature Customer Service Center GmbH
Europaplatz 3, 69115 Heidelberg, Germany

Printed by Libri Plureos GmbH
in Hamburg, Germany